Black Paris

BLACK PARIS

The African Writers' Landscape

Bennetta Jules-Rosette

FOREWORD BY SIMON NJAMI

UNIVERSITY OF ILLINOIS PRESS
URBANA AND CHICAGO

Manufactured in the United States of America
C 5 4 3 2 1

This book is printed on acid-free paper.

Library of Congress Cataloging-in-Publication Data
Jules-Rosette, Bennetta.
Black Paris : the African writers' landscape /
Bennetta Jules-Rosette ; foreword by Simon Njami.
p. cm.
Includes bibliographical references and index.
ISBN 0–252–02066–9 (alk. paper)
1. Authors, African—20th century—Interviews.
2. African literature (French)—History and criticism.
I. Title.
PQ3981.J85 1998
809'.8896'0904—dc21 97-21068
CIP

The author gratefully acknowledges permission to quote from sources granted by the following publishers, institutions, and individuals: Association des Écrivains de Côte d'Ivoire, Suzanne Tanella Boni, president; Éditions Nouvelles du Sud; Éditions Silex; Grove/Atlantic Press; Photothèque of the Musée de l'Homme, Paris; Présence Africaine Publishing House; Revue Noire Publishers; Bolya Baenga; Maurice Bandaman; Manga Bekombo; Calixthe Beyala; Suzanne Tanella Boni; Bernard Binlin Dadié; Paul Dakeyo; Christiane Yandé Diop; Paulin Joachim; Yodi Karone; Edouard Maunick; Simon Njami; Jacques Rabemananjara; Véronique Tadjo; Jean-Baptiste Tiémélé; and Serge Tornay.

Photographs credited to the Musée de l'Homme are reprinted by permission of the Photothèque of the Musée de l'Homme, 17, place du Trocadéro, Paris.

*To the African writers, artists,
and publishers whose dedication
has inspired this book*

CONTENTS

FOREWORD

Simon Njami

It has now been nearly ten years since I met Bennetta Jules-Rosette. She first came to see me at my apartment to conduct an interview for her book on African writers in Paris. For me, this visit represented a double surprise. The first was that, up to now, I have always kept my distance from that literature called African. I have avoided its specific literary circuits that function at best as ghettos. I considered myself above all a writer, and my occasionally violent opinions about African literature, my refusal to make any sort of concession, spared me visits from academics who are more often bearers of received ideas than of truly new ideas. Bennetta Jules-Rosette pleasantly surprised me. Not only had she sought me out, but in addition, she was more anxious to learn and to discover than to develop a hermetic thesis, for which the writers cited would be only an illustration. On the contrary, the material for her book is derived from the interviews that she has pursued and deepened since that time; from the research that she began well before that time—since Bennetta has also been interested in Africa—for over twenty years. The distinctiveness of her book, and its great quality, is thus to broach real questions, whether from a historical perspective or that of today. In African culture of the twentieth century, literature has always occupied a special place. It is not simple narration; it is a form of witnessing. And in this process, Paris has played, and continues to play, a very special role.

This foreword is adapted from Simon Njami's article entitled "Paris: Les Illusions perdues," *Revue Noire* 20 (Mar.–May 1996): 4–9. The original article was translated by John Taylor and has been adapted and reprinted with the permission of Simon Njami and *Revue Noire* Publications.

Everything really begins with the aftermath of the First World War. The colonial system as conceived by Faidherbe is only a few decades old. Paris is healing its wounds through the excessiveness of the Roaring Twenties, pretending to be unaware that the semblant peace will not last. Yet, the Africans who arrive at this time could not care less about the premonitory signs of a coming disaster. They are mere subjects, motivated solely by the goal of climbing the social ladder and, who knows, of winning one of the rare positions in the French civil service that are reserved for native Africans. The history taking place in their midst does not belong to them.

It must be remembered that at the beginning of the twentieth century, the myth of France as a land of political asylum and of intellectual enlightenment was still alive in the consciousness of those who had not experienced the colonial yoke. The myth of the French Revolution of 1789 and the myth of a country without prejudice should, however, have by then been disqualified by the facts. In defiance of all the great revolutionary principles, slavery was not definitively abolished in the colonies until 1848. But little matter. For black Americans, in particular, Paris is the city of tolerance. It must be added that they are given special consideration. They contributed to the victory, as victors, whereas the infantry was viewed, at best, as cannon fodder.

It is probably because of this aura that, as early as 1918, William E. B. Du Bois, one of the pioneers of independent, black American thinking, organizes the first Pan-African Congress in France—in Paris—with the support of Clemenceau. The American lost generation, made up of figures such as Gertrude Stein, F. Scott Fitzgerald, Ernest Hemingway, and Nancy Cunard, fills in the picture. Onstage, Habib Benglia, who will later act in Jean Grémillon's film *Deina the Métisse,* indulges in lascivious dances with scantily dressed white partners. In the cabarets of Montmartre, flocked to by everyone who is anybody in Paris, one is sure to find blacks both onstage and in the audience. The Bal Bullier, with its beguine dancing, and the Bal Nègre of rue Blomet are the hot spots where the night owls of a high society made up of businessmen, artists, and writers searching for exoticism rub shoulders with workers from overseas and students.

While newly arrived Africans begin to experience their exile, black Americans enjoy a situation in which they are finally able to live like other human beings—to drink a cup of coffee, for example, in a café full of whites. Black Americans also exhibit an independence of mind still lacking in Africa. This is especially evident in the various ideological or political movements led by W. E. B. Du Bois, Booker T. Washington, and Marcus Garvey, whose project concerning a boat to Africa will receive a large echo in the black community of the United States. It is naturally in the *Revue du Monde Noir,* founded toward the end of the 1920s by the West Indian Nardal sisters, that texts by black American authors such as Walter White or the communist Claude McKay can be read.

McKay's *Banjo* (1929) is the first book to draw attention to the contradictions of colonialist France.

The French capital will perhaps never play again the role it enjoyed in those days; that is, as the capital of the world. A world which is as strange to the "savages" of the Colonial Exposition as is the world of wit and elegance. Cendrars finishes his *Negro Anthology.* A young black woman who dances while clad only in a banana belt is the idol of the Parisian public. René Maran, a modest Guyanese who had become a colonial government official, wins the Goncourt Prize with a novel—*Batouala: A True Black Novel*—that leaves no ambiguity as to the author's intentions. The French government judges that the writer has not respected his duty to preserve secrecy and relieves him of his functions. But little matter. With Maran, a legend is born.

Soon Marcel Griaule's expedition, in which Michel Leiris takes part, will be ready to depart for Phantom Africa. The world is changing, and the changes are perceptible even if France essentially views its colonies ethnologically; even if a whole series of exotic literature, such as Paul Morand's *Black Magic,* remains rampant. The differences are noticeable in the urgency felt everywhere; in the extremism pushing men in black or brown shirts into European streets. Yes, the world is changing, for the better and for the worse. The blind West sees nothing.

In 1906, Picasso comes across the famous Baoulé mask that will launch what Emmanuel Berl will term "The Negro Revolution." Surrealists from Tristan Tzara to André Breton, as well as several important artists, raise black sensibility to the level of a model to which one must aspire. They hold up the "primitive" gesture, free of all discourse, and the untainted sensibility of a civilization not yet perverted by the social codes of an art world which is already beginning to dig its own grave. It comes as no surprise that the Cuban artist Wifredo Lam will be admitted into the Breton/Picasso circle upon his arrival in Paris in 1938. He brings a new source of inspiration. All avant-garde French intellectuals proclaim the death of reason, which had been raised to a godhead in Western thought. Young African students surge into the breaches that have been opened up, in order to go even further and take in hand the reins of their own destiny. Yet, this new awareness—and such is one of the recurrent characteristics of this kind of Africanness—can emerge only with the support of whites.

Among the theses then in vogue is Lilias Homburger's theory according to which a kinship exists between ancient Egyptian and black-African languages. This appealing theory spreads, finding in Cheikh Anta Diop its greatest interpreter. Other European intellectuals take turns helping another Africa to enter the mind of Europe—Marcel Mauss, but also Maurice Delafosse and Robert Delavignette. Yet, it is from beyond the Rhine, via Leo Frobenius, a German ethnologist who died in 1935, that the opposition between discursive reason and intuitive reason arrives. It is through intuitive reason—the mistress of the senses and thus of poetry, of music, indeed of all the arts—that the black man thinks and conceives the world, whereas the white man merely measures and quantifies. Senghor will later translate these two notions as rhythm and reason when the time comes to create, with Aimé Césaire, the concept of négritude.

The friendship arising between Césaire and Senghor in Paris, during the 1930s, is exemplary in many regards. It reveals one of the fundamental roles played by the French capital. Africa does not exist. Africas exist. Only on a neutral territory, and while facing a common adversary, can a lyrical brotherhood develop which will bring together the children of Mali and Cameroon, of the Côte d'Ivoire, and the West Indies.

During this period, African students and intellectuals begin to form associations—mostly student groups—and start denouncing the situation in the colonies. Now confident in the virtues of independent thinking, which until then had always been questioned, they know that they can think for themselves and that it is up to them to take the bull by the horns. As Nkrumah will state later, "Europe will offer us nothing that we have not torn away from it." An Africa ignored for too long, an Africa that one could not help but experience with shame and guilt, suddenly becomes the rallying cry of an entire generation.

Then comes the Second World War. There is no longer any question of attempting to consider one race as superior to another. The deeds of the Nazis are now forever fixed in everyone's minds. As the struggle for the autonomy of African countries accelerates and is soon transformed into a struggle for independence—the send-off of which is de Gaulle's Brazzaville speech of 1944—the terms of the African presence evolve. Africans no longer grapple with the immediate present, but rather with the future just after the war. Alioune Diop, supported by all African and numerous French intellectuals (Sartre, Gide, Balandier, et al.) founds the *Présence Africaine* journal, which will represent, until the 1960s, the necessary crossroads for all black movements. In 1956, the First International Congress of Black Writers and Artists, organized at the Sorbonne by Alioune Diop, brings together West Indians, Americans, and Africans in order to discuss Garvey's illusory vision of a unified black world.

Two years later, de Gaulle comes to power. All African thinkers are focused on the future of the Community composed of France and its colonies. The filmmaker Paulin Vieyra, assisted by a few fellow students from the IDHEC film school, shoots *Africa on the Seine.* Frantz Fanon publishes *Black Skin, White Masks.* Something has changed. One senses in the air a mutation to which a name cannot yet be given, yet the status of Africans is going to evolve, indeed topple into something else. Having been subjects, they suddenly become foreigners, immigrants, as independence is granted to the former colonies. And another page of African Paris is turned, with its parade of lost illusions.

PREFACE

Strolling through the Latin Quarter of Paris, I often paused to browse and meet colleagues at the Présence Africaine bookstore on rue des Écoles. I was usually on a stopover, traveling to or from an African research site, in search of a missing document or just a good novel to read. Then, in 1988, following a fortuitous telephone call from V. Y. Mudimbe, I began research on an article commemorating the fortieth anniversary of the journal *Présence Africaine.* I had long been fascinated by the philosophy and literature of négritude, but, like many African-American intellectuals of my generation, I tended to dismiss négritude as an odd wrinkle in black intellectual history. As I began what turned into both an arduous research project and a personal quest, I was forced to shake deeply entrenched stereotypes from my mind.

On July 12, 1988, I entered a small cubicle behind the bookshelves and penetrated the backstage of Présence Africaine for the first time. Christiane Yandé Diop, widow of Alioune Diop, the founder of Présence Africaine, welcomed me and introduced me to her colleague, the poet Jacques Rabemananjara. Together, they recapitulated the history of Présence Africaine from the 1940s forward, spoke to me pointedly about the responsibilities of African and African-American writers, and gave me a long list of authors, artists, and intellectuals to contact in Paris. This encounter launched me on a journey that has spanned three continents and several years of research. An amply funded year at a bucolic American research institute with a good library would have made my work much easier, but the resulting book would not have reflected the themes of cultural displacement, uprooting, and diasporic movement so central to African writing in France and to my own intellectual path.

While working my way through Christiane Diop's list of contacts, for which I am eternally grateful, I began serious archival research at the Musée de l'Homme, in Parisian libraries, and in the private collections of African writers. My archival research immersed me in a sea of journals, letters, and photographs documenting the social worlds of African writers and their fellow travelers. I have diligently worked back and forth across these primary materials, secondary critical sources, literary works, interviews with writers, and ethnographic observations. Methodologically, I treat all of these sources as contributions to discourses about an imagined Africa. These discourses are part of larger narratives of longing and belonging that reflect the themes of African writing in France today. Translating this documentation into English has been one of the most challenging and time-consuming aspects of this project.

I wish to thank Muguette Dumont of the photographic library of the Musée de l'Homme for her tireless assistance with my search for photographs, letters, and documentation on the 1931–33 Dakar-Djibouti expedition and the various conferences and festivals sponsored by Présence Africaine. I gratefully acknowledge the permission of the Musée de l'Homme to publish figures 1–5 and 8 in this volume. I would like to thank the staffs of the Présence Africaine and L'Harmattan bookstores for helping me to locate old, new, and obscure publications. I also appreciate the generosity of the writers Bolya Baenga, Paul Dakeyo, Simon Njami, and Jean-Baptiste Tiémélé in sharing their personal archives and unpublished documents with me.

The poet and publisher Paul Dakeyo, founder of Éditions Silex and Éditions Nouvelles du Sud, has followed the evolution of this project across three continents. Dakeyo opened up a new network of younger generation writers to me and introduced me to the many problems and obstacles confronted by African writers and publishers in France. In a series of interviews, I asked the new generation of writers about Présence Africaine's influence on them. Although all of them acknowledged the magnitude of Présence Africaine's impact, they had mixed responses about its personal relevance to them. I became fascinated by two recurrent identity discourses of the new generation—Parisianism, with its focus on the social environment and cultural problems of Paris, and a postcolonial universalism, with its emphasis on cultural inclusion and innovation. In the cinders of négritude, these identity discourses represent new directions that African writers in France have taken.

During the course of this project, I have interviewed in-depth approximately forty writers, critics, and publishers, and I have spoken informally with many others. I would like to thank all of them for their contributions to this book and to the related ethnographic video project entitled *Paris Noir: The African Writers' Landscape.* My contacts with these writers have taken place both within and outside of university environments. The anthropologist Manga Bekombo, of the Université de Paris X, graciously submitted to a series of interviews on the history of Présence Africaine, the activities of the Société Africaine de Culture, and the early African student movement in France. His insights enriched the historical portion of my book and contributed a thickly textured background for subsequent interviews. The poet and journalist Paulin Joachim also provided essential information on the early years of the Présence Africaine publishing house.

The critic and novelist Simon Njami furnished invaluable insights on Présence Africaine in relation to the new generation of African writers and contemporary African art in France. Our work together has gone considerably beyond a series of interviews and has included joint projects, conferences, and coteaching at the University of California. Njami admonished me against making sweeping sociological generalizations and encouraged me to develop the "novel experiment" described in chapter 6. His foreword to this book was a byproduct of our discussions. The novelists Calixthe Beyala and Yodi Karone took me on wonderful real and imaginary trips through the Belleville section of Paris and expanded my perception of problems of immigration in France. Their interviews and our walks through Belleville were eye-opening experiences that provided the sociological tissue and texture necessary to understand their writings.

Benjamin Jules-Rosette and Sanvi Panou introduced me to the worlds of African cinema and theater in Paris. Their participation in the video project on black Paris added a dramatic dimension to African writing in France and opened up new horizons for future research. The dramaturge and poet Jean-Baptiste Tiémélé also contributed to my understanding of the theatrical dimension of African writing. His theatrical performance of Camara Laye's *L'Enfant noir* brought one of the classics of African literature to life. Tiémélé's poetry, discussed in chapter 7, offers a new paradigm for universalism by adapting the spirit of négritude to the contemporary era.

In September 1989, the Mauritian poet Edouard Maunick interrupted his overburdened schedule as a UNESCO administrator to grant me extensive interviews and share his poetry with me. Later, his postcards from Mauritius kept me focused on the brightness and aesthetics of the island so skillfully reflected in his complex poems. In our various interviews and informal meetings, the writers Bolya Baenga and Françoise Naudillon did not let me forget the political implications of universalism and the role of the mass media in African writers' careers and fortunes. Controversial, but fundamentally optimistic, Bolya's Japanese-style Africa, analyzed in chapter 7, points to one way out of contemporary Africa's social, political, and economic crisis.

African writing in France cannot be understood apart from the literary and market contexts on the African continent. Chapter 4 is devoted to the literary and consumer connections that link West Africa to the French publication industry. The environment in which the writers of Côte d'Ivoire work differs markedly from Paris, as does their interpretation of the philosophical legacies of African literature. The portions of this research on literary markets, conducted in Paris and in Abidjan, Côte d'Ivoire, from 1992 until late 1993, were funded by fellowships from the West African Research Association (WARA) and the National Endowment for the Humanities (Fellowship #FA-30958). I thank these agencies for their support of my research and their confidence that African writing belongs in the panorama of world literature.

Yolanda James, a student at the University of California, San Diego, assisted with the interviews and the collection of research materials during my travels to Abidjan in 1992. Suzanne Tanella Boni, professor of philosophy at the Université Nationale de Côte d'Ivoire, novelist, and president of the Association of Writers of Côte d'Ivoire (AÉCI), provided me with crucial background materials on the Ivoirian literary scene and introduced me to an extensive network of Ivoirian writers. Bernard Binlin Dadié, Véronique Tadjo, Paul Ahizi, Joseph Anouma, Maurice Bandaman, and Werewere Liking were also generous with their time and advice, as were all of the members of the AÉCI with whom I met in 1992. I commend them for their courage and creativity.

Along the way, several students and colleagues have contributed their energies to this project or have offered critical feedback. Graduate students in my advanced seminars on the sociology of art and knowledge at the University of California, San Diego, have screened videotapes from the project and engaged in lively discussions of my chapter summaries. Peter Bloom, a graduate student in film studies at UCLA, whose groundbreaking work on French colonial cinema is significant in its own right, assisted with an ethnographic videotape and background research on the African writers' Parisian landscape. The sociologist Pierce Julius Flynn also participated in the video project on the Parisian landscape, and Sandra Peña, a UCLA film student, helped with the editing. The video project included several interviews that have been incorporated into chapters 5 and 6. I am grateful to the Academic Senate of the University of California, San Diego, for providing funding to support the interviews and the video ethnography of black Paris in 1989, 1990, and 1991.

Numerous colleagues have read and commented on portions of this manuscript. Although I did not always follow their advice, I am grateful for their suggestions. In France, these dialogants include Denis-Constant Martin of the Fondation Nationale de Sciences Politiques in Paris; Serge Tornay of the Musée de l'Homme; Michel Maffesoli, Marie-Françoise Lanfant, and Jean Ferreux at the Université de Paris V; Michel Fabre at the Université de Paris III; Bernard Traimond at the Université de Bordeaux II; and the Parisian literary critic Bernard Magnier. My colleagues Christian Coulon and Daniel Bach at the Centre d'Étude d'Afrique Noire (CÉAN) of the Université de Bordeaux IV provided a stimulating intellectual environment in which to complete the writing of this book. Gerald Platt of the University of Massachusetts, Amherst; Bogumil Jewsiewicki of the Université Laval; and Filip De Boeck of the University of Leuven offered incisive comments. Alain J.-J. Cohen, Teshome Gabriel, George Lipsitz, Dean MacCannell, Juliet Flower MacCannell, Allan Mitchell, and Louis Chude-Sokei, my colleagues at the University of California, made pertinent and helpful suggestions about history, literature, and the production of culture. V. Y. Mudimbe's historical precision and synthetic epistemology have been inspiring. By inviting me to attend the fiftieth anniversary of the Fifth Pan-African Congress in Manchester, Richard Werbner, Pnina Werbner, and Simon Katzenellenbogen alerted me to important parallels and divergences between British and French Pan-Africanism. In addition to supporting loyally various aspects of this project, my father, Walter E. Washington, volunteered fascinating reminiscences on the history of Pan-Africanism, and my daughter, Violaine, made original observations on the new generation of African writers.

Other useful comments surfaced during academic conferences at which portions of this work were presented. "Conjugating Cultural Realities: Présence Africaine" was first given at the thirty-first annual meeting of the African Studies Association, in Chicago in 1988. That paper, in which I developed the images and duplicated metaphors of Africa characteristic of the early négritude movement, was published in V. Y. Mudimbe's 1992 edited volume *The Surreptitious Speech: Présence Africaine and the Politics of Otherness, 1947–1987.* It inspired other papers, which eventually became chapters of this book. An earlier and much shorter version of chapter 1 was delivered as "An Uneasy Collaboration: The Dialogue between French Anthropology and the Présence Africaine Movement" at the 1991 annual meetings of the American Ethnological Society in Chicago. Portions of chapter 2 were presented in Paris as "Antithetical Africa: Implications of the 1956 Congress of Black Writers and Artists in Paris" at Michel Fabre's 1992 conference on African-Americans and Europe. The original idea for chapter 5 was presented in "Black Paris: Touristic Simulations" at the 1992 Colloque sur le Tourisme International in Nice. A highly abbreviated version of chapter 6 was summarized as "Rhythms and Images of Black Paris: The Works of Three Cameroonian Novelists in France" at the thirty-seventh annual meeting of the African Studies Association, in Toronto, Canada, in 1994. The essays presented between 1991 and 1994 have been amplified and considerably modified for inclusion in this book and have not been published in this form elsewhere.

A note on sources may be helpful to the reader. African authors often identify themselves using their last names first, for example, Bolya Baenga. These authors have been placed in the reference list under their last names. I conducted all interviews in French, and they were then transcribed and translated into English. French glosses for English translations have occasionally been placed in brackets in the interviews and in other passages quoted and translated into English. I have translated all poetry presented in chapters 3 and 8. Each poem in French is accompanied by its English translation. Certain sources have been cited in their English and French versions (for example, *Les Damnés de la terre,* 1961, by Frantz Fanon). The published English translations for these sources have been quoted unless otherwise indicated. The original French sources and the translations have been given separately in the reference list.

Throughout the entire research period, Sylvia Moeller has provided consistent technical support for this project. Her sensitivity to the poetics of African writing made a substantial contribution to my interpretation of postcolonial universalism, and her attention to detail has made this project feasible. Muriel Vitaglione transcribed a large portion of the early audiotaped materials in French collected between 1989 and 1992. Her cross-checking of bibliographic sources contributed greatly to enriching the interview materials. I would also like to thank the staff of the University of Illinois Press, in particular Richard Martin and Carol Bolton Betts, for their careful attention to the manuscript.

Many threads have been woven into the tapestry of this research. It is my hope that the final product reflects the vitality of African writing in France as a major contribution to twentieth-century literature.

Black Paris

INTRODUCTION

Generations of African Writers in Paris

[O]ur tasks are numerous and exalting. To assume them with full lucidity and passionately is to exercise, from now on, our responsibility in the organization of the world—and to prepare a cultural renaissance that responds to the painful and profound aspirations of all people toward peace.

—Alioune Diop, 1957

It is a brisk December afternoon in 1991. People wander aimlessly into the Présence Africaine bookshop on rue des Écoles in the heart of Paris's Latin Quarter. Some gravitate toward the large shelf of newspapers in the center of the store, picking up fragments of the latest news from Dakar, Abidjan, Lomé, and Douala. Others browse for poetry anthologies or the latest political treatise. A friendly, turbaned woman serves freshly baked cookies and coffee. The radio, playing softly in the background, announces an attempted coup d'état in Togo. A few interested customers ask the saleswoman if she has any more news from Lomé. "It will come in soon," she says. The atmosphere becomes more animated. New customers arrive, along with the perpetual group of authors coming to pay homage to Christiane Yandé Diop, the Présence Africaine publisher and matriarch. Amid all of this activity and camaraderie, no one would ever guess that six months earlier the bookstore almost closed due to crippling financial problems and had barely managed to survive. A customer takes a book from the shelf and asks for it to be placed on hold, while a flamboyant author claims a complimentary copy of his latest book. Spirits are high, and everyone feels better for having passed through the Présence Africaine bookstore on that cold December afternoon.

African writing is the inscription of identity on the walls of history. It may be buried like a hieroglyphic tableau or erased like ephemeral graffiti. The closer you look at the writing, the more difficult it is to decipher. To examine African writing in France is to interrogate the act of writing in the contexts of modernity, Western cultures, immigration, and the decline of the colonial enterprise. Although the influences of African writers were evident as early as the 1920s in France, the 1940s marked the true beginnings of a transformation of the literary landscape. The Présence Africaine publishing house functioned as a cultural and intellectual movement, mobilizing the people, the resources, and the ideas necessary to introduce a new literature to France. For several decades, this publishing house was instrumental in organizing the cultural space, institutional frameworks, and market opportunities for African writing. Later, the role of Présence Africaine was decentered and supplanted by other publishers and international networks for African writers.

The Parisian literary landscape is a collection of memories, images, and symbols emerging in the discourses of African writers. Négritude, an integral part of the African writers' landscape, is one of the most important French-African identity discourses emerging during the mid-twentieth century. Although négritude is not synonymous with the Présence Africaine movement, it is a discourse that was shared for over twenty years by intellectuals associated with the Présence Africaine journal and the publishing house of the same name. Négritude embodies the reactions of African and Antillian writers to European cultural and colonial experiences. Born in Paris, négritude nevertheless draws its inspiration from African cultural expressions, traditions, art forms, and artifacts. During the 1970s, a significant antinégritude movement developed, yet the term continued to be popular among French publishers of African works. Following the decline of négritude in the 1970s, African writers devised a variety of identity discourses that resituated their works in the modern and postmodern contexts of global issues on the one hand, and emphasized the particular distinctions of their African identities on the other. This tension between universalism and particularism permeates the works of African writers in France.

This account of African writing in France includes four complementary perspectives: (1) a sociological study of three generations of African writers, represented by the early Présence Africaine movement, revolutionary writing, and the new generation; (2) a history of the changing relationship between contemporary African literature and French culture; (3) a sociosemiotic reading of the duplicated metaphors of African writing; and (4) an examination of the relationship between African writing and French intellectual discourses. Rather than presenting a literary critique or an anthology of African writing, I explore the writers' worlds in order to disclose the social and cultural conditions under which African works in France have been produced and received.

The perspectives of the writers emerge through interviews with them and through culturally sustained readings of their works. The interviews address the biographies, texts, historical formations, and social milieus of the writers, publishers, and critics under discussion. The interviews introduce a dialogical dimension into the analysis by giving the writers a space to speak for themselves. The writers' identities reflected in these interviews encompass discourses of selfhood and narratives of belonging with reference to place, culture, gender, profession, and life course. Although the question of the national identity of the writers emerges in their discourses, the scaffolding of African national literatures is not the primary concern of this book. Instead, identity is viewed as a mutable social construction that is directly tied to changing images of Africa and France as symbols and literary inventions.

In his analysis of the methods of oral history, Jan Vansina (1985:63) states: "Interviews are social processes of mutual accommodation during which transfers of information occur." Moreover, interviews and ethnographic observations mark the first contacts of researchers with the social worlds they purport to describe. Interviews are phenomenological encounters of subjectivities. The interview experience is transformed into analysis through the categories and technological machinery of academic disciplines. When interviews are incorporated into an ethnographic or historical text, the researcher necessarily abdicates aspects of ethnographic authority (Clifford 1988:34–36; Fabian 1996:211–13). In the tradition established by the early issues of *Présence Africaine,* a reverse anthropology emerges in which researchers and their dialogants are the coproducers of descriptions. This shared anthropology is precisely my goal in moving back and forth among interviews, analyses, and interpretations in order to create a "writing" of African writing (Clifford 1986:1–26).

My excursion into the African writers' Parisian landscape focuses on two periods—1947 to 1969, and 1970 to 1993—even though much earlier material may be documented if Pan-African influences are included. (See appendix 1.) Across both of these periods, I foreground the discourses and texts of the authors, discussed in social context. The year 1947 marks the founding of the journal *Présence Africaine,* and 1969 signals the beginning of the decline of négritude with the Pan-African Cultural Festival of Algiers. Finally, 1993 is the watershed year of retrenchment in which former French interior minister Charles Pasqua's restrictive immigration laws blocked the political and economic progress of many African immigrants in France. In *Les Années littéraires en Afrique (1912–1987),* the Zairian literary critic Pius Ngandu Nkashama (1993:24–25) contends that W. E. B. Du Bois's Pan-Africanism may be viewed as a starting point for African literature in France, but that this point of departure is spurious. He views the Martinican-born Guyanese novelist René Maran's *Batouala, véritable roman nègre* (1921), which won the Prix Goncourt in 1922, as an inspiration for and antecedent of French-African writing.[1] In 1921, Blaise Cendrars also published his *Anthologie nègre*, a collection of the works of black poets in Paris. In spite of these earlier sporadic efforts, I begin my history of African writing in France with a focus on the *Présence Africaine* journal and the publishing house. The first period of significant production covers the years 1947–69, during which the *Présence Africaine* journal was founded and flourished. This period is examined primarily through archival documents and press coverage in the Musée de l'Homme in Paris, the Présence Africaine publishing house, and private collections. The second period of literary production, extending from 1970 to 1993, is explored through interviews with authors, humanist figures, and French and African publishers. At this point, the focus shifts from Présence Africaine to the more recent publication outlets for African writing in France.

The Influence of Présence Africaine

Three points deserve attention in order to clarify the cultural and political role of the Présence Africaine movement. First, the Parisian-based founders of the Présence Africaine publishing house and cultural movement mapped out a long-term intellectual agenda that questioned the primacy of any great civilization over another. Initially, this task meant defining black consciousness, civilization, and history as resources for rewriting a cultural identity discourse. Conferences and colloquia became the means of further refining these issues in relation to literature and politics. Second, writing, which stands in contrast to orality on the one hand and illiteracy on the other, became a useful tool for cultural change. From the viewpoint of black intellectuals in Paris during the 1940s and 1950s, inscribing traditional and historic African cultures was necessary in order to preserve the impact of these cultures in the modern world. Certainly, this strategy has an intellectualist ring to it in the sense that literature, in the beginning at least, is produced by a cultural elite that purports to preserve the history of the people. Popular African writing today, however, is not the sole province of self-proclaimed intellectuals.

The third point is intended to challenge previous interpretations of the roles of sociology and anthropology in developing the early discourses of négritude and black consciousness (Markovitz 1969; Nantet 1972; Arnold 1981; Irele 1981). In this process, African intellectuals took the lead and carved out a liberalizing space for the social sciences. Articles published by French anthropologists and sociologists in the early issues of *Présence Africaine* addressed problems of human dignity and cultural inclusion in ways that were neither current nor popular in scholarly journals of the day. Although the African writers turned to anthropological sources to bolster their arguments, anthropologists, in turn, engaged in a fundamental paradigm shift by adopting the discourses of inclusion and human dignity propounded by the Présence Africaine movement. The uneasy collaboration between Présence Africaine and French anthropology during the 1940s and 1950s was motivated by neither self-serving complicity nor manipulation. Anthropology was not the villain in this scenario. Nevertheless, with the advent of the postcolonial era and new discourses of black consciousness, anthropology's collaboration with black intellectuals became more problematic. The extensive intellectual agendas and profound issues posed by the Présence Africaine movement, in concert with French anthropology, vanished against the backdrop of polarized political and scientific discourses. As the ideological underpinnings of the postcolonial era have once again come under scholarly and political scrutiny, we find that many of the original questions posed by Présence Africaine still beg for answers.

In 1941, Alioune Diop, a Senegalese scholar, poet, and politician, became the leading figure spearheading a new group of young black writers and intellectuals in Paris. Although previous publication efforts surfaced among black students in Paris, these publications were sporadic. Student pamphlets abounded, but they were not able to survive. *Légitime Défense,* a review published by a group of students from the Antilles, first appeared on June 1, 1932. The publication, which called for a return to authentic cultural traditions in literature and the arts, folded after a single issue. *Légitime Défense* advocated political activism as well as cultural change. Soon after this group disbanded, another circle, including the Antillian and African students Aimé Césaire, Léopold Senghor, and Léon-Gontrand Damas, began to distribute a newspaper first appearing in 1934 under the title *L'Étudiant Noir.*

Although Senghor and other concerned African students worked on this publication, the lifespan of *L'Étudiant Noir* was short, and most traces of it have disappeared. Alioune Diop, however, saw his efforts in founding *Présence Africaine* as entirely different from those of any previous group, including the Pan-Africanists and the militant African and Antillian students. Diop (1987:43–47) described his philosophy of universal humanism as a reaction against European cultural assimilation, an assertion of cultural pride, and an effort to create a new cultural movement. In commenting on the early history, Christiane Diop (1988) reiterated her late husband's claims for the originality of his work: "They always confuse us with *L'Étudiant Noir.* They were not our generation. We did not know them." This statement underscores the importance of generational consciousness in African writing and intellectual networks.

The concept of generations of writers requires further amplification. It refers to writers of a specific period, for example, the Présence Africaine authors from 1947 to 1956. Generations are marked by the interrelations of their members and by collective memories of specific events, such as decolonization, liberation struggles, sequences of migration to France, artistic fads, and literary achievements and awards (Mannheim 1952:286–90). In order to contrast the generations of African writers and their challenges in France, I use a combination of factors, highlighting the events and perceptions that create social bonds among writers. Each generation of writers shares a common, though not necessarily uniform, view of the literary enterprise of its epoch and school of thought. Cross-generational dialogues and conflicts pierce frozen stereotypes about the continuity of African literature.

Established in Paris, *Présence Africaine* grew into a larger publication enterprise, spawning an intellectual group and a cultural movement (the Société Africaine de Culture, or SAC). Printed on flimsy folded paper, the first copy of the *Présence Africaine* was 196 pages long and was distributed simultaneously in Paris and Dakar, Senegal, in November and December 1947. *Présence Africaine* initially experienced a period of rapid growth and consolidation, but its visibility on the French literary scene was still relatively low in the early 1950s. In 1949, Éditions Présence Africaine was founded, and Diop published its first book-length manuscript, *La Philosophie bantoue,* by Placide Tempels. Tempels's essentialist argument about the African soul meshed well with the spirit of Diop's universalism. From 1950 until 1954, *Présence Africaine* was not published as a regular periodical but instead appeared primarily in the form of special issues featuring African art, literature, and culture, the problems of African students, and the links between Africa and the African diaspora (Mouralis 1992:7). It returned to periodical publication in 1955, a little over a year prior to the First International Congress of Black Writers and Artists in Paris, held at the Sorbonne from September 19 to 22, 1956. This conference provided a significant boost and a new source of publicity for the journal and related activities.

With the assistance of carefully selected African, Antillian, black American, and French editorial and patronage committees, Diop expanded his publication activities and, in 1956, launched the Société Africaine de Culture. Many of the writers who joined the group had collaborated in student literary circles for at least a decade, and they zealously followed Diop's energetic lead. *Présence Africaine* capitalized on turbulent changes in France. It was the time of desegregation in the United States, the awakening of political protest in Algeria and Indochina, and disillusionment in France over economic stagnation and slow recovery from the war. These social changes triggered ideological challenges to colonialism. African and French participants in the Présence Africaine movement worked together to redefine the colonial literary subject and to express a new form of cultural awareness. As a literary enterprise, the Présence Africaine publishing house served as a cultural broker, or, in the words of the poet and fellow traveler Jacques Rabemananjara, a "midwife," by introducing the works of unpublished authors, sponsoring conferences, creating a forum for debates, and presenting African cultural, political, and artistic developments to an international audience. In fact, Présence Africaine gave birth to a new type of cultural activism in France.

The Présence Africaine publishing house and the cultural movements it spawned, including SAC and négritude, serve as a backdrop for the contemporary African literary landscape in Paris. Even though many members of the new generation of African writers acknowledge Présence Africaine as a pioneer in the field of publishing and cultural activities, they have turned to other outlets. They see Présence Africaine as having advanced an old cultural battle that must now be waged on new and different grounds. I have identified Parisianism and postcolonial universalism as two important genres in contemporary African literature. Although the term "Parisianism" has derogatory connotations bordering on dandyism, my intent is not to employ it in this manner. As used here, Parisianism refers to a literary interest in Paris as the social context for the authors' works, the subject matter of their writings, and the source of their focal audience, while the new universalism involves the re-envisioning of African social and political issues in a global context. Sociologically speaking, universalism emphasizes human dignity, rights, and privileges irrespective of the specificities of cultural origins (Parsons 1960:143). In postcolonial universalism, Africa is a hybridized concept, reflecting the combined influences of the Antilles, the Americas, Asia, and Europe.

In much of the critical literature, the Présence Africaine movement has been seen as a vehicle for African cultural figures to resist colonial domination by redefining the colonial literary subject. Its participants, however, also created a unique and synthetic African literature that contributed to the expression of a universal cultural aesthetics. At the same time that Présence Africaine's vision of the world touted universal values, the movement was, itself, culturally closed. It encouraged a conception of the world based on the dialectics of oppression and reaffirmation. The founders of Présence Africaine formed strong internal bonds, but they did not develop consistent strategies for the inclusion of members of a new generation. Mechanisms for the recruitment of new followers and fellow travelers of Présence Africaine after the first generation were never clearly elaborated. This situation left a space for the development of new literary circles, movements, and genres among writers of a younger generation.

The Pan-African Cultural Festival of Algiers, in 1969, was a crucial turning point for Présence Africaine and the harbinger of a generational rupture in Franco-African writing. At the festival, writers such as Stanislas Adotevi and René Depestre announced the death of négritude and launched sociological, political, and literary critiques of the philosophy as an impediment to political development and creativity. Eventually, the antinégritude movement, which continued to gain momentum throughout the 1970s, was assimilated into négritude as an ideology and a publication strategy, and it is now often reread as a continuation of that approach. In fact, antinégritude was the product of a generational fissure that provided an opening for younger writers to engage in new literary experiments.

The postcolonial generation of writers developed their own publishing outlets, such as Éditions Silex and Éditions Nouvelles du Sud. These writers also began to publish independently with small Parisian publishers and with larger, established publishers, such as Gallimard and Le Seuil. Some of these larger publishing houses introduced special series for African and francophone literature, while others became increasingly receptive to working with African writers who already had some visibility. Like the writers of négritude, the members of the new generation have received recognition, prizes, and accolades from the French literary establishment and have made significant inroads into the publication industry. Without the initial contribution of Présence Africaine to liberalizing the institutional frameworks for African writing in France, however, these opportunities would not have been available. Many of these new-generation writers focus their fiction and critical works on the lives of Africans transplanted in France and on problems of immigration and cultural assimilation. Writers in the Parisianism genre, such as Yodi Karone, Simone Njami, Calixthe Beyala, and Blaise N'Djehoya, use Paris as the ideological and topological foundation for their works. Adherents of the new universalism, such as Edouard Maunick, Jean-Baptiste Tiémélé, Bolya Baenga, and Doumbi Fakoly, are interested in the universal resonance of African identity, and their subject matter encompasses African and French cultural themes. The writers of the new generation, in both the Parisianism and universalism genres, are linked, not only by shared ideological interests, but also through social networks in which they regularly interact in colloquia, seminars, publishers' openings, literary events, radio and television broadcasts, festivals, and other public and private communications.

Narratives of Longing and Belonging

African writing in France expresses cultural displacement and longing. Cultural pride and a desire to belong to the French literary scene fueled the Présence Africaine movement at its inception. The desire to belong is counterbalanced by a wish to retain cultural uniqueness, integrity, and autonomy. Three images of Africa figure prominently in the narratives of longing and belonging: (1) natural or untouched Africa (*Afrique nature*); (2) scientific Africa; and (3) Africa in combat. These images reflect the tension between localism and universalism in contemporary African writing. Paulin Joachim, a Présence Africaine author and journalist from Benin, described natural Africa as a fundamental literary and ideological component of the literature of négritude. In an interview with me, Joachim (1988) explained: "We did not want to be carbon copies. We wanted to assert our uniqueness and originality. We wanted our poetry to have a primordial feeling, with the rhythm of the tam-tam and the violence and gentleness of blackness in our texts. When you read the poetry, you will feel this style."

Nostalgia for a pristine past arises in such works as Senghor's elegy to Africa in his collected poems *Éthiopiques* (1956), and in *L'Enfant noir* (1953), by the Guinean novelist Camara Laye. In poems from *Éthiopiques,* such as "Congo" and "Le Kaya-Magan," Senghor praises the force of a legendary Africa in which the buffalo (the forces of tradition) laughs at the lion (colonial military domination) against the backdrop of beating drums and the heat of a romanticized Africa.[2] In *L'Enfant noir,* Camara Laye remembers an idyllic childhood in a Guinean village, from which he derives the wisdom and strength to leave for France, but also perceives the social rupture created by the colonial educational system that has exiled him from Africa. In spite of Laye's vivid memories, his novel closes as its protagonist's airplane leaves Dakar while he voices the eternal wish for return to Africa. "'Surely, I shall return!' I remained a long time without moving, arms crossed, tightly crossed to hold in my chest. . . . Later I felt a weight under my hand: the [Paris] métro map bulged in my pocket" (Laye 1953:221).

The narrative of longing idealizes holding onto the past while the subject takes a leap into the future. Africa is envisaged as a nurturing mother for whom one longs, and as an authoritarian father whose constraining paternal traditions must be destroyed by an act of patricide (MacCannell and MacCannell 1982:49). Natural Africa never leaves the psychological makeup, or soul, of the writer and is invoked at will through poetic incantations and nostalgia. The narrative of longing clashes with the counternarrative of belonging to a new culture and society—a modern world, which, although tainted, possesses its own symbolic and magical attractions. A powerful fictional statement of the narrative of belonging is contained in the Ivoirian author Bernard B. Dadié's *Un Nègre à Paris,* published by Présence Africaine in 1959. Tanhoé Bertin receives a round-trip airline ticket to Paris. The trip from Dakar to Paris unleashes a Rabelaisian adventure that Bertin recounts in a long, informal letter.[3] With artificial naiveté, Bertin observes the manners, mores, and habits of Parisians, making humorous comparisons to the tranquil and orderly life that he has left behind at home. Although Bertin is a tourist in France, whose return to Africa is assured, he strives to blend in by observing Parisians at a distance without interfering with their lives. Sociologists and critics, examining the experiences of new African immigrants in France, have equated Bertin's journey with the first stages of assimilation and absorption, during which the potential immigrant is impressed and startled by a barrage of wondrous events.

When the African traveler stays on, references to the nostalgic past give way to the immediate environment as a source of new experiences and cultural combinations. The cultural exile becomes an immigrant. *African gigolo,* by the Cameroonian novelist Simon Njami, published thirty years after Dadié's novel, paints a cosmopolitan picture of Paris's vibrant African community. Moïse, the Cameroonian protagonist, demonstrates total fluency with the city and its multiple cultures as he traverses the barriers of ethnicity, social class, and careers. Yet, in the end, Moïse longs to return to an imaginary Africa that he sees as corrupt and confused, but still as a nostalgic homeland. As he receives his last letter from his mother in Cameroon, Moïse sighs (Njami 1989a:222): "It's useless for me to read it. Soon my mother will tell me what's inside." Having achieved an uneasy integration in Paris, Moïse adopts a narrative of longing when he decides to return to Africa to escape the confusion of his multiple European identities. A momentary schizophrenia results from his feelings of loss and alienation.

Narratives of Scientific Africa

The scientific image of Africa reflects the dual cultural narratives of longing and belonging. The late 1920s in France saw a growing interest in *l'art nègre,* jazz, and other manifestations of exotic cultures. In 1925, the *Revue Nègre,* with Josephine Baker, premiered at the Théâtre des Champs Elysées. During the same year, the anthropologists Lucien Lévy-Bruhl, Marcel Mauss, and Paul Rivet formed the Institut d'Ethnologie and began to collaborate on plans for a new museum of anthropology while they explored the uniqueness, integrity, and vitality of "primitive" systems of thought and culture. Popular interest in the exotic rocked the very foundations of French anthropology as artists attracted to ethnology came together with anthropologists dabbling in the arts to design the new museum of ethnology at Trocadéro and mount related cultural expositions.

Facing the Champ-de-Mars, the Palais du Trocadéro was built in eighteen months for the Universal Exposition of 1878. The Eiffel Tower was constructed on the Champ-de-Mars eleven years later. The Palais became the home of France's enlarged museum of ethnography and was the perfect setting for the new anthropology. With a budget from the Ministère des Colonies, and the philanthropic and organizational assistance of the Vicomte de Noailles, the remodeling project at Trocadéro, led by the museum's director, Paul Rivet, and his colleague George-Henri Rivière, began in 1929 (Clifford 1988:135–41). Drawing on his deep connections to the Parisian art world, Rivière remodeled the museum.

Circular display halls were built along sleek corridors, and large windows were constructed to let in more light. By 1932, the stage was set to display one of the largest collections of African artifacts ever taken to France.

Marcel Griaule, trained as a linguist and ethnologist, organized the most ambitious trans-African expedition to date, the 1931–33 Dakar-Djibouti Mission. He developed methods of extensive and intensive ethnology as part of the instructions for the mission. He used every technique possible, from aerial photography to in-depth ethnography, to capture living traces of great African civilizations.[4] The Dakar-Djibouti Mission resulted in the collection of approximately 3,500 objects at Trocadéro, the annotation and transcription of 30 African dialects, and the assembly of 6,000 photographs, 1,600 meters of film, and scores of original documents for the remodeled museum.[5]

A romance with the objects collected during the mission underscored the empire's goal of civilizing its subjects while preserving and appropriating their history. Griaule (1931a:4) asserted that the expedition's objective was a more fruitful and less brutal collaboration between colonizers and colonized people. Later, in "L'Inconnue noire," an article published in the first issue of *Présence Africaine,* Griaule (1947:21–27) used his research among the Dogon to challenge negative stereotypes about primitivism and inferior black mentality and to emphasize the "rich and reasoning mentality" necessary to create the ancient linguistic, metaphysical, and cosmological systems of Egypt and West Africa. A year later in the journal, Griaule (1948a:388–91) published "L'Action sociologique en Afrique noire," in which he asserted of African cultures: "If you will, these magnificent civilizations, where the spiritual greatly influences the material, where every man feels himself linked to nature and to the universe by thousands of invisible ties, where words are felt in the gut, where the notion of the person is richer than anywhere else in the world, these civilizations will not perish" (389).

This statement is at the heart of Griaule's narrative of longing, a romanticizing that characterizes scientific Africa as a pure state of humanity from which modern civilization has deviated. It is not surprising that, in a period glorifying exoticism, an anthropologist portrayed scientific Africa as a pristine source of unity with nature, tradition, and all that is pure. It is interesting and paradoxical that the effort to achieve this purity took place through the collection, display, and analysis of appropriated objects.

During 1925, the same year that planning began for the new museum, political insurrections took place in Morocco. By the time the Dakar-Djibouti Mission ended, Europe was on the verge of entering the Second World War, and the edges of the French empire had begun to fray. Longing for the exotic could be interpreted not only in the appropriation of objects of exotic cultures, but through the incorporation of their peoples and the continuation of colonial domination. We have already seen how African writers expressed the wish to "belong" as part of the process of their interaction with, not only African culture, but also metropolitan France. The scientific response emerged as an expression of tolerance that became the core of a new narrative of belonging.

The sociologist Georges Balandier (1947:31–36) voiced another version of the narrative of belonging in "Le Noir est un homme," which appeared in the first issue of *Présence Africaine.* Balandier contrasted the images of the primitive and the noble savage and attacked dehumanizing discourses:

> In the end, all of these variations of language, with hesitations, turns of phrase, or hypocrisies, show incertitude in the face of who the black man is, a reluctance to classify him among men "like us." These statements are amply sufficient to explain the incoherence of the reactions. Such as the reaction of one of my old neighbors in the countryside, a well educated woman who cried reading the sentimental novel of Harriet Beecher Stowe but trembled upon seeing a black American soldier. It was rumored that they were capable of theft and rape, even having an appetite for the elderly. (Balandier 1947:33)

Balandier proposed that true tolerance means decolonization, equality, and full citizenship for Africans. By incorporating a narrative of belonging, Balandier pushed the image of scientific Africa to its limits, going beyond the assertion of complex and fascinating African cultures and primitive mentality, to a call for social equality that forecasted subsequent political debates and upheavals in France.

The Rupture in Revolutionary Writing

Africans in French colonies were declared to be citizens of France in 1946. Stung by protracted conflicts in Algeria, Indochina, and Africa, Charles de Gaulle and the French government began to take active administrative steps toward the independence of the sub-Saharan African territories. Guinea accepted de Gaulle's offer of "immediate independence," separating itself from the French Community as an independent state on October 2, 1958. Other colonies awaited the 1960 amendment to the French constitution allowing free nations to stay in the French Community. Senegal, Côte d'Ivoire, Cameroon, Togo, Mali, and Niger all proclaimed independence during the spring and summer of 1960. Many Parisian-based African intellectuals returned home to participate in nation building and to put their lofty political theories into practice. Meanwhile, Présence Africaine and SAC moved southward in a relentless round of conferences and publications intended to map out a cultural program for the new Africa.

Among the skeptics associated with the Présence Africaine movement was Frantz Fanon, a Martinican psychiatrist and author, who wrote, in *The Wretched of the Earth* (1963:223), "You will never make colonialism blush for shame by spreading out little-known cultural treasures under its eyes." In *Pour la révolution africaine* (Fanon 1969:45), portions of which had been presented at the 1956 Congress of Black Writers and Artists, Fanon argued that universalism could be achieved only after the yoke of colonialism was broken by political revolution and cultural spasm. Fanon's revolutionary writing documented an Africa in combat that challenged scientific narratives. Citizenship for colonial subjects was no longer merely a plausibility. It now became a political and cultural reality.

The figure of an autonomous Africa, however, does not betoken a unified literary or scientific discourse. Just as French orientalism and ethnology are not unified discourses, the narratives of longing and belonging in revolutionary writing are fragmented (Said 1978:190–92). This fragmentation leads to further diversity on the contemporary Parisian-African literary landscape. Although the image of natural Africa opens itself to a lyrical and nostalgic form of African writing, the issue of decolonization cannot be approached without social and political engagement. A narrative of longing persists, even in revolutionary writing, through invocations of African traditions and the idealistic hope for peace and harmony following the struggle. A counternarrative of belonging also surfaces as part of the effort to restore cultural pride after decolonization.

Paul Niger, a *Présence Africaine* author whose real name is André Albert Béville, wrote a poem entitled "Je n'aime pas l'Afrique" (I Do Not Like Africa) in 1944. The poem, published in Senghor's 1948 anthology, was based on a nightmarish trip that Niger and his poet companion Guy Tirolien made to Africa. Niger saw the emerging Africa in combat as downtrodden, disease-ridden, and corrupt. Unlike the idealists of the *Afrique nature* school, and the scientific promoters of African antiquity, he did not hesitate to denounce what he saw. Niger's poem, quoted here from the translation by Jones (1971:82–83), begins with a litany of faults found in the Africa that he dislikes.[6]

> Me, I do not like *that* Africa!
>
> . . . .
>
> The Africa of men lying down awaiting like a grace to be awakened by a kick.
> The Africa of *boubous* floating like flags of surrender, of dysentery, of the plague, of yellow fever, and of chiggers . . .
> The Africa of "the man from Niger," the Africa of desolate plains.
> Framed by [a] murderous sun, the Africa of obscene loincloths, of muscles knotted by the effort of forced labor.
> (Jones 1971:83)

Although Niger's ambivalent image of Africa in combat creates an effect of reality by incorporating modern political changes, it, too, is a stereotype. Implicit in Niger's image of modern Africa is a longing for the continent to live up to its natural and historic ideal. Dejected and frustrated because the new African reality was not what he had expected, Niger presents an ambivalent portrait of the desolate Africa that he does not like, superimposed upon an implicit ideal. His account is a narrative of longing gone sour when the quest for belonging is unfulfilled. He voices discontent with Africa's neocolonial future. Similar laments can be found in the poetry and plays of Aimé Césaire (1966) and the changing négritudinist literature at the end of the colonial period.

Identity Discourses and Competing Perspectives

No single unifying discourse characterizes African writing in France. African writers' narratives of longing and belonging, and the parallel narratives of French anthropologists, cannot be juxtaposed as simple black-and-white silhouettes. The writers and the anthropologists share exotic images of natural Africa, although they express these images in different ways. During the period from 1947 until 1969, the themes and philosophy of négritude lent coherence to the projects of African writers via the publication efforts of the Présence Africaine group and its numerous conferences and festivals. Négritude conveyed multiple and contradictory social, cultural, and political messages that shifted with each author using the term, and even across the works of single authors such as Senghor and Césaire. It did, however, provide a point of reference and an identity discourse for African writing in France for twenty years. Nkashama (1993:17) argues that, in the end, négritude was not a commercially viable theme for African writers to pursue during the postcolonial period. He made this argument, however, in 1993, shortly after publishing a book on négritude in the poetry of Léopold Senghor (Nkashama 1992).[7]

Négritude reaffirmed the integrity of African cultures and was a necessary philosophical tool for establishing the legitimacy of African literatures. Moreover, négritude served as a vehicle for developing a viable cultural, as well as commercial, identity for African writing in France during the 1950s and 1960s. The impact of the colonial liberation struggles and the emergence of revolutionary writing shattered the colonialist paradigm and ushered in a host of competing philosophies, including black power, Cheikh Anta Diop's Afrocentrism, and various versions of universalism and localism in literary expression. The rising African migration to France during the 1970s and 1980s introduced new concerns into African writing. French publishing houses began to pay more than lip service to African authors, arguing that any author of quality and commercial potential had a chance to be published.

In 1975, Denis Pryen opened the publishing house L'Harmattan, and in 1980 Robert Ageneau created Éditions Karthala after leaving his editorial post as a result of a break with L'Harmattan. L'Harmattan specializes in "Third World" literature and critical studies, with an emphasis on Africa and Latin America. Although Karthala publishes titles exclusively on Africa, the majority of texts are scholarly studies rather than literary pieces. The French publishers Hachette and Hatier produce and distribute African school texts and some literary publications, usually in the form of second and third editions. Hatier has a large commercial interest in CÉDA, the major Ivoirian publishing house. Nevertheless, Présence Africaine remains the only publishing house in France still focusing exclusively on a broad range of African literary, political, and general texts.[8] As early as the 1980s, Présence Africaine began to experience financial difficulties that, by the 1990s, threatened its very existence. Although it has continued to survive, Présence Africaine no longer plays the same cultural and political role that it did in the 1950s and early 1960s. Well before the 1990s, some African authors perceived Présence Africaine as a place to begin publishing, but not to end their careers.

African writing is a visible and recognized field that has come of age in France and has flourished with the rise of an interest in francophonie, or world literatures published in French. Authors now have many publication outlets open to them, and the themes of their works are varied, fluctuating with new fads and trends. In 1993, one editor informed me that she did not wish to consider another book on democratization in Africa. During the course of my research, complaints about African literary stagnation recurred among publishers and among writers themselves, who cited unimaginative colleagues and rigid publishers as the source. In 1988–89, very little published material existed on the new generation of African writers living and working in France. Since then, several publications have appeared (Magnier 1990; Omerod and Volet 1994; Ngal 1994; Nkashama 1994; Coulon 1997). These publications tend to be encyclopedic, containing writers' biographies and textual summaries. Critical literary assessments of the writers' works are still underrepresented. A change has occurred in African writing since the heyday of Présence Africaine, and it may be understood by examining the Parisian social and literary landscapes in relationship to Africa.

African writing in France today is characterized by a psychological inward turn. This trend should be considered in terms of the social context for African writing. Problems of African immigration, assimilation, and marginalization in France are themes that give new meaning to the contemporary authors' narratives of longing and belonging. Emphasis on these diasporic themes, and their political ramifications now, is more personal than négritude's focus on cultural pride and large-scale, Pan-African agendas. Whether this psychological focus is, in fact, pervasive, and whether it betokens fragmentation and literary stagnation are open questions. From the sonorous rhythms of négritude to the fragments of lunatic writing, African writing challenges the dichotomies of modernity: intuition and reason, art and science, the sacred and the secular. There is no doubt that the landscape of African writing is in transition in France as the writers strive to carve out new identities in a postmodern world and a global political economy. These transformations in African writing may be examined from the perspective of its heritage and history and in the context of global markets to which African writers send their artistic messages.

PART ONE

Narratives of Longing and Belonging

ONE

An Uneasy Collaboration: The Dialogue between French Anthropology and Black Paris

> The study of peoples, being purely descriptive, is called *ethnography.* The study of races is of a much higher order; it is purely scientific, and has received the name *ethnology.*
>
> —Pierre Paul Broca, 1876

The year is 1872.[1] The *Revue d'Anthropologie,* publishing the research results of a new synthetic science, has just been created in Paris. Pierre Paul Broca, surgeon, politician, and anthropologist, has recently opened his new cabinet of anthropological instruments, attached to a museum of ethnography, which will soon move and expand. As we enter this dimly lit space, Broca explains (Ferembach 1980:3): "I have just installed, in addition, a room attached to the museum, a cabinet of anthropological instruments where I have assembled all of the anthropometric, craniometric, and craniographic instruments and apparatuses known to date. This precious collection, which is one of a kind, includes both instruments that have only historical value and those that are in use. All of them are at the disposition of researchers; students also find a second set of the more common instruments in the laboratory."[2]

Broca worked in concert with Armand de Quatrefages de Bréau to establish France's first museum of anthropology. In France, anthropology was the earliest and most pivotal "human science." Although anthropology grew out of a long history of enlightenment philosophy (Duchet 1971), its institutionalization in France was a bold scientific and political move. Quatrefages, the first French scholar to teach anthropology and hold a chair in the subject, opened his introductory lecture on June 17, 1856, with a description of anthropology as a branch of zoology in which human anatomy, physiology, and customs could be studied at different stages of their development. He considered "fossils" and "savages" to be the most appropriate objects of anthropological inquiry. In his "Introduction anthropologique" to Jules Rochard's *Encyclopédie d'hygiène et de médecine publique,* Quatrefages (1889:1–18) reiterated his classification of anthropology as a "branch of zoology or mammalogy" in which "man must be studied as an insect or a mammal" in terms of the physiological functions and "hygienic conditions necessary for each race." Both Quatrefages and Broca believed that anthropology was a "synthetic" science encompassing anatomy, natural history, ethnology, and ethnography. The last category, ethnography, however, was considered to have a dubious status. Broca (1876:19) explained: "Ethnology is exclusively anthropological, but this is not the case with ethnography; it includes the relationships drawn from very diverse points of view out of travel narratives based on historical, political, military, commercial, religious, and linguistic facts, etc. Among these scores of facts, we select those that lead us to ethnology, neglecting more or less, the others, which may be very numerous."

Quatrefages saw one of ethnology's major tasks as the classification of human races. Although he supported Charles Darwin's candidacy for the Academy of Science amid much controversy, Quatrefages was leery of British evolutionism. He argued that all humans descended from the same species, and that races, therefore, could, in principle, be equal (Dias 1991:57). Although Broca (1864) disagreed with this view, violently opposing the possibility of hybridity between races, he shared with Quatrefages the belief that the classification of the races, along with the collection of all artifacts necessary to do so, was anthropology's primary task (Young 1995:13–15).

In a treatise on human evolution, Quatrefages argued:

> Trained by certain habits of mind and by a love of race that explains itself easily, many anthropologists have believed that they could interpret the physical differences that distinguish men from one another as characteristics of inferiority and superiority based on simple traits. Because the European has a short heel, and certain negroes a long heel, they wanted to see a sign of degradation in the latter. . . . Does the fundamental superiority of a race really translate itself externally by a material sign? We do not know yet. But when we examine the issue closely, everything tends to make us think that there is nothing to this. . . .
>
> There are no greater differences from one human group to another. It is necessary to take these differences for what they are, for racial characteristics, for ethnic characteristics. The role of the anthropologist is above all to record, to delineate groups, and then to include or eliminate, according to their affinities,

> the races thus characterized. In other words, his work is that of a botanist or zoologist describing and classifying plants or animals. (Quatrefages 1877:58)

The natural-history approach in anthropology serves the purpose of classifying and ranking races. The collection and assembly of artifacts in a museum supports this activity through experimentation and display. Under Quatrefages's direction in 1877 and 1878, the original museum of anthropology mounted several expeditions, including missions to Algeria, Madagascar, and Haiti. These expeditions provided materials for the Universal Exposition of 1878 in Paris, and a new exposition hall was built facing the Champs-de-Mars at the Palais du Trocadéro. The museum moved into the Palais in 1878 and began its new life under Ernest-Théodore Hamy, Quatrefages's former student and protégé. Although Hamy shared his mentor's philosophy, he was determined to broaden and improve the museum's system of classification for ethnographic objects. He devised a complex classification scheme with twenty categories for material culture, ranging from domestic life and agriculture to ornamentation. Nevertheless, Hamy still placed physical anthropology and the classification of races at the top of his conceptual agenda. His scheme remained in use at the museum for decades to come.

The 1878 Universal Exposition was very popular. Hamy and his colleagues presented the results from anthropological expeditions and explained the methods for collecting the materials in lectures open to the Parisian public. The exposition was also the occasion for the publication of one of the first tourist guides to Paris, which included references to the exotic populations (Nubians, Hottentots, and Laps) whose artifacts were on display in the museum at Trocadéro (Moret 1992:97). Over the next two decades, the museum expanded rapidly. After the colonial partitioning of Africa under the Berlin Act of 1885, French colonial expeditions to Africa increased in number and scope, and the museum became the repository for a vast collection of objects. By the 1920s, the museum was overloaded with materials and in critical need of reorganization.

Marcel Mauss, Lucien Lévy-Bruhl, and Paul Rivet, the new, young anthropologists who formed the Institut d'Ethnologie in 1925, had novel ideas about what should be done. They wished to move anthropology away from the exclusive study of biology and race, and toward the comparative study of cultures, behavior, and ideas. Lévy-Bruhl (1923) considered the patterns of thinking by individuals in different cultures to be governed by a system of collective representations. He viewed primitive thought as emotional and prelogical, but he was not tied to Broca's anthropometric views about racial inferiority.[3] Mauss joined Lévy-Bruhl in his interest in the comparative patterning of cultures. Rather than completely trusting unsystematic travel accounts, as Quatrefages and Hamy had in their approach to ethnological studies, Mauss championed the importance of systematic observation and the careful use of ethnographic description for cross-cultural comparisons. Mauss wanted to embrace cultures in their totality.

Paul Rivet shared the interest of his colleagues in total cultures. In 1928, he was named chair of anthropology of the Musée d'Ethnographie du Trocadéro, a title that automatically made him the director of the new museum (Jamin 1982:90). Georges-Henri Rivière, a flamboyant and iconoclastic master of many disciplines, was chosen as the second-in-command (*sous-directeur*), and together they attacked the reorganization of the museum with energy and enthusiasm. In 1937, the Musée d'Ethnographie became the new Musée de l'Homme.

Reorganization of the Museum of Ethnography

Although Rivet did not wish to overturn the legacy of his predecessors completely, he began his tasks by redefining the scope and role of anthropology at the museum (Rivet 1931). In a report on the laboratory of the museum, written with his colleagues Paul Lester and Georges-Henri Rivière, Rivet (1935:507–31) argued that Quatrefages's subordination of ethnography, linguistics, and sociology to physical anthropology was outmoded, and he advocated a culturally centered definition of ethnology. This article states:

> It is regrettable that the word "anthropology," which, in the spirit of all these scientists designated this complex of sciences [i.e., zoology, paleontology, archaeology, ethnography, and linguistics], has little by little acquired a limited meaning, which evokes most often at the present time, the idea of the study of human races from a physical point of view. It is even more regrettable that certain intellects have been victims of this semantic variation to the point of wanting to limit the chair of anthropology of the museum to this study, which is only one of its attributes. In its primitive sense, the word "anthropology" having clearly changed, there is a more and more marked tendency to substitute the word "ethnology" for it. . . . It is certain that, at the present time, the word "ethnology" has taken on the meaning that de Quatrefages, Hamy, Verneau, Broca, and Manouvrier [all founders of the original museum of ethnography] reserved for the word "anthropology." (Rivet, Lester, and Rivière 1935:511)

Rivet and Rivière (1931:7) argued that civilizations consist of complex cultural influences, borrowings, and fusions. There would, consequently, be no pure races or civilizations but, instead, a series of windows into these hybrid fusions. Rivet conceived of the museum as the unfolding of just such a series of open rooms devoted to Africa, Oceania, Asia, and the Americas, where living cultures would be on display. This idea borrowed from the old anthropology an emphasis on cultural difference and the importance of a synthesis of disciplines. At the same time, it brought a humanistic challenge to biological and racial evolutionism. One of the practical functions of the museum was the storing of artifacts from the colonies, collected under the assumption that these objects would provide an enlightened and rational display of the evolution of all human cultures. A humanistic approach to anthropology and museology required a delicate reexamination of the principles of collecting, even if the ultimate colonialist rationale for collecting was not challenged.

James Clifford (1988:139) asserts that the infectious enthusiasm behind the reorganization of the museum masked fundamental contradictions of collecting under the cloak of Rivet's "dream museum." Clifford explains:

> Mauss and Rivet's brand of humanism envisaged an expansion and an opening-out of local conceptions of human nature. No one time or culture could claim to incarnate the mankind on display at the Musée de l'Homme. The species in its totality would be represented there, beginning with biological evolution, moving through the archaeological remains of early civilizations, and ending with a full array of actual cultural alternatives. The different races and cultures of the planet were to be successively displayed, arranged in galleries organized synthetically on one side, analytically on the other. Mauss's *homme total* would be brought together for the first time for the edification of the public. (Clifford 1988:138–39)

The reorganization of the museum was both physical and conceptual. Rivet and Rivière opened up modern spaces, introduced dioramas, and tried to bring cultures to life by exhibiting costuming and artifacts that recreated the sense of whole people and cultures (Rivet and Rivière 1931:4–6; Jamin 1984:39–58). From the very beginning, this reorganization was driven by an effort to keep up with the popular interest in exoticism. The Ethnographic Exposition of the French Colonies, opening in May 1931, was a stimulus for the reorganization of the museum. Displays at the museum emphasized the role of colonizers as explorers and pioneers. (See figs. 1 and 2.)

Conceptually, Rivière propounded overriding the separation of ethnology, folklore, and archaeology in order to enliven the displays. He argued that space should be made for "popular contemporary creative work" such as "auto-didactic paintings," crafts, modern folklore, and jazz (Rivière 1949:208). These changes were accompanied by programs modifying the training of ethnologists by professionalizing them and modernizing their methods with clearer and more sophisticated instructions for the collection of ethnographic materials. Although the anthropometric and linguistic instruction manuals were not abandoned, ethnography joined the other disciplines as a systematic scientific methodology in the museum's laboratories. It is in this atmosphere of experimentation and

Fig. 1. Poster advertising the Ethnographic Exposition of the French Colonies, organized by the Musée de l'Homme, which opened on May 29, 1931. Reproduced, with permission, from the files of the Photothèque, #D.90.194.493, Musée de l'Homme, Paris.

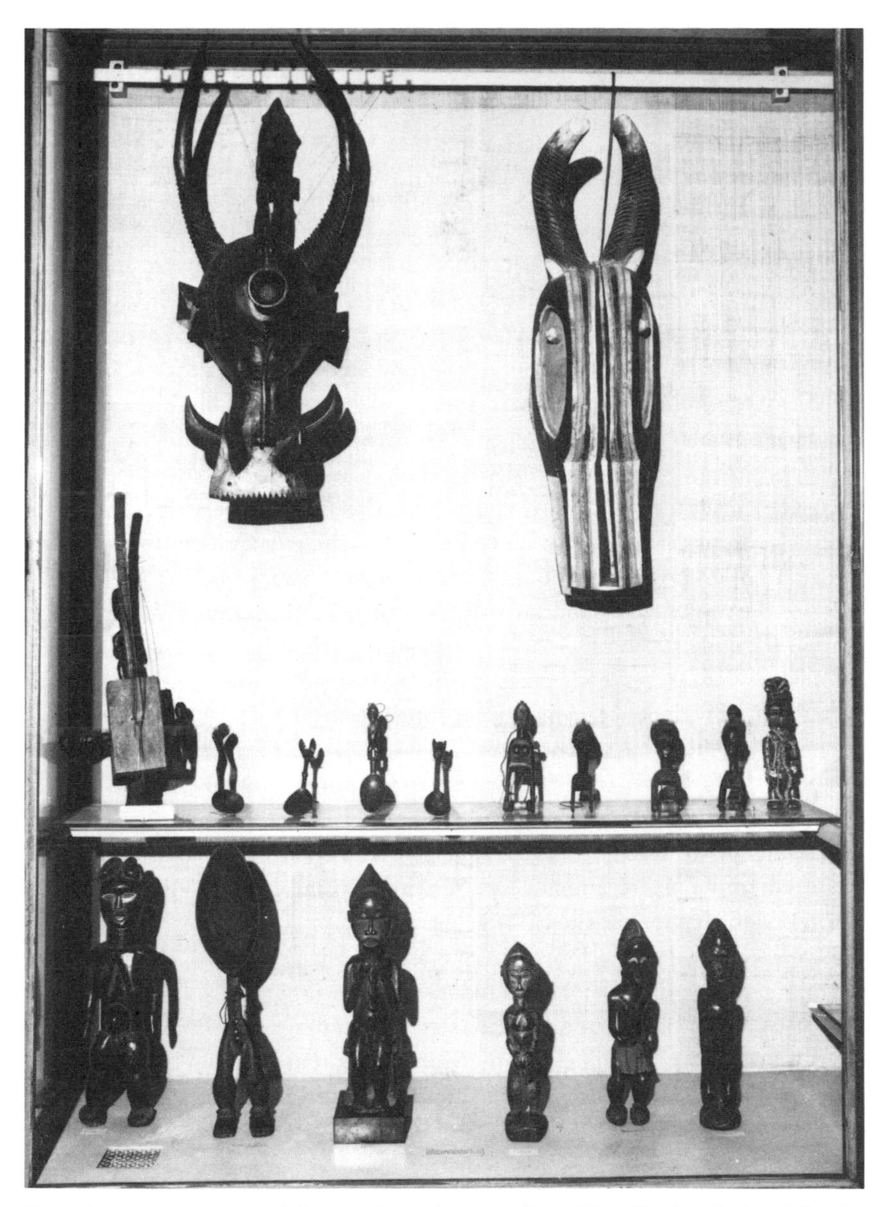

Fig. 2. Museum case containing masks and statues from Côte d'Ivoire, designed for the Musée de l'Homme, c. 1933. Reproduced, with permission, from the files of the Photothèque, #E.73.2042.693, Musée de l'Homme, Paris.

change that Marcel Griaule undertook the organization of the ambitious Dakar-Djibouti Mission in 1931.

Black Paris and the Dakar-Djibouti Mission

The Dakar-Djibouti Mission must be understood both in the context of the old anthropometric anthropology promoted by the colonial vision and in light of the new dream museum that Rivet and Rivière strove to design. Griaule began by devising an instruction manual for the expedition in the spirit of Hamy, Rivet, and Rivière. He wanted to incorporate the new experimental methods of the day, including aerial photography, wax-cylinder voice recordings, filming, and modern anthropometry, into his project. Even the collection of ethnographic artifacts was linked to an updated system of classification that was intended to preserve the cultural meanings of artifacts, rather than merely document the evolution of races and enumerate civilizations. These techniques were all part of Griaule's "less brutal, more fecund, and more rational method" of dealing with colonized peoples as collaborators in building the patrimony of the French empire (Griaule 1931a:4). Griaule's view emphasized that there were various colonial discourses and set the stage for the emergence of contestatory discourses with the decline of the French colonial enterprise.

Given the enormous expenditures involved in remodeling and redesigning the museum, the funds required for a vast trans-African expedition placed considerable strain on the budgets of the museum and the Ministère des Colonies. With his urbane and far-reaching social contacts, Rivière entered the picture as a major force behind the organization of a public fund-raising effort. Rivière was a jazz aficionado and had even written a song for the black American performer Josephine Baker to present at the Casino de Paris (Schlumberger 1974:101). With the visits to Paris of the fighters Jack Johnson and Alfonso Teofilo Brown, boxing was all the rage and provided the solution to the mission's funding crisis. Boxing also fused mass appeal and exoticism. The American-backed Panamanian bantamweight boxer Al Brown was the answer to the museum's prayers (see fig. 3).

After World War I, black American boxers, musicians, and performers began to come to Paris. What they saw as freedom and the appeal of exoticism to the French enticed many of these athletes, artists, and performers to remain. The role played by French anthropology in creating this receptive atmosphere was not negligible. At the same time, anthropology's role was fraught with contradictions that other French intellectuals and artists were quick to recognize.

On March 31, 1931, the Dakar-Djibouti Mission was approved by the French government. Approval spurred further fund-raising efforts, which coincided with the planning of the Colonial Exposition to be held in May of that year. Griaule, then a young assistant at the Laboratory of Ethnology of the École Pratique des

Fig. 3. Publicity photograph of Alfonso Teofilo Brown for the gala boxing match between Brown and French champion Roger Simendé, held at the Cirque d'Hiver on April 15, 1931. Reproduced, with permission, from the files of the Photothèque, #D.80.652, Musée de l'Homme, Paris.

Hautes Études, took charge of planning the mission (Rivet and Rivière 1933:3). Trained in the methods of the Institut d'Ethnologie, Griaule had already completed a successful expedition to Abyssinia in 1928 and 1929. Rivet and Rivière praised his energy, forward-looking views, and competencies as a group organizer. On May 19, 1930, Lucien Lévy-Bruhl, then president of the Committee of Direction of the Institut d'Ethnologie, awarded Griaule a subvention of twenty thousand francs for the expedition from Dakar in French West Africa, via Cameroon, the Belgian Congo, and Anglo-Egyptian Sudan, to Djibouti in the French Somali territory. The mission, including eight researchers, of whom the surrealist Michel Leiris, the ethnomusicologist André Schaeffner, and the anthropologist Deborah Lifszyc are the best known, was to involve collaborative investigations and the collection of a large quantity of ethnographic objects. After the expedition, Leiris strengthened the bond between surrealism and anthropology when he published his famous lyrical reflections on the adventure in *L'Afrique fantôme* (1934). Moreover, Griaule's ambitious combination of new field techniques and teamwork for the expedition revolutionized French anthropology.

The twenty thousand francs awarded by the institute was hardly sufficient for this ambitious task. Additional subventions were given by twenty-three organizations, including three French ministries, the Université de Paris, the national library of France, and the Rockefeller Foundation. An exhibition boxing match featuring Al Brown resulted in raising the sum of 101,350 francs, which was used to purchase and transport a boat for the expedition's crossing to Africa.

The grand boxing gala between Brown and Roger Simendé was organized at the Cirque d'Hiver on April 15, 1931, two months before the scheduled departure of the expedition. Rivière placed a museum guard at each corner of the ring (Arroyo 1982:92). Intellectuals and supporters of the museum were seated in the front rows of a packed room. From this vantage point, Georges-Henri Rivière, Paul Rivet, Michel Leiris, Jean Cocteau (who was very close to Brown and briefly served as his manager), the Vicomte de Noailles, Marcel Mauss, and, of course, Marcel Griaule, were riveted on every move the boxers made. Based on personal communications from Rivière, James Clifford (1988:136) claims that Marcel Mauss had even "shadow-boxed" with Al Brown when the fighter prepared for the match.

The stage was set. According to Brown's biographer Eduardo Arroyo (1982:92), Brown entered and made a short speech in English. "I am boxing," he said, "to contribute to the success of the expedition and to increase the knowledge about and understanding of Africa." Applause followed. Roger Simendé, a stocky métro employee born in Paris's fourteenth arrondissement, stated simply: "I am boxing because I like the sport and also to earn money for my family." Once the ideological terms of the match were announced, the results were almost a foregone conclusion. The crowd waited in anxious anticipation. The match was set for ten rounds of three minutes each. Presumably based on Brown's account, Arroyo (1982:92) describes the fight as brief and incisive. At the end of the second round, Brown sent Simendé reeling against the ropes with a devastating blow. Left, right, left, from Brown to Simendé. The third round lasted thirty seconds. In shock, Simendé stumbled across the ring, fell, tried to rise, and fell again. The referee declared an unconditional knockout to a roaring crowd. Rivière left with 101,350 francs for anthropology—five times more than the Institut d'Ethnologie had awarded Griaule for the expedition.[4]

The anthropologist Jean Jamin (1982:77–78) compares the boxing match to a primitive ritual, glorifying exoticism and dramatizing blackness. He points out the ironies of the setting, comparing the uniformed guards posted at the four corners of the ring to museum guardians protecting a display in a vitrine. According to Jamin (78), Brown was "under surveillance" as a valued ethnographic object. Jamin states: "The black man who fought that night prefigured the '*objets nègres*' that, two years later, the expedition would bring back from the land of his ancestors and display in the remodeled galleries of the Museum of Ethnography, in the proximity of these same guardians: these masks, statues, 'fetishes' which, in their own way, had survived other battles against invisible forces."

Jamin argues that Brown, like the ethnographic objects in the museum, was deprived of his true identity and uprooted from his culture. Although this argument, based in Jamin's words on the "allegory of boxing," offers a symbolic interpretation of the match, it overlooks the impact of Brown's opening speech (Jamin 1982:78). Brown truly believed that he was boxing in order to benefit African cultures and saw himself as reaching back to his ancestral roots. It is too late now to find out whether Brown made these remarks entirely in good faith. He certainly had access to Griaule's statement in the program for the match and to the press release in which Brown was manipulated into the position of a collaborator with the colonial enterprise.[5] Even Griaule's remarks were equivocal as he tried to soften the blow of colonial acquisition and appropriation by tempering it with a spirit of rationality and enlightenment. Anthropology, which ordinarily analyzes the rituals and spectacles of other cultures, was caught up in the contradictions of its own rites. In October 1931, Leiris wrote a nostalgic letter from the field to Rivière reminiscing about Al Brown and the boxing match, inspired by dreams of the romantic Africa that he hoped to find.[6] When the Colonial Exposition opened at the museum, just six weeks after the Brown-Simendé match, André Breton and other French surrealists circulated a pamphlet of protest warning everyone of good conscience to stay away.

Moral apologies for the colonial appropriation enterprise abounded. Anthropologists thought that they were increasing the genuine understanding of other cultures by amassing their artifacts and preserving the remnants of "dying civilizations." In criticizing them, the surrealists assumed the burdens of Western guilt while copying and glorifying African art. Black artists, performers, dancers, and celebrities thrived on the exoticism fad and were not pleased by the French intellectuals' protests and contradictory discourses. In May 1933, three months after the expedition's return, Josephine Baker visited the Museum of Ethnography and posed in several photographs with Rivière and with West African musical instruments and artifacts (figs. 4, 5). She was part of the black artistic world that had supported the expedition and saw its results as uplifting because they enhanced the appeal of black cultures.

Implications of the Dakar-Djibouti Mission for French Anthropology

The symbolic impact of the prizefight emerges more clearly against the backdrop of the Dakar-Djibouti Mission. Ethnographic objects, as defined by the old synthetic anthropology, were props for the study of racial difference. In preparing the Dakar-Djibouti Mission, Griaule (1931b) developed instructions for the collection of ethnographic objects. These instructions outlined special techniques for classifying and inventorying ethnographic objects using a modern system sensitive to their cultural uses. In his methodological introduction to the expedition's report, Griaule (1933:8) argued that the method of extensive ethnography should produce a broad range of observations necessary for collecting and interpreting ethnographic objects. This method should then be combined with intensive ethnography—including in-depth interviews, work with research informants, and research by specialists on language, material culture, and technology. Only a linguist should study language, and someone versed in metallurgy and technology should study ancient technologies. Team field research would yield a comprehensive overview allowing the anthropologists to make sense of their observations and collections in cultural context. Griaule (1933:8) stated: "It is a matter of proceeding from observations that become more urgent from day to day, with a sure and rapid method. This surety and rapidity is based on the division of labor within a group of specialized observers acting in constant liaison. The quantity of results—and one may add the quality—is proportionate to the number of workers. . . . The ethnographer who does everything [*l'ethnographe-à-tout-faire*] is an outmoded conception."

Among Griaule's more controversial innovations was the inclusion of research subjects and informants as collaborators in the ethnographic enterprise. These informants were charged with interviewing other individuals; providing detailed accounts of myth, lore, and cultural practices; and actually analyzing research results. They were also in charge of the collection of objects for the museum. An old Abyssinian painter even contributed some of his own works to the expedition. The collaboration technique was used most actively during the

Fig. 4. Josephine Baker visits the exposition of the Dakar-Djibouti Mission at the Musée de l'Homme, May 1933. Reproduced, with permission, from the files of the Photothèque, #D.84.1119.1933, Musée de l'Homme, Paris.

East African part of the trip. Leiris was assigned Abba Jérôme Gabra Moussié as a research informant. Abba Jérôme was known to be a literate, cultivated, and erudite man. The fact that he could write down his observations made him the perfect collaborator.

In fact, Griaule qualified that literacy was a key element in successful work with research subjects. This type of collaboration made the Abyssinian portion of the expedition at Gondar different from the intensive ethnographic studies conducted in West Africa. Griaule (1932:1) stated: "The collaboration with the

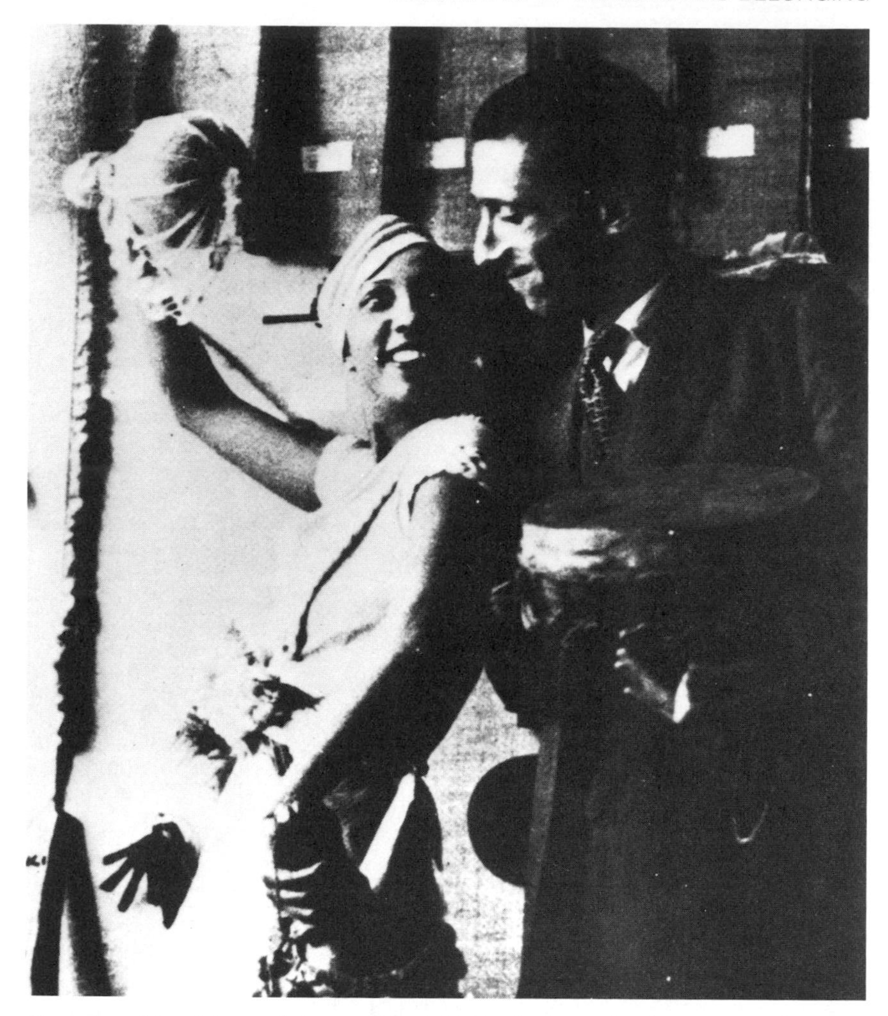

Fig. 5. Josephine Baker and Georges-Henri Rivière in front of a display case at the exposition of the Dakar-Djibouti Mission, Musée de l'Homme, May 1933. Reproduced, with permission, from the files of the Photothèque, #D.84.1072, Musée de l'Homme, Paris.

indigenous element assumed a special importance due to the fact that at Gondar, still a flourishing intellectual center, a number of Abyssinians knew how to write, and to the fact that the period of the expedition was extended."

Writing was not the only factor assuring successful research collaboration and the inscription of valid data. Expertise counted. Thus, several years later, Griaule (1948b) was able to record the ancient mystical wisdom of a Dogon sage, Ogotemmêli, who explained his culture's cosmological system. But this project, not yet in the making at the time of the expedition, was undoubtedly influenced by Griaule's subsequent contact with Présence Africaine and its authors. In the

1930s, Griaule's conception of collaboration was still cautious and centered primarily on literate cultural experts. Nevertheless, acknowledging the anthropological expertise of African informants in any way was a far cry from Broca's anthropometric vision of cultural and racial inferiority.

Although Griaule did not state it directly, his methods and comments revealed two sorts of uneasiness with the old anthropology. First, without overturning the colonial hierarchy, he wished to make the system more reasonable and more sympathetic, as if the liberalizing of the colonial spirit could free anthropology from its guilt over appropriation. Second, he viewed research subjects as constructors of, and experts on, their own cultural systems, the systems from which ethnographic objects are extracted. A problem arises, however, because these subjects are not able to translate their expertise into the codes and conventions of the "science" of anthropology. Literacy is the first step toward this more sophisticated translation, and it made the people of Gondar a test case for Griaule's humanistic vision of a shared anthropology. This humanistic, or more precisely, humanizing vision of anthropology was broadened by another uneasy collaboration—the interaction between Présence Africaine and French anthropology.

Présence Africaine and French Anthropology

African and Antillian students in Paris during the 1930s did not ignore the impact of the Colonial Exposition in 1931. Already disillusioned with the French university milieu, these students embraced a variety of competing influences. They read Marx, dabbled in surrealism, and came in contact with the literature of the Harlem Renaissance in the United States. Paulette Nardal, founder of the *Revue du Monde Noir,* which published only six issues, ran an exciting literary salon that brought together African, Antillian, and black American artists and aspiring writers during the 1930s (Kesteloot 1974:56–57). Although this short-lived salon had an impact that is debatable and difficult to trace, it arose in an atmosphere in which black students and intellectuals in Paris sought alternative avenues of expression. The students had been immersed in the classic texts of French civilization. The philosophies and ideologies that shaped their thinking, while confining, also offered them the tools with which to challenge the foundations of their education and the restrictions of the colonial predicament. Black students at the Sorbonne began to read anthropology and were particularly impressed by the German archaeologist-anthropologist Leo Frobenius's *History of African Civilizations,* which was translated into French in 1936. Frobenius distinguished between Hamitic and Ethiopian cultures and provided an atlas of the great African civilizations and their accomplishments. The students reading Frobenius were less concerned with the specific archaeological and ethnographic facts that he unearthed than they were with his assertion of the integrity and autonomy of African civilizations. These students also came in contact with the works of Griaule, but I believe that they were less impressed, at least initially, with the content of his writings than they were with his ethnographic methods—what Senghor calls his systematic *francité*.[7] There is little evidence that these students, with the exception of Senghor, were especially concerned with the works of Émile Durkheim, Marcel Mauss, Lucien Lévy-Bruhl, or other members of the Institut d'Ethnologie. Instead, they viewed the new anthropology as one tool among many to promote cultural pride and to develop a scientific and humanistic attack on ethnocentrism.

In the introduction to this book, I described the narratives of longing and belonging. Examining the relationship between *Présence Africaine* and French anthropology pinpoints the intersection of these narratives. As the students and young African intellectuals who later became the full participating members of the Présence Africaine movement met in Paris's Latin Quarter during the 1930s, they began to hammer out a response to anthropological discourse that shifted the configuration of the subject-object relationships proposed by the old French anthropology.

In a lecture that the poet Aimé Césaire presented at the Maison Helvétique in Paris on December 4, 1967, he reminisced about the origins of the term "négritude," created in the early student discussions.[8]

> Thirty years ago when Senghor, Damas and I were students in the Latin Quarter the term "négritude" was coined during our discussions and debates. . . . It appears that at that moment we used the term among us as a little bit of jargon. But it happens that in fact I have the dubious honor of having used the word in a literary sense for the first time. Since then, it has become part of a literary repertoire and has been consecrated. Books and articles have been devoted to the term, and I become singularly embarrassed when I personally am called upon to define what we meant by "négritude" in those days. . . . We were students at the Sorbonne then and we confronted a cultural void in the black world. It was a period when the notion of African civilization was very controversial. And for the first time Leo Frobenius's book on African civilization was translated into French. It was extremely revolutionary, extremely shocking. . . . Well, you need to have these facts in mind in order to grasp what we meant when we used the word négritude for the first time.
>
> It must not be forgotten that the word négritude was, at first, a riposte. The word "*nègre*" had been thrown at us as an insult, and we picked it up and turned it into a positive concept. . . . We thought that it was an injustice to say that Africa had done nothing, that Africa did not count in the evolution of the world, that Africa had not invented anything of value. It was also an immense injustice, and an enormous error, to think that nothing of value could ever come out of Africa. Our faith in Africa did not result in a sort of philosophy of the ghetto,

and this cult of, this respect for, the African past did not lead us to a museum philosophy. (Césaire 1967)

Césaire's reminiscences situated activities that would eventually transpire between the 1940s and the 1960s. Senghor commented on the origins of négritude as a form of cultural reaffirmation in a manner that resembles Césaire's message (Senghor 1977b:398).

Alioune Diop was quick to recognize the discontent and questioning of his colleagues. He was the bridge between older, established black intellectuals such as Senghor, Césaire, and Damas, and a new group of young students including David Diop and Paulin Joachim, all of whom met regularly with Alioune Diop to exchange ideas and develop new literary projects. Black American expatriate intellectuals such as Richard Wright were also on the periphery of this world and participated in the conferences later sponsored by Présence Africaine. Paulin Joachim, a journalist from Benin and an early member of the Présence Africaine and SAC organizing committees, explained that Diop became a filter for the energy of the black students' discontent and wanted to develop artistic and literary vehicles for its expression. Alioune Diop was a scholar, teacher, entrepreneur, politician, and devout Catholic (Mel 1995:11–14). Some people considered him a dreamer with an unrealistic vision of African cultural unity because he abandoned his political career as a senator in Senegal in order to devote full time to his publication endeavors (Kesteloot 1974:280). Joachim gave his account of how the Présence Africaine movement began.

We were not alone. There were many of us in the Latin Quarter in those days around Alioune Diop, who was the pioneer, who worked hard to promote African culture. And it was Alioune Diop who assembled around him men like Emmanuel Mounier, founder of the journal *Esprit,* Jean-Paul Sartre, and the surrealist Michel Leiris. These were people who had traveled a great deal and who knew Africa. And so, the initial project started with Alioune Diop and this small group.

At that time in the Latin Quarter, we were students—David Diop, who unfortunately is now deceased, a great poet; René Depestre, a Haitian poet whom you certainly know; Jacques Stephan Alexis, another Haitian poet. He is deceased. He wrote marvelous books. All of us were around Alioune Diop, and our vocation was essentially to insert African culture into the civilization of the white man. It was to affirm our presence, our African presence, because the colonizers had always negated our culture, as if there could be a people without culture. It was a fundamental error. . . . and we wanted to create an African cultural renaissance in Paris, to signify to the European world in which we were immersed that blacks had their own culture and could assert that culture and that presence in the white world. . . . There were about ten students around Alioune Diop. We were loyal followers. First we met at 17 rue Chaligny in the twelfth arrondissement and later

> we moved to 25 rue des Écoles in the Latin Quarter, where all the students could meet easily. (Joachim 1988)

In his description of self-assertion, Joachim contrasts African and European worldviews. He demonstrates how Diop brought representatives of these worlds together. Joachim stresses that the African world of which he speaks exists not only in Africa but in the collective memories of African students and intellectuals absorbed in European culture. Later in the same interview, however, he emphasizes that this vision of Africa, while emanating from Europe, becomes a beacon and signpost for African intellectuals on the continent. Joachim (1988) explains: "*Présence Africaine* was the organ of a cultural movement. And we published. Me personally, David Diop, Depestre, all of the young people who could write at that time, wrote in the journal, which was read everywhere and became a sort of bible that circulated in all of the African hands, everyone's hands in Africa."

Whether the *Présence Africaine* journal actually circulated in all of the African hands is debatable. It was not intended to be an organ of the masses. Yet, Diop constantly cited the youth of Africa as a target audience for the journal. Joachim (1988) quotes Alioune Diop as saying: "In establishing this organ [*Présence Africaine*] we thought first about addressing ourselves to the youth of Africa. It lacks intellectual food. Few echoes come to it from European intellectual life. Left to its own desiccated isolation and adolescent ardor, it runs the risk of asphyxiating and sterilizing, without a window to the world."

But youth was neither the singular nor the primary audience for the *Présence Africaine* journal. Diop took seriously the responsibility for intellectual leadership by the African elite. He argued that the elite should build a bridge across social classes and between Africa and the Western world. In his "Itinerary" for *Présence Africaine,* Diop argued (1987:51): "The elites should take the first step and return to the midst of their people, language, soil, and historical remembrance. They are better equipped to understand the resources of modern life and the new languages the latter is secreting for modern man. Once recognized by their people, they can help them to open themselves and adapt to the new world without danger. The elites must illumine the meeting between the traditional and modern in the life of the people."[9]

Diop cleverly engineered a trilogue among the African elite, French intellectuals, and the African masses. This artful move emerged as early as the first issue of the journal *Présence Africaine* in 1947. Diop (1947:7) began his introduction to the journal, "Niam n'goura ou les raisons d'être de *Présence Africaine,*" by explaining that the publication was to be "open to the good will of all men (white, yellow, or black) who can help to define African originality and hasten its insertion into the modern world." To that end, Diop (1947:13) asserted that European universalism had to be modified to include African elements. Diop (1947:7) envisaged *Présence Africaine* as having three sorts of contributions: (1) examination of African culture by intellectuals of all origins; (2) presentation of African literature (novels, novellas, poems, and plays); and (3) analyses of the modalities for integrating African cultures into civilization. He conceived of the second objective as the most important. The journal, however, strategically began with the first type of entries—commentaries by French intellectuals on African cultures and the importance of an African cultural and artistic presence in Europe. André Gide wrote the foreword, lending his imprimatur to the project of placing African voices in European literature and civilization. Short essays by the French intellectuals Théodore Monod, Marcel Griaule, Jean-Paul Sartre, Georges Balandier, Emmanuel Mounier, and Jacques Howlett, all members of the *Présence Africaine* collective, followed.

These essays shared a tone of confession and apology. They attacked problems of colonialism, stereotypes of African culture, such as Griaule's unknown black spirit; dehumanizing prejudices, such as those cited by Balandier; and the philosophical problem of the absence of African cultures and voices in the European intellectual void, an issue debated by Monod, Mournier, Sartre, and Howlett. The French authors distanced themselves from narrow, ethnocentric views and highlighted the richness of African cultures. Sartre, Balandier, and Howlett touched upon the political implications of colonialism and African inclusion in the European social, intellectual, and cultural panorama.

Sartre (1947:28–29) states: "When we hear about what they call segregation in the United States, we burn with sincere indignation; but at the height of this indignation, we are the most comical and the most guilty. Certainly, Martinicans and the Senegalese come to study here in France and we treat them as our equals. But how many of them are there? . . . After all, at Vassar College near New York, they also accept a student of color from time to time. . . . It is necessary that the African presence be among us, not as a child in the family circle, but as the presence of remorse and hope."

Georges Balandier (1947:35–36) implicates French society and culture in his article on the essential humanity of the black man as he describes the mores of hypocrisy and forecasts the end of the colonial period. Jacques Howlett (1947:53–55), arguing philosophically that the "cogito" implies "presence" and consciousness of others, asserts that modern Western consciousness requires African forms of expression to be complete and come into contact with its authentic roots. He closes his article by proposing that this exploration of African consciousness might someday become a "science" in its own right (55).

Although these arguments are moving and convincing, a larger epistemological question concerns whether they, in fact, influenced French anthropology and human sciences. Alioune Diop's clever strategy of requiring French intellectuals to write pithy articles not exceeding four or five pages, without extensive footnotes and bibliographies, pushed them to address the fundamental question of the African presence in European culture. These short papers were certainly quite different in style and tone from the writings of several of the same authors in scholarly and literary journals within their disciplines.

Griaule cites comparative ethnographic data in his initial *Présence Africaine* article, but he does so selectively in order to emphasize the glories of African antiquity. Sartre's and Monod's philosophical ruminations are hardly technical, and Balandier's sociological insights, while pertinent, are anecdotal. In order to determine whether *Présence Africaine* actually influenced the social science paradigms of the late 1940s and the 1950s, one would have to document these influences to the scholarly works of the authors concerned. This tracing may be achieved without too much difficulty. Griaule's *Dieu d'eau* (1948b) was clearly affected by the objective of uncovering an African system of thought as described in the words of an expert Dogon practitioner, Ogotemmêli. The book, which cites Placide Tempels's *Bantu Philosophy* (1945), an early Présence Africaine republication (1949), as one of its inspirations, clearly carries out the program that Griaule outlined in his 1947 article, "L'Inconnue noire." Balandier's *Sociologie actuelle de l'Afrique noire* (1955) is an exhaustive study containing deep reflections on the impact of the colonial enterprise and its ideological, cultural, and political implications for African societies. Balandier forecasts the advent of African independence, and his bibliography contains citations from the works of African authors associated with *Présence Africaine.* It is, however, debatable whether these works by Griaule and Balandier, which were progressive for their era and have endured the test of time, betokened a genuine paradigm shift in French anthropology. Instead, it is more realistic to consider these publications as opening a window for change.

Winds of Change

The second half of the first issue of *Présence Africaine* contains selections by an international crew of black writers—Léopold Senghor, Bernard B. Dadié, Birago Diop, Gwendolyn Brooks, and Richard Wright, among others. These poems, plays, and short stories stand in stark contrast to the pithy confessionals of the French intellectuals. In 1988, when I asked Christiane Diop and Jacques Rabemananjara, the latter a member of the founding Présence Africaine group, why the French intellectuals had been used to open the journal, their replies were political, as the following interview excerpt demonstrates.

Jacques Rabemananjara: At that time, we were regarded as young revolutionaries. And we needed patrons, like Sartre, Gide, and Camus, to protect us from the spitefulness of what we called the Ministère des Colonies at that time.

Christiane Diop: Otherwise, they would have arrested us or stopped us from publishing. So we needed protection by great names—Gabriel Marcel, André Gide. They didn't dare touch us under the protection of these people.

Alioune Diop, of course, did not present the French input in the same manner within the journal but, rather, took an intellectual stance supporting humanistic universalism and the rediscovery of an African cultural heritage. Kesteloot (1974:283) views Diop's modesty in introducing the first issue of *Présence Africaine* with its French collaborators as a "counterweight to the virulence of the other articles." She argues that the French contributors to the journal in the early days pushed the issue of decolonization to the forefront in their own right by unmasking the purely "cultural aims" of *Présence Africaine* (Kesteloot 1974:288). The conferences sponsored by the Présence Africaine publishing house and SAC revealed that the issue of decolonization was a basic agenda of the early journal and the cultural movement. This fact does not negate the idealistic statements made by Diop and Joachim. All of these accounts are, in some manner, correct. Nevertheless, in an interview, Bernard Dadié (1992) introduced yet another aspect of the problem. Speaking rapidly in French, he emphasized the impact of literary, as well as political, criticism.

> There is a certain way of maintaining a discourse in Africa. We do not insult. We use proverbs. Ah oui, proverbs! With proverbs, one tells a story. Here's how things are: I don't say you are an idiot or become angry. I tell a story, drawing on my traditions, not those of the Russians, the Americans, or the French, because they frame their discourse differently. And here in Africa, we have our own frames of discourse and techniques of criticism that must be respected. I have always said that I reject French techniques for framing discourse. I reject it. I *cannot* do it. You have to escape from occidental methods and, little by little, translate your own method. If you judge me by your methods, it's false. I have always said that you cannot criticize me with methods I reject. (Dadié 1992)

Dadié's short story "L'Aveu" (The Confession), appearing in the first issue of *Présence Africaine,* is an allegorical critique of the entire first half of the journal (Dadié 1947:78–80). He has fully understood the French confessionals but, instead, tells a story about the unjust usurpation of power in an African village. Aka, a wealthy man, visits a diviner who tells him that before the end of the day, he will steal something. Wanting for nothing, Aka dismisses the diviner's revelation and returns to his village. The chief is ill, and Aka secretly wishes for his death. Although the chief survives his illness, he is accidentally shot by one of six hunter's rifles in the village. No one knows who is to blame. Aka assumes the throne, controls the village, and inherits the chief's wife. Only the birds know the truth—that Aka shot the chief. A swallow tells an owl. But the villagers ignore the crazy birds. Aka, say the villagers, is a strong, powerful, wealthy, and noble man. Whether it is possible to read into Dadié's parable the story of colonization and the unjust theft of power in Africa is open to question. Nevertheless, if we examine Dadié's account in the interview, "L'Aveu" might be read as an allegory about the distrust of political domination and the uneasy collaboration between the Présence Africaine movement and French intellectuals.

In many respects, the collaboration between the movement and French anthropology was fruitful. More sophisticated than the early collaboration between French anthropology and black Paris promoted by Rivière during the jazz age, the interaction with *Présence Africaine* went beyond a simple narrative of exotic longing. Although the discourse of natural Africa was present in the négritude movement, a larger agenda of political integration and cultural validation overshadowed naive romanticism. The French intellectual confessionals arguably led to the beginnings of a paradigm shift, or at least a new cultural awareness in French anthropology. Nevertheless, the methods of Mauss's total anthropology and Griaule's systematic ethnography remained intact. And anthropometry did not disappear. The African authors associated with *Présence Africaine* experienced a deception with anthropology. When asked to discuss the ethnologists who had influenced him, Joachim cited Frobenius's *History of African Civilization* and André Gide's travelogues, but he could not remember anyone else. African authors wanted to appropriate anthropology's emphasis on the grandeur and integrity of African civilizations and to emphasize that this greatness was underscored by proven scientific facts. When discussing Frobenius, both Senghor and Césaire avoid the details of his argument and his typology of civilizations in favor of the assertion that great African civilizations once flourished and continue to exist. Anthropology became a discursive tool in the repertoire of négritude. For French anthropologists and philosophers, négritude was a passing fad, an antithetical movement in a cultural and political dialectic.

Mutual uneasiness goes even further. In his criticism of Durkheim's functionalism and Lévy-Bruhl's essentialism, V. Y. Mudimbe (1988:81–82) argues that French anthropologists viewed Africa primarily as a laboratory for evolutionary mutations. Cameroonian novelist and art critic Simon Njami has contended that the anthropometric vision still thrives in French anthropology and art history.[10] Njami (1993:8–9) states:

> Anthropometry is the science of dealing with the measurement of the human body to determine differences in individuals, ethnic groups, and so on. This cau-

> tious examination, whose purpose is to underline differences in human beings, is suspicious in many respects. . . . The aim is to create a dubious fascination. The person in charge of this kind of research is fascinated by his discoveries, and, as his fascination grows, he is less able to see the whole subject of his work. He looks at nothing but the slightest details. He is no longer dealing with human beings but with materials.

Njami believes that anthropometry, which became a tool not only of physical anthropology, but also of ethnology as it was defined by Quatrefages, Broca, and Hamy, is an instrument of cultural domination. He sees the anthropometric vision as guiding the impulses and practices of collecting in contemporary anthropology, museology, and art history. Anthropology was both a source of stimulation and a stumbling block for African writing in France. I do not believe that Jean-Paul Sartre, Marcel Griaule, or any single member of the French patronage group for *Présence Africaine* provided adequate leverage for the négritude movement to consummate its union with French anthropology. Nor do I believe that the debate is over today. Describing the anthropological innovations of Lévy-Bruhl and the Institut d'Ethnologie group, Mudimbe (1988:76) states: "[T]he methodological rules remained essentially the same. They are evolutionary, or functionalist, and still imply that Africans must evolve from their frozen state to the dynamism of Western civilization. The policies of applied anthropology had taken the view of colonialism and focused on African structures in order to integrate them into the new historical process."

It is not surprising that evolutionary models have continued full force in anthropology. Rather, it is amazing that for a small breathing space, French anthropology was influenced by surrealism and the other avant-garde literary and artistic movements of the late 1920s and 1930s, on the one hand, and by a small group of committed African writers and intellectuals on the other. The two shifts in French anthropology, first from the old synthetic anthropology to the protohumanism of the Institut d'Ethnologie/Musée de l'Homme, and then to the psychological and political engagement presaged by the works of Griaule and Balandier, began to challenge anthropometric thinking. The collaboration with négritude, however, did not thoroughly erase the anthropometric vision, or at least a narrow scientistism that separates the new anthropological methods from their historical and epistemological foundations, because both early French anthropology and négritude were colonial discourses. Alioune Diop devised a literary and editorial technique for forcing reflection on the anthropometric vision to take place. But Diop and his literary colleagues could not engineer a shift of paradigms in anthropology or a meeting of minds between anthropologists and the African writers. Many remained skeptical, as Dadié's powerful allegory suggests.

Nevertheless, the *Présence Africaine* journal took a step forward in the dialogue between art and scientism, a step that even the surrealists influencing French ethnology did not make (Clifford 1988:132–34).[11] In order to assert the integrity of African cultures, Diop needed both scientific and artistic materials. Poets and fiction writers made sociological arguments, while anthropologists strove to write poetically. This juxtaposition of eclectic forms, styles, and methods was focused on a single intellectual goal—the cultural renewal and inclusion of Africa in European critical discourse. Although, in my view, this goal was not achieved, French anthropology became a permanent fixture in the scenery of the African writers' Parisian landscape. Anthropology's flirtation with négritude was not forgotten either, as ethnographers broke away from anthropometry to generate new discourses.

The discourses of négritude were forged in an extensive round of conferences and colloquia sponsored by the Présence Africaine movement and the Société Africaine de Culture. These conferences generated research and cultural agendas that would take nearly two decades to explore. It is impossible to describe the contemporary Parisian-African writers' landscape without understanding these debates.

During the various stages of its existence, the goals of the journal remained consistent, but the context of its operations changed with the end of the colonial period. The conferences held between 1956 and the mid-1970s firmly established its international reputation (Mouralis 1992:7–8). Rabemananjara's explanation of the three goals of the Présence Africaine project sets the stage for the conferences.

> I can specify one thing—that Présence Africaine designated a goal. This goal is to renew pride in the black world, the black man. So, first of all, the goal is to revitalize [*réhabiliter*] and reinstate the values specific to the black man in today's world. What I mean is that these values have been despised. They have been ridiculed. Now the role of Présence Africaine is to affirm this revitalization. But Présence Africaine is not content to stop at revitalization. We must go beyond that to illustrate these values, to place them in their proper context. And, finally, Présence Africaine wants to create new values for the African of today, the black man of today, values that belong to the black world. So, there are, in sum, three parts to our goal—first, revitalization; second, illustration; and third, the creation of new values for the black world. (Rabemananjara 1988)

The goal of illustration was achieved through numerous conferences and debates in Africa and Europe. Eventually, Présence Africaine's illustration became the source for devising new intellectual agendas in Africa and France.

INTERVIEW

Jacques Rabemananjara and Christiane Yandé Diop Paris, July 12, 1988

This interview with Jacques Rabemananjara, a Madagascan poet and former politician, and Christiane Yandé Diop, Présence Africaine's director, was the first in a series of discussions conducted at the offices of Présence Africaine. The original interview took place in French and has been translated by the author. Parts of this interview are excerpted in chapters 1 and 2.

Goals of Présence Africaine

Bennetta Jules-Rosette: I would like to start with a few questions on the history and transformations of Présence Africaine. So, Monsieur Rabemananjara, I'd like to ask you in what ways Présence Africaine has changed in the past forty years. Have the needs of African authors and intellectuals changed, and have the goals of Présence Africaine evolved?

Jacques Rabemananjara: It's difficult for me to respond for the simple reason that your question is very broad. Nevertheless, I can specify one thing—that Présence Africaine designated a goal. This goal is to renew pride in the black world, the black man. So, first of all, the goal is to revitalize [*réhabiliter*] and reinstate the values specific to the black man in today's world. What I mean is that these values have been despised. They have been ridiculed. Now the role of Présence Africaine is to affirm this revitalization. But Présence Africaine is not content to stop at revitalization. We must go beyond that to illustrate these values, to place them in their proper context. And, finally, Présence Africaine wants to create new values for the African of today, the black man of today, values that belong to the black world. So, there are, in sum, three parts to our goal—first, revitalization; second, illustration; and third, the creation of new values for the black world. So, if you say that there has been a change in our goals since the early days, it is as a result of the milieu in which we live. Times change. There has been an evolution. Consequently, values become married to their era, which is what Présence Africaine has done in identifying itself with the conditions of the world in which it exists today.

So, there were the writers associated with the first goal, that is to say, revitalization and reinstatement. There were, of course, quite a few who wrote in that vein, like Birago Diop, Senghor, and others who emphasized the values of our ancestors. And then there were the writers who created Présence Africaine and who were there to expand our consciousness and our values. Today, of course, this expansion does not have the same meaning, but the object is the same, that is to renew pride in the black world. Voilà. That's, on the whole, what I have to say about evolution.

Support for Writers

BJR: From the point of view of writers and artists, how do you conceive of the role of Présence Africaine?

JR: Ma foi! The role of Présence Africaine with regard to writers and artists—it's done a great deal. Without being presumptuous, there are many writers who would never have been published without Présence Africaine. Many writers were launched when Alioune Diop created Présence Africaine. He had a turn of phrase that summed up everything. He used to say that Présence Africaine is a midwife who gives birth to authors. That's right, a midwife. So the role of Présence Africaine was to support the emergence and recognition of writers from the black world for the very simple reason that European publishers were reluctant to launch black writers, while the Présence Africaine publishing house took this as a vocation. So truly, Présence Africaine was a midwife that brought forth the talents of black writers. Such great names as Mudimbe, Sassine, and others all passed through Présence Africaine. And our role continues to be that of a midwife, to bring forth as many talents as possible. . . .

BJR: And, of course, Senghor participated in the early days of Présence Africaine. He was active.

JR: Yes, he was our elder. He was our elder because he had already passed his *agrégation* at that time. So, he participated. But he did not organize everything. He came from time to time. We invited him, if you will.

BJR: I see.

JR: At that time, we were regarded as young revolutionaries. And we needed patrons, like Sartre, Gide, and Camus, to protect us from the spitefulness of what we called the Ministère des Colonies at that time.

Christiane Diop: Otherwise, they would have arrested us or stopped us from publishing. So we needed protection by great names—Gabriel Marcel, André Gide. They didn't dare touch us under the protection of these people.

JR: These French writers didn't help us financially, but they assisted intellectually.

CD: They helped us culturally, because we were regarded as subversive. That's very important. Have you understood? Because there are some people who think they helped us financially.

JR: Nothing. Absolutely nothing.

CD: We needed their moral support, their protection. Voilà! That's all. They didn't dictate to us what to write. Absolutely not. And, you know, Jacques, often that astonishes everyone. That we have been able to survive forty years like that. Everyone thinks that we surely had some secret source of support.

JR: Tu parles! Absolutely nothing. No one helped us. We had the faith that we would endure. . . .

CD: It's like Don Quixote: that's where we are. We have this vision of the black world of Africa, and each time that we think that we have arrived there, it's always receding, always disappearing because there is no respondent for us in the cultural domain. Culture is not profitable, you could say. But we have understood the importance of culture.

Language of Publication

BJR: Is the decision that Présence Africaine has made to publish most of its works in the French language intellectual or commercial? Or is this decision based on the needs and requirements of the writers themselves?

CD: No. I think it's based on reality. We have the obligation to learn and to use our national languages. But we cannot afford to miss out on modernity. We have to be realistic. It's important to use our national languages and to enlarge the circle of readers. It's not sufficient to write in our languages. We have to teach children to read in our languages. We have to codify them. Swahili, for example, could eventually become an international language used in conferences. But we need more time for this to happen. . . . In Nigeria, there is a similar debate for the anglophones. Wole Soyinka won the Nobel Prize, but there are other writers who say that he should have written in Yoruba instead of English. It's a false debate.

JR: Yes, it's a false debate. Soyinka is not any less African because he has written in English. By writing in English, he has expressed his true Africanity. His personality cuts across this foreign language. In fact, when we speak French, it is not to become like the French. It's to do something new with the language. In my works, I don't try to imitate Lamartine, Baudelaire, or Mauriac. My work belongs to France, and to the French language, and to something that a French person born here does not have. If not, my work is worthless. . . . And let me add another detail, which relates to what Christiane said. As human beings, we have to know how to communicate. Myself, I come from the island of Madagascar.

BJR: Yes. I know.

JR If I were content simply to write and to speak in Malagasy, would you be sitting here in front of me? I needed a language that enabled me to break away from my insularity. If I have the ambition to be known outside of Madagascar, I must write in a language that others can understand. Certainly, I respect our national language. But I think that one language can enrich another.

CD: But we can be criticized for our efforts to enrich another language.

JR: Certainly. We're in agreement on that, Christiane. But if I express myself in Malagasy, aspects of my French culture show through and influence my Madagascan culture. So, there's a reciprocal enrichment, a type of cultural interference between Malagasy and French.

Conferences and Cultural Activities

BJR: I am personally very interested in the early years of Présence Africaine. Can you tell me about the conferences, seminars, and cultural activities sponsored by Présence Africaine?

JR: The Présence Africaine movement was created by Alioune Diop. Certainly, at that moment, many of us were students, and Alioune Diop assembled us to launch a black cultural renewal. Evidently, that coincided with other movements external to us, but Alioune Diop brought us together and created the idea of Présence Africaine.

BJR: And how did the other writers fit into the picture?

JR: You know, the most fantastic thing was the success of the First Congress of Black Writers and Artists, held here at the Sorbonne. Well, you, the Americans, sent a strong delegation, and we ask ourselves even to this day how so many people accepted to come. There were Americans, delegates from the Caribbean, people from the Pacific, the Indian Ocean, continental Africa, and even India. How do you explain this type of meeting in Paris under the direction of Alioune Diop, who, once again, was not assisted financially? You must remember that no one gave money to finance us at that time. It was Alioune Diop, with his small and loyal team, who united these people from all corners of the world.

CD: They paid for their travel and their stays in France.

JR: Yes. You must keep that in mind. People coming from North America, where you live, from the Pacific—they paid for their stays here. We didn't have any money then. But we had faith. And how did these people from all over the black world come here to debate these themes, which, after all, resulted in some resolutions? I call that a great miracle—the First Congress of Black Writers and Artists in Paris. Writers like Richard Wright were there with the North American delegation. These were the intellectuals from your country. But that does not mean that they shared the same vision of the world. We were all evidently dominated by the cultures that shaped our ideas. But a common cultural base was there. We wanted to express our commonalities across the diverse cultures that separated us.

BJR: And were there genuine conflicts?

JR: Eh bien, there were exchanges of ideas.

CD: And conflicts.

JR: Yes, and there were conflicts, even very bitter conflicts, because what preoccupied us at that time was our colonization. And the Americans did not understand that, because they said they were *not* colonized. They could not understand. And some of them feared that they would not be able to return to the United States after the Congress.

CD: There were political reasons for this, hein. It was a delicate period in America. McCarthy, non?

BJR: Yes, McCarthy.

JR: At the Congress, there were communists. There were Christians. There were Moslems.

CD: Yes, it was fantastic!

JR: Via the Société Africaine de Culture, the role of Présence Africaine was to organize conferences and seminars. The 1956 congress was our first. A certain number of conferences were organized by African nations later, with Présence Africaine as the cultural motor of the conferences. These included Dakar, the great conference in Brazzaville for the centennial of the Berlin conference, the conference on African literature in Yaoundé, and the conference on the family, religion, and values of the black world in Togo. There were also other conferences in Abidjan, in Dakar, and in Paris at UNESCO, and so forth. All of this was a type of illustration. That was the second objective of Présence Africaine. It is a type of cultural animation, which is the normal role of Présence Africaine.

Past, Present, and Future

BJR: And what about today, the present? How do you see the new developments of Présence Africaine?

CD: Well, it's difficult. When you speak to young people about something, you must start from a foundation. Nothing is created out of thin air. Young people say, "Oh, the past again!" If you want to know about the creativity of black writers today, you have to start from the past. . . . But young people are so impatient. You have to begin immediately by speaking about the present. You must understand that the present rests on the past. They think that we are fixated on the past. But if you speak about the present, you must start from a background.

JR: Every person is composed of past, present, and future. It is impossible to separate these three elements. A person has his past—his roots; and his present—what he lives through; and his future—his projects. Good. Every human being and every human enterprise is like that. You cannot cut a person from his past. . . . And the present of which you speak, it's no longer the present. As soon as you speak of the present, it no longer exists. It is past.

BJR: Yes, that's very true. It sounds a little like Henri Bergson. . . .

CD: You know, you might think that we are presumptuous. But the young generation should reread the issues of *Présence Africaine.* Any honest intellectual, in rereading the issues of *Présence Africaine,* will see that we were the first to speak of African cinema. We were the first to organize a conference in Ouagadougou on the topic of African cinema. . . . We have been pioneers in all domains—cinema, African literature, and religion—all domains, even medicine. And we continue today. Voilà! We don't boast about it because our means are limited. But we continue to focus on today's literature. We are now organizing a conference on youth and literature. But, clearly, we don't have the means necessary to enter into the audiovisual arena and the media. . . .

JR: It is certain that Présence Africaine has greatly changed the vision that Europeans have of the black world.

TWO

Antithetical Africa: The Conferences and Festivals of Présence Africaine, 1956–73

> Do you promise or will you promise to contribute to the progress of African civilization to the best of your ability?
>
> —M. A. Seweje, 1959

From Indochina to Algeria, the foundations of the French empire began to shake during the 1950s. In the United States, the legal process of desegregation was underway amid enormous obstacles. An old social order seemed to be crumbling. And, reasoned Alioune Diop, the time was ripe for the First International Congress of Black Writers and Artists, scheduled for September 19–22, 1956, at the Sorbonne. All of the conferences of Présence Africaine, from 1956 forward, may be interpreted as actualizations of different versions of the narratives of longing and belonging in which Africa, as an image and an ideal, is reconfigured.[1] Motivating these conferences was a search for the unity of all black cultures, but this unity was defined in terms of different "value spheres" (Mannheim 1952:153). Some participants were anxious to interpret unity with reference to cultural essences inherent to all black "civilizations." Others saw political oppression as the source of unity and social identity. As the colonial period ended, a discourse of nationalism emerged. In spite of the careful guidelines that Diop and his colleagues developed for each conference, the parameters of the debates were not always clear. The world outside of the conference halls was changing. Inside the conferences, moments of internal conflict highlighted the meanings of terms and the significance of complex papers that addressed cultural agendas on the surface and political strategies underneath. Conference resolutions seldom brought the debates to closure because the organizers tended to ignore conflicts and frame the conference outcomes as intellectually, politically, and thematically unified. The participants, however, did not always share this vision.

Diop and his organizing committee, including Léopold Senghor, Aimé Césaire, and Jacques Rabemananjara, took eighteen months to mount the 1956 congress. The conference was publicized in the August–September 1955 issue of *Présence Africaine* with a letter signed by nineteen African, Antillian, and American intellectuals and artists, among them Louis Armstrong, Josephine Baker, and Richard Wright (Mel 1995:149). The organizing committee invited sixty-two writers, artists, and scholars. Participants came from several African countries and territories—Congo, Côte d'Ivoire, Senegal, Cameroon, Niger, Togo, Angola, and Mozambique. Others arrived from Martinique, Guadeloupe, Haiti, Jamaica, Barbados, India, and the United States. Black American participants included Richard Wright, Horace Mann Bond, Mercer Cook, John A. Davis, William Fontaine, and, as an observer, James Baldwin. The American activist and intellectual W. E. B. Du Bois sent a long and cryptic telegram of support.

Since the end of World War I, Du Bois had actively promoted Pan-Africanism, leading a delegation concerned with African issues to the Versailles Peace Conference in 1914. Du Bois was the motor behind four of the five Pan-African congresses held between 1918 and 1945 (Adi and Sherwood 1995:17–18). Through these conferences, African students, activists, and future leaders, such as Kwame Nkrumah and Jomo Kenyatta, committed themselves to fight for the end of colonialism and imperialism. In the anglophone world, this battle was waged on primarily political, rather than cultural, grounds. Diop (1987:43) emphatically distinguished his cultural movement from anglophone Pan-Africanist activities, even though he considered the end of colonialism as a political necessity. The cultural movement instigated by Présence Africaine was not only a means to facilitate the end of colonialism, but also a way of putting into place a new global vision of culture and civilization. Although Du Bois, who was refused a visa by the U.S. government, was not able to travel to France for political and legal reasons, he may also have disagreed with Diop's perspective.

When theorists of colonial discourse speak of postcolonial rupture, they often forget the efforts made by those who endured the colonial condition to change it. From the early Pan-African congresses to the conference in Bandoeng, Indonesia, in 1955, that paved the way for the decolonization of Asian and African nations, strategies of negotiation and rupture were put into place. The congresses sponsored by Présence Africaine during the 1950s involved a cultural reprise and a profound rethinking of colonialism's consequences. The participants were self-conscious and reflexive about their roles as agents of change.

The 1956 Congress of Black Writers and Artists was a Euro-African celebration of cultural awakening that coincided with the waning of the colonial period in Africa. From a position of exile and observation in Europe, the congress organizers attempted to make sense of radical changes in their cultural and political situations. Africans, Antillians, and black Americans with contrasting visions of the world devised a set of priorities for cultural politics. These efforts were laudable, ambitious, and incomplete. The issues lingered for well over a decade as the same cast of characters, with a few new participants here and there, debated and revitalized their views of cultural and political action.

The ramifications of the 1956 congress were so extensive that Diop immediately formed the Société Africaine de Culture (SAC), an elite cadre of African writers and artists ("*les hommes de culture du monde noir*"), to serve as a research commission implementing the congress resolutions. He established the Présence Africaine publishing house during the same year. (See fig. 6.) In a 1959 interview about the congress, Senghor summarized its significance to him as enabling négritude to be "the efficient instrument of liberation," promoting world liberty (Kesteloot 1974:193).

Considered a success by its organizers, the 1956 congress posed more questions than its participants could ever hope to answer. Most of the delegates to this congress were independent artists and writers, linked by the primary intellectual network of Présence Africaine. From a sociological perspective, issues of artistic and political activism raised by these participants could not be addressed adequately in the absence of local and national cultural organizations and research commissions dedicated to developing a sustained public discourse about art and culture. Although evidence of this institutionalization appeared as early as 1956, the organizational outlets and networks for black artistic and political expression in France were unstable. With heated debates across competing factions, the 1956 congress was high drama, and its energy fueled the Présence Africaine movement and the newly founded SAC for a long round of conferences and colloquia over the next two decades. Each conference partially answered the questions posed by the last and raised new issues and problems.

Having defined the goals of Présence Africaine as revitalization, illustration, and creation of new values for the black world, Jacques Rabemananjara explained his view of the role of the conferences: "Via the Société Africaine de Culture, the role of Présence Africaine was to organize conferences and seminars. The 1956 congress was our first. A certain number of conferences were organized by African nations later, with Présence Africaine as the cultural motor of the conferences. . . . All of this was a type of illustration. That was the second objective

Fig. 6. Bookstore of the Présence Africaine publishing house, rue des Écoles, Paris, July 1990. Photograph by Bennetta Jules-Rosette.

of Présence Africaine. It is a type of cultural animation, which is the normal role of Présence Africaine" (Rabemananjara 1988).

This process of illustration, which included holding conferences and symposia, enhanced the rapprochement of African writing to other disciplines, in particular art history and the social sciences. Illustration and animation opened the doors for difficult political debates as African nations emerged and sought stability. How was "culture" to be defined? What were the roles of cultural tradition and patrimony in political change? And, most significant for the writers and intellectuals, what place did writing hold in the politics of change? As these questions played out, Présence Africaine occasionally found itself on the margins of the very debates that it had initiated and sponsored. The publishing house and the associated social movements stood in the paradoxical position of providing elite leadership for a population that was viewed as subaltern in France. In order to consider how the progressive marginalization of Présence Africaine occurred, it is necessary to begin with the 1956 congress.

Overview of the 1956 Congress

Over a third of the issues of *Présence Africaine* between 1957 and 1969 are devoted to conference proceedings. Numerous accounts of the 1956 congress are available in the journal, the popular press of the day, and the analyses of literary historians (Howlett 1958:111–17; Bâ 1973:22–26; Frutkin 1973:32–36; Kesteloot 1974:103; Mouralis 1984:425–32; and Mel 1995:145–68).[2] A perusal of these accounts indicates that ambiguities inherent in multiple images of Africa and contrasting strategies of political action surfaced during the public debates. Bernard Mouralis (1984:425–61) offers a detailed account of the conferences sponsored by Présence Africaine. Although I also follow a straightforward chronology, I attribute more political weight than does Mouralis to the intensity of the debates, the role of African-American writers, and the rupture with négritude at the 1969 Pan-African Cultural Festival in Algiers. Even though the terms have been reconfigured, the debates emerging during the conferences sponsored by Présence Africaine remain relevant and form the themes of an intriguing and heated discourse on colonialism and Africa. As a result of the 1956 congress, problems with defining Africa as a cultural sign moved from the printed page to the arena of social action.

Three themes motivated the 1956 congress: (1) the richness of black cultures; (2) the crisis in these cultures in relationship to political action; and (3) the prospects for the future. The second theme appears to have received the lion's share of press coverage and is often misrepresented as the theme of the entire congress (Frutkin 1973:32). Three types of presentations were made at the congress: (1) synthetic cultural statements about natural Africa and emerging Africa; (2) scholarly papers based on social science research and observations of particular topics, such as religion in Africa and the tonal structure of Yoruba poetry; and (3) programmatic political statements.

Senghor's "L'Esprit de la civilisation ou les lois de la culture négro-africaine" represented the first approach in its call for a synthetic vision of universal black culture with its roots in African experiences and forms of expression. The second set of exposés on black cultures combined scientific and critical views of emerging Africa in the papers of Mamadou Dia, Paul Hazoumé, and Hampaté Bâ. A third set of papers opened a series of programmatic debates concerning the politics of liberation and African cultures. In "Culture et colonisation," Aimé Césaire argued for the integrity of diverse black cultures in Africa and the African diaspora but stated that all black cultures are united by a common situation of colonial oppression. Richard Wright and other American delegates, including Mercer Cook and John A. Davis, objected to imposing the concept of colonialism on black Americans and argued that their situation of racial oppression was historically different because it involved an active legal, educational, and political struggle within an established national framework. James Baldwin covered the 1956 congress for *Encounter* magazine. In an article entitled "Princes and Powers," Baldwin (1957) expressed mixed views about the relevance of the debates to black Americans and an impatience with the négritude movement.

Along similar lines, Jacques Rabemananjara remarked in his 1988 interview that the Americans did not grasp the intensity of the colonial struggle because they had not been colonized. He also emphasized the justifiable political fear that the Americans had of the scourge of McCarthyism. Some of the American delegates renounced the political agenda associated with the radical decolonization of Africa and chose to focus on the gradual social changes occurring in their country. They did not associate the internal colonial situation in the Americas with what was taking place in Africa. The Americans were leery of what they saw as links between the communist student movement in France and African intellectuals.

Other participants held an upbeat view of the congress. Describing his experiences as founder and participant in SAC, Paulin Joachim enthusiastically reported to me:

> The First Congress of Black Writers and Artists took place here in Paris in 1956 at the Sorbonne. And we were all there. There were Americans who came. I particularly remember Langston Hughes, who was my friend. Eh oui, we traveled to Uganda together later. And there was Richard Wright. We stayed in the Latin Quarter until five o'clock in the morning discussing ideas. In those days, this was our place. It's nothing any more. And there was Frantz Fanon at this first congress. The theme was "Modern Western Culture and Our Destiny." This congress gave a great boost to Présence Africaine. Alioune Diop and Aimé Césaire worked hard to organize it. Black Americans participated and so did French poets. The congress resonated throughout the "Negro-African" cultural movement. They started to take us into consideration and to respect us in France. They began to discover our writings. We were no longer people who absorbed culture. We were the producers of culture. (Joachim 1988)

For Joachim, cultural crisis and conflict were not the fruits of the congress. Instead, he saw respect and public recognition as the principal results. The congress provided publicity and a new forum within which the opinions of African writers could be heard. Problems of definition and debates over terminology faded into the background as Présence Africaine savored its initial successes.

The Image of Antithetical Africa

Cultural integrity and the future of Africa were at the heart of the debates. Senghor and others focusing on cultural, literary, and scientific topics invented a timeless, idyllic Africa as their ideal. Césaire and Fanon invoked the colonial experience as a clarion call for action. Rejecting idyllic or emerging Africa as models, the black Americans described their struggles and experiences of marginality at home, but they were ambivalent about their identification with Africa as a cultural ideal and a model for political activism. Political disputes and personality conflicts not recorded in the congress proceedings figured in these controversies. Nevertheless, the conflicting images of Africa implicit in the broad agenda of Présence Africaine surfaced repeatedly in the conference presentations. Africa immersed in the political combat of decolonization was the antithesis of America undergoing gradual political change.

In an effort to devise philosophical guidelines for négritude, Jean-Paul Sartre (1948:xli) referred to it as the antithetical moment of negativity in a dialectic of race and class. Sartre's vision of antithetical Africa is fundamental to understanding the debates that surfaced at the 1956 congress. I will use the term "antithetical Africa" in order to contrast the cultural ideal of natural and timeless Africa with a combative image of Africa as it emerged from colonial domination. In spite of the anthropological models discussed in chapter 1, it is important *not* to conceive of the movement from idyllic to combative Africa as evolutionary. These images may be combined or contrasted in competing narratives.[3] In his article on black presence, already discussed as part of the first issue of the *Présence Africaine* journal, Sartre (1947:28–29) conceived of blackness as a sign of cultural awareness that induces remorse and hope in France.

In his 1948 essay "Orphée Noir," Sartre reconciled the poetic and political images of Africa by demonstrating that négritude is a source of cultural inspiration in its exotic image and a stepping stone toward universal political liberation in its combative image. The complete statement of Sartre's frequently quoted dialectic of négritude in "Orphée Noir" (1948:xli) is: "Négritude appears to be the upbeat of a dialectical progression; the theoretical and practical assertion of white supremacy is the thesis; the position of négritude, as an antithetic value, is the moment of negativity. But this negative moment is not sufficient in itself, and the blacks who make use of it are aware of this. They know its aim is to prepare a synthesis or realization of the human society without races. Thus, négritude exists in order to be destroyed. It is a transition, not a conclusion, a means and not an ultimate end."

For Sartre, Africa functioned only to highlight the problems of oppression and subjugation affecting the world at large. Antithetical Africa, as Sartre envisioned it, was a logical step in the progression toward the liberation of the human spirit. He considered this liberation to be a fundamental necessity for both European and black writers. Sartre (1948:xxxix) asserted: "[R]ace is transmuted into historicity, the black Present explodes and is temporalized; Négritude introduces its Past and its Future into Universal History." Although Sartre acknowledged that ancestral Africa is an inspiration for black writers—the Eurydice toward which the writers turn—he rejected African decolonization as the sole solution to problems of social injustice. Africa was important as a stunning reminder to European intellectuals that the cultural other exists and that their expressions of liberalism can be undermined by Africa's stark experience of oppression. In the progression toward human liberation, Africa represented the locus of struggle.

In spite of his rational philosophical synthesis, Sartre ultimately reverted to the image of natural Africa by exhorting his readers to consider the consequences of political action. He stated that the African situation may be depicted realistically and without anger: "It will be enough to us to feel the scorching breath of Africa in our faces, the sour smell of poverty and oppression."[4] This "scorching breath" emanates from an idealized, poetic Africa that evokes both natural grandeur and a sense of guilt for the nations that colonized and exploited the continent. In explaining his dialectic, Sartre vacillated between acceptance of the poetic images of a natural and emerging Africa and his conclusion that Africa should be considered as a correlate in the logic of human liberation and universal political engagement.

Finally, Sartre wished to establish a parallel between the condition of an oppressed proletariat in Europe and the situation of blacks on a worldwide scale. His argument is especially timely today, when this source of political unity is being challenged by ideologies of essentialism and changing socioeconomic conditions. Although Sartre acknowledged the social problems resulting from differences in class and race, Fanon considered Sartre's view to be relativistic and distorting. Fanon (1967:133) stated of Sartre's assertion: "When I read that page, I felt that I had been robbed of my last chance." Alioune Diop and his colleagues considered renewing pride in African cultures to be the end point rather than the antithesis of the dialectic (Diop 1949a:3–8; Diop 1949b:154–55). Sartre's perspective was unappealing to the proponents of négritude in its rejection of the primacy and universal significance of African cultures. Yet, his political vision of human liberation attracted the supporters of decolonization, even if they disagreed with Sartre's basic assumptions and strategies.

Debates at the 1956 Congress

September 19, 1956, was a crisp autumn day in Paris. Slowly, Parisians returned for the *rentrée* after their long August vacations. Throughout the summer, Alioune Diop had worked tirelessly, sending telegrams, raising funds, printing programs, and distributing publicity for the First Congress of Black Writers and Artists. From all parts of Africa, from India, and from the Americas, delegates—for many of whom this was a first trip to France—flooded into the dimly lit amphitheaters of the Sorbonne. Walking across gray cobblestones into the large halls, surrounded by images of Descartes, Pascal, and Durkheim, the delegates brought a swarm of questions, challenges, concerns, and complaints. Poets, novelists, playwrights, and journalists, together with politicians and university professors, presented their positions on African and African diaspora cultures in the context of a long-awaited European political awakening.

Diop opened the congress by challenging the group to assume "with lucidity and passion" the responsibility of creating a "cultural renaissance" that would lead toward world peace and international understanding (*Présence Africaine* 1957:6). But this was not "just any" cultural renaissance; it was a reawakening inspired by Africans in Europe. The organizational and political problems involved in staging this renaissance were enormous. Telegrams flew back and forth between Paris and New York, Washington, Boston, Dakar, and Abidjan. Were members of the Communist party involved in the congress? Would the American delegates be blacklisted? Would the African delegates be jailed?[5] In this atmosphere of overt political solidarity and court intrigue, some delegates were even suspicious of others, believing them to be spies for the CIA or the French Ministère des Colonies.[6] The air was thick with fear, euphoria, and creative tension.

Mixed emotions characterized the interpretations of the congress in the Parisian press. Occurring only eighteen months after the Afro-Asiatic Conference held April 18–24, 1955, in Bandoeng, Indonesia, the congress was replete with political connotations. The Bandoeng conference, also covered in *Présence Africaine* (1955:38–44), had focused on problems of decolonization in North Africa and Indochina. Bandoeng delegates resolved that it was time to end the years of servitude, stagnation, and poverty resulting from colonial oppression.[7] The left and liberal Parisian press hailed the 1956 congress as a "cultural Bandoeng," ushering in a new era of artistic protest.[8] In fact, the congress participants, whose cultures and politics clashed beneath the cloak of black solidarity, were not unified in an emphasis on their attack on colonialism. Nonetheless, the conservative Parisian press was alarmed by the entire affair, and failed to recognize the nuances of discourse.

According to Jacques Howlett (1958:112), an article published on September 27, 1956, in *Rivarol,* an organ of the conservative press, mocked "*les nègres et le néant*" and labeled the congress participants "agitators, Arabs, and Communists of every stripe." *L'Indépendant,* a publication that defended colonial interests, printed the opinion that "this supposedly cultural Congress is, in fact, a political enterprise, and what politics! Nothing less than Marx and J.-P. Sartre, those two dreadful characters." *Le Monde* of October 10, 1956, published Alioune Diop's reply in the form of a long article by him dealing with culture, art, and politics (Mel 1995:165). The gap between the conservative and the liberal press coverage of the congress was so wide that it is difficult to believe that the articles were describing the same event.

Humanité and *Démocratie Nouvelle,* publications of the French Communist party, described the congress as rational, sound, and politically engaged. The Catholic press lauded the humanitarian ideals of the congress and considered it an affirmation against racism and in favor of cultural enrichment (Howlett 1958:114–15). These reviews reflected an ambiguous mixture of cultural and political concerns that surfaced in the formal presentations and debates at the 1956 congress. The French university system also provided a source of liberal support. The university offered a venue for the congress at the Sorbonne and bolstered the ideas that sustained the event. In a 1988 interview, Cameroonian anthropologist Manga Bekombo of the Université de Paris X explained: "Senghor was a university person. Césaire was a writer and former French university student. . . . They had fought with their French university colleagues against colonialism, against racism. It's necessary to look at the underlying politics."

A primary debate at the 1956 congress centered around the distinction between a cultural politics rooted in Africa and a political culture with more universalistic overtones. Influenced by Frobenius, Senghor continued to advocate the concept of an essential African civilization that would guide autonomous artistic and literary productions. By 1956, the literary and cultural implications of this version of négritude were common knowledge in Paris, but these ideas were neither accepted nor understood by all congress delegates. In particular, Senghor's application of German historicism to African cultures failed to convince members of the North American delegation, on whom both the political and philosophical implications of négritude were virtually lost in the light of their 1954 and 1955 legal victories against segregation in the United States. Some North American delegates viewed négritude as an abstract and exotic francophone theory with no relevance to their situation (Campbell 1991:108).

Wright responded that although Senghor's presentation lucidly outlined the essential features of African cultural unity, he could not identify with anything Senghor described. In "Tradition and Industrialization: The Plight of the Tragic Elite in Africa," Wright interrogated modernity as a whole and emphasized the economic, political, and technological problems faced by the emerging African elite. While maintaining the illusion of intellectual freedom, argued Wright, the African elite is also tormented by the loss of its cultural roots. During the course of the congress, Wright remarked: "Today, it is not culture that unites men, but technology. Culture will become only an accessory, condemned to disappear by progress. We will no longer think, we will produce" (Rousseau 1957:333).[9] This statement emphasized the extent to which the specter of colonial discourse polarized the congress. Césaire argued that at a congress constituted largely of African representatives and people from the colonized world, it was impossible to pose questions of black culture without situating it in a colonial context.[10] Failing to attack the problem of colonialism would foreclose further debates on the development, uplifting, and diffusion of black cultures.

Fanon went a step further in "Racisme et Culture." In a controversial presentation that was not well received, Fanon analyzed the devastating psychological effects of colonialism and warned against placing too much faith in purely literary and artistic endeavors, to which he referred as "the culture of culture." He questioned the psychological effects of oppression on the colonial subject and advocated direct political action as a remedy. To the dismay of most of the Americans, Fanon did not exclude violence as a response to the debilitating psychological consequences of racism, although he concluded the paper on a conciliatory note. Fanon (1956:131) asserted: "The end of racism begins with a sudden incomprehension. The spasmotic and rigid culture of the occupant, once liberated, finally opens up to a culture of people who have really become brothers. The two cultures can confront and enrich each other. In conclusion, universality resides in this decision to take charge of the reciprocal relativism of different cultures once the colonial statute has been irreversibly excluded."[11]

Cross-cutting the debate on colonialism were the contrasting political concerns of the delegates from the United States. The 1956 congress was one of the first and most significant organized encounters between black American and French-African intellectuals. Tyler Stovall, a historian of black American Paris, states (1996:197) that the 1956 congress was "the single most important example of Wright's ties to French black writers." Nevertheless, Richard Wright and other black Americans in Paris had their own political concerns and fears. A walk in the Latin Quarter, near the congress venue at the Sorbonne, sheds some light on this situation. Wright, who lived at 14 rue Monsieur-le-Prince, just blocks away from the Sorbonne, often spent time at the nearby Café Tournon, which buzzed with American journalists, correspondents, and expatriate artists. During the 1950s, the Tournon was also alleged to have been a meeting place for American government agents and spies anxious to finger suspected communists in the expatriate community. Starving artists were approached to report on each other for a fee.[12] The tension and suspicion in the black American expatriate community in Paris were high. Already cautious about their participation in a French-African congress in Paris, the U.S. delegates confronted this strained atmosphere among their expatriate colleagues. For a variety of reasons, armed liberation struggles were not high on the agenda of discussion for them.[13]

Mercer Cook, professor of Romance languages at Howard University, was a frequent visitor to Paris. For over a decade before the congress, he had worked tirelessly to foster contacts between black American intellectuals and African and Antillian writers in Paris by participating in Paulette Nardal's literary salon and in informal exchanges (Kesteloot 1974:57). Cook believed that the social and political contexts of U.S. race relations were poorly understood in Europe. In his essay "Race Relations in the United States Seen by French Travelers since the Second World War," Cook challenged his African and Antillian colleagues to write more realistic and less lyrical accounts of their experiences in the United States in order to contribute more actively to the international understanding of U.S. race relations (Cook 1957:119–27). Among the U.S. delegates, Cook came the closest to dealing with the psychological effects of racial stereotypes on identity. On behalf of the National Association for the Advancement of Colored People, James Ivy presented "The NAACP as an Instrument of Social Change," in which he focused on black participation in the U.S. political process. John A. Davis (1957:129–47), founder of the American Society of African Culture, an organization modeled on SAC, outlined a history of black participation in the American political process from Reconstruction until 1955 in "The Participation of the Negro in the Democratic Process in the United States." Both Ivy and Davis wanted to demonstrate the benefits of a commitment to gradual political and legal progress leading to an integrated society in the United States. These authors made no references to a specifically "African" spirit of unity or an African "national culture." Nor did they draw a parallel between the African colonial struggle and problems of race relations in the United States, in part because they did not consider violent protest a viable political option. Were these choices a matter of caution or conviction? In retrospect, it is clear that the black Americans were headed toward a more heated political struggle than they ever could have imagined, a struggle that would be influenced by both the rhetoric and strategies of the decolonization of Africa.

In *No Name in the Street,* James Baldwin reminisced about his reactions to the congress and hinted at a source of political concern among the Americans. Part of the suspicion-filled expatriate community, Baldwin explained:

> In the fall of 1956, I was covering, for *Encounter* . . . the first International Conference of Black Writers and Artists, at the Sorbonne, in Paris.
>
> One bright afternoon, several of us, including the late Richard Wright, were meandering up the Boulevard St.-Germain, on the way to lunch. Much, if not most of the group was African, and all of us (though some only legally) were black. Facing us, on every newspaper kiosk on that wide, tree-shaded boulevard, were photographs of fifteen-year-old Dorothy Counts being reviled and spat upon by the mob as she was making her way to school in Charlotte, North Carolina. There was unutterable pride, tension, and anguish in that girl's face as she approached the halls of learning, with history, jeering, at her back.

> It made me furious, it filled me with both hatred and pity, and it made me ashamed. Some one of us should have been there with her! I dawdled in Europe for nearly yet another year, held by my private life and my attempt to finish a novel, but it was on that bright afternoon that I knew I was leaving France. I could, simply, no longer sit around in Paris discussing the Algerian and the black American problem. Everybody else was paying their dues, and it was time I went home and paid mine. (Baldwin 1972:49–50)

Although his impatience with the 1956 congress arose from personal concerns, Baldwin shared two basic beliefs with his compatriots: (1) that American politics set the tone for political debates in the Western world and (2) that the problems of American racism constituted an international crisis.[14] John A. Davis (1957:147) put the question simply: "It is certainly clear that the acid test for American democracy has been the 'Negro question.' It is also clear that the progress since 1933 has been steady and hard fought. . . . These good results are sorely needed because American racism has been deplored by all of the nations of the world since 1946 with the exception of South Africa."

Several of the African participants were concerned neither with the issue of political decolonization per se nor with the local politics of the American delegates. Instead, following Senghor's lead, they focused on renewing pride in African cultures as a route to psychological and political liberation. Based on their attraction to French ethnology, these participants presented detailed anthropological descriptions of specific African cultures and traditions.

"L'Humanisme occidental et l'humanisme africain," a paper by Paul Hazoumé (1957:29–45) of Dahomey (now Benin), raised the importance of preserving and understanding an African cultural patrimony. Hazoumé defined culture as "the enrichment and embellishment of our intelligence and spirit" (29). A large portion of his paper was devoted to an analysis of the misinterpretation of a bas-relief from the ancient royal palace of Abomey, capital of the kingdom of Dahomey. A colonial administrator, relying on the advice of an erudite French colleague, reproduced a series of bas-reliefs in a book on the ancient kingdom. The administrator erroneously described the *ajalala,* a large vase pierced with holes and supported by a figurine, as a "fetish object" intended to provide offerings to the ancestors. Challenging this faulty ethnological interpretation, Hazoumé stated that the *ajalala* was actually a household object used to filter water for the preservation of smoked fish. The *ajalala* was appropriated as a symbol of political unity for the ancient kingdom of Dahomey because many fingers, those of the loyal and devoted subjects of the king, were required to plug the holes in the jar. This gesture symbolized the political unity of the kingdom. In spite of the fact that Hazoumé did not explore the existence of multiple meanings and levels of signification for interpreting the *ajalala,* his parable had a dual target. On the one hand, he argued that correct ethnological understanding requires great familiarity with traditional African cultures on the part of anthropologists and historians. On the other hand, he contended that African intellectuals should reacquaint themselves with their own traditions as a form of cultural and political fulfillment. Hazoumé concluded that African traditionalism enhances occidental humanism, and that this type of enrichment should be the objective of the congress. He echoed Senghor's plea for a unified view of African cultures and civilizations that could be documented in its particulars through the use of ethnological methods. Richard Bjornson (1992:149) refers to Hazoumé's perspective as a contradictory assimilationism in which traditionalism is ultimately undermined by its modernist reinterpretation.

Bernard Dadié returned again with a commentary on the social force of African legends and proverbs that resembled his contribution to the 1947 issue of *Présence Africaine* (Dadié 1957:165–74). N'Sougan Ferdinand Agblémagnon, from Togo, presented a paper on the concept of time in Ewe culture, and Bakary Traoré, of Senegal, gave an ethnographic overview of African theater across the continent. Developed in the spirit of Senghorian négritude, these papers became the ripe targets of criticism from the politicized Antillian contingent. Jacques Stéphen Alexis, of Haiti, and Fanon both criticized the notion of a universal African culture unearthed as part of what Fanon and Césaire called "museum culture." They questioned the utility of any ethnological methods for cultural renewal. Césaire argued cogently for a source of commonality derived from recognition of a situation of colonial domination that united Antillians, Africans, and black Americans in a common struggle. United States delegates objected to this perception of their situation, contending that they were already successfully struggling for racial equality within the legal system of a Western democratic society.

Mamadou Dia, an economist and former deputy to the French government from Senegal, added a sobering modernist perspective to the cultural debates by focusing on the economic situation of African colonies as they moved toward nationhood. Dia asserted:

> It is not by accident that the revival of African cultural consciousness that some have called "négritude" or "negro-African realism" coincides historically with the decline of the imperialist spirit, and the challenge, if not the death, of the Colonial Pact, and the exaltation of economic forms more sensitive to human dignity. . . . [B]ut incontestably, a new dawn is in sight. Yes or no, will the African elites lose this chance? It is by a simple and direct message, the message of an economist to his African cultural brothers, writers and artists, that we respond

> to this question. The situation is too delicate, in this era of the cybernetic revolution and nuclear power, for us not to be more tormented about the economic future of Africa. (Dia 1957:70)

Dia brought together the themes of culture, technology, and economics. He situated Africa in a world economy and bypassed the debate about colonialism in order to look toward Africa's future. Dia's comments have an uncanny relevance today. Nevertheless, his formal contribution to the 1956 debate is often overlooked in critical commentaries on the congress.[15]

After a series of discussions on colonialism, the politics of liberation, and the dignity of African cultures, the congress participants resolved that all countries in the black world should be decolonized and that a scientific inventory of black cultures should be developed. Although the French term *intégration* was used to describe the resolution, the idea might be best translated as recognition of African cultures in an international, and particularly a Western, context. This resolution shaped the more pragmatic Second Congress of Black Writers and Artists, held in Rome three years later. The integration resolution was so general that all debating parties accepted it, even though several participants subsequently wrote mixed reviews about the inconclusive results of the congress for local presses and journals outside of Paris. Invocations of cultural and political unity at the congress masked a situation in which many delegates were "talking past" each other. From the perspective of the *Présence Africaine* steering committee, however, an important outcome of the congress, in addition to the publicity, was the formation of SAC and the establishment of the publishing house to carry out the literary activities of a cultural movement. The Haitian Jean Price-Mars was chosen as the first president of SAC, and Alioune Diop was the secretary general. Officers of the association included James Ivy, Josephine Baker, Emile Saint-Lot, Peter Abrahams, and De Graft Johnson (Mel 1995:171). Together, they began to plan for the Second International Congress of Black Writers and Artists in Rome.

Manga Bekombo, who watched the enterprise unfold, described the operation of SAC to me:

> So, how was the movement organized? Essentially by work commissions. The Société Africaine de Culture of Présence Africaine saw itself as a veritable university. There were commissions that resembled university departments. They worked on history, geography, philosophy, and so on. These were specialized departments. That was the ideal. And on the concrete level it translated into departments that were veritable little societies in themselves. And these commissions operated for a long time, perhaps until the 1960s, and they produced I don't

> know how many issues of the journal. There was the journal itself to publish reflections. And there were books and edited volumes. The objective of all of this collaborative work consisted in bringing Africa into the public view as a human reality, as a great people. Voilà! (Bekombo 1988)

Unresolved Resolutions in Rome, 1959

In order to implement the integration resolution, the SAC organizing committee planned a conference to be held from March 26 to April 1, 1959, in Rome. The 1959 congress was preceded by a relentless round of planning meetings in Paris and West Africa, during which SAC members in Paris debated the intellectual responsibilities of black writers, artists, and scholars. Breaking away from the influence of Western models and envisioning a universal role for African literature and art were the conference goals. Many of the participants from 1956, including Alexis, Césaire, Fanon, Senghor, and Dadié, attended the Rome congress. United States participation continued. John A. Davis returned from the United States, and Samuel Allen and Saunders Redding presented papers on black American literature and négritude. Research and organizing groups of SAC delineated specific problems in African philosophy, art, literature, and culture that were addressed in a programmatic manner throughout the congress.

With respect to the relationship between anthropology and African writing, the 1959 congress took a new turn. The Senghorian approach emphasized using French ethnology and related disciplines as an unexamined support for the tenets of négritude. Little attention was devoted to the epistemology of anthropology, except in its grossest colonialist forms. By 1959, African philosophers, anthropologists, and sociologists, with a firm grasp of their disciplines, attempted to develop ways in which their research and writing could be applied to their societies as a force for social change. A parallel effort took place in the domain of literary criticism, and these activities continued in subsequent SAC-sponsored conferences.[16] From 1959 forward, the role of Présence Africaine and SAC-sponsored conferences was to form a socially responsible and politically conscious intellectual elite primed to bring about cultural change in Africa. Although Europe was the locus and immediate audience for the first two conferences, after 1959 these events shifted to the African continent.

Since 1946, the French Community had been preparing the terms of independence for African colonies, and these terms were finally set in motion in 1958. The congress participants arrived in Rome with a true sense of mission—to begin the work of intellectual and cultural reconstruction for a new, postindependence Africa. Rather than continuing with the inventory of African cultures planned at the 1956 Paris congress, SAC set two new objectives for Rome: (1) to develop a historical foundation for African cultural unity and (2) to define the social and cultural responsibilities of intellectuals, writers, and artists from various disciplines.[17] In reviewing the presentations, it becomes clear that these two goals were actually played out as four themes: (1) invocations of cultural unity (rarely defined but alluded to in every presentation); (2) descriptions of cultural African traditions; (3) efforts to combine tradition and modernity to meet contemporary needs; and (4) discourses on political and social engagement.

At the opening of the congress, Alioune Diop (1959:41) warned against the mystifications of colonial cultural and intellectual domination and called all participants to glorify the essential authority and integrity of African cultures in their work. Senghor reiterated the constitutive elements of African civilization and Fanon and Césaire returned to the issue of decolonization, with an emphasis on the political responsibilities of black intellectuals. Fanon's paper on national culture, subsequently reprinted in *The Wretched of the Earth* (Fanon 1963:206–48), contained a blistering criticism of SAC's political timidity. Unlike the discourses of the first congress, however, these exhortations by the old guard were not the most significant contributions. Instead, new ground was broken by workshop presentations on the social and intellectual responsibilities of novelists, theologians, sociologists, and philosophers. These presentations remain classics in the field of African studies because they developed a unique, although unrealized, agenda for creative and scholarly work.

In his discourse on the African novel and its responsibilities ("Le Roman et ses responsabilités"), Léonard Sainville (1959:42–43) argued that African and Antillian novels should be original, culturally authentic, and uplifting. Taking a jab at Richard Wright, he proposed that the works of the Cameroonian novelist Mongo Beti and the Haitian author Jacques Roumain were more uplifting than Wright's work because they did not pose racial issues in abrasive black-and-white terms but, instead, inspired the vision of a universal culture. While maintaining a politically responsible position, novelists should use their traditions to speak to the modern situation. Sainville urged writers and publishers to support each other in the dissemination of African literature. The conclusions of Sainville's paper were included in a draft resolution on African literature prepared at the end of the congress. This resolution encouraged writers to go beyond fixed Western literary traditions and experiment with new forms of expression reflecting their political engagement. In addition, the resolution outlined the importance of local African languages but, in the context of francophone literature, this respect for local culture did not exclude writing in French or embellishing French with African and creolized turns of phrase.

Abbé Vincent Mulago, of what was then the Belgian Congo, presented a landmark essay on the responsibilities of African theology. Mulago (1959) introduced his theology of incarnation, an African theology inspired by belief, faith, and respect for local traditions within the framework of Catholicism. Mulago pointed to the importance of indigenizing Christianity for Africa and, considering that he was in Rome at the time, argued for a startlingly heterodox rereading of Catholicism.[18] Theology of incarnation became the subject of several conferences later sponsored in Africa, with proceedings published by Présence Africaine and SAC (Howlett 1977:250–54; Mudimbe 1988:60–62). John Mbiti presented a parallel paper emphasizing the importance of Kenyan indigenous religions in relation to Christianity.

The discourse of Taita Towet (1959) on the role of the African philosopher encouraged a return to tradition and oral history while developing reflections on moral philosophy, slavery, colonialism, and social inequality. His paper contained several crucial points, which were integrated into the resolutions, for developing an African philosophy reflecting the traditions, cosmologies, and beliefs of African cultures. A tension between particularism and universalism arose in the philosopher's efforts to distill elements of African cultures and belief systems while preserving the integrity of particular traditions.

The dialogue between Présence Africaine and the social sciences continued as Emmanuel Paul (1959) and N'Sougan Agblémagnon (1959) hammered out the responsibilities of ethnologists and sociologists. Paul stressed that African anthropologists should study their own cultures and insert their intimate cultural knowledge and perspectives into the pool of ethnological knowledge. He did not, however, develop a substantial critique of existing anthropological models or devise specific methods whereby an African ethnology could distinguish itself from any other type of anthropology. Instead, he treated ethnology as a type of literary production to which African insights should be added. Agblémagnon, who had presented a tedious paper fully under the sway of the négritude philosophy for the 1956 congress, returned in 1959 with a more programmatic, and much more interesting, statement about African sociology. He proposed that sociologists should: (1) rethink Western models and take only what is of value from them; (2) develop original methods; (3) engage in an autocritique based on a new sociology of knowledge; and (4) introduce personal experience, understanding of African languages, and a new perspective on African social institutions (Agblémagnon 1959:213). He then concluded that sociology is a "universal vocation" and that nothing separates an African sociologist from any others, except the urgent need to introduce conceptual and methodological reform into the discipline. Operating within the framework of sociology as a profession, Agblémagnon, nonetheless, challenged its fundamental tenets.

At the conclusion of the congress, four specialized commissions published resolutions that synthesized the presentations. These resolutions focused on the position of black artists and intellectuals in the modern world, the problem of the language of writing, and the publication of works by black authors. The outcomes of the commissions drew upon critical papers about African, Antillian, and black American literature that involved questioning the concept of négritude as a definition of cultural identity in the process of political engagement. As mentioned, the responsibilities of African philosophers, historians, sociologists, and artists were addressed in workshops led by experts from these fields. The congress commissions attempted to specify the foundations of a new African literature and the political responsibilities of African intellectuals (Agblémagnon 1959:206–14; Mulago 1959:188–205; Towet 1959:108–28). These concerns were evident in the resolutions of the commission on African philosophy. The commission drafted a recommendation that African philosophy challenge a Western philosophical approach and urged African philosophers to use their own traditions, myths, and proverbs as a basis for developing an outline of African systems of thought. Resolutions of all the commissions at the 1959 congress advocated an "Afrocentric" approach to philosophy, literature, and the arts. SAC used these ideas to plan the First World Festival of Black Arts, held in Dakar from April 1 to 24, 1966.

Bernard Dadié recalled the 1959 congress as the best of all of the cultural encounters. He explained:

> Well, we were all there together. Césaire was there. He was already a deputy, and he became mayor of Fort de France. And Senghor was there. He was the only one to become president of a republic. None of the new African presidents participated in our meetings. We debated the issues of African independence. We touched on just about everything. And then, in 1959, we went to Rome. Frantz Fanon was there. He came and gave his speech, then he left right away. Sekou Touré sent us a message. All of that happened at our cultural meetings. But all of the ideas that we developed then have not been applied today. It's a different ideology, a different conception of human relations. (Dadié 1992)

Back to Africa in 1966

It is now 1966. Six years have elapsed since the independence of most of the states in francophone West Africa. Senghor has returned to the continent as president of Senegal. Nkrumah and George Padmore, who plotted out the terms of political liberation at the 1945 Manchester Pan-African Conference, have tried their hands at applying the new ideas in Ghana (Krafona 1986:61–63). Africa is full of hope—promises not yet broken. And once again, Présence Africaine seizes the opportunity to enter the scene with a cultural redefinition of political autonomy and culture. Ostensibly at least, the colonial enemy has retreated. Europeans are now colleagues and dialogants. Following its established strategy of coalition cultural politics, Présence Africaine seeks the aid of UNESCO to sponsor the First World Festival of Black Arts in Dakar. Shifting from north to south, in 1966, the important task was to bring the message of cultural unity back to Africa while continuing to define the parameters of new cultural and intellectual disciplines inside and outside of universities.

The 1966 festival was one of the most highly publicized and best attended events sponsored by Présence Africaine (Bâ 1973:25). The ministries of culture of several independent African nations assiduously prepared their delegations for the gathering. Bjornson (1991:180) recounts that Engelbert Mveng, then director of cultural affairs of Cameroon and fellow traveler and advocate of the Présence Africaine movement, encouraged the performers, artists, and academics sent to the Dakar festival to reaffirm African values in the style of négritude. Alioune Diop, through his extensive contacts and the activities of his protégés, influenced cultural and literary affairs, not only in Cameroon but also across francophone West Africa.

Although the 1966 festival took place in Africa, the symposium papers had a narrower cast than those presented in Rome. Unlike the two previous congresses, however, the Dakar festival involved the display of art works, theatrical performances, parades, music, and an academic symposium on African cultures and art. This symposium resulted in a series of resolutions concerning the responsibilities of African artists and filmmakers, but most of the papers presented were strictly academic in format and relatively narrow in focus. Participants in the art symposium included European scholars such as Roger Bastide, Geneviève Calame-Griaule, Sim Copans, Jean-Paul Lebeuf, Michel Leiris, Jacques Maquet, and Jean Rouch. African art historians, filmmakers, and musicologists attended. André Malraux, then minister of culture of France, opened the symposium with a discourse on "*art nègre*" and its importance as an artistic resource in European civilization. This was followed by Senghor's commentary on the emotional and rhythmic qualities of *art nègre.* These opening statements set the tone for the calm debates that followed.

Symposium papers addressed methods and theories for the study of African cultures and art from diverse perspectives. In a presentation entitled "Tribality," William Fagg of the British Museum presented an overview of what he termed African "tribal art" based on ancient traditions (Fagg 1968:107–19). Fagg's paper contained severe criticisms of contemporary and commercial art in Africa as degenerate hybrid forms. Other authors from Africa, France, and the United States attempted to redefine négritude and a sense of African cultural identity in the arts.[19] The First World Festival of Black Arts established a precedent for many future meetings that combined artistic display and performance with intellectual debates. Although the 1966 festival appeared to lose the militant enthusiasm that was manifest in the resolutions from Rome, it moved toward an academic and cultural institutionalization of black art, performance, and literature.

Among the most important resolutions made in 1966 were those of the cinema group, which planned to build a visual archive of African cultural traditions and develop an inter-African office of cinematography. In Dakar, with the emphasis on art and performance, cinema emerged as an important strategy for shaping national consciousness and discourses in the arts. Although Paulin Vieyra (1959:303–13), from Benin, had presented a paper on the responsibilities of African cinema in Rome, little attention had been devoted to this domain until the Dakar festival. Here, Vieyra presented a very similar paper (1968) underscoring the need for a trans-African film industry. In his presentation, the French filmmaker Jean Rouch expressed skepticism and concern that cinema and politics might become so intertwined that all creative freedom would be lost (Rouch 1968:523–37).[20] The cinema resolutions crystallized a theme of technological modernization, introduced as early as 1956 in Mamadou Dia's paper on the role of technology in Africa. In spite of these resolutions, little concrete programmatic action was taken in the area of African cinema until the 1970s.

American participation continued at the 1966 festival. Included on the roster were the choreographer Katherine Dunham, who presented a paper and performed, and the poet Langston Hughes. In "Black Writers in a Troubled World," Hughes (1968:505–10) was critical of the psychological violence expressed by a younger generation of militant black authors in the United States. He believed that these authors vehemently expressed their political views at the expense of all literary quality. Hughes complained:

> In Le Roi Jones' play, *The Toilet,* every other word is a word that in times past would have made ordinary citizens blush, and which even today makes ladies stuff their fingers in their ears. Younger Negro writers like Le Roi Jones, Charles Wright in *The Wig,* and the poets of the Village excuse obscenities by saying that America is obscene, and that the only way to show this obscenity is by calling a spade a spade, especially a *white* spade. James Baldwin sends down the "fire next time" on white America, and Le Roi Jones says to whites in print and in speeches, "drop dead!"
>
> In the old days of slavery no doubt Negroes used to talk quite badly about whites "down at the big gate"—but never in the Big House. Nowadays, Negroes talk about whites badly *right in the middle of the whites' own parlors, lecture halls and libraries.* They "tell them off" in profane and no uncertain terms. But the funny thing is that many whites seem to love it. (Hughes 1968:506)

Rather than addressing problems of black art and literature from an international perspective, Hughes preferred to dwell on internal debates among black American authors. He equated négritude with the American concept of "soul," which he defined as "the essence of Negro folk art redistilled" (Hughes 1968:508).

In spite of the academic tone of the 1966 symposium on art, the négritude theme was still alive among African participants who had started to use ideas of cultural pride to develop national policies and university curricula in the arts. Many of the African participants represented official government ministries, and this pattern was to continue at the 1969 Pan-African Cultural Festival in Algiers.

Black Power and Pan-Africanism in Algiers

Although it grew out of the previous congresses and festivals, the First Pan-African Cultural Festival, held in Algiers from July 21 to August 1, 1969, was significantly different from the earlier events. By the time the festival in Algiers took place, many newly independent African nations had already defined their versions of cultural politics. In effect, the colonial period had nearly drawn to a close across the African continent, except in southern Africa. The themes that surfaced in the festival symposium were Pan-African unity, linking North and sub-Saharan Africa, and the emergence of national consciousness as a driving force for cultural creativity. The concept of national consciousness, advanced by Frantz Fanon, contrasted markedly with the earlier ideas of négritude. By 1969, the festival participants had been exposed to the notion that national consciousness and political liberation fundamentally linked the processes of decolonization to psychological liberation and political change. The black American, sub-Saharan African, and North African participants in this festival held similar views regarding the importance of the bond between cultural identity, political activism, and the arts. The concept of black power, from the United States, and the philosophy of Pan-Africanism shared a common ideological space as sources of creative expression motivating the festival performances and symposium presentations.

Many of the delegates to the 1969 festival represented national ministries of culture and local political organizations that were not associated with the primary network of Présence Africaine. Although independent artists and writers were present, their formal communications were in the minority at the festival symposium. This time, Senghor did not attend, and his keynote address on négritude and culture was presented by Amadou Mahtar M'Bow. A young political activist and student in letters and humanities in France at the time of the 1956 congress, M'Bow was minister of culture, youth, and sports of Senegal by 1969. Liberation movements from Angola, Guinea-Bissau, Mozambique, South

Africa, and Palestine were represented, along with the Black Panther party from the United States. The official delegations, including those of the liberation movements, participated in cultural manifestations, artistic displays, film screenings, and parades. They also presented political manifestoes at the festival symposium. Surrounded by dancers and musicians, members of the Black Panther party and African liberation movements paraded down the streets of Algiers in costume. In contrast to the 1966 Dakar festival, the 1969 symposium communications were ideological rather than academic in tone.

Fifty-nine papers were presented as part of the organizing cultural symposium in Algiers. Although some of these papers made favorable references to négritude and praised the longevity of the concept, several papers were extremely critical and sought to do away with the concept. Stanislas Adotevi, minister of culture and youth from Dahomey, and René Depestre, who attended the festival as an independent delegate from Haiti, voiced strident criticisms that sounded the death knell of négritude. In response to the opening address sent by President Senghor, Adotevi and several other delegates expressed strong disagreement with the continued use of négritude as a political and cultural framework for action. United States delegates, including Eldridge Cleaver, representing the Black Panther party, and South African delegates from the African National Congress (ANC) wanted to explore immediate militant solutions to problems of political and cultural domination. (See fig. 7.) Adotevi (1969:8) emphatically summarized his point of view: "Négritude is a vague and ineffective ideology. There is no place in Africa for a literature that lies outside of revolutionary combat. Négritude is dead."

René Depestre (1969) supported the attack on négritude, signing his paper on the sociocultural foundations of identity as a message from Havana. He cited Cuba as the pinnacle of cultural cross-fertilization and artistic achievement. Focusing on syncretism and cultural mixture as unintentionally positive byproducts of colonialism, Depestre argued that philosophies of decolonization such as négritude could not account for the blending of cultures or for the profound psychological and cultural effects of oppression on personal identity. At the 1969 festival, Pan-Africanism, black power, and national cultural consciousness were proposed as alternatives to négritude. The participation of women, although primarily as performers, also increased at this festival.

Some individuals who attended the Algiers festival, with whom I spoke, did not even remember the debate over négritude. Mouralis (1984:461) claims that the ideological schisms in the symposium resolved themselves calmly "within the framework of scientific research," creating a harmonious outcome. Whether or not this assessment of the festival's smooth and productive resolution is correct, a strong challenge to négritude had been made. Representatives from African liberation movements, African and Antillian intellectuals, and militant black

Fig. 7. Members of the Black Panther party mingle with other conference participants in the convention hall of the Pan-African Cultural Festival held in Algiers, July 21 to August 1, 1969. Reproduced, with permission, from the files of the Photothèque, #E83.854.842, Musée de l'Homme, Paris.

Americans all criticized a concept that, in 1956, was still considered a revolutionary breakthrough. The symbolic death of négritude opened the way for more diverse and heated dialogues among African intellectuals.

Reassessment of the 1950s and 1960s

A challenging and complex event, the 1956 congress triggered a series of debates that transpired for more than a decade. Some of these unresolved debates issued from the definition of antithetical Africa, in which black consciousness was an intermediary step rather than a solution to Africa's problems. Delegates at the 1956 congress were unable to achieve an equilibrium between cultural and political action or to define the terms of their artistic expression in a unified manner. Invoking African cultures as a source of enrichment for Western humanism camouflaged these problems. Therefore, the organizers of the 1959 Rome congress took as their primary task the development of research groups and commissions to clarify the cultural and ideological significance of black creativity. The resolutions from the 1959 congress are still pertinent today as theses for the inclusion of black literature, art, and philosophy into a universal corpus of knowledge. Nevertheless, the momentum of these resolutions was not sustained as the congress participants moved into the Dakar festival in 1966. Although there was considerable overlap in participation across all three of these events, a continuous evolution of the discourses developed in 1959 is not evident later.

The First Pan-African Cultural Festival in Algiers marked a political and generational break. Political culture was defined in terms of engaged action instead of aesthetics. Art moved almost exclusively into the domain of performance. Many of the participants in previous conferences still harbor criticisms of this festival's political focus. Nevertheless, the 1969 festival marked a strong rapprochement among American, North African, and sub-Saharan African delegates by virtue of their shared commitment to political activism. Ironically, cultural identity was defined in a manner recalling Sartre's synthesis of the universalistic reconfiguration of négritude. That is, cultural identity was considered to be consciousness of political oppression and marginalization in a transnational context. By 1969, the black Americans were aware of the importance of the civil rights and black power movements as social movements with implications on a worldwide scale. Thus, they were able to share in the discourse of decolonization and nation building that constituted the foundation of Pan-Africanism. Emerging international consciousness supplanted négritude. This new ideology was born in Algiers and transplanted to Paris.

Discourses of national consciousness and Pan-Africanism, however, abounded in Algiers, with less attention devoted to the aesthetic features of black cultural production.[21] The full implications of the 1956 congress were, thus, still unspoken. In order to attain the solutions projected in 1956, a balance needed to be sought between political engagement and aesthetics. In 1956, the balance tipped toward a detached version of literary quality that had moved in a political direction by 1959. In 1966, the balance remained static under the aegis of an academic reinterpretation of aesthetic standards that was not motivated by political commitment. By 1969, the politico-aesthetic balance shifted to the position of political engagement, with a complete transformation of the aesthetic point of view.[22] Even though négritude was questioned and rejected by some 1969 festival participants, it had already become institutionalized by the cultural ministries of Senegal, Côte d'Ivoire, and Cameroon. Négritude, however, clashed with nationalistic ideologies of cultural authenticity and with mass political movements that either viewed négritude as elitist or ignored it altogether. Despite ideological pronouncements of doom, Présence Africaine was far from finished with its projects for the development of literature and the arts.

African Literary Criticism, 1973

Cameroon was a strategic location for the 1973 SAC-sponsored Colloquium on Literary Criticism, which would focus on African criticism, because it stood at the crossroads between anglophone and francophone literary traditions. In addition, Bjornson (1991:172–73) argues, an antinégritude literary and artistic movement, accompanied by the emergence of new publications, was well entrenched in Cameroon by the early 1970s. This movement was largely a response to the view that négritude was linked to the government's policy of cultural authenticity, which the opposition considered both intellectually and politically debilitating. Senghor had made several trips to Cameroon to defend and disseminate négritude during the late 1960s and early 1970s (Bjornson 1991:172). Alioune Diop had trained and influenced leading Cameroonian political and literary figures, such as Engelbert Mveng, and supported the founding of *Abbia,* one of Cameroon's leading cultural and literary journals.[23]

By the 1970s, a number of critics and authors operated out of African universities. They were concerned with establishing a distinctive and flexible form of criticism for African literatures, which would include oral literatures, epics, tales, and new experimental forms. Dadié had been a proponent of this approach at previous Présence Africaine conferences, and Sainville's plea for the authentically Afro-Antillian novel in 1959 foreshadowed the development of a new definition for African literature. No previous conference, however, had tackled the definition of literature and the role of critical discourse. The 1973 Yaoundé conference was the official birthplace of francophone African literary criticism.

The conference brought back several veterans of Présence Africaine symposia and festivals, including Engelbert Mveng and Basile-Juléat Fouda from Cameroon, along with Paulin Vierya, who reiterated his discourse on African cinema in a paper closely resembling those that he presented in 1959 and 1966. Newcomers included young poets, novelists, independent critics, and university professors from recently established African institutions. Over fifty presentations were scheduled into three workshops on the audience of criticism, the role of the critic, and the communication of criticism through education. As usual, the workshop organizers presented a set of resolutions at the conclusion of the conference. The major resolution was a decision to form an Association of African Literary Criticism, to be based in an African country (Société Africaine de Culture 1977:544).

Discussions focused on the formation of national cultures and literatures.[24] Alioune Diop (1977:528–32) was unable to attend the conference but sent a message in which he continued to use the word "civilization" to refer to the amalgam of African cultures. He saw the role of literary criticism as uplifting African civilization. In a brief message, Senghor (1977a:513–15) emphasized that African literature should consist of idea-sentiments, analogical images, and rhythms. The critic should comprehend these ideas and poetic rhythms through feeling concerns that draw on a uniquely African understanding and a meeting of souls (Senghor 1977a:515).

Other participants were more pragmatic, calling for a substitution of the term "values" for "culture" and "civilization" (Nkosi 1977:39) and the development of rational models of audience reception that included the traditional artist and "the people." In spite of exhortations that African criticism should eschew European models, participants, especially the francophones, invoked French philosophers and critics ranging from Descartes to Roland Barthes and Paul Ricoeur.

In 1973, the real drama centered around the locus and language of literary production on the one hand, and the political and cultural role of the critic on the other. The majority of the papers, and all of the resolutions, argued for the inclusion of oral literature as a legitimate form of African literature. The participants acknowledged, however, that new criteria needed to be developed for the recording, preservation, and criticism of oral literature. The resultant products would include ancient epics and tales and a new literature drawing on traditional forms. Although the phrase "artistic innovation," or some variant thereof, was used in many of the presentations, the creative process and the sources of creativity were never addressed. This problem was further compounded by a political definition of the role of the African literary critic as the gatekeeper of the values of national cultures. A key resolution of the workshop on the role of criticism described criticism's importance for political culture: "Its concern should be to discover in works the values that permit consolidating the cultural cohesion of a people in order to allow them to participate fully in national development [*la construction nationale*]" (Société Africaine de Culture 1977:543).

The resolutions on audience reception included discussions of the problem of developing national languages and culture. The workshop on communication and the critic applied these resolutions to the domain of education. In the political reality of the period, however, national languages for instruction were still being hotly debated across the African continent. Popular literatures were just beginning to emerge and were not always greeted favorably by elitist critics, who were encouraging a return to the oral sources of African literature. The larger issue of the political and artistic identity of the African writer lurked behind all of these questions and resolutions. Moreover, not one resolution addressed problems of the commercial distribution of African literature, censorship, and the creative scope of African writers within their political cultures. The issues raised at the Yaoundé conference were doomed to be resolved only by fiat and rhetorical claims.

Analyzing the Yaoundé conference from the perspective of the creative process, Mouralis (1984:468) views the "discourse" on African literary criticism as fraught with ironies and contradictions. He claims that the participation of numerous writers in the construction of this type of critical discourse reflects a "masochistic attitude" characterized by the fundamental contradiction of developing a form of criticism that actually limits the practice of writing. Mouralis's perspective is based on the assumption that writing is a private creative act. In juxtaposing the individual act of writing to the collective standards of criticism, Mouralis points to the dangers of classifying literatures in terms of their national and cultural origins (463–70). For the participants in the 1973 SAC conference, however, the building of recognizable national literatures was the initial step toward specifying criteria for the universal acceptance of African authors in world literature.

Results of the Endless Round

Scores of papers issued from the conferences sponsored by Présence Africaine and SAC from the 1950s to the mid-1970s. The goals of each successive conference became more ambitious than the last. By the late 1960s, UNESCO, various French ministries, and several African governments lent their support to the activities of Présence Africaine. What had started as a small journal gave rise to an international cultural and political movement. Diop, with his collaborators and protégés, directly influenced cultural policy across francophone Africa. The new journal's efforts at bilingualism in French and English increased its appeal.

As African governments developed autonomous cultural politics and home-based writers and intellectuals began to speak out, an antinégritude movement arose. Yet, some antinégritude authors continued to publish in *Présence Africaine* and to use négritude as a counternarrative to sell their books.

The 1969 festival of Algiers introduced a rupture. Ideologies of nationalism and black consciousness challenged Diop's global visions of cultural Pan-Africanism, the universalism of African cultures, and the role of the African elite as the vanguard of literary and artistic production. By the late 1960s, Diop's assumption that the African elite, defined as "men of culture" who were educated in Europe, would return to put Africa back on the cultural map and uplift formerly colonial societies, was viewed in some circles as an unrealistic, neocolonial myth. African governments harnessed their cultural ministries to support one-party rule, national cultural politics, and processes of nation building that were defined in hegemonic, localistic, and anti-intellectual terms. Diop's vision of universalism with an African twist vanished under the weight of glib new slogans of cultural authenticity and political progress, forged against the backdrop of enormous economic hurdles, interethnic conflict, and bureaucratic blockage.

With the battle of decolonization over, Présence Africaine adapted to the times and continued to flourish in Paris. Rabemananjara explained to me that the three goals of Présence Africaine—revitalization, illustration, and the creation of new values for the black world—evolved to reflect changing times. "So, if you say to me there has been a change in our goals since the early days, it is as a result of the milieu in which we live. Times change. There has been an evolution. Consequently, values become married to their era, which is what Présence Africaine has done in identifying itself with the conditions of the world in which it exists today" (Rabemananjara 1988).

Although the Présence Africaine publishing house continues to support debates and discourses on African liberation, both the political environment and the context of publication have changed since the early days of the journal and the first conferences. Other publishing houses in France and on the African continent produce the works of African authors. The mandates of Yaoundé have nearly been forgotten. National African literatures have been anthologized without questioning their origins, boundaries, and identities, while African authors writing abroad challenge the concepts of both national identity and universalism.

Reflecting on the conferences of Présence Africaine, Bernard Dadié (1992) stated: "In Africa, the writer has been the enemy. I don't mean the adversary because we have our tradition of griots [praise singers]. But a writer who does not sing praises, who denounces injustice because he does not share the same opinions as an underling of the head of state, this writer becomes an enemy and has problems. That's why many writers prefer to go abroad to work."

The terms of the African presence in dialogue with Europe shifted during the postcolonial era. Présence Africaine promoted a cultural ideal that based the transition from colonialism to nationhood on a set of assumptions about the leadership role of a vanguard of African elites and intellectuals. The value changes and enormous political developments to which Rabemananjara and Dadié refer altered Présence Africaine's role as a cultural movement. Also, a series of developments in the French and African national publication industries changed the commercial role of Éditions Présence Africaine on the literary scene. The emergence of revolutionary writing as a new literary code and literary genre challenged Diop's vision of universalism.

INTERVIEW

Paulin Joachim
Paris, July 20, 1988

This interview with the poet, journalist, and essayist Paulin Joachim of Benin covers the early years of the Présence Africaine publishing house and the Société Africaine de Culture (SAC). As a young student and author, Joachim was an active participant in the founding of Présence Africaine, and he continues to serve on the editorial committee. His works include several collections of poetry, of which Oraison pour une re-naissance *(1984) is the best known. A journalist for the magazine* Bingo, *Joachim has also written several critical pieces, including* Éditorial Africain *(1967).*

Early Years of Présence Africaine

Bennetta Jules-Rosette: Monsieur Joachim, how do you see the early years of Présence Africaine, and what role did you play at that time?

Paulin Joachim: There were several of us grouped around Alioune Diop, who was a great pioneer in his work for African culture. He brought together French intellectuals such as Mounier, Sartre, and Leiris, the great surrealist. All of them knew Africa. And there was a small group of students: David Diop, a great poet who is now deceased; René Despestre, a Haitian writer; and Jacques Stéphen Alexis, now deceased, from Haiti. He wrote marvelous books. We were all in the small group around Alioune Diop, and we had a mission. Essentially, it was to implant African culture in European civilization, to affirm our presence. And in Paris in those years we wanted to launch an African cultural renewal aimed at the white world in which we had been immersed. We wanted to assert our culture and our presence in this world. The colonizers always negated our culture, as if there could be a people without culture. That was a fundamental error. So it all started with the assertion of our presence, and that was linked to the négritude movement that you know well. It began with the expression of a political position that became a cultural movement.

BJR: And how many people were active during this period?

PJ: There were about ten young people around Alioune Diop, ten faithful followers. We met regularly with Alioune Diop to discuss specific themes. We met in the Latin Quarter and at rue Chaligny in the twelfth arrondissement. Later, the Présence Africaine office moved to rue des Écoles. . . . We were students then. We regurgitated everything that they taught us at the Sorbonne and in the French universities. We were not ourselves. We lived a racial and cultural lie. It was through Alioune Diop and Présence Africaine that we became ourselves, that we discovered our cultural values, our ancestors, and our past.

BJR: And what themes and topics did you discuss at that time?

PJ: First, we discovered black poetry with Césaire's *Cahier du retour au pays natal.* The *Cahier du retour au pays natal* by Aimé Césaire became the bible for all of the young people who met around Alioune Diop. It was our bible, and we were proud of the writings of our elder, Césaire. For a long time, young black poets of the second generation were inspired by Césaire. He created a synthesis. And in Africa, it became a bible. He launched the movement of black cultural renewal, and everything that he wrote became very important for the African intelligentsia. And when the *Présence Africaine* journal was created, it became the organ of our cultural movement. We all published in the journal—me personally, David Diop, Depestre, and all the young people who were writing at that time. And the journal also became a sort of bible that circulated in everyone's hands in Africa. . . . And from that moment on, we were respected.

First Congress of Black Writers and Artists, 1956

BJR: Can you tell me about the conferences and cultural activities of Présence Africaine from your point of view?

PJ: The First Congress of Black Writers and Artists took place here in Paris in 1956 at the Sorbonne. And we were all there. There were Americans who came. I particularly remember Langston Hughes, who was my friend. Eh oui, we traveled to Uganda together later. And there was Richard Wright.

We stayed in the Latin Quarter until five o'clock in the morning discussing ideas. In those days, this was our place. It's nothing any more. And there was Frantz Fanon at this first congress. The theme was "Modern Western Culture and Our Destiny." This congress gave a great boost to Présence Africaine. Alioune Diop and Aimé Césaire worked hard to organize it. Black Americans participated and so did French poets. The congress resonated throughout the "Negro-African" cultural movement. They started to take us seriously and to respect us in France. They began to discover our writings. We were no longer people who absorbed culture. We were the producers of culture. In numbers eight and ten of the *Présence Africaine* journal, you'll find all of the texts from our first congress at the Sorbonne. The first congress was a wonderful impetus for our group, and it attracted a lot of attention. . . . It resounded throughout the black cultural movement.

BJR: What happened after the first congress?

PJ: Well, we discovered ourselves. And I was able to travel to Uganda, to Kampala with Langston Hughes. We went to a meeting with black anglophone writers—Achebe, Wole Soyinka, and others. We were both delegates from Présence Africaine. And that proves the interest that Présence Africaine had in black American writers. . . . I met Langston Hughes during the first congress, and we became friends. Afterwards, we went to the Festival of Negro Arts in Dakar in 1966. . . . It was a real celebration and a moment of rediscovery. We were impressed by all of the art and by our visit to Gorée Island, where our brothers were shipped away to America. I saw many people cry. It was all very moving. And there were conflicts between the francophone and the anglophone writers. Voilà. They reproached us for being too French and for writing long novels about négritude. You know the famous statement by Wole Soyinka: "A tiger in the forest does not proclaim his 'tigritude,' he attacks." You know that?

BJR: Yes, certainly.

PJ: The tiger attacks and bites. That idea was at the basis of our conflicts. The anglophones criticized our writing and our style. They didn't have the same background, and they said that we weren't African enough.

Publications and Writing Style

BJR: What type of writing style did you want to develop?

PJ: We wanted an African style that would make us distinctive. We didn't want to be carbon copies of European writers. We wanted to be unique and original. We wanted our writing to be fauve and rhythmic like an African drum. We wanted our writing to be both violent and sensitive—like Africa. I personally have a calmer style in my poetry now. But in those days, we wrote poems of combat. It was before independence. We had to deal with a colonial situation, a situation in which we weren't accepted as complete human beings. And today, we have managed to place négritude in the French dictionary and even in the Académie Française. The reality of our culture is now accepted by everyone, as a result of the work of our pioneer and spiritual father, Alioune Diop.

BJR: And what are some of the other sources of your inspiration as a writer?

PJ: Voilà. For me, inspiration comes from music and dance and our oral civilization in Africa. That's where one discovers the treasures. In Africa, song and dance preceded writing. . . . I've said this in my most recent book. Song and dance are the origins of African poetry. The griots of Africa composed songs about our history. I remember when we used to meet in the evenings at my grandmother's house. We told stories. Then we stopped the stories to sing and dance. It was wonderful! It was beautiful! And that's how I became a poet.

BJR: And what about your writing today?

PJ: Now, we cannot come to our encounter with universal civilization empty-handed. We have to arrive as producers of culture. We need to renew our traditions, to express ourselves.

BJR: Yes. Can you give me a specific example of what you mean?

PJ: Well, I'll read you a text that I just wrote yesterday.

BJR: Marvelous!

PJ: I wrote: "Remember, and we must not forget, before the erosion of time that will not fail to accomplish its work of destruction, that the general tendency in our latitudes is to imprison a past of shame and cowardice. Young people only have on their minds making those who filtered through the colonial net pay the price for their tardy awakening of consciousness. We must remember the frothy words emerging during our days under the colonial yoke and the passionate dirges of our prophets who tried to clear our tormented skies. We must remember the ambiance and sounds of our liberation in the midst of the false and hypocritical promises of the governors of our colonies: to keep us subjugated. You see! And it is important, and I say it without grandiloquence, that an understanding of the past can and must be our major weapon in the future."

Prospects for the Future

BJR: How do you see the future of African writing?

PJ: In thinking about the future, we must not forget the movements that helped us to liberate ourselves culturally. Young people today want to forget all of that, as if there could be a spontaneous generation. There is no spontaneous generation. . . . We cannot reject the past and everything that we have accomplished. Without those who died in Africa, who were killed by colonial bullets, there would be no independence and no present. Young writers today should not forget that.

BJR: And what are the challenges for young writers today?

PJ: Today, things have changed. Négritude, for example, was a phase, a stage of development. It allowed us to renew pride in African cultures around the world. Now that we have achieved that, after independence, it's time to move on to something else. We can no longer write poems of combat, poems of war. The time has passed for that. It's now time to assert ourselves with a new clarity and creativity.

BJR: What role can young writers play in this process?

PJ: Young writers have to understand that there will always be conflicts between generations. The young always want to kill off their elders, their parents. But one cannot erase the past. You can't erase your past, and I can't erase mine. I'm proud of my past, of the African past. I have found my dignity as a man. Voilà. . . . Because Africa has not been completely contaminated by Europe, there is still a virgin Africa, without pollution and corruption. Even Europeans want to travel to Africa to rediscover its purity. And in this sense, Présence Africaine truly accomplished something. We showed that the purity of Africa, of its culture and its values, has not been lost.

BJR: Yes. That's very important.

PJ: When I return to Africa, I immediately leave the city and go to my home village to reimmerse myself in this memory and to escape European technological civilization. This nostalgic Africa is the land of the dawn of civilization. And through this nostalgia, we become ourselves again. And all of this was part of the work of Présence Africaine.

PART TWO

The African Writers' Challenge

THREE

Revolutionary Writing: Challenges to Négritude

> I am still speaking of négritude. But of négritude across the labyrinth of mystification and the dictionary of neocolonial deception.
> —Stanislas Spero Adotevi, 1972

Algiers, 1969. Disillusionment and hope are in the air. The streets are festooned with banners as members of the ANC, the Black Panther party, the PLO, and the Mozambican liberation movement (FRELIMO) parade down the main boulevard. Art and the politics of liberation are at stake. Behind closed doors in the conference center, official speakers and their guests from North and sub-Saharan Africa, the Caribbean, Europe, and the United States are in the throes of a historic debate as Stanislas Adotevi, René Depestre, Houari Boumedienne, and others prepare a solemn and, they hope, final burial for négritude. The echoes from Algiers, as usual, resonate in Paris.

And these echoes resound within the walls of a crumbling colonial discourse. Infused with notions of progress, evolution, and uplift, colonial discourse is inherently modernist. At the heart of colonial discourse is the chasm separating dominator and dominated, powerful and powerless, other and self (Prakash 1995:5–6). Modernist discourses of liberation, such as négritude, propose a way out of the stifling colonial hot box by transforming a negative identity into a source of empowerment. In its Sartrian and Senghorian forms, négritude is construed as the antithesis of oppression. The raison d'être of négritude, however, is rooted in the very colonial oppression that it wishes to overturn. Négritude cannot exist outside of a colonial paradigm. It is not, as Homi Bhabha (1984:125–33) and Abdul JanMohamed (1985:78–79) have debated, an ambivalent discourse, but is, instead, a vehicle of protest against the colonial condition.[1] As a virtual identity discourse, négritude promises self-affirmation based on a prior experience of degradation. This oxymoron creates a situation in which the specter of degradation must be maintained in order for négritude to make sense. Logically, then, négritude should become superfluous with the end of colonialism.

Colonialism, however, is not merely a discourse. It is also a historical reality and a set of hierarchical institutional arrangements. Examined from the perspective of literary history, the colonial encounter poses two difficult problems. First, the official end of colonial rule in many African states did not eradicate colonial social and economic conditions and ideologies. Second, négritude as a colonial literary discourse also continued to enjoy an active life well into the 1970s, over a decade after the end of colonial rule in French West Africa. Although political history and cultural change seldom mesh in perfect chronology, négritude's tenuous longevity and the conditions of its demise require explanation.

The trajectory to be traced extends from the euphoria of liberation to postpartum disillusionment with the broken promise of modernity in Africa. In turn, this change has stimulated a reconfiguration of artistic and literary identity for African writers. Colonial discourses such as négritude encompass not only monolithic ideas, but also the speech of interacting human beings, espousing different points of view. One need only reexamine the debates sponsored by Présence Africaine on the role of violence in protest (Fanon vs. Diop), national poetry (Césaire vs. Depestre), and colonization and tradition (Wright vs. Césaire and Fanon) to acquire a sense of the contested terrains surrounding négritude discourse. Some literary critics believe that négritude, along with its ideological contribution to these debates, had already started to decline by the early 1960s (Moore and Beier 1963:23; Bâ 1973:159). The clarion call of colonial resistance gave way to a new form of revolutionary writing, which emerged and was transformed during the 1970s. The chronology of these transformations is reflected in competing colonial and postcolonial discourses.

Henry Louis Gates (1991:458–59) warns against the tendency to conflate and idealize theories of colonial discourse. He cites Edward Said's (1989:223) comparison of Fanon and Césaire as anti-imperialist archetypes, and advocates more subtle distinctions among theorists and caution in isolating these figures as global representatives of schools of thought. This problem of ideological distortion is acute in the case of the Présence Africaine movement, where debates abounded. The journal's issues are replete with volleys of contrasting opinions on heated topics such as political engagement, liberation strategies, and national poetry.

Removing these debates from historical context mutes and distorts their nuances. Revolutionary writing is an outgrowth of the interactions arising from these complex dialogues.

In spite of ideological conflicts, the Présence Africaine movement promoted unifying themes that opened the way for new literary possibilities. One of these themes centered around the social and political role of artists and intellectuals. Alioune Diop and his cohort of supporters believed that intellectuals should serve as translators of the voices of their people. Several paradoxes, of which Diop was aware, emerged as a consequence of this vision. Can any individual claim to be the spokesperson for a culture or a people? Are intellectuals, who risk alienation from their cultures, the most appropriate or effective voices of the people? What happens when the work of an artist or writer is singled out for praise and removed from its original cultural context? And finally, what kind of literature is most representative of the people—a regional, national, Pan-African, or international literature?

Trinh Minh-ha examines the tensions between political commitment and art in her comments on a 1957 article by Jacques Rabemananjara.[2]

> In an article, "Le Poète noir et son peuple" (The Black Poet and His People), for example, Jacques Rabemananjara virulently criticized Occidental poets for spending their existence indulging in aesthetic refinements and subtleties that bear no relation to their peoples' concerns and aspirations, that are merely sterile delights. The sense of dignity, Rabemananjara said, forbids black Orpheus to go in for the cult of art for art's sake. Inspirer inspired by his people, the poet has to play the difficult role of being simultaneously the torch lighting the way for his fellow men and their loyal interpreter. (Minh-ha 1989:13)

Rabemananjara's article points to the ways in which African poetry can be political and profoundly sociological. For Minh-ha, Rabemananjara's dedication to the social relevance of art poses the question of whether the artistic "self" is capable of fusing with the other (i.e., "the people") in African writing, or whether this dichotomy of self and other is yet another artistic illusion. Pushing Minh-ha's insights further with respect to the colonial paradigm of African writing, one may ask if it is possible for the intellectual, who has internalized the colonial system, to represent the people.[3] If so, what sort of political and cultural messages are conveyed in this process?

A plausible answer to this question emerges in the discourses of revolutionary writing. In this case, formerly colonized intellectuals throw off their fetters and join "the people" as propagandists, planners, and innovators. For Frantz Fanon, the ultimate goal of this coalition between intellectuals and the masses is the development of "national consciousness." Whether national consciousness also implies a national literature remains an open question.[4] The prospects for national literatures relate to what Gayatri Spivak (1985:262) has termed "worlding," or the construction of cultures and civilizations through literary history. Worlding suggests that literature operates as a tool for both building and suppressing imagined cultural histories (Chambers 1996:50). The "reworlding" of Western and African literatures is a logical outcome of revolutionary writing.[5] As the debates published in the early issues of *Présence Africaine* and the resolutions of the 1973 Yaoundé conference suggest, however, the concept of national literature supports both cultural hegemony and political liberation.

Frantz Fanon and Revolutionary Writing

Revolutionary writing overturns narratives of longing and belonging. Through psychological rebellion, it destroys idealizations of Africa. It also challenges scientific paradigms of ethnological writing by claiming that Africa is not a static museum-piece but a vital source of revolutionary change. This literary transformation issues from a rupture with preexisting structures of colonial domination and control, particularly as they affect culture, the arts, and politics. JanMohamed (1985:79) believes that this rupture is a product of the Manichean anticolonial struggle firmly embraced by Fanon, among others. Frantz Fanon is an early and prototypical writer in the revolutionary genre.

In "Racisme et Culture," presented at the 1956 Congress of Black Writers and Artists in Paris, Fanon (1956:122–31) examined the evolution of racism from biological determinism to a fascination with the exotic. He condemned the anthropometric vision and argued that there are no gradated degrees of racism in any society. The presence of racism implies all of its virtualities from social and political oppression to concentration camps. Nuanced versions of racism, however, play upon an ideological chord by attempting to convince colonized and oppressed people to assimilate into a liberal, dominant society and forget all vestiges of uniqueness and cultural tradition that might be considered inferior. Fanon (1956:131) concludes that the solution to problems of racism lies in revolutionary writing and direct action, whereby a more just society, based on cultural reciprocity, may be developed. Fanon's description of the psychological strategies for overcoming racism by resisting mindless assimilation became the inspiration for political tactics employed by liberation movements in the 1960s and 1970s.[6]

This approach to revolutionary action and writing fell on deaf ears at the 1956 Black Artists and Writers Congress, and Fanon intensified his conflicts with the Présence Africaine leadership at the 1959 congress in Rome. His essay on national culture (Fanon 1963:206–48) forecasts the break between revolutionary writing and colonial négritudinist discourse. Fanon scrutinizes the paradoxes of using violence as a method of decolonization. He attacks some founding members of the Présence Africaine movement for what he considers to be their bad faith in failing to support movements of national political liberation. Fanon states:[7]

> In 1959, the cultured Africans who met at Rome never stopped talking about unity. But one of the people who was loudest in the praise of this cultural unity, Jacques Rabemananjara, is today a minister in the Madagascan government, and as such has decided, with his government, to oppose the Algerian people in the General Assembly of the United Nations. Rabemananjara, if he had been true to himself, ought to have resigned from the government and denounced those men who claim to incarnate the will of the Madagascan people. The ninety thousand dead of Madagascar have not given Rabemananjara authority to oppose the aspirations of the Algerian people in the General Assembly of the United Nations. (Fanon 1963:235)

In the same essay, Fanon argues that an elite intellectual cadre can never designate the parameters of national culture. He states that the efforts of "men of culture" to mold African cultural unity are in vain. All they "amount to is to make comparisons between coins and sarcophagi" (Fanon 1963:234). From Fanon's psychoanalytic perspective, an irony lies in the fact that African men of culture have been emasculated by the European colonial system, which they ultimately internalize in order to reassert their dignity. Instead, national cultures and literatures reject this internalization of European cultures in favor of the shared experiences of colonial combat, suffering, and violence. Therefore, elitist cultural groups such as SAC and Présence Africaine are impotent as sources of leadership for the African masses. Fanon contends that these masses are capable of organizing their own cultural priorities, and that a national culture will emerge spontaneously from the camaraderie of combat. Thus, négritude, as a unifying discourse, is an impediment to the pragmatics of battle. The tactics of the battle on the literary front extend from reviving folkloric traditions to inventing a new literature for the African dawn (Fanon 1963:227–33).

Moreover, Fanon (1963:237) warns against the retarding and opportunistic actions of intellectuals who engage in the "frantic acquisition of the culture of the occupying power," even after decolonization has occurred. Only when intellectuals and writers are no longer alienated from their culture can a truly national literature be achieved. Fanon (1963:240) asserts: "[N]ow the native writer progressively takes on the habit of addressing his own people. It is only from that moment that we can speak of a national literature. . . . This may properly be called a literature of combat, in the sense that it calls upon the whole people to fight for their existence as a nation. It is a literature of combat because it molds the national consciousness, giving it form and contours and flinging before it new and boundless possibilities; it is a literature of combat because it assumes responsibility, and because it is the will to liberty expressed in terms of time and space."

Nevertheless, Fanon offers no specifically literary criteria for evaluating the fruits of combat, nor does he define the parameters of national consciousness, as they are reflected through literature. All impulses toward cultural validation in the aftermath of oppression qualify as national literature. Fueled by the spirit of combat, revolutionary writing is produced from the heart rather than on the basis of the established literary canons of colonized writing. The literature of négritude, in contrast, is inspired and produced by an intellectual elite that invoked, but was often removed from, its cultural roots.

Although Présence Africaine and SAC provided Fanon with venues for public expression, tensions always existed. Fanon was quick to condemn the founders of Présence Africaine for their elitism and complacency. His criticisms surfaced during the 1956 and 1959 congresses and are evident in his commitment to nationalism and revolutionary action. Both in his tribute to Alioune Diop (Dadié 1978:308) and in a 1992 interview with me, Bernard Dadié recalled the abruptness with which Fanon came to the Rome congress, presented his paper, and left immediately thereafter. A contrast in personal styles and points of view between Fanon and Diop's loyal followers obviously sustained this conflict.

Stanislas Adotevi's Antinégritude Discourse

Stanislas Spero Adotevi was a virulent critic of négritude. A university student at the time of the 1956 congress, Adotevi returned to Dahomey (now Benin) to enter politics, eventually becoming the minister of culture and youth. Adotevi's position with regard to négritude served his political purposes by providing him with a means of championing a new form of national power. Adotevi's style of revolutionary writing combines sociological analysis and political critique in his book *Négritude et négrologues* (1972), which he dedicated to Angela Davis. Here, he claims that négritude is a scientifically untenable and politically dangerous philosophy. He was aware that the use of race and ethnicity as a totemic motivation for collective action was a double-edged sword (Comaroff and Comaroff 1992:59-60). Adotevi asserts:

> First of all, négritude in the fashion in which it is broadcast, rests on confused and nonexistent notions to the extent that it affirms, in an abstract manner, the fraternity of all blacks. Thus, because the underlying thesis is not only antiscientific, but also proceeds from fantasy, it presupposes the existence of a rigid black

> persona, which is unattainable. To this permanent persona is added a specificity that neither sociological determinations nor historical variations, nor geographic realities confirm. It makes black people similar beings everywhere and at all times. (Adotevi 1972:45)

Adotevi's critique of négritude, first formulated at the 1969 Pan-African Cultural Festival of Algiers, and elaborated in various lectures and his 1972 book, takes on not only Senghor, Césaire, and the Présence Africaine movement, but also Lucien Lévy-Bruhl and the members of the Institut d'Ethnologie. He equates négritude with neoprimitivism and examines how myths of négritude discourse bolstered, rather than challenged, the process of colonization. His work, along with that of Marcien Towa (1971), contributed to the development of contestatory national literatures in Africa.

According to Adotevi, ethnology's interest in exploring problems of cultural diversity is dubious (Adotevi 1972:192). Not having evolved since the Victorian period, ethnology may be faulted as an arm of colonial domination and as a questionable set of theories that perpetuate distorting and destructive views of the cultural other (Adotevi 1972:195; Adotevi 1973). The remedy for the obstacles posed by the colonial discourses of négritude and ethnology is the development of a new kind of writing—the African book—that overturns the balance of power and invents new and richer images of other cultures (Adotevi 1972:279). Adotevi's 1972 book stops short of providing examples of this new form of revolutionary writing. We are presented with a series of social and political criticisms of existing genres and only the barest glimpse of what might replace them.

René Depestre and Yambo Ouologuem's Farewell to Négritude

The Haitian poet René Depestre saluted the advent of négritude, but he also bid it adieu with his conceptions of cultural syncretism, hybridity, and *marronnage* (i.e., the autonomous cultures of escaped slaves in the Caribbean). The terms *marron* and *marronnage,* which appear frequently in the works of Depestre, Césaire, and other Antillian writers, appear to have been derived from the Spanish term *cimarrón,* meaning "runaway slave" (Eshleman and Smith 1983:402). Depestre contended that négritude was an inadequate philosophy because it did not take into account the hybridity of cultures and the processes of domination and survival that have influenced blacks in the new world. In *Bonjour et adieu à la négritude,* Depestre (1980:88–89) states: "As Haitians, we must respond to the following question: Why did anthropological knowledge and the négritude that it nourished, after having their beginnings in the social sciences, literature, and the arts, illuminating and passionately enriching the political consciousness of the oppressed people of the Americas, quickly become recuperated and reintegrated in an organic and operational manner into the imperial or neocolonial problematic?"

Responding to this question, Depestre argues that anthropological works on escaped slaves and their cultures demonstrate that the essentialist theses of négritude are unworkable. Cultural hybridity and combinations occur in a variety of ways, often as a consequence of political domination and reactions to an oppressive culture (Young 1995:22–26). Although it is born of oppression, cultural syncretism is a robust alternative to négritude because it reflects the power of history. For Depestre, négritude as a philosophy explains neither the subtleties of these cultural combinations nor the political conditions under which they take place.

As part of his 1978 contribution to a festschrift for Alioune Diop published by Présence Africaine and the Italian "Friends of Présence Africaine," Depestre provides a frank overview of his attitudes toward the publishing house and its philosophy. Addressing a quasi-confessional letter to Diop, Depestre asserts:

> My radical and fiercely "Stalinist" anticolonialism could not conceive of a journal as a place of dialogue, a forum for the free confrontation of opinions of men from different horizons. I acknowledged fellow travelers from our ranks of the extreme Left, but I did not see myself in the inverse situation: a fellow traveler of a young and groping apparatus of decolonization. I could not imagine myself dialoguing freely with you, nor with Richard Wright, Balandier, Claude Julien and the other intellectuals who frequented 16, rue Henri-Barbusse. I was still on my guard vis-à-vis André Gide, Sartre, Camus, R. P. Maydieu, Merleau-Ponty, Griaule, Naville, and Senghor, who formed the Patronage Committee. At that time, I took as an enemy or an agent of our enemies anyone who was not on exactly the same wavelength as us, in philosophy, aesthetics, human sciences, or any other domain of culture. As a student in letters and political science, I was incapable . . . of perceiving what was anticolonial, that is to say *true,* in *Présence Africaine,* in regard to our revolutionary struggle against the pomp and workings of colonization. (Depestre 1978:59–60)

Depestre comments that this critical approach characterized his attitude toward *Présence Africaine* as a youth in 1947. In 1955, under the influence of Aimé Césaire, Depestre changed his tune somewhat as a result of a debate in Paris on national poetry sponsored on July 9 of that year by the Société Africaine de Culture and subsequently published by *Présence Africaine.* In spite of his disagreements with Césaire in this debate, Depestre found that his opinions were welcomed, or at least tolerated, by the journal, and he altered his view of the operation. In his letter of homage to Alioune Diop, Depestre thanks the publisher for his open-mindedness and assistance in the publication of his poems and two books. Depestre (1978:60) states: "You never proposed as a condition of the publication of my texts that I stop attacking the négritude of Senghor and his essentialist approach to the coupled notion of class/race in the history of our societies. You did it neither in Paris nor in Algiers at the Pan-African Festival after an offensive that many African and Antillian intellectuals had just mounted against the increasingly ambiguous intentions of négritude." While clinging to his critique of négritude and his firm belief that a nearly ideal deracialized society had been achieved in Cuba, Depestre nonetheless congratulates *Présence Africaine* on the creation of an open dialogue on politics and culture.[8] Depestre's genre of revolutionary writing is both a protest against négritude and an idealization of the utopian, multiracial society that he believed already existed in the Caribbean.

Tackling the demise of négritude from another revolutionary perspective, the Malian novelist Yambo Ouologuem, in *Le Devoir de violence* (1968)—translated as *Bound to Violence* (1971)—criticizes imperialism and neocolonialism. He argues that all phases of African development, from the colonial to the postindependence periods, are linked by a common theme of violence and deception (Palmer 1979:200). Oppression is not only a byproduct of imperialism, but is prolonged by elitist and distorting philosophies such as négritude, which divide classes and cultures. His allegorical history of the legend of Saif rulers in West Africa illustrates the ways in which oppression and degradation were perpetuated by African leaders who deceived, enslaved, and tortured their people. The Saif empire is rife with corruption, intrigue, and injustice. Ouologuem won the prestigious Prix Renaudot for his book. At the time of its publication, Ouologuem's book was regarded as controversial. This controversy was compounded by accusations of plagiarism associated with his description of the fictive Saif empire. Ouologuem retorted that he had not plagiarized but, instead, was reappropriating European knowledge about Africa and placing it in a more relevant revolutionary context. The literary critic Christopher Miller (1990:21) argues that the complexities and parodies in Ouologuem's text, including its veiled criticism of négritude and its subtle treatment of alienation, warn against a simplistic interpretation of the relationship between African literature and anthropology. Ouologuem's prizewinning novel has been praised for its combination of oral traditions and new narrative styles. It marked a path-breaking entry of postnégritude African literature into the mainstream French publication market. His work creates a bridge between the epic novels of the 1950s and the new African literature, critical of modernity's broken promise.

During the 1960s and 1970s, an antinégritude movement swept across francophone West Africa. Left without a unifying philosophy, writers sought inspiration from a variety of sources and leveled heavy criticisms at Africa's neocolonial leadership. Bjornson explains:

> Novelists such as Yambo Ouologuem . . . depicted Africa in a way that contradicts the principal tenets of Senghorian Negritude. Philosophers and cultural critics such as Stanislas Adotevi, Paulin Hountondji, and Ferdinand Agblémagnon argued that Negritude perpetuates European stereotypes of Africans, distracts attention from the real causes of economic underdevelopment, and blocks the evolution of African states toward more equitable forms of government. By this time, Senghor had become a symbol of political conservatism for the younger generation of francophone Africans, and although he continued to elaborate his conception of Negritude, it was increasingly viewed as a questionable basis on which to construct a viable sense of collective identity in Africa. (Bjornson 1991:172)

Although it was by no means unified, the antinégritude movement that Bjornson describes was based on market as well as ideological considerations. The emergence of a new elite reading public on the African continent made possible a break with négritude's pre-independence idealism. Additionally, a cross-over audience of political activists outside of Africa created a commercial niche for the publication and reception of the works of such authors as Fanon, Adotevi, and Ouologuem by mainstream French publishers. In this case, the intermediary commercial role previously played by Présence Africaine could be bypassed. The power to produce African literary works passed on to a new generation.

Alioune Diop's Reply

Alioune Diop wished to build a sense of cultural unity and universal coherence for African cultures, not a single collective identity. In response to the criticisms of négritude, Diop argued that the role of African authors and intellectuals should be to reconfigure the African past in terms of a set of traditions and cultural programs pertinent to the present. Diop and Senghor both traveled across West Africa to meet with political leaders and intellectuals in an effort to foster journals, cultural associations, government ministries, and university programs that reflected their humanistic views of the role of African intellectuals as leaders in molding a Pan-African culture (Mel 1995:281–84). In his summary of the history of Présence Africaine's publications, Diop states:

> There has been no linguistic unity among Blacks since time immemorial. Their historical awareness has been fragmented into many worlds whose horizons are at least as *limited* as their linguistic areas. In Africa, our cultures are *oral* and our

> *wooden* monuments are not weather-resistant. Our political authority is limited in space. Our spiritual personality is easily thrown out of balance. The intellectuals and the people (who are deprived of writing) do not scientifically or really master our heritage. No common vision of the future of the world sustains our co-existence on earth. Deprived of the means of thinking correctly about modern life, which stem from sufficient information and adequate exchanges, we allow strangers to build our future for us and to impose ideals upon us which we ourselves have not forged from a personal experience of the history and administration of the world. (Diop 1987:50)

Diop conceived of Africa in motion as it catapults from its proud past to an unstable present. He proposed a solution to the problems of fragmentation, isolation, and oppression when he argued (Diop 1987:46): "A real cultural solidarity of our people is, thus, indispensable to our salvation and our faith in ourselves. But this solidarity among black people must begin with an organic solidarity between the Westernized elites and their own people." The Africa described by Diop is not just a geographical location in time and space. It is an ideological construct and a cultural sign. Africa's existence and unity depend upon conscious political and social acts.

Literary pioneer and mentor to scores of black writers, Diop tirelessly mounted conferences, scaffolded new cultural programs, and published the works of African writers. He fostered links between African and French intellectuals while maintaining an analytic distance from their particularistic philosophical and ideological debates. Occasionally critical of Sartre, Fanon, Depestre, and even of négritude, Diop brought to public attention many of the issues that are still fundamental to contemporary African writing. Christopher Miller (1992: 431) views Diop's universalism as contradictory and, in certain instances, self-destructive. Diop's philosophy of the African elite's responsibility, along with his strategy of foregrounding the inclusion of African writing in the pantheon of European literature, presaged debates about literature and cultural integration current in France during the 1990s. This approach initially met with opposition from local intellectuals and grass-roots cultural activists as new national literatures began to emerge in Africa. Miller (431–32) considers francophonie, or the attempt to institutionalize African and Antillian literature in France and worldwide, one of the legacies of Alioune Diop's philosophy. In fact, Diop's idealized universalism was far bolder than francophonie. It was an attempt to demonstrate the ways in which all forms of African artistic creation are manifestations of the human spirit and to institutionalize the structures necessary to foster this creativity in Africa and Europe. Revolutionary writing attacked this dream with its claims that idealized universalism was divorced from the political realities of autonomy, nationalism, and populism.

Literary examples emphasize that revolutionary writing was a transitional genre. It sought to break away from the constraints of the politics of Présence Africaine, the négritude movement, and a dependence on naive anthropologizing. Many of the revolutionary writers were trained in the social sciences and philosophy. They attempted to incorporate ideologies of colonial liberation movements and postcolonial development into their works. They highlighted diversity, oppression, fragmentation, violence, and political deception as the challenges of a new Africa. Revolutionary writing used social protest as its unifying theme, but beyond that, it did not develop a clear set of stylistic and rhetorical principles for a new literature. Although African literary criticism arose in tandem with revolutionary writing, African intellectuals in their new universities did not set forth standards for African literature that tackled the thorny thematic issues posed by revolutionary writing. To further complicate matters, writers such as Adotevi, Depestre, and Towa may be interpreted as having continued the legacy of négritude by keeping its debates alive in their antinégritude discourse. Thus, even after the decline of négritude, the concept continued to survive as a literary theme and a source of debate. As a consequence of this mixture of styles, themes, and forms, the literary metamorphosis of African writing during the 1960s and 1970s is difficult to analyze, chronologically and critically.

Revolutionary writing was linked to a number of cultural manifestations, including the 1969 Pan-African Cultural Festival in Algiers, the Second World Black and African Festival of Arts and Culture (FESTAC) in Lagos, Nigeria, and local forms of street theater across the African continent. These cultural performances broadened the scope of African literary expression. They challenged earlier formats and genres of literary presentation and eventually influenced the styles of African writing in France during the 1970s and 1980s.

Paul Dakeyo's Concept of Revolutionary Love

A key transitional figure who warrants consideration at the close of this chapter is Paul Dakeyo, a Cameroonian sociologist, publisher, and poet. (See fig. 8.) An unusual combination of literary and political interests energizes Dakeyo's work. Born in Cameroon in 1948, Dakeyo represents the first wave of the postindependence generation. His anthologies of poems, including *Les Barbelés du matin* (1973), *Chant d'accusation* (1976a), *Le Cri pluriel* (1976b), *Soweto: Soleils fusillés* (1977), *J'appartiens au grand jour* (1979), *La Femme où j'ai mal* (1989a), and *Les Ombres de la nuit* (1994), emphasize a search for personal identity in the midst of political conflict and upheaval. Because of his activities as a writer and publisher critically positioned between Europe and Africa, Dakeyo may be viewed as a leading author responding to négritude and bridging antinégritude and the

Fig. 8. Paul Dakeyo in his office in the Ivry suburb of Paris, October 1, 1991. Photograph by Bennetta Jules Rosette.

new generation. His poetry of revolutionary love preserves the fervor of combat while simultaneously focusing on problems of exile and psychological suffering. In addition, his work as an editor and publisher of the writings of the new generation makes Dakeyo instrumental in the world of African publishing in France. This institutional linkage to the world of publishing, which is reinforced by Dakeyo's creative work, positions him as a prime mover facilitating a new African literature in France.

Dakeyo uses the metaphor of love in human relationships as a way of demonstrating a narrative of longing for a destroyed Africa and a quest for belonging in a new and autonomous political order. Dakeyo's later writings ostensibly deal with the pain of ruptured romantic relationships, but in fact they voice a lament about broken political promises in Africa. He transforms revolutionary writing into a personal exploration of problems of psychological torment and pain. In so doing, Dakeyo blends the literature of combat of the 1970s and the more introspective literature of the intimate generation of the 1980s and 1990s.

In his early poem *Chant d'accusation* (Song of accusation), Dakeyo develops a narrative of longing in which he juxtaposes his love for an idyllic Africa with his distress over its destruction. He speaks from a position of exile about a homeland that he has left but not abandoned. Some social critics argue that Paris, from the postwar period forward, was a place in which Africans experienced a sense of belonging because it became the staging ground for Africa's future (Mouralis 1992:4). Dakeyo's sense of exile, however, is not based on external social conditions but, instead, on his precarious and hyphenated sense of belonging to Africa and to France. From this precarious position, he uses the language of passion to express his desire to bring about political change.[9]

> Je ne t'apporte ni ciel
> Ni crépuscule
> Mais ma peine absolue
> Douleur sèche
> Comme un hurlement
> Sans issue infinie
> Avec mon chant qui vibre
> Toute notre souffrance.
>
> Je continuerai à colporter
> Les insomnies
> Le long de mes nuits
> agacées
> Jusqu'à l'ulcère final
> Alors qu'on me porte hautement
> Sur ma terre de granit rouge
> Parmi l'herbe fraîche
> Où paissent les vaches
> . . . .
>
> J'ai cherché ton souffle
> Jusque dans les entrailles
> De ma terre vorace
> Portant au fond de moi
> L'écharde de l'exil
> Mon univers constellé de meurtres.
>
> Je reviendrai comme une lave bleue
> A l'aube parmi les récifs
> L'essence de ma parole dressée
> A la dimension de mon souffle
> Sûrs mes pieds calleux
> Par-dessus tes montagnes feutrées
> Avec des mains qui referont le jour.
> (Dakeyo 1976a:18–19)

[I bring you neither daylight
Nor dusk
But my absolute grief
My arid pain
Without end
With my song that resonates
All of our suffering.

I shall continue to peddle
Insomnia
Throughout my tormented nights
Until the final ulcer
When I am transported high
Upon my land of red granite
Amidst the fresh grass
Where cows graze.
. . . .

I looked for your breath
In the entrails
Of my voracious land
Arousing in the depths of me
The splinter of exile
My universe studded with murders.

I shall return like blue lava
At dawn among the reefs
The essence of my erect words
In the measure of my breath
My steady callous feet
On the felt-covered mountains
With hands that will remake the day.]

Out of grief and torture, Dakeyo reaches for Africa from "the splinter of exile." Although his commitment to Africa intensifies with separation, his faith in revolutionary action is fractured by his diasporan location. His poetry contains a hyphenated discourse inspired by Africa, but filtered through Europe. He vows to "return like blue lava" to redress injustices and set his homeland aright. The idyllic image of a "land of red granite amidst fresh grass where cows graze" is contrasted with a voracious land "studded with murders." In certain respects, *Chant d'accusation* is reminiscent of Aimé Césaire's 1960 poem "Afrique," from *Ferrements.* There is, however, an important difference. While Césaire (1983:347) exhorts a passive Africa "not to tremble" in the wake of the new fight of neocolonial change, Dakeyo positions himself as an active combatant who, although in exile, longs to return and take on the crisis. He does not promise, as does Césaire, that a new land will emerge from dormant rhythms but, instead, commits his personal force and energies to the battle in the form of the "plural voice" of the poet-activist. This type of revolutionary writing is subtle because it does not challenge others to rise up in direct protest, as did Fanon, and does not criticize ineffective political action, as did the antinégritude polemicists. In contrast, Dakeyo expresses a lament of psychological loss, and the unfulfilled wish to transform that loss into political action.

In his 1979 epic poem *J'appartiens au grand jour,* Dakeyo further asserts his personal commitment to return to a struggle for justice in Africa. *J'appartiens au grand jour* is divided into three parts: the memory of Africa, the painful longing for Africa, and the projected return to African soil. The poem opens with the elegiac remembrance of Africa's suffering. Dakeyo (1979:14) presents poignant images of the violence of Sharpeville and the streets of Soweto, declaring that his "word opens on the entire space." The Sowetos and Sharpevilles evoke Dakeyo's revolutionary consciousness, but these are painful images of Africa that are part of the author's memory and ruins of the past (Gabriel 1993:214–16). The refrain of belonging maintains Dakeyo's lament for a lost land to which he is certain he belongs.

Envoyez-moi des nouvelles
Des nouvelles de notre terre
Sans Nord sans Sud
Envoyez-moi des nouvelles de
Notre terre
De notre terre que je veux prendre
Dans mes bras comme le vent nu
Qui porte mon chant
Aux confins de l'aurore
Envoyez-moi des nouvelles
De notre terre
De notre terre que je veux
Porter parmi les soleils
Parmi les fleurs
Libre comme mon corps
En transe
Libre comme le temps
En friche
Envoyez-moi des nouvelles

De notre terre
De notre terre de diamant
Et de vent
(Dakeyo 1979:11)

[Send me news
News of our land
Without North, without South
Send me news of our land
Of our land that I want to take
Into my arms like the naked wind
That brings my song
To the confines of dawn
Send me news
Of our land
Of our land that I want
To transport to the stars
Among the flowers
Free like my body
In trance
Free like time
Lying fallow
Send me news
Of our land
Of our land of diamonds
And of wind]

Ma parole s'ouvre sur l'espace entier
Tout l'espace
Et ma voix plurielle
N'est pas usée par la nuit
Qui torture mon âme
Mais comment effacer ma douleur
Il y a tous les Soweto
Et tous les Sharpeville

Je vais hisser l'histoire
Au haut bout du jour
Et les morts invinciblement présents
Sur ma terre écailleuse
Qui se redresse avec ses townships
Et ses grabats sordides
ITINÉRANTS de mort

Comme un linceul
Sur le sable étale
Ma fraternité seule
Dans la grandeur de l'aurore
(Dakeyo 1979:14)

[My words open upon an entire space
All of the space
And my plural voice
Is not worn out by the night
That tortures my soul
But how do I erase the pain
There are all of the Sowetos
And all of the Sharpevilles

I am going to lift up history
To the highest extremities of the day
And the invincibly present dead
On my rocky land
That flattens with its townships
And its sordid pallets
ITINERANTS of death
Like a shroud
On the sand expose
My lonely fraternity
In the grandeur of the dawn.]

Dakeyo projects a wish to belong to a new African dawn characterized by both progress and the terror that he wishes to eradicate. In *J'appartiens au grand jour* (1979), he requests news of Africa in order to transport the continent to new heights through the plural voice of the poet-activist. At the same time, he laments the conflicts and deaths of Soweto and Sharpeville. The "invincibly present dead" blanket the townships with a shroud of sorrow as the poet's voice reaches out in political unity with those who suffer. Dakeyo's activist poetry is written in terms of virtualities. The theme of belonging to a cause, to a downtrodden land, and to those who suffer within it recurs. The narrative of longing found in *Chant d'accusation* is transformed into a narrative of virtual belonging in *J'appartiens au grand jour.* This sense of belonging is fueled by political undertones foreshadowed in *Soweto: Soleils fusillés,* dedicated to those who died in Soweto in search of the "final word, love" (Dakeyo 1977:32). Dakeyo views love as the outcome of suffering and as a metonym for commitment, belonging, and death. His poetry challenges early négritude's idyllic images of Africa, and replaces them with the personal quest to rebuild a new continent. In contrast to Fanon, Depestre, and the early critics of négritude, he personalizes revolutionary writing by introducing ruptured romance as a key element. In his 1989 poem *La Femme où j'ai mal,* dedicated to his ex-wife, Dakeyo (1989a:54) intones: "You will go, my beauty, under the warm flowers of my country when the songs break out like the conqueror, and your face will be reflected on the horizon. But you will return." Traveling to Africa represents an ephemeral political commitment on the part of the woman who will eventually abandon Africa for her native France. For Dakeyo, love and longing always carry with them the possibility of abandonment, deception, and suffering.

To amplify the plural voice of the poet, Dakeyo joined with a group of writers to form Éditions Silex in 1980. His avowed motivation was to take the poetry of activist African writers published in France back to Africa. Dakeyo explained:[10]

> Well, Éditions Silex was created in 1980 under the initiative of three poets whose works were published by Éditions Saint-Germain-des-Prés—Alfred Melon-Degras of Martinique, Hédi Bouraoui of Tunisia, and myself, Paul Dakeyo of Cameroon. We realized that, as African writers, our works were published in France, but poorly distributed in Africa. We thought that the best way to promote our literature, our creations, our work, and other African productions was to form our own publishing house with the goal of creating a space for the exchange of reflections. (Dakeyo 1989b)

For over a decade, Dakeyo has combined his role as a literary figure with his entrepreneurial activities as manager of Éditions Silex and Éditions Nouvelles du Sud. As a publisher, Dakeyo has solicited literary works in Paris and across West Africa in an effort to compile a new African literature that goes beyond national boundaries, and beyond the bounds of négritude and the Présence Africaine movement. Éditions Silex began by publishing African poetry and then moved into literary criticism and political essays. According to Dakeyo, the publishing house experienced several years of prosperity. Because it attempted to create active links with African writers, but without large government subventions or a strong sales base, it eventually encountered financial difficulties. Dakeyo has initiated coeditions with African publishers who suggest authors and share publication costs. More recently, he has collaborated with Parisian colleagues at Présence Africaine and Éditions L'Harmattan to publish works in France and Africa. In 1991, Éditions Silex went out of business and was replaced entirely by Éditions Nouvelles du Sud. Dakeyo continued with his managerial activities and a more active plan of collaboration with African publishers as he returned to his homeland to seek out new authors, titles, and sources of financial support. He converted the art and activism of the 1970s into the new entrepreneurship of the 1980s.

The literary critic Françoise Cévaër (1991:106) emphasizes the ideological challenges faced by members of the new generation of African publishers such as Dakeyo when she states: "Publishers are not yet ready to welcome their modernist, innovative discourse that dispenses with an archaic world in which négritude and decolonization remain dear to 'third worldist' and anti-colonialist ideologues. No one wants to take the risk. Neither the older African publishers located in Paris, nor the French publishing firms whose policies, sometimes inadvertently, confine African literature to a sclerotic immobility. Within this context, the project implemented by the group of writers at Silex may play a decisive role in the emergence of a truly modern francophone African literature."

Dakeyo's editorial group presents a literary and political challenge to the older approach of Présence Africaine. Dakeyo has transformed cultural brokering into his own brand of political activism. In contrast to French publishers of African literature, Dakeyo promotes African creative works that represent the voices of new writers. A philosophy of revolutionary love, born of a diasporic separation from Africa, motivates Dakeyo's quest to develop a new and autonomously published African literature. The following chapter explores how this process works for Dakeyo and for local publishers on the African continent.

INTERVIEW

Paul Dakeyo
Paris, September 11, 1989

Born in Bafoussam, Cameroon, in 1948, Paul Dakeyo is a pivotal figure in the postindependence generation of African writers in France. His poetry of revolutionary love creates a bridge between the writing of combat and the works of the intimate generation of Parisianists. Dakeyo's collections of poetry include Les Barbelés du matin *(1973),* Chant d'accusation *(1976a),* Le Cri pluriel *(1976b),* Soweto: Soleils fusillés *(1977),* J'appartiens au grand jour *(1979),* La Femme où j'ai mal *(1989a), and* Les Ombres de la nuit *(1994). In addition to his writing, Dakeyo was a founding editor of Éditions Silex and is the editorial director of Éditions Nouvelles du Sud. These two publishing houses have provided important literary outlets for African writers.*

Publishing in France and Africa

Bennetta Jules-Rosette: As you know, I'm working on the history of the Présence Africaine publishing house and the evolution of African writing in France. Along these lines, please tell me about your literary and publishing activities.

Paul Dakeyo: Well, Éditions Silex was created in 1980 under the initiative of three poets whose works were published by Éditions Saint-Germain-des-Prés—Alfred Melon-Degras of Martinique, Hédi Bouraoui of Tunisia, and myself, Paul Dakeyo of Cameroon. We realized that, as African writers, our works were published in France but poorly distributed in Africa. We thought that the best way to promote our literature, our creations, our work, and other African productions was to form our own publishing house with the goal of creating a space for the exchange of reflections. So Silex was founded in 1980 and now has published more than three hundred titles, consisting of poetry and critical essays on economics, general literature, and the social sciences. We publish about forty titles a year, which is a heavy production task, considering that it is necessary to be competitive and to renew our publication base constantly. Because books have a life, as soon as your major titles are sold out, you have to think about publishing new books.

BJR: Does that mean that you are under pressure to seek out new writers?

PD: Yes, well, we have developed a program to search for new talent. We helped to launch new young novelists such as Yodi Karone. Because we are taken very seriously, we have also been able to publish writers with well-established reputations, such as Jean-François Brière, Jean Métellus, and the literary critic Bernard Mouralis. We publish academic research on African literature, as well as literary works.

BJR: And does your publishing house have a specific philosophy or outlook on African writing?

PD: Let's just say that we believe, without any complexes, that Africans are just as capable as anyone else to create and to produce. So, Silex has existed to give a voice to those who didn't have a forum from which to speak. Because the African continent exists, we must speak about it, whether it's on the economic, sociological, historical, or literary level. There are those who can redefine the problems of the continent, and Silex exists to make a space for their literary work, their research, and their thoughts.

BJR: What's the difference between Éditions Silex and other publishing houses, such as Présence Africaine and L'Harmattan, that also concentrate on Africa?

PD: There's a fundamental difference. All of our founders were African, with perspectives that differed from Présence Africaine and L'Harmattan. We concentrated on different problems, and we wanted to be the voice for those who didn't have a voice and a space in which to express their ideas. . . . To be frank, in contrast to Présence Africaine, we wanted to create another renewal, and to place the power of expression back in the hands of the African continent. Voilà. And the essential difference between us and, let's say L'Harmattan, is one of sensitivity. We were all Africans, conscious of the political and social problems faced by Africa. That placed us in a special position, a situation different from a European publishing house working in Africa. As Africans working on Africa, we were, in my opinion, better equipped to define and express the problems of Africa. Voilà.

BJR: And what type of market did you want to develop for your books?

PD: I think that the problem is to consider a book as a product. And, as a product, a book deserves a great deal of attention. It needs time to live and breathe. But this time is necessarily limited. After two years, you know if a book is going to survive or is going to die. All right. There are rigorous commercial parameters that we must follow. Sometimes, for example, the works of young authors don't correspond to market demand, especially on the African continent. And today, the African continent revolves around national literatures. So, when you go to Dakar, and you present a list of books to vendors there, they respond: "But this one is by a Cameroonian author. It doesn't interest us!" So now, with regard to the African market, you have to deal with the phenomenon of nationalism. And this nationalism influences the African market, unless the African author is dealing with continental problems that have an impact on everyone. Take the case of my own book, *Soweto: Soleils fusillés.* It's read in Dakar, in Abidjan, and in Lomé because everyone is concerned with the problems of South Africa. And, for example, my book *La Femme où j'ai mal* touches practically everyone who had experienced a deception in love, whether they are French, Dutch, Belgian, American, or some other nationality. I'm talking about my relationship with a woman. So at the Festival of Avignon last July, everyone reacted positively to my presentation of this text because it discusses universal problems.

African literature has passed through stages. First, African authors spoke about their daily lives, that is, their families, their economy, and their communities. They discussed slavery, colonization, and, later, neocolonialism—let's say the great sociopolitical problems. Voilà. But I think that young writers today want to interrogate new problems, their existence and their freedom. When I was a student, I asked myself, "What is freedom? Does it come after combat?" Today I say, as I did recently on a radio broadcast at France Culture, that freedom is the result of direct action. It doesn't emerge in relationship to anything. I exist, so I am! And my existence depends on my capacity to write and produce books of high quality. I mean of high technical and literary quality. Then we package them. We put them in cans like sardines. And that interests me too. Then people pick up the book. They turn its pages. Either they buy it or they don't.

BJR: You have spoken about the African market for your works. Can you say a bit more about the French market?

PD: In certain respects, we are fortunate because our publishing house, legally speaking, is French. It's African because I'm the director of publications. But we have received much more assistance from France than from any African country. We don't have problems of censorship. We've never had anything like that. We just don't receive subventions from African governments. At the meetings of the Association for African Publishers, they declared that we were French. I responded, "It's not a problem of geography. You have only to look at my catalog. Show me your catalogs, and I'll show you mine. We publish forty titles a year, and we've launched a number of young African authors." If you look at my anthology of African literature in France, you'll see that at least 40 percent of the authors have been published by Silex. And that's a lot of work for less than a decade of publishing. In the nine years that we've been on the market, we've accomplished a lot.

Poetic Inspirations and Writing Poetry

BJR: Now, let's talk about your work as a writer. Tell me about your conception of poetry and your writing.

PD: All right. I think that a good poet should adhere to his genre, that is, the type of poetry he wants to create. For me, poetry is the search for the absolute. It's the search for something primordial. And it's difficult to express this sense of the absolute in, let's say, a novel. Some have tried, but it's difficult, and they usually don't succeed. I once tried to write a play, but I quickly abandoned that project and returned to my poetry.

BJR: How do you go about your work as a poet? What's your approach to writing?

PD: Well, I search for a turn of phrase. Some people ask me, "How did you come up with that? Do you enter a state of trance in order to write?" I answer that for me, it's simply a matter of putting myself into a context. Just as in an interview, you have a person in front of you and something happens. There's a certain chemistry that makes you want to communicate. It's the same way with poetry. In poetry, there's a total communication. Aimé Césaire once said that the secret of great communication is great combustion. And I think in the case of poetry, that's exactly what happens. When something takes place between two people, there's a discourse. Writing poetry is like that. . . . Some academics think that all you need is a certain background, then you can write. For them, it's like building a house. You have the foundations, the cement, and the roof. All you need is a mason to put it all together. Well, writing poetry is not at all like that. It's special. When I go through my library, I can immediately pick out the good poets. Some collections, I can read them in four minutes. They're not poets worth the time. There are other poets whom I adore, and I regularly read and re-read them.

BJR: What are some of your sources of poetic inspiration? Who is your favorite poet?

PD: My favorite poet [laughter]—my favorite poet, without a doubt, is Pablo Neruda. I have a very special relationship to his poetry because he speaks of all the themes that interest me—love, society, and politics. Of course, I've read the poetry of négritude. And, as a black person in search of my identity, I've gone past that stage. There are problems in every independent African country, not to mention South Africa, and there is a total absence of political culture. We need to write about universal themes.

Challenges Facing African Writers and Publishers

BJR: What are some of the challenges facing African writers and publishers today?

PD: What we lack in African literature today is choice—a range of books and the infrastructure for their publication. We need to stimulate talent and to provide the structures for publishing new talent, whether in the form of subventions, bookstores, or continental and national prizes to promote the books. When a young author says to me, "I'm a writer. I've sold a thousand or two thousand copies of my book," I respond, "That's not a writer!" To be a writer, you have to create on a regular basis and produce books that are recognized and adopted, for example, in instructional programs. But we also have to change the standards. There are many excellent young writers today, for example, Bolya, Yodi, Beyala, and Njami. They have a new vision of Africa, its problems, its economy, and its history. We have to make a space for this new literature. But with the way things are today, it will be torpedoed. Schools continue to teach our students texts in the style: "Black woman, clothed in the color of your skin, you are beautiful," that sort of thing. We have not yet gone beyond these outmoded discourses that have betrayed Africa economically, politically, and culturally. . . . But the real problem is political and not economic. In Africa, bureaucrats who have no literary standards deal with books. In European publishing houses, there are a number of criteria for a good book. The most important criterion is the subject matter. Is a book interesting and is it commercially viable? If it's not well written, it can be revised. That's not a problem. But a publisher is not a philanthropist. He has to ask himself whether a book will sell and how many copies. He can't just publish the speeches of the head of state! . . . A publisher has to have a passion for literature and has to be able to discern whether a book will sell.

BJR: How do you see the prospects for the future of African publishing?

PD: In Africa, the schools, especially the high schools, buy the books. You have to be on the educational program. And that's a question of politics. For example, some works of African authors who write about society and politics—for instance, Sony Labou Tansi, in the Congo—can't be found in their home countries. These works are too politically sensitive, and you won't find them in the windows or on the shelves of local bookstores. Eh bien, that's what I call "autocensorship." And there's not much that we can do about that. Voilà. I'll leave you on that note.

FOUR

Green Beans and Books: Côte d'Ivoire and the Parisian Literary Landscape

> A publisher is not a philanthropist. I think I have devised a project to permit the African book to live and breathe . . . with financial support.
>
> —Paul Dakeyo, 1992

Africa is not just the source of nostalgic imagery for Parisian-based writers, it is an autonomous site of literary production. It is important to examine African publishing in order to understand the global market for francophone African literature and the publication and marketing challenges faced by African writers at home and abroad. Seen from the vantage point of an African metropole, the Parisian literary landscape is both attractive and daunting, empowering and exploitative. The dilemmas of publishers of African literature in Paris are linked directly to literary and economic conditions on the African continent. A journey to Abidjan, Côte d'Ivoire, highlights the connections and contradictions between the Parisian and African literary worlds. African literary works are both cultural texts, produced by dedicated authors, and market commodities, edited and sold by publishers. Although some of these authors regularly move back and forth between Africa and France, their survival strategies differ considerably from those of the Parisian-based writers. The marginality of postcolonial African writers is not only an artifact of cultural domination, but also a byproduct of the limited markets available for them to publish their works on the continent.

Literature has a well-developed history in Côte d'Ivoire. Bernard Dadié, the nation's literary grandfather and giant, was an active member of the Présence Africaine movement and has inspired many young authors. Dadié moved from journalism and critical writing to poetry, novels, and theater. His early work was thoroughly imbued with the spirit of anticolonial protest. But times have changed since Dadié began his literary career, and a new space has opened up for younger Ivoirian writers.

Green Beans and Books

It is the summer of 1992 in Abidjan. From the spacious patio of an Ivoirian author-journalist, we look out on his colorful tropical garden in the muggy afternoon heat. "Green beans!" he shouts. "Publishing in Africa is like the sale of green beans." He explained that this year's crop of green beans in Senegal was excellent in spite of the drought. There was a substantial surplus of green beans to sell throughout West Africa at a low cost and still make a profit. For reasons of foreign exchange and supposed safety, however, the beans were frozen and shipped to France, where currency exchanges for the international banks take place. After sitting for a month or two, the beans were then shipped back to Africa for resale at a higher price, with the overhead for shipment, storage, and international custom's duties subtracted from the profit for Senegal. Direct inter-African exchange was avoided. In the author's view, the green beans served as a metaphor for the local publishing situation, which he labeled as one more instance of neocolonial control. Covering problems of censorship, reading publics, and royalties, we continued to lament over the problems of African publishing until sunset, when we left for a meeting of the Ivoirian writers' association in the Deux Plateaux residential area of Abidjan.

This journalist's allegory highlights the dependence of African metropoles on the West for intellectual and commodity exchanges.[1] Even CÉDA (Centre d'Édition et de Diffusion Africaines à Abidjan), the largest publishing house in the country, engaged in the common practice of sending completed manuscripts to France for printing, and returning them to Côte d'Ivoire for resale at elevated prices. Caught in a vicious cycle of slow manuscript-referee processes, followed by foreign printing and pricing of their manuscripts, some writers in Abidjan complained that they had waited up to eight years from the initial acceptance of their manuscripts to final publication. And these were the lucky authors whose manuscripts were accepted with minor revisions on the first submission. When the manuscripts returned to Africa as published books, prices were so high that local consumers, even the elite reading public, could not afford them. Some authors bypass this system by making sure that local bookstores, such as the

Librairie de France and the Maison des Livres, always keep in stock a small supply of their books. They accompany friends and potential buyers to the bookstores, show them where the stash of books is hidden, and even volunteer to help pay for the purchase of their own works.

Self-publication is another innovative solution to the costly and inefficient distribution problem. Ivoirian writers engaging in self-publication use their own word-processors or the services of a professional desktop publisher. In this regard, they are fortunate to be in Côte d'Ivoire, where computers are accessible and no import duties are levied on word-processing software (Jules-Rosette 1990:110–12). With this technique, they prepare a limited number of copies of their manuscripts for promotional sale. The poet and playwright Amoa Urbain, who also teaches at Abidjan's École Normale Supérieure, told me that self-publication is the only viable solution to the dual problems of the time lag in publishing and overpriced books. "It's a sort of literary self-help program," he explained (Urbain 1992b). For Urbain and many others, the goal is to place books quickly into the hands of people who appreciate them. Combined with village and community theater, self-publication is an effective strategy for expanding the public for African literature.

But self-publication is risky for a professional writer whose goal is international recognition. Maurice Bandaman, an Ivoirian novelist and playwright who has engaged in self-publication, described the stigma associated with it. "If you opt to publish your own book, people think you're not able to get it published by any other means" (Bandaman 1992). Urbain, who published his own 1992 poetry anthology, *Les Braises de la lagune* (1992a), and other champions of self-publication retort that it is far more important to produce and circulate creative works locally than it is to worry about the prestige of publication outlets.

Niangoran Porquet, playwright, producer, and inventor of the theory of "griotics," chose a more radical solution to the problem. He wrote and produced his works in the form of plays and griotics theory. Drawn from the term *griot,* a West African storyteller and praise singer, griotics offers a way of understanding how oral traditions may be transformed into contemporary literature and theater. Porquet assured the reception of his work by wearing many hats—producing his own plays, analyzing them on radio talk shows, and writing up the critical commentaries. He pushed the self-publication strategy to its extreme limit.

The Municipal Club Debate

Hidden behind the winding treelined boulevards of an affluent residential section of Abidjan sits the Club Municipal de Deux Plateaux. Not far from a decadent tennis and country club, the Municipal Club houses the CARAS cultural center, run by André Acho. It is here that Suzanne Tanella Boni—novelist, professor of philosophy, and dynamic president of the Association des Écrivains de Côte d'Ivoire (AÉCI)—has scheduled the July 30, 1992, meeting of her group. Tonight, Boni has invited a special guest speaker from France, the poet/publisher Paul Dakeyo. (See fig. 9.) Completing the final leg of a West African promotional tour, Dakeyo has chosen to lecture on a topic that surprises no one who knows him well: "The African Publication in Question: The Examples of Silex and Nouvelles du Sud." By popular demand, and because this is, after all, a writers-guild meeting, Boni has asked Dakeyo and some of the other participants to give poetry readings as part of the session. In the audience are Côte d'Ivoire's leading writers, members of the fifty-person association: the novelist and social critic Jean-Marie Adiaffi Ade, whose prizewinning first novel, *La Carte d'Identité* (1980), was praised in Paris; the poet, actor, and journalist Bernard Zadi Zaouru, who later became minister of culture; the poet and past president of the association, Paul Ahizi Adiapa; and Micheline Coulibaly, author of children's tales and secretary of the association.[2]

As the session opens, Dakeyo intones:

> Silex was created in 1980 by Alfred Melon-Degras, Hédi Bouraoui, and myself with French and African associates, with a goal to giving a voice to everyone who could not easily find a space to publish poems. But we quickly realized that poetry was not profitable. So, eventually we proceeded to create new collections—anthologies and critical essays on the economy, general literature, and the social sciences. And the catalog of Silex reached 350 titles, with an average of 40 titles—yes, 40 titles—per year, some of which sold, some of which didn't sell. And it is from this experience that I wish to open tonight's debate.

I began to fidget in my chair and to feel uncomfortable. Rapidly, I checked the sound levels on the tape recorder. I had already heard this account once before in Paris, and I wondered whether Dakeyo would modify it for the benefit of his Ivoirian audience. Everyone else appeared so eager and enthusiastic that I questioned how a Parisian-style contestatory debate could ever emerge in this atmosphere. Then, although Dakeyo's tone remained calm, suddenly the discourse shifted. Dakeyo continued:

> Well, Silex enjoyed, shall we say, a period of ten years of prosperity until the tax commission of Ivry—because we are located in Ivry—investigated us and asked for 360,000 francs to be reimbursed over a ten-year period. The case is now in the tribunal. I have written to President Mitterand and to several African heads of state. It's all political. Well, now, following these difficulties, we have transferred our operations to Éditions Nouvelles du Sud, with a capital of 100 million French francs,

Fig. 9. Maurice Bandaman (left), Paul Dakeyo (center), and Suzanne Tanella Boni (right) at the Municipal Club debate, Deux Plateaux, Abidjan, Côte d'Ivoire, July 30, 1992. Photograph by Bennetta Jules-Rosette.

> in order to maintain all of the contracts and the translated works, and not to stop our activities. Two solutions were adopted. First the associates of Silex are not the associates of Nouvelles du Sud. I am the only person to belong to the two structures by collaboration. Second, we had a meeting in Dakar a month-and-a-half ago, sponsored by UNESCO. About twenty publishers and African book wholesalers met to create a consortium to permit the African book truly to exist on the market in Africa as well as elsewhere. I thought that this UNESCO project would provide a place for the African book to breathe by the organization of cultural events, the reading of texts, and encounters between writers and journalists passing through Paris and living in Paris. This project should begin in 1993. . . .
>
> The major problems are the absence of any strong projects by our ministers of culture, and the disdain for African books with regard to their presentation in bookstores, where stockers prefer to display tourist guidebooks to African literature. So there is work of consciousness-raising to do on all levels so that the African book will be on the first row in African bookstores. There is also important work to be done by writers' associations to see that the African book receives the place of merit that it deserves. And I take this occasion to thank the Ivoirian Writers' Association.

On this note, the debate began. Jean-Marie Adiaffi Ade opened the discussion with comments on intellectual freedom and censorship.[3] Using his own book, *Silence, on développe* (1992), published by Éditions Nouvelles du Sud, as an example, Adiaffi described his publication battle with CÉDA. The Ivoirian publishing house asked him to reduce the manuscript from 900 pages to 500 pages and to remove all politically inflammatory comments. When the book was cut to 500 pages, the publishers still found it too long and wanted to censor it. The battle lasted nearly a decade, after which Dakeyo finally published the book in Paris. Adiaffi explained:

> The case of *Silence* poses the problem of the status of the African writer and African writing. . . . Do you think that the African writer is free? The African writer is not free. For me, liberated African writing does not exist. The free African sermon does not exist because whites dictate what we write. Why? Because the cultural game is linked to an ideological game. The question of our independence has not been examined by our presidents for the past thirty years. It's sad to say, but these truths are hard, raw, and cruel. But we must say it because it is our only means of salvation. After independence, you know, paper presidents were put into place, and they governed in the place of France. In other words, instead of governing directly, France governs by interposed presidents. It's in this situation that the cultural game emerges, because the presidents know very well that one must not be preoccupied with culture, that the future belongs to technology. But they also know very well that it's not possible to be independent without being culturally independent. It is as if God made man without a heart. Culture is the heart, and you cannot live without it.

Dakeyo responded positively to Adiaffi's remarks by reinforcing the responsibilities of African leaders in the area of cultural development. "The fault," he assured everyone, "does not lie with the publishers." Other questions ensued about the situation of Éditions Silex and Nouvelles du Sud in France, about the publication market, and most notably, about how new young authors might be published for the first time. Dakeyo responded that Éditions Nouvelles du Sud was now looking for "great authors." He explained that if a new manuscript from an unknown did not come in with a recommendation from a well-established author, he would throw it in the dustbin. This comment elicited gasps of horror from the audience. "A publisher," retorted Dakeyo, "is not a philanthropist. When we publish a book, we want it to sell, so that we can cover our costs. The costs include not only printing, but also the salaries that we must pay our employees, phone calls, postage, time to travel to see authors, dinners in restaurants, and so on." These remarks drew little sympathy from the crowd. The atmosphere grew tense. Once again, Dakeyo defended himself skillfully: "It's not me. It's not even the market. It's the 'system' in France that's to blame. What we need is south-south cooperation." The audience rallied to this response. And Dakeyo continued, "I cannot be a publisher in Paris and a book salesman in Abidjan, Dakar, and Douala."

A conciliatory voice emerged from the audience. "Wouldn't it be possible to sponsor a publication prize with Nouvelles du Sud and the Association des

Écrivains de Côte d'Ivoire?" Dakeyo responded that a new all-African literary prize had been considered at the recent Dakar publishers' and wholesalers' meeting. Larger sums of subvention should be obtained from ministries of culture so that prizes of 150,000 French francs (approximately $30,000, U.S.), equivalent to a year's salary, could be given to authors to finish their books. Although some of the writers looked astonished, others nodded in agreement. Everyone had hoped for a clearer commitment of resources from the Parisian-based publisher. Dakeyo reminded the members of the AÉCI that he had the page proofs for their new poetry anthology in hand, and he would thereby introduce many of them to an international audience.[4] The tension abated. Boni called the debate to a close in order to open the second part of the program—poetry readings and performances. As the guest of honor, Dakeyo was asked to begin the readings, and did so with the dramatic recitation of the opening stanzas of his 1979 poem *J'appartiens au grand jour.* Zadi Zaourou followed with a recitation, as did several others. The evening ended with André Acho's moving rendition of a black American spiritual in English and French. For weeks, members of the association continued to discuss Dakeyo's puzzling visit. Some were encouraged by his efforts; others were completely disillusioned. Still others clung to the strategy of self-publication as the only effective way to bypass the exploitative system that Dakeyo and Adiaffi had described.

The Ivoirian Authors Respond

In 1992, Ivoirian authors were preoccupied by several pressing problems, including their creative autonomy, dependence on French publication outlets, alternative avenues of publication, and obstacles, such as censorship and severe local criticism, encountered in the publication and distribution of their works. I spoke at length with sixteen authors about their literary projects and future plans. As president of the AÉCI, Boni was among the most vocal. Long committed to improving the lot of local writers, she used her position to promote a series of public debates on the role of the writer, the purview of press criticism, and the mechanics of publishing manuscripts. She spearheaded a literacy campaign among adults and primary- and secondary-school students to enlarge and uplift the literary public in Côte d'Ivoire. Challenged by the magnitude of her task, Boni never admitted defeat. She continued her public activities at a breakneck pace, along with her personal literary projects. She outlined her cultural and literary goals.

> Starting in November of 1991, I tried to put into place a new group of writers, and we've attempted to animate the cultural and literary life of Côte d'Ivoire in a gen-

eral manner. Now, what we want to create and set in motion is a credible writers' organization. When I say credible, I mean that we must be open to ourselves and the external world. We must establish contact with other organizations, and all of those who share the same passion as we do. Since the new office was put into place, we have organized several public debates. The first debate was with journalists, and the theme was "Creation and Press Criticism: Information or Confrontation?" [laughter] That was the theme of the debate that we organized in March of this year. And since we started to function, that's what we've done. . . . After the first public encounter, we organized another debate, "From the Manuscript to the Book," because our association also wants to defend the moral and material interests of its adherents. And we've noted that one of the major problems that we've confronted within Côte d'Ivoire is that of the publication and distribution of our works. Practically since 1989, the large publication houses in Côte d'Ivoire have held no literary openings [*rentrées littéraires*]. The literary openings serve the purpose of showing the whole population in Côte d'Ivoire all of the new works produced by these publishing houses. . . . That gave visibility to new books in the country. But, since 1989, we have remarked that this doesn't take place anymore. (Boni 1992b)

Later, Boni emphasized that problems with the publishing houses coincided with the advent of an economic crisis in Côte d'Ivoire. She did not, however, excuse their diminished productivity. CÉDA was established in 1961 and was privatized in 1992, with 75 percent of its operations taken over by Éditions Hatier in Paris. The major focus of their publications (90 percent) is now on schoolbooks. Thus, CÉDA has become a restricted outlet for African literature. This situation was confirmed by a commercial editor at the French administrative offices of Hatier.[5] Nouvelles Éditions Africaines (NÉA) is the second-largest publishing house in Côte d'Ivoire. Both CÉDA and NÉA have experienced major publication difficulties since 1985, even though they have received financial support from the local government (Sié 1996:27). In 1990, NÉA closed its Abidjan office but remained active in Dakar. As a result of this financial crisis, manuscripts submitted to these publishers often disappeared entirely from view. Boni lamented this unfortunate situation.

At CÉDA publishing house, in either 1987 or '88, a new series was put into place. It was a children's literature collection, directed by one of my colleagues from the university who specializes in children's literature. She is in the Department of Communication, so she was named general editor for this collection. She received several manuscripts, but she published only four, just about four. She even organized a conference to promote children's literature in Côte d'Ivoire. The manuscripts resulting from this contest were copyedited and corrected by the authors

> and resubmitted to the press, but they have never been published. We regard this as a real problem, almost a scandal. (Boni 1992b)

Although Boni wanted to use her association to defend the rights and privileges of authors, she found herself blocked by social and economic circumstances. An educational crisis, beginning in 1990 in Côte d'Ivoire, slowed down sales of schoolbooks, the bread and butter of the local publishing houses. Without the schoolbooks to fuel sales, CÉDA, in particular, became increasingly reluctant to publish general literature. Since 1992, Côte d'Ivoire has experienced uncharacteristic social and economic unrest.[6] An attempted coup d'état in 1992, followed by the election of Henri Konan Bédié, successor of Félix Houphouët-Boigny, left the country politically unstable and turned it, nearly overnight, into a poor financial risk for external investors. Cultural and literary activities were the first victims of this instability, and writers found themselves stranded with neither local publishers nor a clearly defined literary audience. Boni's literacy campaign functioned as a stopgap in this stagnating situation. Individual authors sought subventions, and, ultimately, if possible, sent their works outside of the country for publication. Along with her public activities, Boni formulated the act of writing as the first step to promoting her association's activities. She was literally brimming with new projects, ready to be published in Abidjan and abroad.

> Since 1990, I've been writing a novel, and I'm very determined to finish this novel. In terms of length, I think it's going to be more voluminous than my previous novel, *Une Vie de crabe,* and the setting is also very interesting. I'm just in the first draft right now, and I hope to be able to finish between now and the month of December. The novel is very interesting and very important to me. And I think if I succeed, this will be a definite plus in my career as a writer. . . . In addition to this large novel, I am also writing some stories for children. In 1991, I had a novel published by NEA/Edicef called *De l'Autre côté du soleil,* and I also have another collection with the same publisher, which is called *La Fugue d'ozone* [1992]. It takes up ecological problems and African children at the end of this century. . . . Also, the AÉCI is putting together an anthology of the poets of Côte d'Ivoire, to be published by Paul Dakeyo, with Éditions Nouvelles du Sud. We've already completed this project, and it's in press. (Boni 1992b)

In the end, Boni's projects moved into print. The AÉCI's anthology of Ivoirian poets was published after much negotiation. In September 1995, at the Festival International des Francophonies in Limoges, France, Boni read excerpts from *La Fugue d'ozone* (1992a) and described her upcoming projects to an eager audience. Since our 1992 interview, she had been a visiting artist in Limoges and had further solidified her contacts with French publishers. *Une Vie de crabe* (1990), Boni's first novel, was published by NÉA of Senegal. By the end of 1992, she had moved into the intercontinental world of publishing through the francophonie circuit while retaining her interest in local literary affairs. In other words, she became one of the fortunate local writers able to make the leap from Abidjan's publication ghetto into an international literary market.

The Cameroon-born artist, playwright, and theater director Werewere Liking assembled her own combination of strategies to deal with Abidjan's stagnating publication scene. In addition to forming a theater troupe and cultural collective, the Groupe Ki-Yi M'Bock Théâtre, for which she writes and directs plays, Liking has explored self-publication, subvention, and the exportation of her written and performed works. Her projects include theater, fiction, and critical writing in the arts (Liking 1984, 1987, 1988, 1992b; Liking and Hourantier 1987). Now internationally known, especially in the French-speaking world, Liking bolsters her literary projects with work in the performing and plastic arts, combining all three elements in a kaleidoscopic collage. Liking explained her innovative artistic approach:

> As for me, I'm trying to express myself, but I can't, for example, paint every day. I can't paint 365 days a year and I can't write every day either. But when I don't paint, I might want to write, or dance, or sing. For me, it's always the same thing. It's always the same motivation, so I can't say that one form of art pleases me or attracts me more than another. I can only say that art is the language of the soul, and that expresses itself by poetry. And poetry can be visual. It can be sonorous, coming from sound, and it can be artisanal. So, when I express myself, I say that I express myself as a poet in all of these media. (Liking 1992a)

Although she has successfully promoted her works in various venues, Liking has experienced cultural isolation. She, too, has used the Festival International des Francophonies in Limoges as one way of bringing her plays and writings to Europe.[7] The label of francophonie disturbs some French-based African writers and artists, but those authors producing in Africa use Limoges and similar festivals as ports of entry into the international market. In this regard, Liking viewed Abidjan with mixed feelings.

> Everyone is not stimulated by the same thing. I've done a great deal of work in Abidjan, primarily because I'm alone. That is, I'm a bit isolated from the artists of my generation. I'm practically alone. I don't work with a lot of people here. There are not really a lot of exchanges. I hope that one day we'll correct this situation of isolation and lack of exchanges. But, in any case, this isolation has permitted me to produce a great deal. There are people for whom this environment

works very well, and who are stimulated. One thing is certain—Abidjan is a crossroads. In Abidjan, one meets people from all over Africa, and that is very, very important. And also on the political level, at least until now, it's been relatively "cool," except for the incidents of February. But these incidents have not kept artists from creating. So, you can say that Abidjan is a favorable environment in the sense that there is not an enormous repression in the domain of the arts. (Liking 1992a)

Liking cited the new activities at the Institut National des Arts, the rise of the *vau vau* artistic movement, which is a contemporary trend drawing on the ritual and magical meanings of traditional art, and creativity in the plastic arts as part of Abidjan's appeal. She was skeptical, however, about the worlds of literary and theatrical production. She explained that she had a subvention for the play that she was then producing, *Un Touareg s'est marié à une Pygmée* (A Touareg married a Pygmy) (1992), in rehearsal at the time of our interview. "We did have a subvention, but it arrived so late that it was just like not having any support at all. And so we had to run around and make do with things as though we didn't have any money," she complained. "I said to myself, this is the last time I'm going to use the subvention system. I'm going to organize myself differently in the future."

The playwright's clever solution to her problems was to work in a variety of media—theater, film, literature, and the plastic arts—using the revenues and royalties from one venture to support new work in another domain. This artistic entrepreneurship is typical of many artists living and working in Abidjan, although Liking carries it to a skillful extreme. The strategy resembles what Kenneth Little (1974:32–34) has termed "urban opportunism" in Africa, or the combination of multiple employment ventures for economic survival. Fortunately, in Liking's case, these entrepreneurial strategies have led to an international artistic recognition that fuels her projects at home. *Un Touareg s'est marié à une Pygmée,* in rehearsal in July and August 1992, went to the Limoges festival in September of that year, and on to Tokyo and Paris. In sum, Liking used local resources and outlets as a means of building an international reputation. This reputation has bolstered her theater troupe and local artistic pursuits.

The novelist, poet, and journalist Jérôme Carlos, originally from Benin, has similarly combined strategies in producing and marketing his work. He began as a journalist for *Ivoire Dimanche,* a newspaper that had a twenty-year lifespan. When I interviewed Carlos in August 1992, he had just started as a founding editor and journalist for the *Nouvelle Presse,* a weekly newspaper that was then just two months old. He had already written a collection of poems entitled *Liberté* (1973) and a novel entitled *Fleur du désert,* published by CÉDA in 1990. In mid-1992 he also was at work on a second novel, *Le Miroir.* Besides these impressive literary credentials, Carlos was known in Abidjan as a public figure who did not shy away from expressing his opinions on a variety of social, cultural, and political issues. He hosted a television talk show, with two broadcasts per month, entitled *Le Livre ouvert,* in which he interviewed local authors. He had also recently collaborated on a documentary film about the construction of the cathedral at Yamoussoukro, birthplace of Félix Houphouët-Boigny. As with Liking, he used the revenues of his diverse side ventures to support his purely literary pursuits.

Carlos was pessimistic about the privatization of local publishing houses and the consequent obstacles posed for writers attempting to publish their works in Côte d'Ivoire. He outlined his views in a lengthy discussion with me.

> Ah, the publication situation is very, very difficult for African writers here. From my point of view, I must say that my first manuscript was accepted by CÉDA because I'm a journalist, and I'm well known here. Sometimes, because the publishers don't know writers, they place their confidence in journalists who are well known. There are a lot of young people writing today who are unknown because they can't get published. In my case, I was very lucky, but this kind of opportunity doesn't come to everyone. (Carlos 1992)

Elaborating on Abidjan's publication situation, Carlos echoed Boni's frustrations about the economic crisis and the neocolonial overtones of the publication industry.

> We have to say that for publishers who are here in Côte d'Ivoire, general literature doesn't count for very much. It's good for their catalogs and for their visiting cards. But it's the schoolbook that holds the primary interest for these publishers. In general, literature comes afterwards. Novels, short stories, and poetry come afterwards. And this situation is going to become more complicated with the new wave of privatization. The publishing houses are no longer owned by the state. So, in the new situation, CÉDA is dominated by foreign capital—French and Canadian. I wonder if they're going to be interested in national literature and its development, because national literature will sell badly for them. And the people who come here to represent these publishing houses are basically businessmen. I wonder if they're really going to care about cultural affairs. (Carlos 1992)

Equally skeptical about prospects for publishing in Europe, Carlos stated that French publishers often throw books by African authors in the dustbin if first sales are not promising. The European reading public poses an obstacle because of oversaturation, lack of interest, and cultural insensitivity. The resultant problems constitute a tragedy for international African writers' markets.

> I am concerned because French publishers are not publishing us a great deal either. In France, there is not a large public for African literature and African books. We know the unfortunate experience of *Les Tambours de la mémoire,* published by Senegalese author Boubacar Boris Diop. We are aware, as well, of the experience of Véronique Tadjo, with her book *A Vol d'oiseau,* first published by Fernand Nathan in 1986. Both books were remaindered. There were not enough readers, so they were stockpiled. These were books written by Africans, but published by French publishing houses. There weren't enough readers to buy these books in France, and in Africa, we don't have enough readers in the reading public. In France, there aren't enough people interested in our books. So we risk writing to put the books in our own desk drawers. This is, a little bit, how our problem presents itself now. (Carlos 1992)

In spite of these problems, Carlos was enthusiastic about the new turn that his literary career had taken. His collection of poems, *Cri de la liberté* (1973), established a solid African reputation for his works. He used these works to convey a message of social criticism. Yet, this message was often cloaked in allegory and metaphors of displacement. His novel *Fleur du désert* (1990) takes up the problems of African dictatorship and exile in which the revolutionary hero, Jésus Muntu Marx, fights for his life and the freedom of his people in a fictitious African country. This allegorical tale allows Carlos to have a free hand in criticizing neocolonial injustice. But he remains protected behind the fictional trappings of his narrative. Carlos explained his political motivations: "You can see that I, myself, by virtue of my works, I'm very present and active in society. I'm a liberal. I don't think we have a right to dictate a direction of thought for writers. We shouldn't tell writers what to write. . . . But if a writer fulfills his central contract, which is the contract of being aesthetically worthy, then there we have an authentic writer" (Carlos 1992).

The interview concluded with a discussion of Carlos's notion of "social witnessing." He argued that witnessing is capturing the spirit of an era, with all of its successes and failures. Although his own writing has often been cautious in this regard, Carlos explained that witnesses report what they see and feel by turning the work itself into a historical document. He explained, "A work is historically dated. That is, a work bears the imprint of a person who has lived in a particular era and written under specific circumstances. A work may be eternal, but at the same time, it is time-bound. The witnessing in my work is based on the signs of a particular era. That is to say, the truths and realities of an epoch, of which I am a witness. It's not the author who is actually a witness. It's the work that witnesses for the author" (Carlos 1992).

This philosophy of witnessing is closely tied to Carlos's practices of writing, in which he bears witness to social problems but mutes political criticism with a poetic aesthetic. This strategy has garnered him considerable success and the reputation of an outspoken creative writer and journalist who is, nonetheless, sheltered from censorship and political reprisal.

Véronique Tadjo, whose 1986 book *A Vol d'oiseau* is mentioned in Carlos's interview, is an important Ivoirian writer. (See fig. 10.) Born in 1955 in Paris and educated in Côte d'Ivoire and France, Tadjo travels frequently from Africa to the United States and Europe. She forges important links between the Ivoirian and French publication scenes. Tadjo received recognition early in her career by winning a local poetry contest. She writes novels, poetry, children's books, and critical works on African and African-American literature. Her collection of poetry, *Latérite,* won the 1983 prize of the Agence de Coopération Culturelle et Technique and was published by Hatier, Monde Noir Poche, in 1984. The multifaceted novel *A Vol d'oiseau* (1986) was her second book, followed by *La Chanson de la vie* (1990b), a children's book published by Hatier in 1990. *Le Royaume aveugle* (1990c), an ambitious poetic novel about a fictitious African kingdom, was published by L'Harmattan. I first interviewed Tadjo in Paris on July 23, 1990, and spoke with her again after her move back to Abidjan in 1992 as a professor of literature. She is among the minority of writers in Abidjan whose works have been published successfully and regularly in Europe and Africa. In spite of the problems of distribution experienced with *A Vol d'oiseau,* Tadjo remained optimistic about her career.

She recounted the beginnings of her literary career:

> My mother was a painter, so there was always an artist in the house. But I never really thought that I would be a writer. I wrote poems, and I was encouraged by my parents. And I also received support from Bernard Zadi Zaourou, a poet in Abidjan who was a personal friend. The Agence de Coopération Culturelle et Technique sponsored a contest. I decided to assemble my poems and determine what logic existed in my writings. So, I sent in the collection, and it was accepted. I won the contest. They asked me then, "Would you like to be published by Hatier?" and I said, "Yes, of course, no problem. I certainly would." And that's how my work was first published. I became known as a result of the prize from ACCT with the publication of *Latérite.* (Tadjo 1990a)

Tadjo's successful first publication launched a fruitful career, which she describes as "a great journey." As a result, in her words, "I never had to go door to door, from one publisher to the next." She was likewise spared the problems of initial entry into a European market. Everything happened at once. Yet, she was unable to control the French reception of her work. Although the reviews were favorable, her complex and sensitively written *A Vol d'oiseau* (1986) was not a bestseller. She described her feelings about the situation.

Fig. 10. Véronique Tadjo, Ivoirian author, born in Paris and residing in Abidjan, works at her desk in Paris, July 23, 1990. Photograph by Bennetta Jules-Rosette.

> I have a lot of friends who are African writers. They spent all of their time encouraging me. "You must absolutely continue. Don't let your writing go! I loved your novel." And they wrote positive articles about my work. Then other people followed, you see! . . . So, now I'm relatively well known in Côte d'Ivoire, and my writing has been well received. France is another story. It's more difficult on the level of distribution. Only those interested in African literature buy the works, because you're not in the big networks [*les grands circuits*], at least I'm not. (Tadjo 1990a)

After the publication of her ambitious novel *Le Royaume aveugle* (1990c), Tadjo's confidence soared. Nevertheless, for personal and career reasons, she returned to Abidjan. There, she continued writing, with the respect and encouragement of the local circle of writers and intellectuals. *A Vol d'oiseau* was republished, with greater success, by Éditions L'Harmattan in 1992.[8]

Maurice Bandaman, novelist, poet, and active member of the AÉCI, provides a final case of African writing in Abidjan. Born in 1962 in Toumodi, Côte d'Ivoire, Bandaman began the serious writing of poetry and short stories while teaching at a lycée in Abidjan. His first book, *Une Femme pour une médaille* (1986), was published by CÉDA. Undaunted by problems of publication access and distribution, he published a collection of short stories, *Le Sang de la république* (1991), at his own expense with Inter/Afrique Presse in Côte d'Ivoire. An allegory about dictatorship and political repression resembling, in some respects, Carlos's work, this book stimulated Bandaman to continue his writing career. *Le Fils de-la-femme-mâle,* a novel, was published by L'Harmattan in 1993, earning Bandaman the Grand Prix Littéraire de l'Afrique Noire and praise as "one of the most promising voices in African francophone literature" (Éditions L'Harmattan 1995:49).[9] He was also the lead editor of the anthology of Ivoiran poetry entitled *Portrait des siècles meurtris,* published in 1994 by Dakeyo's Éditions Nouvelles du Sud.

When I interviewed Bandaman on August 9, 1992, he was upbeat about his recent successes and new projects. He was on the brink of breaking into an international literary market.

> Now, as for my projects, I always have several! I just published a collection of short stories, *Le Sang de la république,* and I have manuscripts that are already completed and in press. I just finished a novel that will appear soon with L'Harmattan entitled *Le Fils de-la-femme-mâle* (The son of the male-woman). It's a rather complex title. The "*femme-mâle*" is a woman who is both female and male. This idea has its roots in African mythology, where the first creatures were androgynous—both male and female. They were giants with supernatural powers, capable of putting into motion everything surrounding them. They were able, then, to change the world. And in this book, the subject is actually changing the world, in particular, Africa. It's a book that consists of three stages that correspond to three drawers that can be opened—creation, destruction, and rebirth. . . . At each stage, it's a matter of changing the world, and these mythical beings are so strong, so exceptional, that they can raise society to a higher level. (Bandaman 1992)

Both *Le Sang de la république* (1990) and *Le Fils de-la-femme-mâle* (1993) are allegorical criticisms of dictatorship and corruption in Africa. Bandaman's literary and stylistic strategies have reinforced his career goals of moving from a local to an international market. His self-published book brought him visibility and contacts in France. Participating in various conferences and workshops also took him to France. When I interviewed Bandaman in 1992, he had just written a play for his lycée and was working on a film scenario, in addition to his books. As it happened, I saw him again in 1995 at the Festival International des Francophonies, where he was an artist-in-residence. He had moved from a local setting with strong intellectual and network ties into the international arena of francophone literature.

Other authors I interviewed in 1992, such as the poet Amoa Urbain and the playwright Niangoran Porquet, were on the verge of making a leap into the international market. Although Urbain proclaimed a preference for self-publication as a means of disseminating his works to the local public, he also traveled to France and Germany whenever possible to explore alternative outlets. Porquet had recently completed his voluminous draft manuscript on "griotics," the methods of African storytelling applied to theater, literature, and the arts. Unfortunately, this work remained unpublished at the time of his death in 1995. Scores of other writers, members of the AÉCI and "independents," tried to break into Abidjan's moribund publication world and held out hopes of someday moving into international circuits. The Ivoirian writers' responses to the Municipal Club debate and the aloof world of foreign publishers were optimistic. When necessary, they used self-publication and artistic combination as strategies for gaining international recognition.

African Books in France

Since the early days of Présence Africaine, a number of French publishers have started to produce literary and critical works by African authors. Publishing houses, such as Le Seuil, Gallimard, and Seghers, have developed special series on African and Afro-Antillian literature, and on francophonie. Hatier's Monde Noir Poche series includes important novels produced with an eye toward inexpensive classroom sales. Hatier's role in the reorganization of CÉDA provides a direct connection between the French publishing house and the African literary scene. Two other, smaller publishers, Éditions L'Harmattan and Éditions Karthala, play critical roles in filling the literary and publication space initially opened up by Présence Africaine in the 1950s. L'Harmattan is devoted to Third World literatures, with the largest concentration of its titles (approximately 34 percent in 1990) based on African topics, or written by African authors (Ruppert 1991:156).[10]

Founded in 1975 by Denis Pryen, a former Catholic missionary in Africa, L'Harmattan began with a small budget and lofty ideals. (See fig. 11.) Pryen wanted to give a voice to authors who did not have access to publication outlets in their countries, and to fill a gap in the French market for Third World publications. Over the past two decades, he has succeeded in expanding the French literary space for African authors with the Encres Noires series. According to Sophie Ruppert (1991:158): "Among the Africans whose works have been published by L'Harmattan, one of the primary reasons for writing has been to liberate themselves—and, by extension, their fellow countrymen—from the silence that surrounds them." Ruppert (157) claims that most of the African authors published in L'Harmattan's Encres Noires literary series were born after 1940 and are part of the new generation of francophone African writers.

In 1993 I interviewed Armelle Riché, senior commercial editor at L'Harmattan in Paris. We discussed the problems and prospects of African literary production and the current publication situation at her press.

Fig. 11. Bookstore of L'Harmattan publishing house, rue des Écoles, Paris, July 1990. Photograph by Bennetta Jules-Rosette.

> The distribution of books in Africa—that depends on the country. We work with francophone Africa, principally because the anglophone market has been practically closed to us. Our success depends on the country, but, overall, the situation has become worse everywhere. The most dramatic decline occurred in Cameroon, which once had a fairly dynamic market with two major cities. Now, it's in trouble. And then there are other countries, like Niger, that don't have a single bookstore. . . . We work primarily with bookstores that we know, and they are not too numerous. And, parenthetically, they must be solvent. That is, we can't work directly with small bookstores. There is an established network of wholesalers, but our operations depend on the country and on the people in charge. This has worked very well in Gabon and somewhat well in Senegal. (Riché 1993)

Although these strategies are commercially viable for L'Harmattan, Riché was aware of the problems they pose for local consumers. She noted that small popular book shops are forced to buy from the wholesalers, creating a cycle of sales that could increase the prices of books on the local African markets and make them virtually inaccessible to many consumers.

> If the owner of a small kiosk places an order with me, I tell him: "But, finally, you see, it's complicated. You have to find a place for the book in your merchandise. Go to the wholesalers and order it." . . . But this doesn't resolve what I call "the inundation of books." It means that you have to finance a production so that it won't be expensive. I mean, finance it at a loss so that the book can circulate. (Riché 1993)

Riché was also concerned about the scarcity of high-quality manuscripts. She claimed that by 1992 L'Harmattan had produced over five hundred titles, about a quarter of which were about Africa.[11]

> You sort through the piles of manuscripts. You look at what's arrived. The flow of manuscripts is steady because we're relatively well known and local publishers can't absorb the production. But, even so, the production now is not extremely strong. The good manuscripts coming from Africa have diminished. We publish what Europeans write on Africa, and we publish Africans. There are these two aspects of our production, and both are diminishing. I think that one can analyze this situation in several ways. There is an economic crisis. People are thinking more about survival than writing manuscripts. The situation is blocked, and there is no new reflection, no innovation at the moment. Another manuscript on democracy! They arrive in an endless stream, and the same thing is always repeated. (Riché 1993)

Given Riché's pessimism about the quality of some of the material she received in 1993, I asked her whether she had in mind an ideal book that she would enjoy publishing. She responded evasively in terms of the literary market.

> I can't really talk about an ideal book as a commercial editor. The ideal book is a book that sells itself and develops a good reputation. We have to publish good material. But, it's not so much an ideal book that interests me, as an ideal author. The ideal author is one who collaborates, who understands the problems of book distribution, and who is willing to help out. There are some authors who, once their child is born, never take care of it. So, I think that the notion of an ideal author is very useful. (Riché 1993)

A mirror image of the experiences described by Ivoirian authors, Riché's account highlights some of the obstacles faced when African authors confront French publishers. In some respects, L'Harmattan offers these authors a halfway house and a bridge between local publishing and the French market. The cases of Bandaman and Tadjo illustrate, from different perspectives, the ways in which L'Harmattan has furthered the literary careers of African authors. For Bandaman, L'Harmattan offered an escape from self-publishing and a means of literary mobility. In Tadjo's case, L'Harmattan picked up a book that was well reviewed but that sold poorly and republished it. At a certain point, publishers and authors meet on the same terrain, where they share frustrations about the limited audience for African titles and the future of book sales on the African continent.

In April 1980, Robert Ageneau, a founding member of Éditions L'Harmattan, broke away and established Éditions Karthala, with a focus on scholarly and informational and academic writing about Africa and the Third World. According to Karthala's publicity summary (Éditions Karthala 1990:1), the objective of the publishing house is to "support the emergence of approaches representative of African contemporary realities, whether they are expressed in terms of research and scientific reflection, political engagement, domains of development (agriculture, education, and health), or literary writing." Although this approach resembles that of L'Harmattan, internal differences among the personnel, and the opening up of new market possibilities, made Karthala a viable, independent venture. Karthala's primary emphasis is on francophone Africa. Since 1987, the publishing house has sponsored a contest to attract new titles. By the end of 1990, Karthala had published 320 academic and literary titles. A specialty house with a limited number of publications, Karthala has, nevertheless, enriched the African publishing scene in France by introducing seven collections in the social sciences, development studies, and literature.

In August 1993, I interviewed Farida Benbelaid, commercial and publicity editor for Karthala. She qualified that Karthala is "small," even by comparison to L'Harmattan, and that its primary focus is a university market.

> We are experiencing a drastic deterioration of bookstore networks in Africa, which is not surprising in the light of Africa's chronic economic problems. . . . We sell directly to local libraries in different African countries. We work well with some countries and not so well with others. And, as I said earlier, the network has become terribly restricted. . . . The content of our works is very diversified. We publish practically all genres, but we publish very few literary works, and no theater or poetry at all, for purely commercial reasons. These genres are very difficult to commercialize, at least in France. Our colleagues at Présence Africaine are in a much better position to publish African literature in the format of inexpensive paperbacks [*livres de poche*], which are more accessible to an African public. (Benbelaid 1993)

I questioned Benbelaid further on the publication policy and the number of books printed in the Karthala collections.

> I'm a commercial editor, so I convert everything into francs! For our academic collections, such as Hommes et Sociétés, we print about 1,500 copies. But we also have another collection, the Méridiens, which is intended for the general public. The Méridiens series introduces particular countries in a general manner—daily life, society, political life, geography, and history. It's really very general, destined for a larger public. In this case, we print 2,500 to 3,000 copies with the possibility of reprinting the work if it sells well. As a monthly average, up to the 1990s, we printed three titles per month. Now—and this corresponds happily with a normal evolution—we print six to seven titles a month. (Benbelaid 1993)

Benbelaid expressed a clear preference for the generalist works published by Karthala. She explained: "It's necessary to recognize that readers are often reticent and standoffish when they know that a book has been written by a scholar or researcher. They approach it with a certain prudence. We would like our authors to write more simply, knowing that they are going to reach not only an audience of academics, but also the general public." Benbelaid claimed that Karthala was in the process of developing some new editorial policies that would stimulate sales, but she was reluctant to discuss these developments. "We can't unveil everything about the publishing house," she concluded. Nevertheless, the interview with Benbelaid disclosed Karthala's strategy of filling a specific niche in the African-oriented market by leaving literary publication largely to Présence Africaine and L'Harmattan while focusing on scholarly and general nonfiction books. Although Benbelaid complained about the weak African markets for Karthala's publications, the publishing house adopted a strategy of targeting the French and selected African academic markets with limited printings of between forty and eighty titles a year.

In contrast, Hatier occupies the opposite extreme of the French market for African publications. Hatier's 1993–94 catalog contained hundreds of African-oriented titles, mostly schoolbooks, and a more limited series, the Monde Noir Poche, with about fifty-five fiction, poetry, and theater titles by well-established African authors. Authors included the Ivoirian writers Jean-Marie Adiaffi Ade, Bernard Dadié, and Véronique Tadjo. The titles were published as inexpensive pocket books targeted toward an educational, although not exclusively scholarly, audience. The school textbooks outnumber the Monde Noir collection ten to one and provide economic support for Hatier's literary experimentation. Hatier's copublications with CÉDA in Côte d'Ivoire include titles in the Monde Noir Poche collection. According to Caroline Ogou, commercial editor at CÉDA, these copublications are not really a cooperative enterprise (Cévaër 1994:204). Hatier selects the titles, chooses the printer, produces the book, and merely sends the bill to CÉDA, creating yet another instance of the "green beans" export phenomenon.

Claude Connickx, editor for Hatier's francophone West African desk, explained the problem as one of commercial viability. According to him, copublication facilitates distribution of affordable books for an African public by cutting out import taxes and opening up new local markets. Connickx viewed this process as a fruitful collaboration and not a case of foreign intervention in publishing. In a 1993 interview at Hatier in Paris, he elaborated on his point of view.

> So, the problems of distribution rely essentially on the economic fabric of each country. That is, in circumstances where the economic crisis and poor remunera-

> tion break up the social fabric of the country, the structure of distribution collapses. Consequently, the bookstores and points of sale disappear. It's certainly useless to send schoolbooks or literary works to African capitals where the books don't leave the airport. So that's the first problem. The second problem is the financial resources of students' families and the buying public. And I would say that a third problem that is equally important is thematic. Often, African authors write about the same themes that they began with five or ten years ago. There's no innovation [*renouvellement*]. As a result, the potential public that could be reached by these works is a little discouraged from reading. (Connickx 1993)

Connickx lamented the lack of originality and innovation in African literature. He continued: "I think that the problem is more innovation than originality. Originality exists, but it's simply that African authors who produced a literature of political engagement have not changed their themes or formats. Now there is a popularization of African writing that has become a bit homogeneous." This type of argument, of course, is not new. It places the blame for weak sales of African literature on the shoulders of unimaginative authors without examining the marketing context for their works.

Although he complained about the quality of African literature, Connickx admitted that literary works constitute only about 10 percent of Hatier's African titles. Schoolbooks, Hatier's bread and butter, have assured sales based on large contracts with African ministries of education. These educational sales help to keep prices down and permit the publisher to take some risks with African literature.

> Literature represents about 10 percent of our publications, with between 50 and 55 titles in one of our collections, Monde Noir Poche, created about ten years ago. The principle is this: you often have books published in France that sell at 65, 80, or 100 francs. In Côte d'Ivoire, the same book will cost five times as much. To react to this situation, we want to make books available locally at reasonable prices. This is not at all a philanthropic mission. We do this by selling 90 percent of our publications to ministries of education and culture. . . . We also have copublications with CÉDA, including a youth collection for schoolchildren between 7 and 12 years old. (Connickx 1993)

In concluding his interview, Connickx emphasized the commercial basis of his enterprise: "We work with ministries of national education and with teachers working in the field. We have two objectives—the first is to make our publications known and see if they appeal to the educational system and, then, the second is to interest them in buying our books."

Publishers interviewed in Paris complained about declining African book sales and the stagnant market. They adopted a broad spectrum of strategies to cope with this situation. Karthala, for example, focused on primarily academic publications with limited circulation in France and Africa. L'Harmattan had a more extensive French and African distribution, venturing into literature, theater, and poetry with the Encres Noires collection, while maintaining a stable base of nonfiction publications. Of the three publishers interviewed, Hatier had, by far, the largest operation, but its literature collection did not exceed that of L'Harmattan. Although Hatier's methods might be considered the literary equivalent of the "green beans" export phenomenon, the approach to copublications did not actually differ from the other publishers. All three publishing houses engaged in coeditions with African publishers, including CÉDA, and, in most instances, the French publisher selected and produced the book in France, selling the final product back to the African-based publisher. This cycle is yet another case of the dependence of African institutions on the technology and distribution networks of the West (Rodney 1972:35). This vicious cycle of external production and reproduction, characteristic of neocolonialism, is at the heart of African publication enterprises.

One may ask what effect the economic base of African publishing has on the literature itself. An idealistic response to this question is "no effect." Claude Connickx of Hatier criticized the quality of African literary production as though it were autonomous from the commercial distribution base. Ironically, however, he noted the tedious redundancy of popular books that sell well. Although the commercial base of publication does not determine the quality, or even the themes, of works produced, the reward system of publication sustains the distribution of certain kinds of books while excluding others. Thus, we have seen that two out of the three publishers (Karthala and Hatier) generally avoid poetry and keep literary publications to a minimum. At least two methods are available to authors who wish to break into this restrictive system: (1) producing a prizewinning or noteworthy manuscript that catches the publisher's eye or (2) using self-publication as a vehicle to enter the publication loop with an unusual piece of work.

In the worlds of art and culture, buyers and sellers and artists and audiences often have very different interpretations of how creative works are produced and circulate. Interestingly enough, the authors and publishers working out of Côte d'Ivoire shared similar views of their environment. Authors were keenly aware of the publishers' commercial strategies, and publishers understood the limitations of their market. Only the reading public, through lack of resources and interest, seemed powerless to make its views known. Instead, a multitiered series of middlemen, culture brokers, and sales points emerged, including the wholesalers, bookstores, local shops, and small stands. By dealing primarily with the wholesalers and large bookstores, French publishers bolster their profits at the expense of reaching a larger reading public. When their stock of complimentary copies is depleted, African authors have a difficult time obtaining copies of their own books, which are stockpiled and destroyed before they ever reach local bookstores.

To the three French publishers discussed here, we may add the Parisian-based African publishers such as Présence Africaine and Éditions Nouvelles du Sud. By virtue of their literary activities and contacts, these publishers may have greater access than the French publishers to local African authors, but they, too, are affected by economic conditions. Although the African publishers often take more risks than their French colleagues with new and unknown authors, they place limits on their experimentation. They are also caught in the vicious cycle of exporting books from Europe to Africa and engaging in asymmetrical copublication arrangements with African-based publishing houses.

The Marketing Loop in African Literature

The publication syndrome in Côte d'Ivoire opens up important questions about the marketing and future of African literary efforts that are overlooked in critical studies of literary texts. Although the Ivoirian authors I interviewed in 1992 were prolific, they had varying degrees of success in breaking into international publishing. Most of them began with a focus on the local market, which, they complained, was stagnant for both economic and ideological reasons. A few, such as Carlos and Urbain, claimed to have found success primarily in Côte d'Ivoire and were content to remain in a regional African market. Even this market, however, is highly dependent on European sources for production and distribution, as the interviews with French publishers suggest. Self-publication is the only semi-autonomous facet of this market. Hence, a commercial loop between Africa and Europe shapes the internal Ivoirian literary market, overshadowing it with a latent neocolonialism. This marketing loop exists in other forms of African contemporary cultural production, including the plastic arts and music (Baudrillard 1972:124–25; Jules-Rosette 1984:16–22; Ewens 1991:126–57; Jules-Rosette and Martin 1997:17–19), but in certain respects, it is more pronounced in literary production, where sales, as the publishers emphasize, depend on a literate and solvent commercial audience. In some African countries—Cameroon, Kenya, and Nigeria, for example—a growing market for self-published street literature is emerging (Barber 1987:48–53; Griswold 1987:1–35).[12] This market is not yet active in Côte d'Ivoire and is not sufficiently developed to account for the successful crossover careers of popular street writers. Thus, self-publication either becomes a dead end or, more positively, the first step that writers take toward Pan-African and international literary markets.

Another trend evident in Côte d'Ivoire is the multiple artistic career, in which writers simultaneously explore various forms of expression from journalism and theater to the plastic arts. Although for different reasons, authors are as concerned as publishers about the financial success of their works. A purely literary career, however, is possible for only a select few in Côte d'Ivoire. Most writers there engage in journalism, teaching, or related pursuits to support themselves. Artistic combination, as seen in the cases of Werewere Liking, Jérôme Carlos, and Maurice Bandaman, offers another interesting strategy for maintaining literary careers.

As they look toward Paris and the international publication scene, Ivoirian authors face a multilayered economic market that has many complexities. The cycle of literary production begins with the artist and the local market and may be blocked at several points before the author's work ever reaches an international market. Even works that remain primarily in the local publication circuit are often printed and distributed from Europe, reinforcing the closed circle of neocolonial literary production. Although the content of writers' works may transcend this neocolonial marketing cycle, becoming examples of so-called postcolonial or world literature, the production and marketing remain within a neocolonial economic framework. Figures 12 and 13 illustrate this process.

What have the writers accomplished when and if they finally enter an international market? The economic dependency of Africa is perpetuated in the cultural domain by the economic and editorial control of foreign publishing houses. On the local level, this control is apparent in the privatization of publishing houses such as CÉDA and the purchase of their controlling interests by a majority of foreign investors. Individual writers have the illusion of escaping this trap by sending their works directly to Europe, or, in some cases, North America, for publication. In this instance, however, the writers are caught in an insidious game of category and genre classification developed by foreign publishers. These

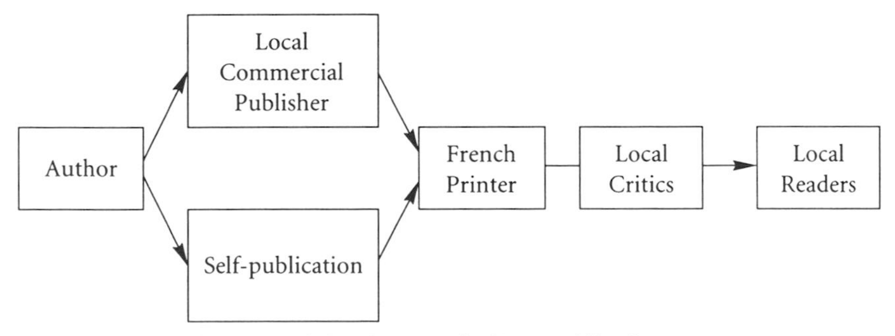

Fig. 12. Local production and distribution of African publications.

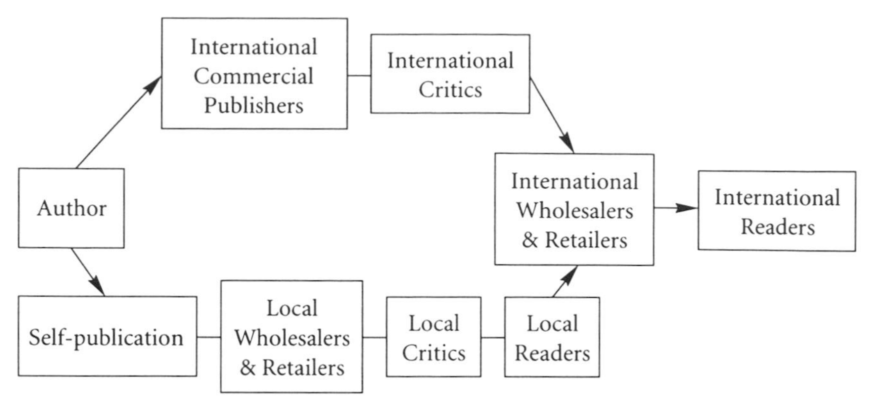

Fig. 13. International production and distribution of African publications.

systems of classification are not identical internationally. For example, French markets differ from U.S. markets in their classification and distribution schemes. In both cases, however, African fiction is generally labeled as a category apart from mainstream writing and is targeted at specialty academic or ethnic audiences. Although publishing works classified under the label of "francophonie" offers opportunities for new artists and writers, it has the negative side effect of ghettoizing the works of African authors.[13] Thus, reaching an international audience may ultimately amount to reaching a newly configured, restricted audience, or another ghetto that is international in name only.

The marketing loop links African writers to an international audience without assuring them a place in world literature.[14] Publishers' marketing and classificatory schemes block the distribution of some works, resulting in low visibility and sales for African authors. These books, as Jérôme Carlos suggested, end up in "desk drawers." There is no quick economic fix for this situation. The only solution appears to be one that the writers of the AÉCI have already adopted: educating publishers and the general public about the richness and variety of African literary productions by developing a broader, content-based schema for marketing "African" literary works. Changing this schema requires a more active relationship—a type of dialectical exchange—between African producers and foreign publication houses, with the addition of more sensitive editors and new authors.

Reflections on Francophonie

On the rainy day of September 23, 1995, three years after my initial interviews, I met Tanella Boni and Maurice Bandaman at the Festival International des

Francophonies in Limoges. Cordoned off in this provincial French city, so well known for its classic porcelain, was a tent that served as the festival's center. Inside, African authors and a handful of French critics and publishers rubbed shoulders. The festival gave the writers a chance to exchange ideas freely, debate, and make new contacts.[15] The atmosphere was warm and animated. The theatrical productions were especially moving. On the surface glimmered the promise of a new acceptance of African cultural productions in France.

Leaving the tent and walking into the rainy city, I noticed that very little had changed. Although the authors benefited from their sabbaticals in France, their books were nowhere to be seen outside of the festival. Local townspeople benignly tolerated this momentary African intrusion as yet another occasion to profit from the tourist trade. Since my last encounter with the Ivoirian authors, they had published the books that they had discussed with me and much more. A tone of optimism reigned, but the contours of the French publishing houses had not changed, and more African authors had just been removed from the official reading list for French baccalaureate exams. As I walked away from my meeting with the authors, the festival tent faded into the background, a flimsy nomadic structure, sheltering the writers from the rest of the world.

INTERVIEW

Bernard Binlin Dadié Abidjan, Côte d'Ivoire, August 10, 1992

Bernard Binlin Dadié is one of the best known writers of Côte d'Ivoire and has been a leading figure in his country's cultural and political activities for several decades. (See fig. 14.) Born Koffi Binlin Dadié in Assinie, Côte d'Ivoire, in 1916, Dadié was educated in Bingerville, Côte d'Ivoire, and in Dakar, Senegal. During his youth, he was active in colonial protest movements. After meeting Alioune Diop, he participated in the conferences and cultural activities of Présence Africaine. Following independence, he served as minister of culture of Côte d'Ivoire. His prolific writings include numerous novels, autobiographical pieces, short stories, poetry, plays, and works of political criticism. Many of these works were originally published by Présence Africaine. His novels include Climbié *(1956),* Un Nègre à Paris *(1959), and* Un Patron de New York *(1964). The latter two novels are foundational pieces for the new generation of literature of Parisianism. He published the short story "L'Aveu" in Alioune Diop's first issue of* Présence Africaine *in 1947. His three-act play* Béatrice du Congo *(1970) is considered one of the most innovative masterworks of African theater.*

In sum, Dadié is a living legend and a cultural reference point for many younger African writers.

There is a copious critical literature on his works, and there are several English translations (Battestini, Battestini, and Mercier 1964; Brench 1967; Vincileoni 1986; Hatch 1994; and Patterson 1994). My interview with Bernard Dadié in August 1992 focused on his early involvement with the Présence Africaine movement and his views on contemporary African writing.

Early Years as a Writer

Bennetta Jules-Rosette: Monsieur Dadié, your writings are well known throughout the world. I'd like to begin by asking you about your background as a writer and some of the important events that influenced your career.

Bernard Dadié: I entered the École Primaire Supérieure of Bingerville in 1930. At Bingerville, we took an exam that allowed us to compete for entry into the École William-Ponty, which grouped together students from all eight French colonies. The École William-Ponty was located on Gorée Island. It

Fig. 14. Bernard B. Dadié and Bennetta Jules-Rosette in an interview, Abidjan, Côte d'Ivoire, August 10, 1992. Photograph by Yolanda James.

had several sections—administration, cinema, and medicine. I took the courses in the administrative section, and I finished in 1936. At that time, I decided to stay on in Dakar and try to work for the local government. I started in the Department of Education. Then, in October, I met a young archivist and lawyer, Monsieur André Villard. He came by looking for an assistant. And they told him, "We have a young man here. He's very good, but he doesn't get along with anyone." [laughter] So I said to Monsieur Villard, "I just finished school. If you have confidence in me, your work will go well. If you don't trust me, everything will fall apart." He said, "I like that. At least, you're frank." From that moment on, we became friends. And we spent day and night studying, writing texts, and discussing politics. I wrote newspaper articles in Dakar. It was a great adventure, and I was fortunate to meet Villard. We worked in the archives of the Institut Français d'Afrique Noire (IFAN), a very interesting milieu in which to learn everything. . . . And in Dakar, it was around 1936, I also wrote *Assémien Déhylé,* my first play. It was performed in front of the cardinal and later across all French West Africa and in France.

BJR: How long did you stay in Dakar?

BD: I was in Dakar until the war in 1939. The months from July to December were a very difficult period. There were bombardments in France, and there was trouble in Senegal. Then, after the war, the chiefs of state came. And I met a young senator who approached me at the national library in Dakar. His name was Alioune Diop. And at that time, he spoke to me about his projects, his plans to establish a journal. There was already one journal called *Griot d'Haïti* in which a lot of writers and politicians were publishing. But Alioune Diop proposed something different. There was a good deal of political activity in Dakar at that time around the RDA [Rassemblement Démocratique Africain]. Dakar was a great political center. But I didn't belong to any political party then.

BJR: What happened when you returned to Côte d'Ivoire?

BD: I was back in Abidjan at the time of the general strike in 1947. There was a strike of railroad workers and government personnel. It was a difficult time for the African economy. And from 1946 to 1947—after the war—things changed. There was a law that made us French citizens, and we could create our own newspapers. We had already started a paper called *Le Reveil* in Dakar, and we started another one in Côte d'Ivoire. It was also the time of the first congress of the PDCI [Parti Démocratique de Côte d'Ivoire]. I presented two reports at the congress—one on youth and the other on the press. I was already a member of the editorial committee of *Le Reveil.*

BJR: What were some of the consequences of your political and journalistic activities?

BD: After the war, things began to change in Europe, on metropolitan terrain. . . . And in 1949, there was a sort of retrenchment, a change in local government. It was as if we had lost everything we gained. They wanted to put us on alert. They were afraid of the Communist party. There was a meeting at the Comacico movie house in Treicheville. It was organized by the Bloc Démocratique on February 6, 1949. We all came to this meeting. And we learned that some people who came were armed. But the government was behind that. We were tricked. And they described our meeting as pillage and violence. It's still written like that in the government documents of accusation. And they picked us up then. I've written about it in *Carnets de prison.*

BJR: So, you were arrested on February 6, 1949. How long were you in prison?

BD: After a little over a year, our case came to trial, on March 22, 1950. I was given three years with grace, so I was released just before Easter in 1953. During this period, they kept appealing our case. I was released twice, briefly, but I had to go back until 1953. They took us to a prison camp where we had to sleep on the ground for the first night until our wives could bring us mats. They didn't want to take us to trial. So we had a hunger strike. There were eight of us journalists who had been picked up with the others. . . . They didn't brutalize us. They didn't insult us. The guards knew that I was a writer, so they were careful. But they searched us regularly. I had written an article against Governor Péchoux and had passed it along to my wife. I was writing a second article when they came to search me. I heard them coming, and I tore the article into little pieces and ate it.

BJR: You ate your article? That's incredible.

BD: Yes. I ate it. I really ate it because the guard was coming to search me, and I knew what he was looking for then. They had already confiscated one document. It's interesting. When you're in prison, you become very clever, and you learn to size up your adversary.

BJR: And did the experience in prison change your outlook on life?

BD: You learn to refuse certain things in politics and life, to refuse to compromise. It's an attitude based on respect—the respect you don't receive in prison. It's not a question of color or race. You learn to respect people and to value humanity. Voilà. That's my personal struggle, my battle to value life and humanity. All of my books are about that.

Paris and Présence Africaine

BJR: I'd like to discuss your career in the 1950s and your relationship to the Présence Africaine movement. Earlier, you mentioned meeting Alioune Diop in Dakar. Tell me about your experiences with Présence Africaine in Paris.

BD: I had a ticket for France in the month of July of 1956. It was then that I wrote *Un Nègre à Paris.* The sequel was *Paris à la loupe,* but our friends who read the books that are good to publish didn't like *Paris à la loupe* because they said that I was praising the go-betweens. So that book was never published. Good, but why? Because I said that in Paris, women adorned the streets and the boulevards from Saint-Denis to Sébastopol, from the Madeleine to the Champs-Elysées, making the boulevards joyous for strangers to see. I was just doing a documentary report. There are films that say this, but it was, perhaps, too daring to write at that time. Then September came, and we all attended the famous Congress of Black Writers and Artists in Paris, which was a very great cultural and political movement. . . . Alioune Diop had invited all of us. And I already knew Jacques Rabemananjara. He was a great friend. He had telephoned me before the congress to discuss certain topics.

BJR: In your view, what were some of the results of the congress?

BD: Well, we were all there together. Césaire was there. He was already a deputy and he became mayor of Fort de France. And Senghor was there. He was the only one to become president of a republic. None of the new African presidents participated in our meetings. We debated the issues of African independence. We touched on just about everything. And then, in 1959, we went to Rome. Frantz Fanon was there. He came and gave his speech, then he left right away. Sekou Touré sent us a message. All of that happened at our cultural meetings. But all of the ideas that we developed then have not been applied today. It's a different ideology, a different conception of human relations.

BJR: In spite of the problems, what importance do you attribute to these cultural encounters?

BD: They were very important because they permitted black writers from all backgrounds, territories, colonies, and nationalities to study the political situation. It allowed them to describe how they were treated as citizens of a state. Even though we were technically citizens in 1946, we were not independent. These meetings created an occasion to discuss our plans and to create friendships. A certain sense of solidarity developed during these meetings, and there were Europeans among us who shared in this spirit of friendship and camaraderie. We experienced this in Paris and in Rome. And the Société Africaine de Culture developed ties with the Société Européenne de Culture. Many people don't realize this. So, an entire program developed. It was a new environment. And the dialogue among people who wanted to change things was very fruitful. But if in France, in Europe, men of culture can influence the course of events, this is not always the case in Africa.

Writing in Africa Today

BJR: What are some of the problems facing African writers today?

BD: In Africa, the writer has been the enemy. I don't mean the adversary because we have our tradition of griots. But a writer who does not sing praises, who denounces injustice because he does not share the same opinions as an underling of the head of state, this writer becomes an enemy and has problems. That's why many writers prefer to go abroad to work. Oh, myself, I've been known to say one can criticize everything. But if I say to someone, "You're not very cultivated," I insult him. If I say "You haven't read a lot," I incite him to read. Voilà. You must say everything in Africa in a certain manner.

There is a certain way of maintaining a discourse in Africa. We do not insult. We use proverbs. Ah oui, proverbs! With proverbs, one tells a story. Here's how things are: I don't say you are an idiot or become angry. I tell a story, drawing on my traditions, not those of the Russians, the Americans, or the French, because they frame their discourse differently. And here in Africa, we have our own frames of discourse and techniques of criticism that must be respected. I have always said that I reject French techniques for framing discourse. I reject it. I *cannot* do it. You have to escape from occidental methods and, little by little, translate your own method. If you judge me by your methods, it's false. I have always said that you cannot criticize me with methods I reject.

BJR: Are these problems confronted by writers consequences of an economic and political crisis in Africa?

BD: Some say that African independence experienced a rocky start—a false start. If we look around the African continent today, there is war everywhere. There is conflict everywhere—Liberia, Somalia, Ghana, Angola, South Africa. But we have to try to make peace and stop hatred. We're all in the same boat. It's not just Africa that's off to a false start. These problems are global. In the midst of all of this conflict, it's not the role of the writer to reproduce, but to prevent and denounce. People without any understanding are in power. There's the problem. There's the drama of the authentic writer. . . . When Victor Hugo criticized Napoleon, he said that Napoleon had a battery of cannons, but he had a pen. And the pen has remained much longer than the cannon fire.

Advice to Young Writers

BJR: What advice do you have to pass along to young writers?

BD: I'm not in a good position to give advice to young writers. Writing is very difficult, especially today. There are certain norms and standards. It's not enough to criticize colonialism. That's over. And then there's the problem of publishing. In Africa, it takes patience. Some young writers think that if they leave a book with a publisher, it will appear automatically. But a publisher is in business. There is a whole system with many elements at play. If you're impatient to see your name in print, you're in the wrong profession.

BJR: Do you have a few words of encouragement for young writers?

BD: They should read a lot, observe, and listen. Having an extensive vocabulary is very important. When I have to stop to search for a word, my inspiration and my concentration are cut. When I find the right word, my inspiration returns. It's all connected. And when I'm writing, I don't eat and I don't sleep. I'm never hungry or tired until I've given birth to my work. That's the kind of passion that a writer needs. That's all.

FIVE

The African Writers' Parisian Landscape: A Social and Literary Panorama

For me, Paris will always be a mirage in the wilderness.
—Bernard Dadié, 1966

Small streets crowded with bargain shops, one-room cafés, beggars, and curiosity seekers criss-cross black Paris. Sights of Africa and odors of the Orient blend and signal the crossing of an imaginary border. Black Paris is not an American-style ghetto. It consists of many communities sprinkled across the city, creating an exotic subculture that lurks behind the official monuments. As new immigrants pour into the city, Paris reluctantly makes room for them. This alternative environment has become the incubation cubicle for a new style of African writing.

From 1960 to the mid-1980s, the social and cultural context of African writing in France transformed. The end of the French colonial period in 1960 marked a watershed for African writers with the appearance of revolutionary writing. Many African intellectuals turned their attention toward building a social and cultural infrastructure on the African continent. At the same time, seeds were present for the growth of a cosmopolitan style of Franco-African writing known as Parisianism. The roots of Parisianism may be traced to Bernard Dadié's landmark book *Un Nègre à Paris* (1959). Dadié's novel records the habits of Parisians through the eyes of Tanhoé Bertin, a naive first-time visitor from West Africa, who writes a lively letter home about his startling experiences in the metropolis from July 14 through August 2, 1956. His version of the Parisian journey is the predecessor of a long line of novels about travel and displacement. The term "Parisianism" is not a genre description current among literary theorists. There is little critical work on this relatively new genre, but the quantity of new works and their thematic similarities warrant classification and recognition. In addition, the term is particularly appropriate because the authors use it to describe their own works and to assert their cultural claim of belonging to French society.

In the 1980s, the Parisianism genre experienced a rebirth because social conditions in France opened a new window through which African writers could see themselves as a vital part of French society and intellectual life. Their participation differed from the contestatory impact of the Présence Africaine publishing house that used France as a staging ground for African liberation. Writers with a reinvigorated version of the Parisianism style (Yodi Karone, Simon Njami, Calixthe Beyala, Blaise N'Djehoya, and Félix Bankara, to name a few) were the beneficiaries of an incredible world of opportunity in which many aspects of French social and cultural life were open to them. Although access to this environment was fraught with obstacles skillfully described by the writers, the fruits of their struggles were within reach, and they viewed Paris as their own city. These writers participate in networks that are not as structured as the early Présence Africaine movement with its centralized leadership and research commissions. Nevertheless, they are in regular communication with each other directly, and through public and private dialogues in the mass media, at festivals, and in colloquia. These contacts are centered in Paris but extend to the rest of Europe, Africa, and the Americas. The authors also read and occasionally publish each other's works.

Literature reflects society on many different levels. For example, it is possible to analyze the ways in which writers develop their topics, the author-audience connection, the role of publishing houses, and the influence of literature on political debates (Griswold 1987:28–32). In his study of contemporary *beur* (North African immigrant) fiction in France, Alec Hargreaves (1991:47) counsels against making a "one-to-one" correlation between social experiences and literature. An examination of the works of Parisianism in the light of the legal and social conditions of the late 1980s and early 1990s in France, however, suggests that these publications were fueled by conditions of cultural promise existing in the society at that time. The Parisianism of the 1980s would not have been possible without political pressure to liberalize legal and social attitudes toward immigration in France and to combat xenophobic sentiments. In this complex and changing environment, France saw the emergence of a new category of black writers.[1]

From 1960 to 1992, the number of sub-Saharan Africans residing in Paris virtually exploded. The rising African migration rates do not include the considerable Antillian population from Martinique and Guadeloupe. Antillians, whose numbers in France were also on the rise, are French citizens by law and are dealt with under separate categories for census purposes. The growing black presence in Paris expanded the audience for African writing and cultural productions, and became a rich source of material for African fiction works, theater, and social science writing. A new African literature flourished under these social and cultural conditions.

The migration patterns in France over the past thirty years afford a concrete basis for examining African writers' interpretations of the Parisian landscape. The 1982 French census showed 127,322 Africans from former French colonies living in France, in comparison to 18,000 recorded in the 1962 French census, which contained only a partial breakdown of immigration statistics (Dewitte 1987:18). (See appendix 2.) According to the 1990 census, 1,633,142 North and sub-Saharan Africans of various nationalities resided in France. By 1991, the term "immigrant" applied to 4.5 million people out of a national population of 56 million (Lloyd and Waters 1991:51). Of the individuals acquiring French nationality by naturalization in 1989, 37.5 percent were reputed to be of European origin, and 34.5 percent of North African and sub-Saharan African origin.[2] In a report sponsored by the Institut National d'Études Démographiques (INÉD), Michèle Tribalat (1995:224–25) found that the new immigrants were, on the whole, better educated and culturally equipped to meet the challenges of French society than were their predecessors. The new arrivals in Paris migrated to areas where they could find affordable and convenient housing, in the eighteenth, nineteenth, and twentieth arrondissements and in working-class suburbs such as Charenton, Issy-les-Moulineaux, Ivry, Montreuil, and Pantin. These locales became the dispersed centers of black Paris. They contain shops, cafés, bars, beauty parlors, churches, and mosques catering to the immigrant population.

As a collective physical and ideological space, black Paris is a landscape of memory that encompasses the subjective perspectives of African writers. Through the environment of black Paris, experiences are communicated and memories reinvented (Gabriel 1989:59).[3] The expression of community in terms of ethnicity as a simulation and a lived experience is evident in the emergent discourses of black Paris. With the increase in immigration, these discourses have filtered into the public domain.

One of the few compilations dealing with the geography and social life of black Paris is a tourist guidebook entitled *Guide actuel du Paris mondial* (Équipe du Guide Paris Mondial 1992). This book resembles Parisian weekly entertainment guides such as *Pariscope* and *L'Officiel des Spectacles* that advertise upcoming events for tourists and local residents. The guide to world Paris, however, selects events and locations pertinent to specific groups and provides social and political commentaries on their art, music, and cultures. It opens with a long and lively chapter entitled "Paris Afro-Antillais." The discussion begins with an ideological justification for the conversion of black Paris into a set of touristic simulations. The guide explains:

> The shock of cultures may end in the dilution of traditions, a loss of identity, and the notion of a "nègre blanc." Certain ancestral rites challenge French law (we remember the trial for excision; we know less, on the other hand, about the problems of subsistence of the marabouts, veritable guardians of the traditions and morality of the African community here even more than in Africa . . .).
>
> Finally, racism, which is rising with unemployment, and white nationalism will create new barriers and lead to disillusionment expressed by a sort of modern blues (especially among the Antillians, French by law).
>
> The former colonizer, coiled up in his hexagon, forgets the benefits of this exchange: cultural métissage, indirect aid to Africa, evolution of certain classes of African society, in particular women, education, and the importance of maintaining francophonie. (Équipe du Guide Paris Mondial 1992:16)

These strident political justifications are unusual statements for a tourist guidebook. Not only does the guide provide a list of African and Antillian cafés, restaurants, bars, nightclubs, book shops, movie theaters, and record stores, it also contains profiles of authors, artists, musicians, and cultural figures who make *Paris noir* come alive. These figures include the Cameroonian novelist Simon Njami, who has written about the sights and sounds of black Paris in *Cercueil et cie* (1985) and *African gigolo* (1989a); Pascal Legitimus, a Martinican actor; the Cameroonian jazz musician Manu Dibango; and MC Solaar, a Chadian rap musician. Readers of the guidebook are taught to identify the literary figures, musical styles, artistic trends, fashions, and foods of Africa and the Antilles. They are even introduced to African dialects, Antillian creole, and Afro-Antillian slang.

Entering black Paris means leaving the sacred sights of monumental and historic Paris behind (MacCannell 1989:42–48). The *Guide actuel du Paris mondial* does not reveal all of the secrets of black Paris. It merely presents a map of the territory. A leisurely touristic stroll through certain sections of Afro-Antillian Paris is difficult. As one leaves the métro Barbès-Rochechouart and walks up to the Goutte d'Or district and the Château Rouge commercial area, the overwhelming feeling of being in an African city surfaces. Shoppers swarm into Tati, the local bargain department store, and crowd into the open-air African market, Marché Dejean. (See figs. 15 and 16.) Strangers are approached by Islamic beggars and met by cold stares from suspicious residents. Members of

Fig. 15. A busy street in Afro-Antillian Paris in 1991. Photograph by Bennetta Jules-Rosette, Black Paris Collection, 1991.

Fig. 16. The Marché Dejean was listed in the 1992 *Guide Actuel du Paris Mondial* as selling the best African fish in Paris. Photograph by Bennetta Jules-Rosette, Black Paris Collection, 1991.

this community protect themselves from intrusion and are cautious about casual outsiders. Residents are justifiably wary in the light of the changing legal and social conditions of immigration in France. Guy Boudimbou's 1991 anthropological study of the habitat and lifestyles of African immigrants in France contains a detailed analysis of the difficulties posed by substandard housing and social stigmatization. Boudimbou (1991:51) emphasizes that subsidized low-income housing (the HLM) "symbolizes all of the difficulties of integration" into French society and the sentiments of disdain and marginalization encountered by the immigrants.

Legal and Social Dimensions of Immigration in France

In France, a heated debate surrounds definitions of citizenship and nationality. Access to French nationality is based on two principles, birthright (*droit du sang*) and residence (*droit du sol*). Law #93-933, of July 22, 1993, popularly referred to as Charles Pasqua's law, made it difficult for French-born children of immigrants to acquire French nationality (Costa-Lascoux 1994:18–19). The status of being born in the country and growing up there does not automatically assure French citizenship. Instead, nationality is traced back to the grandparents' place of birth. Second-generation immigrants must petition for citizenship through an arduous process, the results of which are not assured. An ironic turn of events has taken place over several years. Some young North and sub-Saharan African immigrants elect not to assume French nationality, even when offered the legal possibility to do so. This perplexing situation has baffled French authorities, who, despite posing obstacles to French nationality, always expected that all immigrants would ultimately want it.

On Friday, August 23, 1996, three hundred Africans whose papers were not regularized were arrested and expelled from their place of refuge in the Église Saint-Bernard in the eighteenth arrondissement of Paris (Desportes 1996:4). This incident, along with a series of other expulsions and extraditions in 1996, gave rise to the Sans Papiers movement, in which unregularized immigrants joined French citizens to change the 1993 immigration laws. The goal of the Sans Papiers movement is to protect the legal rights of immigrants, whether they are citizens or not.

Social scientists, journalists, and political commentators analyzing this situation have described three options in the immigrants' adjustments to France: *insertion* (retaining one's own nationality and cultural practices while living in an isolated enclave in France); *assimilation* (adopting the customs and practices of France, with or without assuming nationality); and *intégration* (adopting French nationality while attempting to retain a balance between one's culture of origin and French culture and society).

Harlem Désir, former leader of the militant political coalition SOS-Racisme, has suggested that immigrants without French nationality be given the right to vote, especially on issues that affect their communities. He believes that immigrants need not assimilate or adopt French nationality in order to participate in public debates affecting their welfare. The sociologist Véronique de Rudder (de Rudder, Taboada-Leonetti, and Vourc'h 1990:305–22) describes cases in which North African, Portuguese, and sub-Saharan African immigrants argue that French nationality is not the fundamental issue. What they want is equal legal protection and economic access to the benefits of the country in which they have chosen to live. A 1992 French commission on the legal conditions of integration concluded that solutions such as Désir's are viable as cultural, but not legal, alternatives for immigrants in France. The republican ideals of centralization and universalism discourage the persistence of cultural particularism. In 1992, the Haut Conseil à l'Intégration (High Council on Integration) condoned the development of immigrant and minority welfare associations in the cultural domain, but decried legal particularism. The "official line" presented by government agencies, the mass media, and national organizations drowns out the individual voices of immigrants and their associations, relegating the latter groups, especially the *beurs* and the blacks, to the status of powerless cultural commentators on their own condition.

Several reports prepared by the integration council, organized by Marceau Long under the Mitterand administration in 1992–93, have attempted to clarify French policy on immigration. By the end of 1992, many of the council's more liberal suggestions were challenged by other government agencies and by the rising voice of the new right in France. For example, in its 1992 report on the legal and cultural conditions of immigration, the council urged separation of cultural and legal conceptions of integration by encouraging new immigrants to conform to French law in public, while relegating their personal religious, cultural, and familial choices to their private lives. Thus, the council initially championed a fairly open conception of integration, including the maintenance of cultural particularism in the private domain. In a 1993 publication, however, it revealed a less liberal attitude about the conflict between legal foundations of human rights on the one hand, and the cultural privileges of particular minority groups on the other. The Haut Conseil (1993:35) supported what it termed a "logic of equality" in contrast to a "logic of minorities." Beginning with the premise that equality, established by the French Revolution, is the right of all citizens, the council argued that no special concessions should be made for immigrant and minority populations. The British and American models of minority rights, contended the council, dilute the legal basis of the French concept of nationality. Accordingly, in its report the council asserted:

> The Haut Conseil thinks that integration should be conceived of, not as some sort of middle path between assimilation and insertion, but as a specific process. Following this process, what is involved is instigating the active participation in national society of various and different elements, while accepting the survival of cultural, social, and moral specificities and in holding as a truth that the whole is enriched by this variety, by this complexity. Without denying the differences, in knowing how to take them into account without exalting them, it is on the basis of these resemblances and convergences that a politics of integration ultimately puts the accent on, in the equality of laws and obligations, creating the solidarity of the constitutive ethnic and cultural differences of our society and on giving to each person, whatever his origin, the possibility of living in this society, of which he has accepted the rules and of which he becomes an integral element. . . .
>
> Is our concept shared by the immigrants themselves? Naturally, those who confront insecurity and xenophobia will look toward the warmth of community or religious identification as a refuge against exclusion. But it seems that the majority among them—adults and, even more so, the young—only see there a temporary support to validate their claims, while these claims tend to make them, as rapidly as possible, French "like everyone else." (Haut Conseil à l'Intégration 1992:34–36)

In its 1993 publication, the council concluded that while religious and ethnic loyalties provide ephemeral sources of support for members of immigrant communities, these identifications ultimately obstruct the process of becoming French "like everyone else" ("*des Français comme les autres*"). These conclusions followed a series of ethnically related uprisings in housing projects of Paris, Lyon, and Marseille during the mid-1980s and the 1989 Muslim veil incident, in which three young North African women were expelled from a public school when they refused to remove their veils (Corbett 1994:96–98). Again, the council found itself in a constitutional dilemma as it deliberated on religious freedom with respect to the immigrant community. In its 1992 report, entitled "Conditions juridiques et culturelles de l'intégration," the Haut Conseil (1992:29) cited a 1905 law ensuring religious freedom in the context of public order. Religious freedom, argued the council, must not interfere with public order and tranquillity. Thus, the Haut Conseil (1992:31) observed: "That is, for example, the meaning of the judgment rendered by the Conseil d'État in the affair of the Muslim veils." According to this view, the definition of human rights supersedes cultural and religious particularism and stresses the individual's responsibility of conforming to the norms of a secular society (*laïcité*). The council's conception of legal rights of citizenship begs the question of what it means to be French "comme les autres."

The Haut Conseil next addressed women's rights as they pertain to immigrant populations. In this instance, it once again grappled with the public versus the private definition of individual rights and privileges. Following a legal decision made by a local tribunal in the Montcho polygamy case of July 11, 1980, the council supported the right of a husband to bring his second wife to France when the marriage had been contracted in the country of origin and the "normal" family was held intact. According to the Haut Conseil's report (1992:14): "[F]or a polygamous immigrant from Benin, a normal family implies the presence at his side, in France, of his two wives. This decision thus offers the legal basis for a polygamous grouping, with the reservation that all conditions concerning the housing and resources of the head of the family are strictly met in accordance with government regulations." In contrast, under no conditions did the Haut Conseil condone female circumcision and excision rites. Anthropological studies note the persistence of legal and illegal polygamy in France, as well as excision rites (Fainzang and Journet 1988:87–113; Nicollet 1992:138–51; Amselle 1996:172–78). Cultural practices cannot be legislated into and out of existence. This climate of cultural clash presents a series of paradoxes for the Haut Conseil and other legal bodies in France.

A major problem issues from the fact that integration is a cultural process with legal and social ramifications. The legal aspects of integration involve the status of citizenship and the rights and privileges that it entails. The integrated individual is, or eventually becomes, a citizen and, ideally, exercises the attendant political and economic rights and privileges without reference to history, cultural origin, race, or religion. As long as cultural particularism was restricted to the private domain, remaining outside of schools, courts of law, and public spaces, the Haut Conseil did not consider it harmful to the state and saw it, in some instances, as enriching. If, however, the expression of immigrant cultures transgressed these boundaries, the council viewed it as a threat to public order. Several contradictions surface in this approach to integration: (1) not every immigrant has the possibility to, or wants to, become a citizen; (2) the line between public and private life is often muted, as in the cases of religious institutions and the family; and (3) the state reserves the right to intervene in the private domain.

Some social commentators, such as Julia Kristeva in her 1990 open letter to Harlem Désir, argue that the private domain contrasts with the *esprit général,* or commonly shared norms. Laws must protect the private practice of customs, which, in turn, should not challenge the public spirit. Kristeva (1993:61) states: "The vast domain of the *private,* the land of welcome of individual, concrete freedoms, is thus immediately included in the *esprit général* that must guarantee through law and economy the private practice of religious, sexual, moral, and educational differences relating to the mindset of confederate citizens. Simultaneously, while the private is thus guaranteed, one is committed to respect the *esprit général,* in the bosom of which there is a place for its own expansion." Access to citizenship underscores Kristeva's version of integration and assimilation. Her approach resembles that of the Haut Conseil. But this perspective excludes the marginal immigrants whose cause Désir champions.

In their study of strategies of adjustment among immigrants in France, de Rudder, Taboada-Leonetti, and Vourc'h (1990:293–94) distinguish between the past and present subjective orientations of immigrants as these individuals cope with legal and social problems. Some first-generation immigrants, as might well be expected, retain strong ties to their countries of origin by sending money home, making regular return trips, and planning for eventual retirement in the old country. Others adopt the aggressively future-oriented stance that Kristeva describes by becoming naturalized citizens as soon as possible and fully engaging in the customs and conflicts of their new country. Between these two extremes of nostalgia and cultural amnesia lie the "double-rooted" individuals who, in the terms of de Rudder, Taboada-Leonetti, and Vourc'h (1990:305), are "neither here, nor there" (*ni ici, ni là-bas*).[4] These individuals tend to be second-generation immigrants who feel marginal in France but also remain alienated when they return to their home countries. The study argues that the degree of attachment of these double-rooted individuals to France depends on their success in school, work, and social situations (de Rudder, Taboada-Leonetti, and Vourc'h 1990:325). Social and economic failure are blamed on discrimination and blocked situations in which the immigrant's cultural identity becomes a point of reference.

Blockage leads to pessimism about France and a negative narrative of belonging. At this point, the immigrants' responses include self-hatred, antisocial behavior, and aggression toward the society, rather than simply falling back into the comfortable fold of the immigrant community. This type of response was vividly depicted in Mathieu Kassovitz's 1995 black-and-white film *La Haine,* about the anger of Jewish, North African, and sub-Saharan African youths in the Parisian suburbs. The social historian George Lipsitz (1994:126) aptly summarizes the complexity of the immigrant's situation when he asks: "What if immigrants leave a modernizing country that turns anti-modern and fundamentalist while they are gone? What happens if the host country becomes deeply divided between anti-foreign activists and anti-racist pluralists? Which culture do immigrants carry with them? Into which culture do they assimilate?"

Sociological evidence about immigration strongly suggests that the Haut Conseil's paradigm of integration, insertion, and assimilation is erroneous. Another unsettling option looms outside this paradigm: rejection of the host culture and internalization of the host culture's perceived rejection as self-hatred. Legal reports and sociological studies describe the external features of the immigrant's environment as a combination of contradictions. France welcomes and protects the rights of assimilating citizens while condemning active expressions of cultural particularism. The official ideology of opportunity coupled with responsibility does not coincide with immigrants' lived experiences of social blockage, discrimination, and disillusionment. Many of these experiences are subjective and, in order to better understand them, it is helpful to return to the works of African writers.

Moving to the subjective level requires a shift to the experiences of African immigrants in Paris. As already noted, de Rudder, Taboada-Leonetti, and Vourc'h (1990) developed a sociological typology of immigrants' responses of attachment to and involvement with France. Their approach assumed that, although immigrants' attitudes may change and evolve over time, they remain more or less consistent during any given phase of involvement. Thus, the assimilating immigrant is always future-oriented, while the double-rooted immigrant switches perspectives when challenged by crises and obstacles. In contrast, the authors who write in the Parisianism genre present a more nuanced and finely tuned view of life as Africans in France, with an emphasis on subjective reactions to specific circumstances. These writers advance a philosophy of inclusion, but also emphasize the psychological suffering that results from assimilation. Narratives of longing and belonging motivate the writers' characters as they cope with the alienation of daily life in France and dreams of Africa.

Writers' Gazes on the Parisian Landscape

Contemporary French society is reflected in the literary gazes of three Cameroonian novelists: Yodi Karone, Simon Njami, and Calixthe Beyala.[5] Works of other writers using the Parisianism genre will be mentioned as they relate to the techniques and issues introduced by these authors. The gaze to which I refer is a "look" that encompasses gender, ethnicity, and class as these identity categories relate to the experiences portrayed by African writers in France. The gaze implies a discursive stance that positions the reader with respect to the narrator and creates a bond between the reader and the observing subject, or protagonist (Fontanille 1989:17–21). This discursive stance is transformed into action through the narrative. Although the gaze is topological, constrained by the landscape (specifically the perimeters of black Paris), its meaning is subjectively rooted in the identities and trajectories of desire that the authors construct for their characters. The gaze locates, bonds, and disrupts subjectivities. It configures, refigures, and disfigures them. Demonstrating the evolution of characters and events, the gaze is also temporal. The three levels of the gaze move from inaction (the gaze of virtual desire), to cognitive and emotional action (the gaze of loss), and finally to social action (the environmental gaze), which also involves physical movement across black Paris. The environmental gaze totalizes and unites the gazes of desire and loss.[6]

The three levels of the gaze parallel the movement from a narrative of longing, through which the characters confront their environment and desires, to a narrative of belonging, in which they situate themselves in relationship to Paris and to Africa. The gaze is dialectical. People give and receive gazes, and they are transformed by the "looks" of others. Yodi Karone described one manifestation of the triple-level gaze as a forced look. "There are people who look at you and all of that. Here in Paris, I mean, you can be an illustrious anonymous individual. Nobody cares. At the same time, you exist. From another perspective, you have existed as a result of the look of the other. Nevertheless, I think that in Paris, one can avoid that look because some people share the same criteria. . . . So, you can find yourself because you share the same common sensibility" (Karone 1991).

Exclusion and marginalization are the unspoken consequences of "the look," or the disfiguring gaze. The environmental gaze, however, goes beyond the look by incorporating everything in sight and unifying the subject and object at a single glance.

The Virtual Gaze in Yodi Karone's *A la Recherche du cannibale amour*

Born on March 15, 1954, in Cameroon, Yodi Karone (*nom de plume* for Alain Dye) has written four novels: *Le Bal des Caïmans* (1980b); *Nègre de paille* (1982), winner of the Grand Prix Littéraire d'Afrique Noire; *A la Recherche du cannibale amour* (1988a); and *Les Beaux gosses* (1988b). (See fig. 17.) He has also published one play, *Sacré dernier* (1980a). Karone's novels are set in West Africa, Paris, and New York. He is one of the leading young novelists in the Parisianism genre. He has published with a variety of Parisian publishers, including Éditions Karthala, Publisud, Nathan, and Silex (Nkashama 1994:164–67). Also a musician and sculptor, Yodi draws on rhythms and visual images to enhance his narrative.

Eugène Esselé, the protagonist of *A la Recherche du cannibale amour*, begins his romantic search for inspiration to the accompaniment of an amateur jazz saxophonist playing in the Châtelet métro station. "The notes rise along the walls and resound in the corridor, smothering the murmurs and rushed steps of hurried travelers," writes Karone (1988a:21). The saxophonist plays a bossa-nova tune with blues accents just as Eugène, an African novelist, drops and loses his manuscript in the métro station. On these notes of jazz, a fervent search begins, transporting Eugène from Paris to Cameroon, from West Africa to Harlem, and back.

Fig. 17. Yodi Karone (Alain Dye) at home in the Belleville quarter of Paris, July 17, 1991. Photograph by Bennetta Jules-Rosette.

The scene in which Eugène loses his manuscript begins not only with jazz notes, but also with a gaze. Karone narrates:

> My métro stopped at Châtelet.
>
> The doors just opened when I was surprised by an equivocal gesture of this young woman seated on the platform in the station. She burst out laughing, as if at a good joke. Finally, our gazes crossed ineluctably. I painfully swallowed my saliva. A soft warmth ran up and down my spine. I pressed against the bar of the door, giddy from the odor of love that I imagined coiled between her thighs. The young woman smiled at me timidly. Suddenly, the signal for closing the doors sounded. I hesitated to get off while she stood up. Her face quivered. The doors slammed shut. My manuscript was caught, and fell on the platform at the feet of Philodia, who moved forward.
>
> The train pulled off and I had just enough time to see her pick up my work. . . .
>
> I would have gone crazy, but deep in my soul, I knew that my book had fallen into good hands. That's why I continued my route, comfortably installed, waiting for a new sign of destiny. (Karone 1988a:23)

The ineluctably crossing gazes of Eugène and Philodia begin a search for identity, love, and belonging. Eugène's virtual gaze maps out a trajectory of desire that is oriented toward Philodia, an attractive young Antillian woman sporting dreadlocks and a red, green, and yellow t-shirt. Powerless to act on his desire for Philodia, Eugène assumes a passive gaze at level one. On the second level, he moves toward emotional action, but is still powerless to pursue his gaze. Eugène's second-level gaze follows his lost manuscript, which he concludes has fallen into the hands of fate. The gaze of loss moves the operations of discourse and observation toward narrative action. Philodia returns the manuscript to Eugène the next day, and one part of the love story begins. Thus, the gaze of virtual desire sets in motion Eugène's soul searching. The second-level gaze combines the potential for fulfillment and loss. The gaze of loss also represents Eugène's longing for Africa, which has receded into a mythical dream during his stay in France. On the third level, the environmental gaze traces Eugène's search across Paris and two continents. This gaze articulates with the Parisian setting of the novel because it takes in Eugène's total environment. He looks at, as well as listens to, the vibrant activities in the métro station, where people of multiple cultures rub shoulders. The environmental gaze that occurs on the third level allows the subject to drink in the intercultural and interracial relationships that are so characteristic of Paris.

Philodia and her new acquaintance, Adélaïde, an African American, represent Eugène's longing for the new world and his links to the African diaspora. His love affair with Philodia, who inspires his work, and his affection for Adélaïde are integral to his search for inspiration (*cannibale amour*), encompassing a return to Africa and travel to New York. Philodia, who runs errands for her grandmother, a local voudon cult priestess, continually reminds Eugène of ties to African mysticism and its transplantation in the diaspora. Eugène tries to resolve his desire for Philodia as part of his tricontinental search. The atmosphere established in this search has an undercurrent of music—in particular, jazz—as Eugène listens to it in Paris, Africa, and New York. The first-level and second-level gazes are, thus, intertwined in Eugène's trajectory of desire and search for identity.

The environmental gaze sets the stage for each scene of the novel. In *The Critique of Dialectical Reason,* Jean-Paul Sartre (1976:238) argues that everyone produces a signification of self based on "material exigencies." Here, he is referring to signs of social class, but he could just as well have included gender and ethnicity. When he observes other Africans in Paris, Eugène situates himself vis-à-vis their social conduct, appearance, and material conditions. The environmental gaze fixes Eugène's social and material location and clarifies the motives for his actions.

On the day after he meets Philodia, Eugène takes the métro again and emerges at the Forum des Halles. He observes a patchwork of cultures interacting and sets himself apart from the ethnicolor mutants. Karone explains:

> There is not a place of communion stranger, a crossroads more extravagant than the Forum des Halles: gigantic bubble of pleasures in microcosm. Artificial heart, luminous arteries that drain all of Paris. The well-dressed dandies [*homos sapés*] take their place on the terraces of cafés. Ethnicolor mutants invade fast food shops and, at the far end, a horde of negropolitans occupy the steps of the temple. Those anointed by paradise [*les pétrolés du paradis*] say nothing, out of habit. They traffic the bits of their dreams and troll with little hope for white women. (Karone 1988a:35)

In the midst of this bustling environment, Eugène meets Philodia at a Chinese restaurant, the Mandarin, in the Forum. At this point, the environmental gaze and the gaze of desire are united. Karone is at his best when he uses the environmental gaze to describe the parading of the young negropolitans, *sapeurs* (modern dandies), and ethnicolor mutants. The term *se saper,* meaning "to dress well," derives from the impressive uniforms worn by the nineteenth-century French military and police, known as *sapeurs.* The term is also an acronym for the society of well-dressed persons originating in Congo Brazzaville. The *Société des Ambianceurs et des Personnes Élegantes,* popular in Brazzaville and Kinshasa, requires an initiatory trip to Paris to obtain the fashions and accouterments of prosperity (clothing, portable telephones, televisions, boom boxes, and fax machines) that are the apotheosis of Western modernity and success.[7] Karone picks up the currents of interracial fantasies and failed dreams of the sapeurs. In another passage using the environmental gaze, Karone describes the African population of the eighteenth arrondissement—the heart of black Paris. Against this backdrop, Philodia first meets Adélaïde. Once again, the environmental gaze and the trajectory of desire are combined as the two women who are most important to Eugène appear in black Paris. Karone (1988a:41) introduces this setting: "The métro Barbès-Rochechouart disgorges about fifty Senegalese, dressed in long *bou-bous* and multicolored caftans, and immaculate Wolofs, who sway on the Parisian pavement."

As it turns out, Adélaïde, who works at the Ministère de la Coopération, serves as a guide for this group of Senegalese tourists. Nevertheless, even without Adélaïde's presence at the scene, the description of this African group in Barbès would have been true to the environment of the area. Karone combines a sensitivity to the presence of Africans in Paris with his ongoing narrative by intertwining all levels of the gaze. Since all three gazes have both existential and narrative dimensions, they provide a means through which the author demonstrates both the fantasies and blocked possibilities of his protagonist.[8] Eugène imagines the relationship with Philodia before it occurs. The relationship that unfolds differs from his expectations. The journey provides a strategy for fulfilling Eugène's quest for love and inspiration.

By means of the environmental gaze, Karone juxtaposes images and stereotypes of Africa and highlights Eugène's feelings of marginalization in Paris. As the book closes, Eugène reflects on his voyage to Cameroon in search of his roots and inspiration. In the Harlem apartment of Jason, an African-American jazz musician, Eugène reflects upon the fragments of his existence. Karone (1988a: 184) remarks: "Jason is crazy about literature and musical revolution. He spends hours telling me about the lives of the giants of jazz—Coltrane, Armstrong, Mezzrow; one day he makes me listen to one of his own compositions, something strange with funny rifts. I start to laugh. He complains sharply: 'Does one even sneeze when Miles plays?' For him, I remain an enigma."

Eugène describes to Jason his experiences as an African writer in Paris and West Africa. Haltingly, he reads a rough English translation of a passage from his new book. In tears, Jason exclaims that now he understands the African dream, and this dream will be the theme of his next musical composition. The African is suspicious and reflects: "for him, the American, Africa appears to be a land of prefabricated souvenirs: raffia houses, savage warriors, crazed dictators, and half-nude women with burning bodies" (Karone 1988a:185). But Jason protests that he truly understands Eugène's inspiration, and that he will put into music this meeting of black minds and spirits: "I'll tell the whole world what a great artist you are!" (185). In this case, jazz forecasts a moment of harmony, but the moment is fleeting, and the harmony is fragile. Eugène feels fragmented in New York and in Paris, and his harmonizing artistic search in Africa remains a faint memory.

Karone admits that the idea of integration was one of the themes of his writing, but he situates integration exclusively with respect to Paris. He argues that the cosmopolitan character of Paris masks cultural differences. Thus, his character Eugène could feel both part of and distant from this environment. Belonging, which is the seduction of Paris, does not erase longing for Africa. In the interview, Karone elaborates:

> The specific situation of Paris revolves around the sentiment, that is the idea, of integration. I suppose that the notion of integration is not as strong elsewhere as it is in France because it is specific to a certain French mentality. You come to Paris, and you are American, Spanish, Italian, or Polish, anything you want, and you are attracted by the place. You become a Parisian. To be a Parisian does not mean to be French. It's another mentality and another specificity. When someone asks me for directions in Paris, I feel a part of the place. I would never ask a European, even one who lives there, for directions in Douala. But here in Paris, it's natural. . . . On the whole, to be Parisian does not mean to be French. I am Cameroonian, but I am also Parisian. (Karone 1991)

The Erotic Gaze and Trajectories of Desire in Simon Njami's *African gigolo*

Simon Njami, born of Cameroonian parents in Lausanne, Switzerland, on January 4, 1962, is a novelist, journalist, and literary and art critic (Nkashama 1994: 273). (See fig. 18.) He is editor-in-chief of *Revue Noire,* France's leading African art magazine, and has written four novels: *Cercueil et cie* (1985), *Les Enfants de la cité* (1987b), *African gigolo,* (1989a) and *Les Clandestins* (1989b). His works also include three critical pieces, *Ethnicolor* (1987), edited with Bruno Tilliette, *James Baldwin ou le devoir de violence* (1991b), and *L. S. Senghor,* a forthcoming biography with Éditions du Seuil.

Cercueil et cie (1985) places two of Chester Himes's characters from *Cotton Comes to Harlem* (1965), Coffin Ed and Gravedigger, in a Parisian setting, where they solve a crime with the assistance of an African journalist, Amos Yebga. *African gigolo,* set in Paris of the late 1980s, is the narrative of Moïse Ndoungué, a Cameroonian student, who has squandered the money sent to him from home and makes a living as a gigolo and dilettante art dealer. The novel is set in Paris, Deauville, Amsterdam, and Venice, and is a foundational work in the literature of Parisianism. The struggles and failures of Moïse's assimilation in France are played out against the worn refrains of canned disco music and African Jazz. At the New Morning, a jazz club in Paris's tenth arrondissement, Moïse first meets Mathilde, a stylish French society matron who launches him on a treacherous voyage of self-discovery. In the background, Tala André-Marie, who is described by Njami as "a sort of Cameroonian Stevie Wonder," sings failed solos with an inexperienced African jazz band. The dreary banality of the music forecasts the problems that Moïse will experience with Mathilde and with Parisian society as a whole.

A former student and self-styled expatriate who refuses to accept his isolation, Moïse manipulates young women as a means of daily survival in Paris—until he meets Mathilde. An older woman who has lost her husband in Cameroon, Mathilde is well connected in the Parisian art world. Through her close contacts, she sponsors Moïse in a career of art collecting, appraisal, and purchase that moves him through the galleries of Paris, Venice, and Amsterdam. While desperately attempting to escape his ties to Africa and his dying father, Moïse is drawn more deeply into two contrasting aspects of Parisian society: Mathilde's world of the sixteenth arrondissement and fashionable galleries, and the bustling black Paris of the tenth, eighteenth, and twentieth arrondissements. In the subterranean world of black Paris, Moïse frequents jazz clubs and cafés with his Cameroonian philosopher friend Étienne.

Fig. 18. Simon Njami in his study in Paris, July 18, 1991. Photograph by Bennetta Jules-Rosette.

Lost and uprooted, Moïse grasps for any sign of Africa that he can find in the European maelstrom—Mathilde's beautiful young Ivoirian protégé, immigrants from Surinam in Amsterdam, and a fascinating Antillian prostitute who becomes his downfall. Jazz clubs crammed with faceless dancers moving to the hollow sounds of pop music constitute the backdrop of Moïse's intense but fleeting encounters with black Europe. The music of Michael Jackson and James Brown punctuates his conflicts with African bureaucrats and European art collectors. The gaze of erotic desire occurs at the moment of his initial encounter with Mathilde at the New Morning club. Njami describes this event:

> The African advanced toward her, not knowing exactly what he was going to say to her, insensitive to the supplications of Étienne, who tried to hold him back. She raised her head, almost frightened. At first, she said nothing. Only her eyes interrogated. She found him handsome, suspected him arrogant. He also said nothing. This lasted several minutes. The song ended. Then Moïse started:
>
> "Swell, isn't it?"
>
> She took a few seconds to realize that these words were addressed to her. Her companion stared at Moïse.
>
> "Not bad," she responded politely. "A little naïve and awkward, however." She could not prevent herself from passing judgment. "You came here as a teacher?"
>
> "Excuse me, that's not what I meant."
>
> "But you said it."
>
> She did not respond, and turned her head. Moïse smiled. This adventure was going to be perilous. (Njami 1989a:38)

Moïse's virtual gaze transects boundaries of gender, class, ethnicity, and nationality. The pleasure and excitement of Moïse's perilous adventure derives from the taboos surrounding it. Breaking these taboos entails risks, but the ultimate promise is Moïse's acceptance into a society where he is anonymous and marginal. The stare of Mathilde's suave French companion fixes Moïse in the status of an African interloper. Mathilde's silence and refusal to look at Moïse is a challenge. The averted glance is transmuted into a stare of longing and desire.

Movement across space with the environmental gaze signals narrative tests that Moïse faces and recapitulates the imaginary potential of the gaze of desire, as well as the blockage of the gaze of loss (Fontanille 1989:61). At a critical moment, Moïse hesitates. After their frosty but appealing encounter, he waits a day before making his first telephone call to Mathilde. When he does so, he melodramatically claims he will die if he does not see her, and she takes the supplication seriously (Njami 1989a:47–48). This call occurs immediately after Moïse has received a letter from his mother, initiating the second-level gaze of loss. The call also instigates the third-level, environmental, gaze, in the form of a trip across

Paris, from rue Léon-Cosnard in the seventeenth arrondissement to the chic district of Passy in the sixteenth arrondissement.

In *African gigolo,* Moïse's trajectories of desire are complicated by three French women—Sophie, Mireille, and Mathilde—and three women of African descent—Mathilde's godchild and protégé, Sarah; an Antillian prostitute in Amsterdam; and Moïse's mother, a constant presence who makes her shadowy appearance only through letters from home. Before his initial phone call to Mathilde, Moïse actually opens the first letter from Cameroon in which his mother requests he return immediately to take care of his ailing father (Njami 1989a:45–47). Repeated signifiers that suture key scenes, the rest of the letters from Cameroon remain unopened. In other words, Moïse averts his gaze from his mother and Africa (the motherland), while longing at a deep level to return. These letters from Cameroon constitute the gaze of loss at level two.[9] The third-level gaze emerges as Moïse traverses Paris in search of Mathilde and, like Karone's Eugène, totalizes the environment at a single glance. For Moïse, all three gazes are intertwined with a sense of thwarted desire, loss, and marginalization.

When Moïse first meets Sarah, while on a vacation in the south of France with Mathilde, he is moved by her eyes and her gaze. As Njami describes it:

> She [Mathilde] disappeared immediately, and reappeared five minutes later, escorted by a young man with brown hair and a pleasant face, and a black girl [*une fille noire*] with bronze skin and gray-green eyes. What a funny idea for a negress who was not mixed [*une métisse*], thought the Cameroonian distractedly.
> . . .
> "Here is Sarah. I met her when she was a child in Côte d'Ivoire. I am her godmother." . . . Moïse turned around to see better. He had the sun in his eyes and put on his dark glasses. . . .
> Sarah was dressed in white. She stared at Moïse with insistence. It was apparent to him that she did not like him. That she, a negress, detested encountering a black [*un nègre*] in this milieu, and being constrained to play a part written by others.
> "Do you like Brahms?" she asked.
> "No, not too much. I prefer Dvorak."
> "One says Dvorjak." (Njami 1989a:135)

The first encounter between Moïse and a subject of passion again takes place against the background of music (or a discussion of music) and amidst a volley of gazes. These gazes, too, transect gender, class, and cultures. Sarah, however, remorsefully reminds Moïse of Africa. Initially ambivalent toward her, he ultimately initiates a haunting and abortive love affair. When Sarah reappears later in Paris, their gazes change, and the exchange fleetingly becomes one of muted desire. Njami writes: "When they met again, Sarah held Moïse's hand for a long time in hers, fixing him with her gray-green eyes. 'I hold an excellent memory of our last encounter.' The Cameroonian averted his eyes" (Njami 1989a:154).

Moïse's ambivalent emotions upon encountering the young African woman are complicated by his recurrent memories of Africa and his futile attempt to escape the omnipresent maternal gaze. The first letter from home reaches Moïse just before his encounter with Mathilde, and a second letter appears when he reflects upon his rupture with Sophie, the French girlfriend whose indifference launches him on a career of aimless searching for false companionship. Moïse finds the second letter unexpectedly at his apartment on rue Léon-Cosnard. "The letter was there. He did not need to see it. He knew it was there, palpitating like a freshly torn-out heart" (Njami 1989a:62). The last maternal letter arrives on the closing page of the book and is transported to Moïse by Mathilde, who finds him alone and dejected in Amsterdam. As he prepares to return to Cameroon, Moïse states flatly: "It's useless to read it now. Soon my mother will tell me what's inside" (222).

The letter announces the death of the protagonist's father and is the narrative motor for Moïse's ultimate return to Africa. Moïse refuses to read both letters and averts his gaze from them. More than simple rejection is involved in these averted gazes. In this imagery, Africa is the longed-for mother, but in abandoning Africa's traditions, Moïse also commits an act of patricide (MacCannell and MacCannell 1982:48–50). Throughout his European sojourn, Moïse questions his identity, the philosophy of négritude, and the legacies of European and African civilization. In a brief banter with Étienne, Moïse remarks:

> "You see," he finally concluded, "words like négritude are not scientific enough. Not true enough. Zuluique or Peul-like. There are words that ring true."
>
> "You're joking, my friend. But one day you'll regret it. It's the destiny of Africa that you're short-selling in thinking that you can elevate yourself above this millenarian debate." (Njami 1989a:31)

The environmental gaze catapults the narrative forward by fulfilling Moïse's desire to please Mathilde. He absorbs the landscapes of Paris, Venice, and Amsterdam with an African eye, constantly looking for and turning away from signs of his natal origins. In Amsterdam, he is confused by Dutch-speaking black immigrants from Surinam. In Paris, Moïse traverses boundaries of race, class, and culture at a single glance. But, fundamentally, Moïse remains a loner, alienated from the settings in which he lives.

Environmental gazes usually occur before a significant encounter with a woman: Sophie, Mireille, with whom he occasionally shares the apartment on rue Léon-Cosnard, Sarah, or Mathilde. Before one of his early calls to Mathilde in the chic sixteenth arrondissement, Moïse engages in an environmental gaze in paratopian space:

> It started to rain at the Place des Abbesses [eighteenth arrondissement], and he had to take refuge in the métro. The tramps prepared their spots for the night, and dined on a can of sardines and some bad red wine. Women alone, frightened by the unsavory fauna of their midnight surroundings, walked rapidly along the quais, gripping their handbags. A punk with hair dyed red by some bizarre coloring cried out his hatred of the world and the bourgeoisie. A train came. Moïse rushed to a seat and rode haphazardly to the end of the line. He stared at the rare passengers who got on and off, rushing to a precise point inscribed in a fixed itinerary. He sailed aimlessly by the stops. The last métro dropped him at the Place de la Nation [thirteenth arrondissement]. He took a taxi to rue Léon-Cosnard [seventeenth arrondissement], where his first reflex was to call Mathilde. (Njami 1989a:66)

This roving environmental gaze reinforces Moïse's alienation. Njami's protagonist is a dislocated subject.[10] He is both African and European, and yet neither. Moïse regards the classical arts of Europe from a distorted, commercial viewpoint and is skeptical of African traditions. His sense of dislocation creates a series set of fragmented images, and a narrative that is not easily recounted in linear fashion. His journey toward self-discovery is disjointed, dissonant, and deceptively spontaneous. Moïse's final decision to return to Africa in search of his father's posthumous blessing remains unfulfilled as the novel closes. He carries with him idyllic images of Africa cross-cut by the daily struggles of black Paris. Resolution of the conflicts of Euro-African identity remains as an evanescent dream.

Contrasting Examples of the Environmental Gaze

Blaise N'Djehoya, author of *Le Nègre Potemkine* (1988), is another representative of Parisianism. *Un Regard noir* (1984), by N'Djehoya and Massaër Diallo, dissects African gazes on Paris and is a lively and original example of the Parisianism of the early 1980s. The book contains two contrasting case studies describing African environmental gazes on the Parisian landscape: N'Djehoya's account of the adjustment of Makossa, a young Cameroonian who comes to Paris to begin his university studies, and Diallo's ethnography of West African marabouts (diviners) and their clients in Paris. Together these accounts provide a kaleidoscopic vision of black Paris. N'Djehoya's fictional character, Makossa, duplicates the experiences of Dadié's Tanhoé Bertin. He is naive and wide-eyed in his literal interpretation of French culture and customs. Although he believes that he has adjusted quickly, Makossa remains a cultural outsider with a telescopic gaze. N'Djehoya describes Makossa's mixed reactions:

> A trimester after his arrival, one could say that his adjustment was really moving along. The period of socialization was barely coming to a close when the snow began to fall. The natives, in their imperceptible mutation, changed their shoes for boots, their T-shirts for pull-overs or coats of rabbit, rat, bear, or synthetic fur, like a sort of metamorphosis that gave them the appearance of beasts. Their hands, gloved in leather or naked, red and white, emphasized the strangeness of their mouths that exhaled vapors of oxygen resembling the long beards of men who adorned the shop windows full of gifts costing ten thousand francs. . . . Makossa lived through these events with curiosity, noting with scientific objectivity the common destinies and magico-religious practices of Christians in Paris, Ouagadougou, or Manila. Since he knew neither how to ski nor how to erect snow men, it appeared to him hazardous to venture outside for fear of triggering a latent and chronic malarial fever that veered toward delirium tremens with the approach of Christmas. (N'Djehoya and Diallo 1984:22–23)

N'Djehoya expresses Makossa's alienation through a humorous juxtaposition of his character's perceptions and French customs. Makossa's naiveté sustains an environmental gaze that is tinged with pathos and disillusionment. He stands in sharp contrast to Njami's sophisticated Moïse and to Félix Bankara's cynical autobiographical character (Félix), both of whom master the Parisian scene with cunning.

Bankara's *Black Micmacs* (1988) and the 1986 top-grossing French film of the same name, produced by Monique Annaud and Thomas Gilou, blend psychological marginality and a quest for belonging. Describing his experiences, Bankara (1988:11) writes: "My name is Félix. . . . I am a Black [*sic*] whose papers are in order. Having arrived on the shores of the Seine at age fourteen, I worked with a mechanic who had polished the language of Voltaire on the zinc counters of every bistro from Belleville to Ménilmontant. From him, I learned to express myself in a different way than an African recently arrived from his village. This permitted me to become a journalist for *L'Africain de Paris.*"

L'Africain de Paris is the lens through which Félix sees the streets and subterranean nightclubs of black Paris, from Belleville to the Goutte d'Or district of the eighteenth arrondissement. But some French spectators have found that the film of *Black Micmacs* left a bitter aftertaste (Dewitte 1987:19). They considered the rapid and uneven montage of Paris to be distorting. While Bankara remains on the exterior of black Paris with an environmental gaze, the novelists Karone and Njami excavate its interior by exploring the changing sense of identity that black Paris fosters. Yet another literary gaze on black Paris emerges in the works of Calixthe Beyala, whose subtle reflexive approach emerges in her use of the televisual gaze.

The Televisual Gaze in Calixthe Beyala's *Le Petit prince de Belleville*

Calixthe Beyala was born in Douala, Cameroon, in 1961, and lives in the Belleville quarter of Paris, which is also the setting for two of her novels about a young Malian immigrant's life. (See fig. 19.) She has written seven novels: *C'est le soleil qui m'a brûlée* (1987), *Tu t'appeleras Tanga* (1988), *Seul le diable le savait* (1990b), *Le Petit prince de Belleville* (1992), *Maman a un amant* (1993), *Assèze l'africaine* (1994), and *Les Honneurs perdus* (1996), which received the 1996 literary Grand Prix from the Académie Française, followed by an unwarranted polemic over the originality of some of the book's passages. She has also written one nonfiction book, *Lettre d'une africaine à ses soeurs occidentales* (1995). The alienation, isolation, and entrapment of African women, both in African cities and Paris, are themes of Beyala's work (Nkashama 1994:58–63; Omerod and Volet 1994:43–45).

Tu t'appeleras Tanga, Beyala's second novel, develops a resonance of identity between two prison cellmates—Tanga, a neglected prostitute from the slums of Douala, and Anna-Claude, a Jewish refugee who listens to Tanga's last story. As Tanga recounts her narrative of exploitation, poverty, and prostitution, Anna-Claude loses the ability to disentangle herself from the saga. In the dark prison cell, Anna-Claude adopts the personality of Tanga. This transposition of identities creates a convoluted echo effect in which the older European woman assumes the personality of the young African. Anna-Claude's madness is located in a utopian space where cultures and subjectivities blend without boundaries. This discourse space weds two cultural universes in silence.

In *Le Petit prince de Belleville* (1992), Beyala unites the virtual gaze of desire with the gaze of loss. The narrative is presented through the eyes of Mamadou Traoré, or Loukoum, a second-generation Malian migrant who is seven years old when the novel opens and grows into adolescence in Beyala's fourth book, *Maman a un amant* (1993). Loukoum lives with his polygynous family in a small Belleville apartment. The family's poverty does not bridle Loukoum's imagination. As his mother, a second wife and undeclared immigrant, dies, the young boy attempts to understand his environment by watching televised news broadcasts featuring François Mitterand and George Bush. In the silence of the televisual space, Beyala's protagonist comes to terms with his cultural isolation. The silent void of the televisual image points to Loukoum's alienation and his inability to reconcile the differences between his own lifestyle and the images of political figures and fictional characters portrayed on television.

The virtual gaze in televisual space is one of desire, as Loukoum reaches out toward his imaginary French interlocutors. Recognizing that the characters on television do not share his background or culture, he turns away with a sense of

Fig. 19. This photograph of a publicity shot of Calixthe Beyala was taken during an interview with the novelist at her apartment in the Belleville quarter of Paris, July 27, 1990. Photograph by Bennetta Jules-Rosette.

loss. Beyala describes a scene in which Loukoum watches a televised news broadcast with his father, Abdou Traoré:

> When we came home, my papa was seated in front of the television. He looked at us, then changed the channel. I sat next to him.
>
> "Is it true that the fascists are going to chase us away?" I asked my father.
>
> "Shut up!"
>
> Then I concentrated on what was taking place on the screen. I don't like the television news. But the broadcast would not stop. I put my hands in front of my eyes in order not to see. There were people building a dam in an area where Indians always lived and caused them to move. Then there was a film of a guy who assassinated lots of old women. And it was the same actor who played the judge and the assassin. And you know what they decided to do to this official who had stolen lots of money? Nothing at all!
>
> The best of all was to wait for Inspector Malcolm, who came on after the TV news. He is so intelligent that he always wins in the end.
>
> When it was all finished, my father turned off the set, even before I could see Inspector Malcolm. Then he rolled a kola nut in his hands. (Beyala 1992:22–23)

Loukoum identifies with the illusory space in which Inspector Malcolm pursues his exciting adventures, but he covers his eyes during the news broadcast of atrocities and injustice. Shocked by what he has seen on television, seven-year-old Loukoum decides to write a letter to President Mitterand offering his support in the battle against racism.

> Monsieur le Président,
> ... Permit me to say that you have all of my support, and that with just one signal from you, I shall throw myself completely into the assault of our enemy—right in the middle of his political group....
> Monsieur Le Pen, our mortal enemy, plans to chase us all out of here. But I know that you, master of the invisible and the visible, you who are so wonderful, you will not let him do this ghastly thing. (Beyala 1992:24–25)

Through the gaze of virtual desire, Loukoum breaks the barriers of power, class, and ethnicity, figuratively jumping inside of the television screen. He converses with presidents and dignitaries, becoming part of the powerful fantasies that he watches. According to Jean Baudrillard (1981:54–55), television mutates the real into the hyperreal by moving from representation to simulation in infinitely receding image flashes.[11] Loukoum enters this loop of simulation by shifting rapidly from the gaze of desire to the alienated gaze, through which he perceives loss and injustice. Initially, he averts his eyes. Then he takes action, entering the fantastically real world of French politics as the president's dialogant.

Television empowers Loukoum with the ability to observe his own community at a distance through an environmental gaze. Remarking on the plight of immigrants, Loukoum walks the streets of Belleville with his father, his friends, and alone. Beyala's use of the environmental gaze in Belleville encompasses gender, ethnicity, culture, and isolation. Through Loukoum's eyes, Beyala describes Belleville in the spring.

> Spring is here. The weather is wonderful. A little brisk as usual around Easter. Everything is already very green in Paris. It's beautiful. And, at night, all of the immigrants come out to the Boulevard de Belleville. Some sit in cafés. They talk. And they are silent. They have nothing to say. Except about everyday life. They watch the young women stroll by. Some say gross words about the behind of one woman or the gait of another. The immigrants enjoy this. You must understand. It's easier for them to talk than to act, since most of them have left their wives in Africa. (Beyala 1992:206)

Loukoum's seemingly innocent environmental gaze inspires him to reflect and to act. Observing the immigrants lust after passing women, he decides to write to Lolita, the young schoolgirl on whom he has a crush. His parents disapprove of the budding relationship, and the school counselors and social workers pick on Lolita. Loukoum blames the televisual gaze. He remarks (Beyala 1992:204): "Everyone believes that depravation comes from television and all the bad things one sees. They call that negative influences, or something like that that I don't understand very well. They've done a lot of research on it. In the end, they have concluded that kids are really difficult, ungrateful, and all of that. If you can explain that to me, I'll be eternally grateful."

By using the televisual gaze as a tool, Beyala dissects Loukoum's surroundings and combines the environmental gaze with the gaze of loss. She demonstrates Loukoum's marginality but also emphasizes his refusal to accept a subaltern position. Loukoum floats between his fantasy world and life on the streets of Belleville, between childhood and adulthood. His televisual gaze leads him to political action in a vacuum where he waits for Superman and Inspector Malcolm to save the day. All the while, the oppressive social realities of Belleville's blocked immigrant community surround Loukoum without smothering him.[12]

Beyala's 1995 essay, *Lettre d'une africaine à ses soeurs occidentales,* is an open letter to French women about feminism. In this nonfiction work, she situates the mediated gaze differently. Responding to comments on her own works by the mass media, Beyala examines the plight of African women in a global context. She contrasts their struggles for autonomy and self-determination with the situation of women in the West and develops a philosophy of "*feminitude.*" Beyala urges women to express their uniqueness, which she believes is universal, while remaining cognizant of cultural differences. Insofar as the open letter is a product of the Parisian milieu, geared principally toward feminists, other French intellectuals, and a popular audience, it, too, is an example of Parisianism. At this point, it is important to emphasize—as is evident for the works of Karone, Njami, N'Djehoya, and Beyala—that Parisianism contains an underlying rhetoric of social commentary, influencing both its literary style and content.[13]

Cultures of Black Paris through the Writer's Lens

Karone, Njami, and Beyala express their experiences of cultural fragmentation through the vehicle of the triple-level gazes of desire, alienation, and observation. N'Djehoya and Bankara use the environmental gaze as a descriptive device. These gazes demonstrate the tension between belonging to the environments of black and official Paris and a sense of loss, betrayal, and exclusion. The authors convey their cultural uniqueness through memories and reconstruction of Africa. Karone describes Eugène's longing for his African cultural roots via his love affairs and transatlantic search for self. Njami emphasizes Moïse's ambivalence toward Africa and France by juxtaposing an erotic gaze and the omniscient gaze of the mother, who calls Moïse back to his natal land and social responsibilities.

In contrast, by using the vehicle of Loukoum's childhood narrative, Beyala breaks through the three gazes, recuperating all levels in the televisual gaze. This gaze encompasses passive observation, desire, and alienation. Loukoum wants to be part of what he sees on the screen, yet he knows, deep within him, that the imaginary characters on television are very far away. Their media images have nothing to do with his life in Belleville (Humbolt 1991:17–18).

In addition to using the gaze as a narrative and rhetorical strategy, the authors employ it as a means of highlighting the disillusionment and ambivalence experienced by Africans living in France. New immigrants, whose experiences of exclusion are reflected in Eugène's alienation, Moïse's social climbing, and Loukoum's bewilderment, flood into the official city, but they find its gates closed. Political groups such as SOS-Racisme, formerly headed by Harlem Désir, call upon followers to be suspicious of assimilation and militant against the rising tide of racism in the National Front, France's most conservative political party (Désir 1990:2).[14] Although the African writers' Parisian landscape has changed considerably over the past forty years, the insulation of black Paris is broken by the writers' cultural imagination, sustained and reflected through the literary gaze.

Each writer constructs a different version of the cultures of black Paris. Karone's Eugène uses black Paris as a staging ground that pushes him back to Africa. Njami's Moïse derives identity and comfort from black Paris. Bankara's autobiographical character engages in a cynical manipulation as he reports on black Paris for his newspaper. Makossa and Loukoum approach their respective environments with childlike naiveté by revealing the contrasts and contradictions between their own lives and French customs. Although these authors do not treat black Paris in an identical manner, the themes of marginalization and the desire for inclusion resonate across their works.

Whether they wish to be or not, the African writers in France are influenced by the contemporary social and political atmosphere. The French government and its administrative councils have engaged in a delicate balancing act with regard to the immigration issue. The scales swing from liberal attempts to accommodate immigrants to an underlying fear of other cultures, particularly those influenced by Islam (Roman 1995:148–50). The legal cases of the 1980s, involving religious freedom and family rights, challenged the line between public and private behavior. Contrasting international models of ethnicity and multiculturalism, particularly those emanating from Britain and the United States, have posed disturbing political challenges to French concepts of nationality and legal universalism. These challenges have been so threatening that they have triggered official governmental responses. Yet, within this legal framework, the lives of individuals migrating and settling in to make the metropole their home have continued. The outsider's ethnographic gaze on French culture has begun to crystallize, not only through new forms of community life, but also through a new culture and literature.

To the extent that literature is a vehicle for the construction of public culture, African writers play an important role in responding to the French social and legal situation by creating alternative images and avenues of opportunity. The writers bring into focus the experiences of large numbers of marginal people. In addition, it must not be forgotten that French publishing houses produce and disseminate these works. All of the authors cited in this chapter have published with French houses that are not exclusively devoted to African issues. Thus, in addition to representing a new generation, Parisianism attracts a broad, popular audience. Parisianism contributes to French debates on integration, assimilation, and multiculturalism. Thus, while underscoring the uniqueness of African experiences in Paris, the Parisianists make distinct claims about the universality of these expressions.[15] Parisianism provides a map and a cultural template of the contemporary African writers' reality.

PART THREE

Parisianism and Universalism

SIX

Parisianism: The African Writers' Reality

> Looming over the heads of all of its creators is the too precarious genius of *art nègre.* Perhaps in order to liberate themselves totally, they should accomplish the sacrilegious act, patricide, by burning what their parents, grandparents, and great-grandparents adored. Perhaps they should erase statuettes and sacred masks from their memories in order to finally enter the [twentieth] century
> —Simon Njami, 1987

What happens when tradition is no longer idealized and is, instead, transmuted after its diasporic voyage across the ocean? Parisianism, one of the fruits of this voyage, challenges the canons of African literature. It questions old narratives of African belonging, turns away from pure orality, undermines African cultural specificity, and reconfigures point of view and characterization in writing. One of the most important literary and social contributions of Parisianism lies in its authors' descriptions of the influence of an African gaze (*un regard africain*) on French society and the power of this gaze to transform the literary landscape. By examining the works of three major writers of Parisianism—Yodi Karone, Simon Njami, and Calixthe Beyala—I will place in social context this challenge to the canon of African literature. I will supplement the analysis of these authors' texts with interviews in which they elaborate on their styles and the underlying assumptions of their approaches. Both the written and oral texts contain discourses about exclusion, marginality, and exile. They also embody the wish to belong to French society. The basic premises of Parisianism cannot be separated from larger debates about African identity and its universalization.

Postcolonial literatures from various sources share the common themes of displacement and identity construction. Anthony Appiah (1992:141) defines "postcolonial" as that which goes *beyond* the colonial, even though it may be rooted in the history of domination. In their analysis of postcolonial literature in Britain, Ashcroft, Griffiths, and Tiffin (1989:9) assert that "concern with the development or recovery of an effective identifying relationship between self and place" is a major theme of postcolonial writing. Parisianism is not an exception to this norm, but the social circumstances under which it developed differ from those in Britain. As early as the 1960s in Britain, African and Caribbean writers formed active artistic networks that reconfigured their cultural identities. Anne Walmsley (1992:xviii) argues that the Caribbean Artists Movement (CAM) played an important role in "the transformation of Britain's West Indian community from one of exiles and immigrants to black British." In both the French and the British diasporan cases, as Iain Chambers (1996:53) points out, "These altogether less obvious and more complicated modes of identification hint at a sense of 'flexible citizenship.' Identities are articulated across the hyphen, the transition, the passage between, rather than firmly located in any one culture, place or position."

Decolonization and diasporic movement changed the social environment in France and Britain. Rapid increases in the immigrant population in France during the 1980s and 1990s provided fertile ground for new artistic and cultural movements. At the same time, social and political movements in Britain, ranging from black power to Rastafarianism, opened up alternative discourse spaces for the expression of black British identity (Lipsitz 1994:128). New immigrants in both Britain and France were able to select from several different ideologies to adapt to the metropole. Although the case of Parisianism resembles the black British example in spite of the time lag, it also exhibits subtle characteristics that are unique to the French social and political scene.

During the course of my interviews, one writer posed an unsettling methodological question about my understanding of literature and society. How, he asked, could I venture a genuine critical analysis of the new developments accompanying Parisianism without having written a novel in the genre? The project attracted me as an exercise in applied anthropology and a personal adventure. After much consternation, I eventually responded to his challenge by producing the draft of a novel in my version of Parisianism. Besides encountering many of the problems and criticisms faced by novice fiction writers and evoking perplexed reactions from the author who challenged me, I ran headlong into the literary and social issues posed by Parisianism. What sort of voice does an outsider assume in addressing France and Africa? How does the writer balance contrasting images of France and Africa? How does an author retain the environmental gaze, which is essentially an external ethnographic viewpoint, while developing the characters' psychological dimensions and inner voices? In order to elucidate my understanding of Parisianism, I will examine these questions in the section entitled "The Novel Experiment." Thus, this chapter will range from the social and philosophical to the personal registers in order to describe what Parisianism, as a genre and an identity discourse, means to writers and how it is received by publishers, critics, and the general public.

Parisianism and African Literary Traditions

If Parisianism could be packaged as a national literature, critics would be at ease. In fact, attempts have been made to situate the works of its authors in this manner. Bjornson (1991:416–20) views Beyala's first two novels, set in Cameroon, as examples of a feminist brand of Cameroonian national literature. The subject matter of the novels and the nationality of the author make his choice logical, but his approach renders classification of her subsequent novels, including the prizewinning *Les Honneurs perdus,* set in Paris, problematic. On the positive side, critics of Parisianism praise the authors as promising, perceptive, and original storytellers and cultural critics (Magnier 1990:103–7). Their trendy and lively prose is appealing. For example, the Senegalese journalist and political critic Jean-Pierre N'Diaye (1991) commented in an interview: "There are some very good young novelists, like Yodi Karone. Formidable! They write very, very well." On the negative side, Parisianism has been criticized for using too many clichés and stereotypes, and for being too predictable in its style and its outcomes. Some critics believe that it is too psychological, while others claim that it is too descriptive, or journalistic, and not psychological enough.[1] Still others assert that it is too "African," or not "African" enough. These remarks emanate from both French and African sources. Deliberately defying the Senghorian tenets of Africanity, sonority, rhythm, and heroism—legacies of the early days of Présence Africaine—Parisianism takes a rebellious stance. Although it is not a literature of protest that exhorts readers to act collectively, Parisianism is unconventional. Its antiheroes mirror the shortcomings of the society in which they live, and this mirroring results in social criticism.

Standard anthologies of African literature avoid Parisianism because it is a hybrid genre. In his *Dictionnaire des oeuvres littéraires africaines de langue française,* Nkashama (1994:166–67) devotes two lines to Karone's *A la Recherche du cannibale amour* (1988a), set in Paris, and well over a page to his *Les Beaux gosses* (1988b), which takes place in Abidjan. Describing *Cannibale amour,* Nkashama (1994:167) states that the book develops "the theme of a novelist in search of his 'writing,' and who meets his inspiration on the quais of a certain métro." He is equally brief in his discussion of Njami's *African gigolo* (1989a), which he tersely summarizes as explaining "the difficulties in the existence of an African immigrant, who hangs out on the sordid streets of Paris, Amsterdam, and Deauville" (Nkashama 1994:273). Although he presents a more substantial analysis of Beyala's *Le Petit prince de Belleville* (1992), her 1993 sequel, *Maman a un amant,* is barely mentioned (Nkashama 1994:61–63).[2] Nkashama is not alone in viewing these accounts of alienated urban life in France as disturbing and somehow unclassifiable in the classical schema of African literature. The vulnerable protagonists of Parisianism are not exemplars of national glory. In fact, they often reject their cultures of origin and are equally cynical about France. Although cultural pride is not absent from their works, the atavistic attachment to an idyllic image of Africa, characteristic of the literature of the 1950s, has vanished. Finally, Parisianism presents a conceptual challenge to literary criticism because it implies what Michel Maffesoli (1992:256–60) and Paul Gilroy (1993:38–39) have termed a "politics of transfiguration" that extends beyond literary styles and genres to blend culture, art, and politics. A strong link may be established between the literature of Parisianism and contemporary works emerging on the African continent. *Fleur du désert,* by Jérôme Carlos, discussed in chapter 4, and the novels of the Zairian writers Emongo Lomomba (1989) and Djungu-Simba Kamatenda (1988) illustrate this critical gaze on contemporary urban life. Works of Congolese writers such as Sony Labou Tansi and Jean-Baptiste Tati-Loutard also resonate well with the themes of Parisianism.

The Novel Experiment

As part of my critical analysis of Parisianism, I ultimately responded to the challenge of writing in the genre. My novel, entitled *Bundu: The Stolen Mask,* was set in Paris, Brussels, and four African countries. In accordance with the themes of Parisianism, I situated African characters in a contemporary Parisian environment. Tassili Edwards, the protagonist, an African-American anthropologist searching for a valuable African initiation mask stolen from London, works with Agrippa, an African journalist and magazine editor, based in Paris. Using international fax, computer, and telephone communications, Agrippa contacts Tassili from Paris as she tracks down the mask in Africa. He engages his half brother Moussa Demba, a small-time hustler and art dealer, to help out with the search on the African continent. Ferdinand Tshilumbu, a failed Zairian nightclub musician, also befriends Tassili and concocts secret art deals with Demba. All of these characters contribute to the Parisian ambiance of the novel.

After completing a draft of the novel, I gave it to the author who challenged me. He responded that the psychological portrait of my main character and her reactions to Paris should be deepened. Following the ideal that Parisianism is a literature in which the authors "think in terms of individuals," he emphasized the internal development of the characters as its touchstone. He was not satisfied that I had written a convincing novel in the genre. Publishers and literary agents in the United States found the novel to be puzzling. Was it a mystery or an adventure story? They finally classified it in the general category of "contemporary women's fiction," which provided a commercial classification that sidestepped conventional genre categories.

One of the major problems that I encountered writing the novel revolved around orchestrating the environmental scenes as they unfolded across three continents, while developing depth in Tassili's character. This tension was, in part, a byproduct of novice fiction writing, but it also stemmed from a technical difficulty inherent in the Parisianism style. The environmental gaze discussed in the last chapter comprises a distant look at Paris and other French social settings. Using this gaze as a literary tool opens a psychological chasm between the main characters and their social worlds. To make a subject's motivations believable, aspects of the social and cultural environment have to be internalized by the character. Karone's Eugène and Njami's Moïse exhibit the same sort of technical problems of character construction. The authors resolve these problems through the skillful use of shifters (Greimas and Courtés 1979:79–82) that move the characters across settings without changing the authorial point of view.

Referring to Moïse as "the African" whenever he encounters French women and other representatives of French society, Njami uses Moïse's proper name when his character interacts with other Africans. Although he maintains the third-person point of view in both cases, Njami (1989a:20–21, 27, 44, 52–53, 61, 85, 101, 219) increases the cultural distance between Moïse and the French characters by labeling him as "the African" or the "Cameroonian." For example, Njami (1989a:20) states: "The African loved to explain . . . that a woman who has waited was a conquered woman." Moïse Ndoungué's full name appears only once in the novel, when he is introduced to a French bureaucrat at the New Morning nightclub (Njami 1989a:50). When Moïse confronts social situations of exclusion, or power struggles with the French authorities, he reacts as an African outsider. Only with other Africans and Antillians does Moïse dare to unmask his emotions, and at these moments Njami addresses him by first name. This technique allows the author to contrast the thoughts and values of his African and his French characters. Similarly, when he wishes to add depth to his characterizations, Karone shifts the environmental gaze in *A la Recherche du cannibale amour* (1988a) from Eugène to other characters (Philodia and Adélaïde) as they traverse the Parisian landscape. He employs Eugène's tricontinental voyage to heighten the intensity of his loneliness and highlight his internal motivations. In spite of Njami's and

Karone's clever use of psychological techniques, some critics of Parisianism (Mukabamano 1991; Nkashama 1994:167, 273) question the authors' success with character development and the literary value of the genre.

My literary excursion into Parisianism was tentative. Although I attempted to portray the lifestyles of Africans in Paris within the framework of my plot, my leading character was an African-American woman who did not fully share the experiences of the French-African characters. She had no need to assimilate into French culture. She was just passing through Paris and Brussels, with the ultimate goal of returning to Africa in search of a precious lost object and her spiritual self. There is a precedent for the introduction of African-American characters into Parisianism, most notably Njami's use of Chester Himes's characters, Coffin Ed and Gravedigger, in *Cercueil et cie* (1985:34–39), and the French author Guy Maçou's *Voyage au bout de la négritude* (1994), a fictional biography of Harvey Rollins, an African-American from New Orleans who travels to the Niger delta in search of his roots.[3]

A larger question involves how Paris is represented as a signifier in the social and political discourse of Parisianism. The city holds out a promise of the ultimate dream of success and social inclusion, but it also blocks this dream. The barriers of nationality, race, and class are ever present. The authors continually question what it means to be Parisian, French, and African. Through the adventures and existential struggles of their characters, the writers develop coping strategies that allow the characters to resolve their personal and cultural problems. The outcomes of these narratives include the characters' acquiescence, their assimilation, and their rejection of French society through insanity, anger, and death. Speaking of contemporary life, especially in Paris, Michel Maffesoli (1992:257) points out that describing these outcomes "in the jungles of rock that characterize our civilization of asphalt" requires a profound type of writing that goes beyond "our classical and too rational instruments of analysis." Since my novel did not restrict its principal character to the Parisian setting and focused on her psychological and spiritual quest in Africa, I deviated from the ground rules of the Parisianism genre. This problem, combined with other technical difficulties, made my work an anomaly within a hybrid genre.

The novel project pushed me to learn about the international reception of Parisianism. No framework currently exists for the translation of Parisianism into the commercial markets of the anglophone literary and publication worlds. Category fiction in the American publication market refers to novels classified as romances, mysteries, thrillers, adventures, science fiction, cyber-fiction, and so forth. Thus, a novel is classified in terms of its plot structure and superficial aspects of its content. Although these categories serve as convenient commercial tags for literary agents, publishers, and book outlets to gauge audience appeal and sales, they result in stereotypical and distorting labels for the novels. In this commercial context, Parisianism as a genre simply does not exist. It merely refers to a locale for the writing and a specific style. I contend, however, that Parisianism is not only a unifying theme, but also a distinctive genre with identifiable strategies for literary construction, plot and character development, and narrative. These strategies include the point of view of the Parisian gaze and the narratives used to describe the problems of exclusion and marginalization experienced by African writers and their characters. Consequently, French publishers are able to identify Parisianism as a concrete marketing category, although they prefer to use alternative terms such as "new wave African writing," "new generation writing," "African travel writing," and "African autobiography" to classify these works in order to enhance their commercial appeal.

The concept of a genre is a double-edged sword (Fabian 1996:194–96). Although sales require packaging by genre, freedom of expression is constrained by being boxed in by genres with rigid conventions. The formulae of genre writing, like the conventions of classical poetry, discipline and constrain authors. The Parisianists both rebel against and reinvent the genre in which they work by pushing its stylistic boundaries to the limits, then returning to its characteristic themes and structures. Thus, a narrative continuity is evident between, for example, Dadié's novels on Paris and Beyala's *Petit prince de Belleville* series. Both sets of novels contain narratives of self-discovery (the French *roman d'apprentissage*), but their social context, messages, and styles differ. Tanhoé Bertin's wonderment is replaced by Loukoum's naive yet cynical criticism of the failures of social justice in France.

The Social and Political Messages of Parisianism

Following is a series of interviews juxtaposed with written texts that address the themes of Parisianism and reflect the identity discourses of a new generation. This new-wave literature has its roots in the 1950s, when writers began to discover Africa on the Seine. The contrasting viewpoints illustrate the range of variation in Parisianism as a genre and an identity discourse. Bernard Dadié summed up the contrast between the old and new approaches.

> I had a ticket for France in the month of July of 1956. It was then that I wrote *Un Nègre à Paris*. The sequel was *Paris à la loupe*, but our friends who read the books that are good to publish didn't like *Paris à la loupe* because they said that I was praising the go-betweens. So that book was never published. Good, but why? Because I said that in Paris, women adorned the streets and the boulevards from Saint-Denis to Sébastopol, and the Madeleine to the Champs-Elysées, making the boulevards joyous for strangers to see.(Dadié 1992)

Dadié continues with a contrast between works on Paris, which he considers to reflect a joyous and even frivolous atmosphere, and the "great cultural and political movement" sponsored by Présence Africaine. He establishes dichotomies between documentary reportage and literature, between joyous expression and serious social commentary. This tension between the aesthetics of joyous expression and the social responsibility of the artist is a recurrent theme in the works of the writers I interviewed. The interviews delve into the social and political uneasiness of the artist, the representation of the individual in Parisianism, approaches to plot, narrative, and characterization, and innovations in the use of language. Several of the writers were interviewed up to three times over a four-year period and occasionally changed their views.[4] Writers' assessments and descriptions of their own work challenge conventional literary canons and contain projections and justifications that may subvert what their critics have to say about them.

Should the writer be an activist, a witness, or an engaged artist? The narrative structure of Parisianism pushes the writers toward witnessing the world by assuming an ethnographic and journalistic gaze on their social environments. The concept of witnessing is a recurrent theme and strategy of African writing. Witnessing turns the gaze toward the social other, toward the environment to which the African subject and writer adapts. Njami (1989c) summarizes this witnessing stance: "Recently, there was a public debate, and not more than a week later, I was invited to France Culture. Paul Dakeyo was also there with Bolya Baenga and Calixthe Beyala. They asked us about the role of the African writer, and everyone had a definition. For my part, I said that the writer doesn't have any role. The writer doesn't have a role more than anyone else. And if Africans don't have a point of view, they shouldn't count on writers to give them one. . . . A novel or an essay is not the Bible."[5] Later, Njami (1991a) elaborated on his point of view more eloquently: "I think that it is more powerful to show a man and a woman in a country where blacks and whites cannot mix, to make a painting of a black man and a white woman embracing, than to write ten pages on the horrors of apartheid. The role of the artist is to show. Any good artist has open eyes, and what shocks the artist's eyes will shock the world. For me, the artist is a medium between the public and the world. The artist is able to make the world transparent, and to convey the rhythm of the world in words and images."

By subtly manipulating the term "African" in juxtaposition to a personal identification for Moïse in his 1989 novel, Njami achieves this type of social statement. For example, he contrasts Moïse's sense of belonging and joy at encountering his Cameroonian friend Étienne with his cynical alienation from the crafty French art dealer, Durand: "The bell rang. Moïse, upset, went to the door. It was as if the stupid instrument had not stopped ringing in his head for several days. It was Étienne, evidently. . . . Étienne settled in on the cushions, silently. Moïse smiled joyously" (Njami 1989a:43).

Moïse recognizes the distant bond that he has with his collaborator, Durand, but remains suspicious of the French art dealer because of their cultural differences. Njami describes the relationship between Moïse and Durand: "Underneath his false airs of a blasé priest, Durand loved life, all of its forbidden pleasures. Actually, he only rejoiced fully in the feeling that he was making a mistake. In that respect, Moïse resembled him, except that they did not share the same concept of a mistake. While for the African it was a profoundly solitary notion, something abstract in a way, for Durand it was a question of a challenge leveled at society, a kick in the face of good morals, what he called a concrete affront" (Njami 1989a:97). The vengeful murder that Moïse commits in Amsterdam and his ambivalent longing for Africa are personal secrets that he keeps as he glides through his fast-paced life in the capitals of Europe. The author conveys a social message about Moïses's alienation without ever using the word.

Discussing the role of the novel, Karone echoes Njami's keynote of revelation in individual expression and artistic demonstration. Karone describes the task of the novelist as one of showing an imagined world, but he transfers the critical dimensions of the problem from interior revelation to explicit social commentary.

> We artists in the black community have the power to express our own fantasms. Artists have the formidable hope of being able to show something. As soon as artists have shown something, they have, between parentheses, resolved a part of the problem. I believe that when we show the problem, the question has already been posed. One has advanced the beginning of a response. And that's important. Everything that one hides and that one does not show is in bad faith. You're cheating. What I am trying to express is precisely that a novel is a way of posing questions, not necessarily of answering them, but at least posing them. (Karone 1991)

In a powerful scene from *A la Recherche du cannibale amour,* Karone depicts Eugéne's alienation and soul-wrenching identity quest.

> Thursday.
>
> An ambulance stops just in front of the house.
>
> "Is there someone dying in the neighborhood?" asks Philodia, astonished as she follows the reverse movements of the vehicle. Angèle finishes her embroidery and pushes back her glasses.
>
> "There's no doubt. It's a bad sign." Suddenly, a heavy-set man with a graying beard and an intelligent forehead enters the courtyard, followed by two guys in white shirts, with jockey caps turned backwards.
>
> "Does Monsieur Esselé live here?" asks the heavy-set fellow at the bottom of the stairs to the verandah. . . .

> "Yes, why?"
> "Are you his wife?"
> "Yes, what's it to you?"
> "Boiló Boiló, psychiatrist at the hospital of Écuelles. I've come to get Monsieur Esselé who is mad as a hatter, according to the law." (Karone 1988a:143–44)

Eugéne's search for inspiration and his failure to adjust to life in France drive him to the brink of insanity. There is no way out for him. Karone demonstrates the negative effects of the social pressures of immigration on the individual psyche.[6]

As part of her approach to social and political action, Calixthe Beyala develops the notion of "feminitude." This concept takes her identity as an African woman and a writer as its point of departure. Beyala explained how much her personal identity influences her work.

> I am a woman and I am a writer. This precision is very important. And whether it is in France or in Africa, it is a shock. I am young. Something which is not accepted because the image of sexuality is glued to the black woman. I live and experience this situation. That is, there is a desire to deny me my intelligence because I am a woman and because I am black, especially because I am black. . . . It's necessary to work ten times harder than everyone else to be published and to be accepted. That's an everyday reality. It's a daily combat. . . . It's a palpable reality for me as a black woman writer here in Paris. (Beyala 1990a)

Beyala (1995:76–78) elaborates on identity construction as an African woman in her open letter to Western women. In this lively essay, she exposes the political, social, and legal problems facing French and immigrant women. She attacks discrimination, inequities in employment, and problems of political participation. Nostalgically, she looks back upon the French feminism of the 1960s, but also claims that the era of mass movements is over. Each woman must create her own identity and her own destiny. Beyala (1995:20–21) states: "In conformity with your models, my independence was my first means of destruction according to the machos. More construction, according to me, it led me, during the 1980s, to a definition of my feminitude—very close to feminism but different to the extent that it is not based on equality between men and women, but on the egalitarian-difference between men and women. Another word was necessary to define this new woman who wants three sources of power: career, motherhood, and an emotional life."

The balance of models that Beyala seeks arises from her blend of French and African ideals. When I traveled in Cameroon during the late 1970s, speaking to the leaders of women's groups, many women explained that complementarity between the sexes was what they sought in lieu of a Western style of feminism. Beyala's feminitude resembles the Cameroonian notion of complementarity with one subtle difference. She aspires toward, and has achieved, a brilliant, award-winning career as a writer in Paris, and feminitude is part of her public persona. These achievements, based on the commercial support for and reception of her work in Paris, are influenced by her choice of Parisianism as a literary genre for five of her major works (Beyala 1992, 1993, 1994, 1995, 1996). Beyala's feminitude reflects narratives of both longing and belonging. She longs for the traditional comforts of family life and the image of a solitary African community. Yet, she proclaims her independence in a competitive, modern world far from the traditional African home, which she has never experienced and now rejects. This simultaneous idealization of individuality and desire for community characterizes not only Beyala's version of feminism but also Parisianism as a whole.

Individualism surfaces as a persistent theme in the literature of Parisianism and the interviews with its authors. The protagonists' encounters with French society are seldom smooth or easy. Although the authors handle situations of conflict with irony and humor, the options that they offer their characters are often bleak. Their heroes are witnesses of the tragedy of failed assimilation.[7] Trapped in an identity crisis, Njami's Moïse lashes out against European society by murdering a man and threatening his own life chances. Njami describes Moïse's dilemma:

> The rupturing of the umbilical cord. In this country, he [Moïse] had left a man dead on the cold slab of a suburban house. Once again, he alone knew. And this secret proved to be perfectly useless. To have shared it with an Antillian prostitute proved nothing. Death had been the ultimate thing for which he felt nothing. Even death had lost its allure. It was a banal, sordid formality. Men died just as they had lived, without luster, without panache. They lost consciousness like losing a button. Almost without perceiving it. And that changed nothing in the course of things in the world. (Njami 1989a:212)

From Fanon through the writers of Parisianism, madness has been used as a metaphor for failed African assimilation (Mouralis 1993:146–47). Although Moïse does not reflect on it, his existential isolation creates a silent madness. Beyala and Karone are more direct in their descriptions of the madness resulting from cultural clash and the pathology of displacement. In Beyala's *Tu t'appeleras Tanga* (1988) the European character Anna-Claude assumes the personality of a Cameroonian prostitute, Tanga, in a schizophrenic search for self-validation. Beyala returns to the theme of madness in her 1992 novel *Le Petit prince de Belleville.* Young Loukoum's father, Abdou Traoré, is arrested for receiving social assistance under false pretexts to support his wives and children in Belleville. Traoré reflects:

> I've gone mad. Besides, they've come after me. No, don't cry for me my friend. Cry for yourself, for your son. I know today what it means to be here, locked up. I knew other people in prison before, here, away from the world, but I never had such a clear and precise idea about it.
>
> I thought I experienced agony. I have touched it. . . .
>
> I thought I was defeated. I am defeated.
>
> My faith has evaporated. (Beyala 1992:245)

Following Abdou's confession, Loukoum and his family are asked to pose for newspaper pictures. Although everyone in Belleville thinks they are famous, the newspaper caption reads: "An immigrant family declares false births and steals several million centimes of familial allocations" (Beyala 1992:247). The vicious cycle of poverty and exclusion has entrapped Traoré and his family, leaving them practically no way out. Traoré's madness is his only solace.

Eugène's erratic behavior, in *Cannibale amour,* is misinterpreted by the medical authorities, and he is incarcerated. Under the pretext that Eugène is suffering from a malarial fever, Philodia is able to delay his hospitalization, but only for a few days. His condition worsens as he vainly seeks the source of artistic inspiration (the imaginary *cannibale amour*) in dreams and delusions.[8]

In *Un Regard noir* (1984), N'Djehoya and Diallo propose less tragic options. Makossa, the naive Cameroonian student, is neither angry nor anguished. He remains in a constant state of wonderment, a continuous cultural shock that allows him to interact with his French hosts at arm's length. He is a perpetual tourist. Diallo's description of the West African marabouts in the second half of *Un Regard noir* reveals another strategy of adaptation. Threatened by arrest and deportation as illegal immigrants and charlatans, the marabouts craftily turn their trade to their advantage. Like the folk healers of Africa, they are psychological entrepreneurs who promise relief for clients and play upon their insecurities (Jules-Rosette 1981:129). Diallo explains that Ameth, a masterful marabout, uses clever techniques to convince a policeman of his powers. Following a séance or two, the policeman hires Ameth as his private marabout. Ameth comments: "After all, the police are also men; and as such, they can have 'problems with people, problems of melancholy' (to paraphrase a well-known song)" (N'Djehoya and Diallo 1984:185). Ameth succeeds in using manipulative strategies to convince the authorities to share his culture and point of view.

The cultural and psychological strategies used by characters in the literature of Parisianism are closely tied to narrative format and plot structure. Seldom are the problems of adaptation and assimilation resolved. The stories end with a promise of escape through fantasy, madness, the idyllic return voyage to Africa, or an uneasy compromise with French culture. The outcomes remain open-ended, suggesting that the gap between cultures can never be closed.

Parisianism uses innovative language. It breaks through the barriers of sound and syntax in French. Crisp and salty French argots are interlaced with classic turns of phrase and Africanisms. No effort is made, however, as it was in the poetry of négritude, to imitate the oral literatures of Africa or to validate the use of African languages. Njami is emphatic about this point when he refers to language as a "machine" that should run well and be useful. Language also reflects the intersection of cultures. The Moroccan sociologist and novelist Abdelkebir Khatibi, whose works closely parallel the works of Parisianism, contends that language is the point of emotional intersection for cultures. In *Love in Two Languages* (Amour bilingue), Khatibi (1990:5) asserts: "The idea imposes itself as I write it: every language should be bilingual! The asymmetry of body and language, of speech and writing—at the threshold of the untranslatable." Khatibi's notion of the *bilingue* is fueled by the desire for a utopian communicative space in which dislocation and marginality are transcended through the artifices of language. Behind the idea of bilingual space are the immigrant's experiences of exclusion and the dream of devising an open discourse that incorporates all cultures.[9]

Beyala frames the problem of language in terms of the debate over francophonie. She believes that francophonie—or the separation of French literatures outside of France into a special category—restricts African writing to the inferior status of a literature without a center of gravity. When francophone writing is labeled as an exotic expression of French, the writer's claims to originality and universality are blocked. Beyala states:

> For the present—I am speaking of France—there is a rejection of the ex-colonial toward the culture of the colonized. There is a disdain that envelops not only the African writer but black literature in general. That is, people don't see any good coming from it. Francophonie is invented to assure the survival of the French language and culture. But we are an incontestable element in defense of the French language. This is not the French of Baudelaire, but a reconfigured language that will enrich French culture, language, and values, as in the case of any blending. Because of this, African literature is the literature of tomorrow that will give life to French culture and make the language more dynamic. (Beyala 1990a)

Both Beyala and Njami view the debate over francophonie as critical to creating utopian language spaces. Beyala sees African writing in French as a source of cultural enrichment, while Njami regards French as a necessary tool that should not be marked by signs of positive or negative cultural value. The debate about francophonie is not new. The writers associated with the Présence Africaine movement struggled with the domination of the French language, the influence of creolization, and the techniques that could be used to inflect French with an African flavor.[10] Bjornson (1991:14–18) regards African writing in French as a legacy of the colonial period's valorization of European languages and education. He argues that European languages have historically functioned as symbols of success in Africa. They are associated with education, political power, and technological mastery. In addition, Bjornson considers writing in European languages as an international marketing device. Appiah (1992:149) makes the point that national literatures in European languages have been influenced by the transition through the colonial period. Some of these literatures reconfigured language into a postcolonial tool, while others have retained older paradigms and styles. Eloise Brière (1988:34–39) adds an interesting note concerning the translation of French-African writing into English. She criticizes the omissions in English translations of such works as Camara Laye's *L'Enfant noir* (1953) as failures to take into account the cultural background of the works. These perspectives often clash in heated debates about the language of writing.

Since it does not reify or idealize African models of expression, the literature of Parisianism departs from earlier concerns about African inflections in language and postcolonial literature. The authors move toward ethnographic realism in language by conveying how people speak colloquially. Although this ethnographic realism contrasts with the stylized poetics of the négritude and creolization movements, its outcomes may, in fact, be similar. In the end, both the old and new generations of African writers test the limits of French expression in order to envelop their cultural experiences into the language. This use of language entails a politics of representation that questions what it means to be French and to be African.

Although the new writers embrace the use of French, Parisianism challenges myths of modernity by stretching the language to its limits. The influences of rap, reggae, hip-hop, and international popular culture give a new flavor and fast-paced tilt to Parisianism. This intriguing mixture of argot, African rhythms, colloquialisms, and puns makes stylistically accurate translation of the novels difficult. N'Djehoya and Karone are masters of the upbeat and colorful style of Parisianism, using irony, urbanity, and witticisms to convey the experiences of the new generation. N'Djehoya and Diallo's *Un Regard noir* contains a pertinent example.

> Jurez et prêtez serment sur la Bible, la vérité rien que la vérité, au commencement, c'était bien avant l'érection de Babel-City, tu sais bien, athée, au commencement était le Verbe, bien avant la génération spontanée, sponti ou mao-spontex, au jardin d'Eben. Ébony and Ivory [*sic*] marchaient à nouveau le long des quais, entre le trafic d'un soir et les bateaux-mouches qui remontaient le fleuve. Ils croisèrent les visiteurs de la tour Eiffel, visiteurs du soir, puis remontèrent vers

les beaux quartiers, jours tranquilles à Passy, rive gauche, ta fourchette toujours à gauche, ton portefeuille à droite, silence hôpital, don't disturb, il est tard monsieur, tout de même, enfin. (N'Djehoya and Diallo 1984:48)

[Swear on the Bible, the truth and nothing but the truth, in the beginning, well before the erection of Babel-City, you know, atheist, in the beginning was the Verb, well before the spontaneous generation, sponti or mao-spontex, in the garden of Eben (Ebony). Ebony and Ivory walked along the quais, between traffic of the evening and the bateaux-mouches (river boats) that sailed down the river. They passed visitors from the Eiffel Tower, evening visitors, then returned to the beautiful sections of town, tranquil days at Passy, the left bank, your fork always on your left, your wallet on your right, silence hospital, don't disturb, it's late sir, in any event, finally.]

Contrasting Discourses of Ideology and Utopia

When Parisianism is situated with reference to other discourses about integration and assimilation in France, it assumes a special place. It is both rebellious and acquiescent, politically activist and individualist. In a modernization of Mannheim's (1936:55–59) theory, Stuart Hall (1981:31) emphasizes that ideologies are not just isolated concepts. They entail a series of cultural meanings with social consequences. Parisianism is a discursive formation that is at once active and passive (Foucault 1972:138–40). Without making a collective political statement, Parisianism is, nonetheless, connected to liberal and individualist, antiracist ideologies. It reflects a cognitive utopia that unifies literature, politics, and social life (Tyler 1985:93; Gilroy 1993:37).

The French legal discourses of republicanism, secularism, and state-sponsored universalism receive scant attention in the literature of Parisianism. The writers are, instead, concerned with the space left vacant by the republican ideal—the private domain of thought and action. This private arena, however, clearly impinges on public action. Fear of the authorities, arrest, death, and insanity recur as narrative obstacles in the novels. Political repression is a literary reality in Parisianism. While négritude idealizes images of Africa, Parisianism questions their existence. In Parisianism, the return voyage to Africa culminates in a disappointing fantasy. In spite of their emphasis on Paris as a setting and an ideological space, the writers of Parisianism reject Kristeva's notion of responsible assimilation in favor of solitary rebellion. They eschew labels and limits without denying the persistence of discrimination, blockage, and racism.

Minority discourse theorists in the United States disagree with this perspective. They argue that ethnic and minority literatures must survive autonomously by using alternative canons that are not dominated by conventional cultural and literary norms. Abdul JanMohamed and David Lloyd (1987:9) assert: "For, to date, integration and assimilation have never taken place on equal terms, but always as assimilation *by* the dominant culture." This approach requires the expression of particularism in literature and cultural politics. The final results of minority discourse are ambiguous. It may lead to a "politics of transfiguration," where the "tribal" part enriches the global whole, or to a dead end of marginalization.

In yet another type of discourse on exclusion and marginality, Jean Baudrillard introduces the notion of hatred (*la haine*) as an emotional excess of postmodernity.[11] According to Baudrillard (1995:201–2), hatred is the expression of disdain and visceral denigration that appears among "people other than Western" in their encounter with Europeans. It creates a permanent gap between universal (namely, French) culture and "others" and is the "phantom of the excluded" that haunts Western societies. The writers of Parisianism approach this problem in reverse by exploring how social barriers are internalized by excluded individuals and lead them to the extremes of insanity, aggression, and death.

A final sociological discourse on marginalization worthy of mention centers around the process of retribalization (Maffesoli 1988:17–19; Maffesoli 1992:257–58; Barber 1995:132–44). According to this notion, the postmodern world is engaged in a regressive movement in which the anonymous and universal aspects of public legal, political, and economic life are counterbalanced by a private retreat into small family, gender-based, subcultural, and interest groups. This retribalization into microcommunities creates a dichotomy between private and public life, and it is in this private sphere that immigrants and minority groups reaffirm their particular identities. Each group operates as an island unto itself until some aspect of the group's lifestyle and mores transgresses public legal and social codes. Although liberal constitutional democracy supposedly remedies these problems of difference in the public domain, it fosters further exclusion by creating the legal and social conditions in which the retribalized groups flourish. Parisianism challenges this thesis by demonstrating how fragile the impulse toward retribalization is and by questioning the instability of attachments and individual identities within these groups. It also overturns the foundations of retribalization by emphasizing that the external society plays a role in perpetuating retribalized groups through stereotypes, racism, and other practices of exclusion. Thus, Parisianism calls into question the dominant discourses about citizenship and inclusion. Implicit in Parisianism is a special brand of universalism based on the integrity and risks of individual expression. It is impossible for the African subjects of Parisianism to be "French like everyone else." But in attempting to achieve this goal, the antiheroes of Parisianism encounter menacing obstacles that serve as the ingredients for good stories.

The writers of Parisianism engage in a freestyle harmonization that destroys nostalgic images of Africa and replaces them with signs of the conditions of displacement and transition. From the hero's madness to the manipulation of marabouts, the writers explore the emotional texture of living in France. Although their works do not champion political causes or reinstate a new cultural politics, these writers are engaged in various ways in public action. Beyala considered running for political office in her neighborhood of Belleville. Njami was a founder of the ethnicolor art movement, promoting multicultural artistic and political expression. They have established niches for themselves with Parisian publishing houses and have a loyal reading public. Their works have achieved recognition and moved into the mass media through radio, film, and television. Although they deny the status of role models, these writers are undeniably cultural leaders with a new voice.

What place does universalism hold for them? Their bid for recognition in French cultural life is, in itself, a test and expression of universalism. Although they are cynical about "being French like everyone else," they do not shy away from being "writers like everyone else."[12] Thus, without making grandiose philosophical claims, Parisianism incorporates a postcolonial universalism. Its emphasis on the theme of the individual coincides with a liberal political ethos that is threatening to some African states where this perspective is considered both decadent and dangerous. Bernard Dadié has referred to this problem as the role of the writer as the enemy in African societies. Resembling the double-rooted immigrants described in the sociological literature, the authors of Parisianism are influenced by, but not living in, Africa, are "neither here, nor there" (*ni ici, ni là-bas*). But the cultural reality and images that they describe are increasingly becoming the "here and now" of the Parisian landscape. Parisianism as a discourse makes a space for changing expressions of African identity in France. Without Parisianism, the new universalism would be impossible.

INTERVIEW

Simon Njami
Paris, July 18, 1991

Simon Njami is an important figure in the new generation of African writers in France. A novelist, essayist, poet, and critic, Njami moves with fluency across several literary genres and cultural spaces. He has written four novels, including his best-known pieces, Cercueil et cie *(1985), translated into English as* Coffin and Co. *(1987), and* African gigolo *(1989a). Njami's critical works include* Ethnicolor *(1987), with Bruno Tilliette;* James Baldwin ou le devoir de violence *(1991b); and* L. S. Senghor, *a forthcoming biographical work. He is a founding editor of* Revue Noire, *France's leading contemporary art magazine, and is an active contributor to the new criticism of African contemporary culture and the arts. The following interview is one in a series of four formal interviews I conducted with Simon Njami between 1989 and 1991. This interview focuses on the social and political context of African writing in France.*

Art and Social Commitment

Bennetta Jules-Rosette: Is it possible to make art for art's sake, especially for the black artist—whether African, Antillian, or American—or is the black artist caught in a situation where it's necessary to be socially and politically relevant?

Simon Njami: This is a debate that has always interested me very much. I am passionate about literature. Not only do I produce it, I also consume a great deal. And this is a debate that has considerably shaken up the postwar literary scene in France. It's a debate in which Gide and Sartre engaged. I think that all art involves a commitment. Every artist is an engaged artist doing political work. But we must interpret politics here in the correct sense. The Greeks said that politics was the administration of the city-state. Thus, the citizen participating in the city-state should take an active part in its organization and politics. But let's be clear about this! Engaged art does not mean writing in one's book that so and so is a bastard or a jerk—and that's where there's a dichotomy that people don't perceive very well. Someone can write a poem on the moon at night that appears to be completely abstract, and that can be politically relevant. I think that what one wants to express fundamentally, and that can take different forms—when one describes someone who's crying, for example—that's a type of engagement. When one describes someone who's dying, that's a form of engagement. And I think that every good artist produces an engaged work, even if he does not start by saying: "Look, this book, I'm writing it to combat apartheid, or racism, or this and that." But the good artist is the one who, in the end, when one has finished reading his book, seeing his play, or looking at his painting, stimulates a reflection provoked by images that one must grasp in the second, or third, or fourth degree. I also think that art doesn't have to be explicit to be strong. I think that it is more powerful to show a man and a woman in a country where blacks and whites cannot mix, to make a painting of a black man and a white woman embracing, than to write ten pages on the horrors of apartheid. The role of the artist is to show. Any good artist has open eyes, and what shocks the artist's eyes will shock the world. For me, the artist is a medium between the public and the world. The artist is able to make the world transparent, and to convey the rhythm of the world in words and images. If he is lucky, he can convey these images to others. The artist is the one who has the distinction, when looking at an object, to say: "Fine, I'm going to look at it this way and, suddenly, that will change things." So, I think that engagement, to return to that, is something that every artist can bring to his work. And it assumes strong accents, even stronger implications, when the context is bad. That is to say, if one is not in a war, if one can't see a war going on, one is not bathed in the atmosphere for writing about war and people who die in war. If one is in a war zone, that necessarily impregnates the work.

BJR: Yes, you can't escape it.

SN: So, to come back to Africa, there is so much chaos. There are so many problems that the artist can't escape them, even in the first degree. He can only be influenced by what takes place around him.

BJR: Now, I'm going to ask another question. Bernard Magnier has recently written an article about the new generation of African writers in Paris. He has used the terms *beurs noirs, negropolitain,* and *gallo-nègres* to describe these writers. What do you think about this?

SN: I hate labels. I am not a negropolitain, or a gallo-nègre, or a gallo-anything. First of all, I was born in Switzerland. But to come back to the article that Bernard has written, I think that what's interesting in what he says is that political engagement is different today. Formerly, when one spoke of racism, it was always conceived of as issuing from the white person toward the other. From a semantic and semiological perspective, when you listened to people, someone black or Chinese wouldn't be racist. And with respect to Africa, the African writer had to say that Africa was governed by tyrants. If one is African and one lives in Paris, this creates considerable problems. An artist should not be governed by a geographical map. I have always been bothered by the labels "African writer," or this type of writer, or that type of writer, as if everyone has a domain reserved for him out of which he cannot move. But today, the new generation of which we speak—and I am part of that generation—has no frontier. That's what Bernard emphasized in his article. My first novel takes place in Spain, Paris, and the United States. My second novel unfolds in Italy, Holland, and Paris. My third novel takes place in Berlin and Côte d'Ivoire. One has ideas and expresses them where they are. That's how ideas will come across with their full force and meaning. I want to be defined by what I write. So, I can only be defined ultimately once I'm dead. For the present, I refuse to be put in a box. You can put me in a box later, after I no longer have anything else to say.

BJR: What you have said about labels is really interesting. They certainly can't cover the mutable and changing identities of a person or an artist. Along these lines, I'd like to ask you about the term you've coined, "ethnicolor." What does it mean?

SN: From time to time, during conferences, lectures, and debates, people have not understood exactly what I mean by "world civilization." But what I mean by that is that there can be no world civilization without the specificity of individuals. If you and I are able to hold a conversation, it's because you are Bennetta and I am Simon, and we don't have an identical view of the world. But at the same time, we share a common base. If we didn't both speak French and English, for example, dialogue would be impossible. So what I mean by ethnicolor, is that the world is a rainbow. The rainbow is a whole. One can't say that just the color red is the rainbow. It's not that! It's blue, red, green—the entire declension of the prism of light. At the root of ethnicolor is ethnic. That is, each individual has a specificity, a color. And all of these individuals form a whole in the same world. Africa is the cradle of this world, the source of humanity. The first human being was found in Africa. The first car was invented in Egypt, and so on. . . . One can't escape one's roots. One has a certain culture. But it's funny, these experiences with black Americans in the United States—they have discovered the limits of that culture. It's good to have a lyrical illusion like that, to attach oneself to something because, historically, it's true that something existed. But, after three hundred years of being out of Africa, they have found that things have changed.

The Language of Writing

BJR: Let me ask you a question about use of the French language in African writing. What do you think about that for writers of African origin?

SN: During a recent conference, a woman asked me, "Don't you feel guilty writing in French when there are so many beautiful African languages?" I responded, "Look, my good woman, when I drive a car, I am not preoccupied by whether the car is Japanese or whether it was made in Cameroon, because if I were, I would walk. I drive according to the rules of the road, which say that there is a first gear and a second gear, etc. There is a machine. There is a tool. I use it without posing any other questions. . . . And I am not going to return to Africa in an absurd and vain gesture to learn a language and start writing in it, because that would not be natural.

Advice to Young Writers

BJR: And now, to change the subject a bit and to conclude, what advice do you have for young writers?

SN: One of James Baldwin's phrases comes to mind. When someone asked him that question, he said, "Put that face on the paper." And I think that there is no other solution, no further advice. There is not a school where you can learn to be a good writer. You can learn techniques, that's all. Your only tangible resource is yourself. You have to write with this type of mirror, and reread to see if that's what you wanted to say. Apart from that, you will be published, or not published. You should never write to be published. That will finish you. For me, writing is a vital necessity. If not, you can always put it off until tomorrow. To be a writer, to use a popular phrase, you have to come clean [*se foutre à poil*]. And it doesn't do any good to deceive yourself. There are lots of young people who say that they want to be writers, but who are not cut out for it.

BJR: You never know if you don't try.

SN: That's right. You never know if you don't try. And it's not on your brilliant ideas that you'll be judged, but on the paper that you've covered with ink.

BJR: That's certain!

SN: You can be beautiful, intelligent, and charming, but you'll be judged on the book that you've produced. So my final advice to young people is: "So, you want to write. Okay. Eh bien, do it."

INTERVIEW

Calixthe Beyala
Paris, July 27, 1990

Calixthe Beyala, born in Cameroon in 1961, is one of the most visible, successful, and controversial African writers of her generation in France. Born in a situation of poverty, Beyala attended high school in Douala and began to write seriously in 1984 through her own personal efforts and inspiration. She had no special literary training. Beyala now has to her credit several novels, a critical piece on African feminism, and the 1996 grand prize of the Académie Française for best novel of the year. She is politically active in France and is a frequent commentator in the mass media on issues concerning feminism, francophonie, and the cultural integration of minority populations in France. Her novels, discussed in chapters 5 and 6, include C'est le soleil qui m'a brûlée *(1987),* Tu t'appeleras Tanga *(1988),* Seul le diable le savait *(1990b),* Le Petit prince de Belleville *(1992),* Maman a un amant *(1993), and* Assèze l'africaine *(1994), and the award-winning* Les Honneurs perdus *(1996). Her nonfiction work includes a treatise on African feminism entitled* Lettre d'une africaine à ses soeurs occidentelles *(1995).*

Beyala's work has been covered in several critical anthologies and articles on new African literature including Bjornson 1991; Volet 1993; Nkashama 1994; Omerod and Volet 1994; and

Coulon 1997. I have analyzed Beyala's work in the context of the genre of Parisianism, but it may also be considered with reference to new Cameroonian national literature.

Literary Background

Bennetta Jules-Rosette: Calixthe, tell me about your literary background and how you became a professional writer.

Calixthe Beyala: I came from a very poor family in the bidonvilles. What can I say? In our primary school, there were 150 to 160 students to one teacher. So, I finally passed my baccalaureate exam (bac). I was able to come to France. And I passed my bac in France. And I completed a BTS degree in secretarial training, because, you know, in our family we didn't have a lot of ambition. We had limited horizons. Then I said to myself: "What are you going to do? You have to work. No, I don't like office work too much, so I'll study accounting." I studied accounting and received a diploma. Afterwards, I studied Spanish literature.

BJR: So you speak Spanish, as well.

CB: Yes, I speak Spanish very well, I think. [laughter] And it's after my studies in Spanish literature that I began to write. I've never written in Spanish. I've always written in French. I finished my first novel, *C'est le soleil qui m'a brûlée.* Once the book was done, I published it very quickly. Four months after I gave the book to the publisher, it was out in the book stores. It was published by Éditions Stock.

BJR: That's every writer's dream!

CB: Yes, I've been fortunate to publish with major French publishing houses. That plays a very important role, I think. In Africa—not only in Africa but elsewhere—many people approach writing as a pastime, but writing is a career. For me, writing is a career that must be approached not only from an artistic perspective but also as a professional. And it's important to approach it that way in order to put forward one's ideas and improve one's literary style.

BJR: In your novels *C'est le soleil qui m'a brulé* and *Tu t'appeleras Tanga,* relationships among women, in particular mothers and daughters, are important themes. How do you view these relationships? Are they changing in Africa today?

CB: Well, first of all, you have to admit that Africa is a feminine continent, completely dominated by women. That is, women hold the economy together, even if it's not always evident. The thoughts and spirits of women guide men. So, in my novels, women emerge as very strong characters. The mother-daughter relationship is part of this matrix. In fact, it is only a consequence of this matrix. The mother-daughter relationship is an essential element because mothers transmit values to their daughters and their sons. On the African continent, the father is often absent, and the task of educating children falls on the mother's shoulders. The mother is always there. Even when the father is present, the mother assumes total responsibility for the children. As far as I know, Africa was originally a matrilineal and a matriarchal continent. The interactions across the sexes that appear today result from external religions and civilizations—the influence of Islam and Christianity. In southern Africa, three famous queens headed empires. But most of Africa has now lost its matrilineal character. Even so, women still dominate everyday life. And that's why I give women a central place in my novels.

BJR: Yes, women seem to play an important psychological role in your novels. They contribute to the psychological depth of your work. Do you use women characters in a special way psychologically?

CB: If you are speaking about the use of the unconscious in my works, I am not well placed to talk about that. I think that a writer cannot make a critical analysis of her own works. Others are better placed to describe the implications of a writer's work. I appreciate the fact that there are many different readings of my work. Some critics say that my writing shocks them. But I don't try to do that. My writing is an extension of my personality. That's all. If it's well received, fine. If it's not, too bad. But, up to now, my novels have been well received.

BJR: And have your experiences growing up in an African bidonville, as you have described it, greatly influenced your writing?

CB: Certainly. If one asks me to speak about Africa, I can't talk about the Africa of traditions, so-called beauty, lyricism, and pastoralism. I was born in a bidonville. That was my world. For me, that's Africa. For many, Africa is the world of air-conditioned cars, beautiful clothes, and *boubous.* Not for me. I saw those people pass by at a distance. For me, Africa is also the Africa of tomorrow where cultures mix and blend. It's the Africa where children make toys from the refuse of civilization. That's my Africa—the Africa where I was born, and that has made an impression on me.

Writing as a Woman

BJR: How do you experience your situation as an African woman writer in France?

CB: I am a woman and I am a writer. This precision is very important. And whether it is in France or in Africa, it is a shock. I am young—something which is not accepted because the image of sexuality is glued to the young black woman. I live and experience this situation. That is, there is a desire to deny me my intelligence because I am a woman and because I am black, especially because I am black. An image of a certain type of sexuality stereotypes me as a black woman writer. I have experienced this repeatedly, and it makes me work ten times harder at what I do. Excuse me, but this is a daily reality and a daily battle for me as a black woman writer in France! Every time that I produce a new novel, I begin all over again.

BJR: Do you think that this situation is more difficult in France than elsewhere?

CB: I think that a black woman writer in France has to work ten times harder than everyone else to be published and to be accepted. People do not take you seriously as a writer. But you can't change four centuries of history in ten years. It takes time to change things, and that's not easy. I don't think that black women writers will be fully accepted during my lifetime.

BJR: Both you and playwright Werewere Liking have spoken about lunatic writing. Explain what you mean by that term and how it applies to the women in your novels.

CB: What I have written about is madness. For me, madness is not a drama in itself. It results from an excess of intelligence in a world where many people have lost their identity and their sense of self. So madness can be conceived of as an excess of intelligence, a sort of intellectual and spiritual superiority. When no one else understands what's happening in the world, when no one analyzes what's going on, the person who does understand goes mad. So, I'm not talking about the furious and angry madness that one encounters in a psychiatric hospital. I'm talking about a very special madness that results from the intelligence of people who have a clear vision of things in a world where everyone closes their eyes. Lunatic writing reflects this clarity of vision. Through weakness, other people run away from it. Let me give you an example. In African bidonvilles, everyone has a clear vision of the future. They always speak of tomorrow. For these people, the present and the past don't exist. That's crazy. Everything is conjugated in the future tense. "I'll buy a house." "I'll buy a refrigerator." "I'll go to school here or there." It's always in the future. Never "I've bought," always "I'll buy." And this language reflects a moment of loss. And when you try to understand the present with this language, you go mad. Life in the bidonville denies the present because one lives on hope. Everyone thinks that they're in transit to a better tomorrow. They think that life in the bidonville is transitory—never fixed, never definitive. No one stays there out of sheer pleasure. So, you conjugate verbs in the future tense. And it's in that space between the present and the future that lunatic writing develops.

Speaking of France and Francophonie

BJR: How do you see the current situation of African writers in France, and what are the prospects for the future?

CB: For the present, I am speaking of France, there is a rejection of the ex-colonial toward the culture of the colonized. There is a disdain that envelops not only the African writer but black literature in general. That is, people don't see any good coming from it. Francophonie is invented to assure the survival of the French language and culture. But we are an incontestable element in defense of the French language. This is not the French of Baudelaire, but a reconfigured language that will enrich French culture, language, and values, as in the case of any métissage. Because of this, African literature is the literature of tomorrow that will give life to French culture and make the language more dynamic.

BJR: So, do you think that African literature has the capacity to revitalize French literature?

CB: In certain respects, French literature is moribund. It turns inward on itself. Why has English held up so well for writers? Because English has integrated the languages of the empire. Have we received a Nobel Prize in francophone African literature? Not yet, but there has been one in anglophone African literature! Is this because we lack good francophone African writers of the quality and dimensions of Soyinka? No, of course not. It's because France has rejected the African literatures and cultures which can enrich it.

BJR: What do you think is the source of this problem of stagnation?

CB: Well, it's evident that Africa has many languages and cultures. And no one accepts the language of others. In Cameroon, for example, there are more than 280 languages spoken. Who will accept someone else's language? No one. Language generates tribal and ethnic wars. It's unimaginable! But I think that there can be an evolution inside of the French language, if African writers introduce their own languages and turns of phrase into French. You have to superimpose your language onto the French language to enrich it. That's what I do in my books.

SEVEN

Universalism: The African Writer's Dream

> In my work as a poet, I want to say to others, no matter from what country they come, what language they speak, or what culture they represent, that they too have an identity, and that this identity can become an affair of passion. And once this passion is understood, they will develop a national passion for their countries, and they will also want, as I do, to rejoin the universal.
>
> —Edouard Maunick, 1989

Universalism, the search for a distinctive place in world literature, is the African writer's dream. It includes a set of cultural attitudes, economic strategies, and political tactics. In sum, universalism is a philosophy, a way of life, and a dream. Some African writers, especially those of the new generation adhering to Parisianism, are skeptical that universalism's veiled Eurocentrism excludes anyone who asserts a marginal identity. The versions of universalism advanced by négritude and the postcolonial universalists emphasize the equality of different cultures. Léopold Senghor defined universalism as a sense of complementarity in which African cultures enhance the legacy of European civilizations (Senghor 1977b:341). Alioune Diop (1987:45–47) viewed the universal contribution of black civilization to the world as a spiritual and social expression of the maturity of African values. Political and social agendas lurked behind these expressions of universal culture. On the one hand, African intellectuals and writers could mold, out of their knowledge of traditional cultures and their formal training, a new transcontinental collective identity. On the other hand, this collective identity would develop into a source of pride, combating the debilitating effects of colonialism and providing a cultural space for African literature. This expression of universalism paves the way for a new egalitarian society in which new world citizens—those whom Edouard Maunick (1987:28) calls "the birds of the third millennium"—fly freely.

The laudable goals of Senghorian universalism were fueled by the struggles of African intellectuals in Europe during the end of the colonial period and in their home countries at the dawn of independence. Recognition of African literary accomplishments opened new avenues to publish and establish a secure place for at least one Parisian African publishing house, Présence Africaine. The founders of the journal *Présence Africaine* envisioned a strong network of African intellectuals who would link the publishing ventures, conferences, and festivals organized in their home countries to France. African independence in the 1960s introduced further challenges, including establishing institutional legitimacy and financial support for the arts and culture in emerging nations beset with a host of economic and political problems. In this context, universalism met with local opposition as a value, a goal, and a strategy.

African politicians often grouped the arts together with sports and youth in government ministries. Art and literature were considered frivolous sources of entertainment, secondary to national economic and political development. The role of "black men of letters and culture," promoted by Présence Africaine and the négritude movement, came under fire. New nations needed to be organized by people with technical training—activists ready to become bureaucrats. Nationalism replaced universalism as the rallying point for collective identity. When literature was on the political agendas of new nations, mounting national literatures in opposition to the old colonial legacy was the order of the day. In spite of these countervailing forces, universalism has persisted as a theme in the works of new African writers—the birds of the third millennium—and as a distinctive feature of African diasporic writing.

Poetry's Universal Message

Poetry has long been at the core of literary debates about universalism among African writers in France. This chapter examines the work of two poets, Jean-Baptiste Tiémélé and Edouard Maunick, and one essayist and novelist, Bolya Baenga. Before discussing the poetry by Tiémélé and Maunick, I find it useful to review the terms of the debate on national poetry sponsored by Présence Africaine on July 9, 1955. Once again, *Présence Africaine* provided a foundation and crystallizing point for understanding the history of African and Afro-Antillian poetry in France. Not only did *Présence Africaine* devote considerable space to the publication of this poetry, it also sponsored the keynote conference on the role and forms of African poetic expression.

The debate on national poetry was inspired by Louis Aragon's publication of three classical French poems in the December 2, 1953, issue of *Lettres Françaises* (Mouralis 1984:432–34; Mateso 1986:118–21). Aragon argued for a return to classical forms of verse, such as the alexandrine, the octosyllable, and the sonnet, and for a greater awareness of French poetic styles and conventions. He wished to solidify the boundaries of a French national poetry and to ensure its high quality. Nevertheless, in the process, Aragon forgot about francophone poets outside of France. He left no room in his schema for French-speaking African and Antillian poets. In fact, Aragon was even critical of free verse, which he labeled alternatively as modernist individualism and cosmopolitan pretension. In 1954, Aragon assembled a collection of what he considered exemplary poetry in *Journal d'une poésie nationale.* Aragon's position triggered a virulent response from René Depestre, who published an editorial letter in the June 16, 1955, edition of *Lettres Françaises.* Depestre's argument was that a Haitian national poetry, conforming to its own formal conventions and standards of quality, was possible alongside of, but autonomous from, French poetry. This Haitian poetry had African, French, and creolized elements. Depestre's letter provoked a response published by *Présence Africaine* in the form of an ironic and scathing poem, "Le Verbe marronner," which Aimé Césaire (1955a:113–15) dedicated to Depestre. The famous line "marronnerons-nous Depestre, marronnerons-nous?" (Shall we escape like slaves Depestre, like slaves?) opens this poem. Clifford (1988:179–81) emphasizes Césaire's neologism in creating a verb from the noun *marron* (maroon), meaning "escaped slave." This neologism is part of Césaire's larger argument that poetry, no matter what its national origin, should be a form of individual creative expression.[1] Césaire's clever argument touched on several points, which may be summarized as a defense of the individuality of poetic expression. According to Césaire, no particular African or Antillian form of expression should characterize poetry. Poets should use all of the tools and techniques available to recount their experiences. If technical mastery is achieved in expressing inner feelings and experiences, a universal poetry necessarily results. In his second response to Depestre, Césaire states:

> What is essential for a poet is to approach a poem, I will not say with all his soul, I will say with all his being. That appears to me to be the only condition of poetry. . . . I think that if a poet is engaged in a truly total manner in the poem, I think that his poetry, if it is African, cannot fail to be an African poem; that is, if the poem is good, that is, if the poem comes from sufficiently far away, the poem can only carry with it the mark of the poet, his essential mark, that is, a national mark. Who, thus, more than a poet, is of his time, of his milieu, of his people? (Césaire 1955b:41)

Césaire, however, did not conceive of a unique route to this mark of distinction. Why, he asked, should an alexandrine be considered a more national form of French poetry than the *Song of Roland,* or why should rhyme be more appropriate than free verse? This view challenged both Aragon and Depestre because Césaire, whose roots were in surrealism and experimental poetry, did not want to be constrained by classical French forms of verse or folkloric African and Antillian styles. At the 1955 poetry conference, Césaire presented his views, and they were supported by several other writers. Although Depestre could not attend the conference, he reviewed the tape-recorded proceedings and answered Césaire in an article entitled "Response to Aimé Césaire: Introduction to a Haitian Poetic Art," published in the October–November 1955 issue of *Présence Africaine.*[2] Depestre (1955:55) argued for a Haitian poetic art based on specific stylistic forms and cultural-historical experiences. He claimed that this Haitian poetic realism would eventually lead to a universal realism (*un réalisme universel*). He believed that this realism could be achieved via a dialectic, with the totality of the experiences of poetic language as its thesis, the search for technique as its antithesis, and "critical assimilation," linking tradition and poetic invention, as its synthesis (Depestre 1955:60).

Use of the term "assimilation" was a red flag for further debates. Césaire criticized Depestre as an "assimilationist" whose techniques were no different than those of Aragon. Amadou Moustapha Wade, a West African poet, supported Césaire in the debate, arguing for freedom of poetic experimentation and expression without national boundaries. The Senegalese poet David Diop (1955:63) entered the fray by publishing his poem "Un Enfant noir" in the 1955 special issue of *Présence Africaine,* devoted to the debate, and following it with an article entitled "Contribution au débat sur la poésie nationale" in the February–March 1956 issue of the journal. Diop (1956:113–15) made the case for a politically engaged national poetry, which, nevertheless, should not fall into the traps of being maudlin, folkloric, or structurally and aesthetically substandard. He was concerned about the ghettoization of African poetry, and he wished to see it situated in the ranks of world literature.

Sponsored by Présence Africaine, the debate on national poetry had the broad impact of contributing to the definition of universalism in African literature. Specifically, the debate refocused questions of poetic form, content, and style with respect to cultural issues. Should a national poetry exist in the context of Africa and the African diaspora? In what ways should or could this poetry reflect local languages, dialects, histories, and social experiences—including colonialism and oppression? To what extent should such a poetry be folkloric, and what balance could be achieved between "exoticism" and "realism"? In this debate, universalism may be interpreted in at least two ways: (1) as the individual author's quest to express personal emotions and responses in a universally acceptable form (Césaire's position), and (2) as an effort to reflect one's nation and culture with a unique style and message that would eventually achieve a distinctive place in world literature (Depestre's position). Various nuances developed between these two positions, and the arguments waxed and waned. As usual with the debates sponsored by Présence Africaine and later by SAC, this one had no real end-point. African and diaspora poets continued to debate the issue of universalism in their creative and critical writings. Two poets, Jean-Baptiste Tiémélé and Edouard Maunick, extend this debate by presenting complex views of universalism as a value and a strategy. They criticize, readapt, and modify the approaches of the négritude poets and Présence Africaine as they grapple with the relationship of identity to universal cultural values and world literature. The views that they express are widely held by the adherents of postcolonial universalism.

Tiémélé redefines the philosophy and practices of négritude for the 1980s and 1990s by emphasizing the shared elements of the human condition and the importance of universal values derived from human suffering and compassion. Maunick stresses cultural blending and métissage in his literary pact with his country and the world. His passion for universal cultures drives him to fit his personal and cultural identity into a larger panorama. Although he is not a poet, the Zairian author and social commentator Bolya Baenga uses incisive criticism and journalism to call universalism into question. He highlights the relevance of the Japanese model of modernity for Africa. These three approaches to universalism, through extending and challenging the legacy of négritude, emphasizing cultural diversity and blending, and overturning the myths of modernity, breathe new life into the Senghorian tenets of universalism and situate universalism as a viable set of values and strategies for contemporary African writers. All three writers have worked in the literary environment of Paris with the freedom to reconfigure an "African" national and personal identity as they wish. They are directly connected with overlapping Parisian publication outlets for their works. They have all published with Éditions Silex or Éditions Nouvelles du Sud. Consequently, universalism, while bringing a distinctive flair to their works, is also a beneficial literary and political strategy for them.

Jean-Baptiste Tiémélé: Pleasures and Pains of Africa

Born in 1933 eighty kilometers north of Abidjan, in Agboville, Côte d'Ivoire, Jean-Baptiste Tiémélé is a poet, playwright, and actor residing in Paris. (See fig. 20.) He completed primary school, receiving a Certificat d'Études, in Agboville and was sent to Rennes, in Brittany, to attend lycée. After completing secondary school, he attended the Université de Paris, where he studied first linguistics and

Fig. 20. Poet and playwright Jean-Baptiste Tiémélé standing in a garden that inspires his poetry, Paris, July 19, 1990. Photograph by Bennetta Jules-Rosette.

then urban geography. Although he received a degree in urban geography, he never took up this profession. During the 1960s, Tiémélé became fascinated with poetry and published his first collection, *Chansons païennes,* with Éditions Pierre Jean Oswald in Honfleur. He contributed financially to the publication of this book, in return for which he was able to purchase copies at a 30 percent to 40 percent reduction. The first printing was of a thousand copies, many of which the author distributed himself. This practice is fairly common for the publication of poetry, and even more so for the works of African authors.[3]

Tiémélé's second collection, *Ce Monde qui fume,* was published by Éditions Saint-Germain-des-Prés in 1981. Copies of this collection were difficult to find, even shortly after its publication. Saint-Germain-des-Prés used the same subsidy system as Oswald but concentrated less on the distribution of the book. In 1987, Tiémélé published his third poetry collection, *Aoyu suivi de Yaley,* with Éditions Silex. My first interview with Tiémélé took place on September 15, 1989 when *Aoyu suivi de Yaley* was still in circulation.

Thoroughly committed to cultural and intellectual life, Tiémélé added theater to his repertoire in the mid-1960s. In 1965 he obtained a role in *Chant public devant deux chaises électriques,* produced by the Théâtre National Populaire (TNP) in Paris. He then began taking acting courses while searching for other roles. In 1989 Tiémélé completed a play about Thomas Alexandre, a general in the French Revolution and the father of Alexandre Dumas. Tiémélé wrote *Thomas Alexandre* to commemorate the French Revolution's bicentennial and to illustrate the role of black soldiers in the Revolution. The play was performed once but has not been published. Tiémélé's work in progress includes "Essan, le savant du vingtième siècle," a play about a modern scientist experimenting with in vitro fertilization in a traditional African village. In order to support his poetic and theatrical writings, Tiémélé acts in a variety of Parisian productions and performs African folktales for children at the Musée Dapper. He plans to publish a collection of these folktales as children's stories.

A cross section of poems from Tiémélé's *Chansons païennes* and *Aoyu suivi de Yaley* with a commentary by Tiémélé illustrates his contribution to universalism. Tiémélé begins by explaining the notion of identity as a dream.

> Identity has an imaginary side. But when is a dream real and when is it a fantasy? It comes from the unconscious, and that is real. . . . one lives a dream, if even just for seconds. And that reality has a fiction glued to it. Identity is like that. I exist as a person, different from other people, and around me is a halo of values in which I bathe. This halo consolidates my values and aspirations, finally, everything that I represent for myself and others. We all bathe in the same universe with different personal elements. In this halo of values, differences appear as transparent realities. (Tiémélé 1990)

Separation of the subject from the object of desire creates alienation and longing. The joining of subject and object results in a universal vision and harmony. Tiémélé's poetry plays upon the poles of longing and belonging, of comfort and pain. Living in France is a source of comfort for Tiémélé, and thoughts of Africa create anxiety. At the same time, Tiémélé expresses the sense of belonging to Africa, and longing for acceptance in France. In describing his mission as a writer, he emphasizes the importance of Africa as a theme. Tiémélé states:

> My objective is, above all, to try, not only to make Africa in some way present in my writing, but also to try to consolidate—in my manner—to toss my small stone into the consolidation of African culture and of the black world in general. And that is my vocation. But through my work I would like to develop a more fraternal dialogue among blacks who are dispersed around the world, whether they are here or in Honolulu, because we live in a world where there is a reciprocal interaction among societies, and we cannot be absent from it. . . . We must recognize ourselves as such, and we need to assert ourselves. (Tiémélé 1989)

Contributing to the consolidation of Africa while focusing on a universal context highlights the axis of comfort versus pain. The black writer is part of the black world (*le monde noir*), yet lives in a broader society. Belonging to the black world involves the paradox of exclusion from other cultures. Thus, longing and belonging operate in opposition, simultaneously engendering the pleasures and the pain of Africa. From Tiémélé's perspective, politicians create much of the pain of Africa and the world. They are responsible for suffering, hunger, political divisions, instability, and genocide. Moreover, political decisions about culture complicate the African writer's fate by creating conditions in which books are censored, cannot be sold, and are never read. Tiémélé emphasizes:

> A problem that arises for writers is that in Africa, no one reads. In any case, they read very little. And this is a genuine problem basically because at the level of politics, they prefer that writers become known elsewhere, and not in their countries, because it's less dangerous. . . . As a result, many black writers are published in Paris. And very few are published in Africa, and, in the end, this is regrettable because when one writes, one speaks out for Africa, and Africa is the last to read us! It is as if we are screaming in the desert. (Tiémélé 1989)

According to Tiémélé, African writers are alienated from their audiences, whether these audiences are in Europe or Africa. European publishers and reading publics ghettoize African literature, while the African audience remains weak and undeveloped. Consequently, African writers "scream in the desert" without a clear direction, audience, or response, and their writings reach Africa only in what Tiémélé terms "homeopathic doses." Efforts to rectify this problem include philosophical developments such as négritude, which provided a space for African writers to express themselves in France and at home. Nevertheless, Tiémélé is critical of négritude's contribution. He argues that the word *nègre* is not accepted by everyone, even though the movement of négritude had a strong philosophical basis. The container that envelopes the movement is flawed, but the content of the philosophy is strong. To replace négritude, Tiémélé suggests a type of universalism that begins with self-awareness and an understanding of cultural identity, and then moves beyond the self to humanity as a whole. Amplifying this idea, Tiémélé asserts:

> When I write, it is with reference to Africa and to the black man [*l'homme noir*] because I know that the battle of tomorrow will be the battle of humanity. But before we can reach the battle of humanity, there is the battle of races. This is what I think is happening, and I do not think that we should deceive ourselves on this issue, because if we delude ourselves about the battle of tomorrow, it will be lost because we have no soldiers. (Tiémélé 1989)[4]

This theme of universal and particular cultural battles resembles the dialectic of négritude. Tiémélé, however, approaches this problem from the perspective of an African battle—or the combat of races—as the first and essential step toward achieving a victory of universalism. Once again, it is possible to return to the contrasts between the comfortable and the painful, the agreeable and the disagreeable, in order to understand why Tiémélé believes that suffering precedes the triumphs of universal harmony. This point is well illustrated in Tiémélé's 1969 poem entitled "Le Chemin de la liberté" (The road to liberty). The poem opens with a quote about banana republics in which the "ripe bananas" can never detach themselves from the tree. For Tiémélé, the road to freedom is a long and rocky road, in which many obstacles must be confronted and several battles fought. He argues for self-reliance in overcoming suffering through courage and persistence.[5]

> *"Le régime de bananes mûres ne se*
> *détache jamais de lui-même du bananier."*
> (Proverbe africain)
>
> Le chemin de la Liberté
> n'est pas un long ruban de soie
> que l'on déroule sur plusieurs kilomètres
>
> Le chemin de la Liberté
> n'est pas celui que l'on fait assis
> dans un fauteuil de bambou ou de cuir
>
> Le chemin de la Liberté
> Ce n'est pas celui qui consiste
> à compter à l'ombre d'un palissandre
> Le nombre de kilomètres parcourus par les autres
>
> Le chemin de la Liberté
> C'est cette sente rocailleuse
> à travers les ronces jalonnée par les monts
> et les plaines et qu'on arpente soi-même hardiment!
> (Tiémélé 1969:40)
>
> [*"The regime of ripe bananas never*
> *detaches itself from the banana tree."*
> (African proverb)
>
> The road to Freedom
> Is not a long silk ribbon
> that unfolds across several kilometers
>
> The road to Freedom
> Is not traveled seated
> in a bamboo or leather armchair

The road to Freedom
Does not consist
of counting under the shadow of a tree
the number of kilometers traveled by others

The road to Freedom
Is a rocky path
across brambles marked by mountains
and plains that one crosses boldly!]

Displeasures of oppression, exclusion, and alienation emerge in Tiémélé's poem "Les Conquistadores" (The Conquistadores), which is a commentary on the massacre of Amazonian Indians in 1986. Tiémélé pleads for a more humane world that is not dominated by greed and violence or riddled by bullets. His poem appears to be a reflection of current events after morning coffee. Underneath this musing, however, is a bitter protest against the agonies of suffering and genocide. By implication, Tiémélé's poem about the Amazonian Indians also refers to colonialism and neocolonialism in Africa—the rape of the land, the dispossession of the people, and mass murder.

Qu'apprend-on en ce onzième jour de janvier 1986?
Des Indiens d'Amazonie
dans leur réserve
marchent sur de l'or!

Des Indiens d'Amazonie
tout nus
couchent sur de l'or!
Le réveil ce matin est bien douloureux

Les conquistadores ont resurgi de leurs cendres
Leur prétention? La cession par les Indiens
de leur lit d'or!

Soixante récalcitrants
longs à se mettre debout
longs à fuir
sont occis criblés de balles!
Est-ce là le XXe Siècle Humanitaire!
Janvier 1986
(Tiémélé 1987:85)

[What does one learn on this eleventh day of January 1986?
The Amazonian Indians
on their reservation
walk on gold!

The Amazonian Indians
completely nude
sleep on gold!
Waking   this morning   is very painful

The conquistadors have reemerged from their ashes
Their pretext? The Indian's repossession
of their bed of gold!

Sixty recalcitrants
slow to take a stand
slow to flee
are massacred   riddled by bullets!
Is this the Humanitarian XXth Century!
January 1986]

In another poem, entitled "Messieurs les savants" (Learned gentlemen) (1987:39–40), as well as in his unpublished play, "Essan, le savant du vingtième siècle" (1997), Tiémélé denounces the role of scientists and modern consumers in destroying the environment and the harmony of the universe. He singles out "men of science" and consumers, including himself, as immoral. He warns scientists

mais quoi vous avez finement extrait
de ce monde exceptionnel
des choses qui tuent
NAPALM
BOMBE
BOMBE
NAPALM
Ah! le jour où vous inventerez la joie
vous aurez l'ingéniosité
de lui insuffler un rien d'air vicié
Messieurs les savants
vous êtes immondes
(Tiémélé 1987:39)

[but what you have carefully extracted
from this extraordinary world

things that kill
NAPALM
BOMB
BOMB
NAPALM
Ah! the day when you invent joy
you will have the ingenuity
to fill it with a void of noxious air
Men of science
you are immoral]

Harmony of the environment affects tranquility of the soul. The balance of the individual depends upon the balance of the universe. Relationships between humans and the environment reflect relationships among humans themselves, across races and cultures. In "Statue de bois" (Statue of wood), Tiémélé (1969:19–20) begins by affirming his black identity and his reverence for traditional religion—a statue of wood whose magic protects him. The statue stands in lieu of Africa. In turn, Africa blends with the universe. When an imbalance occurs through Africa's suffering, the individual (that is, the poet, himself) and the rest of the universe are troubled. These haunting rumors of trouble and imbalance presage the present state of Africa and the world. Tiémélé declaims:

Statue de bois
j'ai eu peur l'autre soir
Statue sans voix
Fais qu'au travers
de ces fumées
je dénombre
les étoiles de l'universe
Mais fais aussi que ces rumeurs
ne troublent point mes espoirs
et l'harmonie des couleurs
de ce monde.
(Tiémélé 1969:20)

[Statue of wood
I was afraid the other night
Statue without a voice
Allow me through
this smoke
to count
On the stars of the universe

But also stop these rumors
from troubling my hopes
and the harmony of the colors
of this world.]

The individual's condition is reflected in cultural displacement. Tiémélé uses personal terms to talk about longing for his mother country, while attempting to belong in a new "country of marvels." Two poems by Tiémélé, "Abidjan, ma belle" (Abidjan, my beauty) (1987:25) and "La Lettre de ma mère" (Letter from my mother) (1987:21), poignantly demonstrate the poet's ambivalent longing for Africa in the midst of a new life. In "Abidjan, ma belle," he portrays Abidjan as a beautiful woman to whom he is engaged. Although the engagement is never broken, the marriage is postponed by his long journey abroad. The fiancée cries and suffers, longing for her lover—who is also her native son—to return. Tiémélé orchestrates this lament of lost love:

Je t'ai quittée un jour de grand soleil
Tes joues luisaient couvertes de larmes.
Sur une nef antique fouettée par les lames,
Je m'embarquai pour un voyage sans pareil.

. . . .

Je partis à la recherche des plus jolies fleurs,
Crois-moi, pour nos prochaines épousailles.

Mais des ans ont passé. Du pays des merveilles
Je ne suis point revenu et, je sais, notre amour
Qui te fit pleurer tant, te fait pleurer toujours.
(Tiémélé 1987:25)

[I left you on a bright sunlit day
Your cheeks glistened, covered with tears.
On an ancient ship whipped by waves,
I embarked on an incomparable voyage.

. . . .

I left in search of prettier flowers,
Believe me, for our future wedding.

But years have passed. From the country of marvels
I never returned and, I know, our love
That made you cry so much, still makes you cry.]

"La Lettre de ma mère" once again exhibits Tiémélé's longing for Africa, metonymically represented as his mother. His mother's distant pain causes the poet to suffer, yet news of her is sublime. These mixed emotions lead him to re-read and tear up the letter. His longing is repressed by turning away from the maternal message in solitude.

Ta lettre ma première lettre
Je t'entends
Me dire tout bas les nouvelles
De la famille
Et l'inquiétude qui sourd en ton coeur
A cause de mon absence
Je te vois confier
Ta pensée à cette feuille d'un cahier d'écolier
Enfin ta Parole
Je te sens là
Présente
Pour la première fois
Depuis ce grand départ
Où je me suis noyé
Dans la nuit du silence
Ta voix maintenant s'élève nette
M'emplit la tête
M'enveloppe
Quels instants mystérieux sublimes
Cette lettre vient de toi
De l'autre côté de la mer
Elle a traversé l'air
Ou peut-être fendu l'Océan
Elle est venue jusqu'à moi
. . . .
Dans ma solitude
Je la relis pour te retrouver
Mais ta peine y est si lourde
que de peur je l'ai déchirée
(Tiémélé 1987:21)

[Your letter my first letter
I hear you
Telling me very softly the news
Of the family
And the uneasiness that resounds in your heart
Because of my absence

I see you confiding
Your thoughts about this family to a page of a student notebook
At last your Word
I feel you there
Present
For the first time
Since this great departure
Where I have drowned myself
In the night of silence
Now your voice is raised clearly
Fills my head
Envelopes me
What mysterious moments sublime
This letter comes from you
From the other side of the sea
It has crossed the air
or perhaps plowed through the Ocean
It has reached me
. . . .
In my solitude
I reread it to find you again
But your suffering is so heavy
That out of fear I tore it up]

Semiotic axes of the comfortable, or agreeable, and the disagreeable are conjoined in this poem. Africa is a source of maternal solace, memories, and strength, but it also raises the specter of suffering. The author's absence from his native land inspires guilt, but his memories carry with them the consolation of comfort, belonging, and mystery.

"L'Âme des feuilles" (The soul of leaves) expresses Tiémélé's universalism in its purest form. He laments the sadness of autumn when the trees lose their leaves. As winter approaches, the swallow departs, and the infinite wind carries off the soul of leaves. One reading of this poem interprets the swallow as a metonym for the poet, who flees from his African homeland. This poem has deeper psychological connations. A universal sense of longing and lament is expressed with the flight of the soul of leaves. More important, Tiémélé has written this poem with reference to nature and universal human emotions. It represents the "battle of humanity" that follows the conflict of cultures. He touches upon a common chord of sadness and longing that can be shared by readers regardless of their backgrounds.

Les Arbres
Au ciel monotone
Tendent leurs mains exsangues rudes et dures

L'Hirondelle, quant à elle, à tire-d'aile
Inquiète s'enfuit
Vers d'autres horizons
Car le Vent à l'Infini
Dans son envol emporte l'âme des Feuilles.
(Tiémélé 1969:25)

[The trees
In the monotonous sky
Extend their bloodless rough and hard hands

The Swallow, as for her, at full speed
Restless flees
Toward other horizons
Because the Infinite Wind
In its flight carries off the soul of leaves.]

Tiémélé's approach to universalism is reinforced by his concept of "the halo of cultural values." He emphasizes that physical differences among people are irrelevant. The rainbow of cultural values makes the world exciting. More than tolerance is required to accept these values. We must strive to preserve difference in the midst of the universal. Tiémélé concluded a 1990 interview with me by asserting: "And finally, sometimes, one situates oneself at a level where one loses pride. Because one possesses one object more than another, one says that one is *above* the other, while the person in question is merely different from you" (Tiémélé 1990).

Throughout his poetry, Tiémélé examines questions of culture, race, and difference. He reaffirms his own blackness, while placing cultural differences in perspective. He longs for Africa, but does not leave Paris. He criticizes politicians, scientists, and soldiers, but admits his own guilt in passively accepting their deeds. He denounces, but takes responsibility for, the suffering that he decries. Tiémélé borrows from négritude a concern for African culture and the "battle" of the universal. He accepts what he terms the "content" of négritude, but not its "container," or form. The poet assimilates fully into the Parisian world of letters, but never abandons his longing for Africa and his guilt over its suffering.

In terms of an economic market, Tiémélé's poetry reflects the problems of many African writers in France. He publishes with French houses, but shares the costs of the editions. His poems have been placed on the academic roster for Ivoirian schools, but the books never arrive. He writes from Paris, for Africa, but fears that his voice is a "scream in the desert." What is the true audience for Tiémélé's universalistic message? On the one hand, his dilemma resembles that of the Ivoirian writers at home in search of publishers in Africa. On the other hand, he lives and works in Europe with access to French publishers. His message is tailored to a multifaceted Euro-African audience. The responses are essentially positive but troublesome enough to raise serious questions about the future of universalism as a literary strategy.

Edouard Maunick: Passion for Universalism

Born on September 23, 1931, in Port-Louis, Mauritius, Edouard Maunick is now considered one of the leading poets of his country and enjoys an international reputation. In addition to writing poetry, Maunick has had a distinguished career in the field of cultural affairs. At the age of twenty-seven, he became head librarian for the municipality of Port-Louis. At that time, he had already received several literary prizes for his poetry. After working at the library briefly, he moved to France, where he eventually went to work as a radio broadcaster and journalist. He has published several books with Présence Africaine, Éditions Silex, Saint-Germain-des-Prés, Publisud Paris, and L'Harmattan, among other publishers. His best-known collections of poetry include *Ces oiseaux du sang* (1954), *Mascaret ou le Livre de la mer et de la mort* (1966), *Fusillez-moi* (1970), *Ensoleillé vif* (1976), *Saut dans l'arc-en-ciel* (1987), and *Mandéla, mort et vif* (1987).

After working as a journalist in France, Maunick became director of Radio-Caraïbes Internationale, in Saint Lucia, then he returned to France to work for the Agence de Coopération Culturelle et Technique (ACCT). He has also been a visiting professor at the University of California, Irvine, and has lectured throughout the world on African, Mauritian, and Caribbean literature. When I interviewed Maunick in 1989, he was working as a cultural director at UNESCO, where he was in charge of African literary acquisitions and projects. His job involved collecting a cross section of African literary works in various languages and overseeing their translation into French and English for French, Belgian, British, and Canadian publishers. He was also in charge of the UNESCO Arts Traveling Exhibition (Rowell 1989:491). He assumed a position as head journalist and editor at *Jeune Afrique* magazine before being named Mauritian ambassador to South Africa.

In his poetry, Maunick resuscitates the memory of what he calls "the Source" in the district of Flacq, at Port-Louis. He spent his childhood there and describes the universe of sight and sound that surrounded him. Maunick describes his childhood experiences: "The world, the universe, began with my friends there. At night, we met and walked around together. We looked at the sky and counted the stars of the tropics—the southern cross, Antares, the scorpion. We read the sky first, then, afterwards, we came back to earth. You know, we were thirteen, fourteen, and fifteen years old. . . . all of us had reinvented the world" (Maunick 1989b).

This childhood memory flavors Maunick's writings on the variety and beauty of his country. He also emphasizes the cultural and linguistic mixtures of Mauritius. Maunick states: "I am profoundly creole. My language is creole. That is to say, a certain French, which is a language of proverbs, a way of writing, a way of expressing images. Creole has its proverbs that I use to be universal" (Maunick 1989b). A commitment to creolization allows Maunick to link his diasporic attachment to Africa with Mauritius, the Caribbean, Europe, and the United States. Maunick uses creolization as a driving force for the political commitment of his poetry. He explains: "And because I am mixed [*un métis*], I have occidental blood. I have African blood. I have Asian blood in me. The drops of black blood that flow in my veins are poisoned when they imprison Mandela, and I am obliged to cry out, not for myself but for him. . . . I also cry out because, through Mandela, millions of people are condemned to silence" (Maunick 1989b).

Universalism, as expressed by Maunick, begins with a sense of personal identity that is rooted in one's own country of origin, language, and experiences. Building on this sense of identity, which is already a mixture or creolization, he establishes a link to the suffering of others around the world. His 1987 poem *Mandéla, mort et vif* (Mandela, dead and alive) emphasizes the universal chords touched by Mandela's imprisonment. In the context of world history, if Mandela suffers, those who imprison him, those who watch him, and those who support him are also victims of the same injustice. Maunick explains that he is the most revolted by injustices that touch a large number of people, for he identifies with everyone who suffers or is oppressed. He explains: "Thus, there are in me the roots of a man in revolt, the branches of revolt, the trunk of revolt, the leaves of revolt. I am a tree that grows, that is, that destroys a little bit of space on the earth where it exists, with its roots, that makes a hole in the air when it takes its place in the sky. Because I have the right to a place, and each human being has the right to be a tree—the tree that he is—and to grow in everyday life" (Maunick 1989b).

Each individual is a tree that takes up space in this universe by displacing natural forces and others. Poets have at their disposition the use of words, which transcend this universal space and can be used to rectify injustices. Ideologies and philosophies are also like trees that take up space in a universe of discourse. Rather than defend these ideologies, Maunick argues that there can be a "natural cohabitation" among people and philosophies. As with Tiémélé, Maunick struggles with the balance that can be achieved among race, culture, and identity. He is dissatisfied with simplistic solutions to conflicts resulting from cultural differences. In his view, the poet creates a bridge across cultures by reflecting first on personal identity and nation, and then on the world. This movement from personal to global identity is what Maunick calls "the passion for the universal." A writer, however, must display more than this passion. The writer's work is based on dedication, inspiration, and talent.

When I asked Maunick about his current goals as a writer, he responded:

> I do not have any current goals. My objective was born the day that I decided to fully embrace my career as a writer. The term "career as a writer" might appear a bit pretentious, but when I discovered one day that I had talent to write, it was necessary, in recognizing that gift of nature—that gift that nature gave me—that I make a decision. And it is there that was born the objective of my career as a writer. . . . I am, essentially, a poet and, for me, the work of a poet is not to sing about little girls or young women, beautiful flowers and nature. One may do that, but in the interior of a project the objective of a poet is very simple. It is to always question myself and to arrive at an understanding of the heart of my identity. (Maunick 1989b)

For Maunick, identity is not merely personal. It is tied to memory, family, country, and the part played by the individual in a universal panorama. Maunick's collection, entitled *Saut dans l'arc-en-ciel* (Leap into the rainbow) (1985), is divided into thirty-one separate poems. In *Saut,* poem 17 links the roots of Maunick's universal tree to the world (Maunick 1989b).

. . . Amsterdam Amirantes
  San Francisco la nuit
Valparaiso le jour
  mais l'arbre est foudroyé
mon banian amiral
  et mes frères sont partis
sans me laisser d'adresse
  un cyclone me hante
et la voix de mon père
  me distrait de la mer
(Maunick 1985:47)

[. . . Admirable Amsterdam
  San Francisco at night
Valparaiso by day
  but the tree is crushed
my miraculous banyan
  and my brothers have left
without leaving me an address
  a cyclone haunts me
and the voice of my father
  diverts me from the sea]

In this poem, Maunick addresses the appeal of the exciting cities of the world—Amsterdam, San Francisco, Valparaiso. He is attracted to travel and to the call of the universal, but he is summoned back to his origins—the banyan tree—by the voice of his father. As with the poetry of négritude, once again, the father's voice represents the constraints of tradition. Maunick demonstrates the complex tension between longing for his native island and the desire to belong to a wider world. A cyclone of change and movement haunts him; those of his generation—his brothers—have all left to live abroad. The author is caught in myriad reflections about his Mauritian past and his diasporan future. As he yearns to travel on the sea, his father's voice calls him to return to an irretrievably lost past.

Saut dans l'arc-en-ciel forces the reader to jump into a rainbow of cultural and natural images. The poems in this collection are poignant telegraphic flashes of journeys back and forth between the author's island home and the world at large. Maunick uses a creolized style in which multiple meanings invested in French words and image-analogies reflect the sonority and feelings of his native island and its speech. Thus, it is often difficult to uncover the manifold layers of meaning in Maunick's very rich and compact texts. Nevertheless, the polarities of longing and belonging recur throughout the poems, as does a constant juxtaposition between stability and wandering (*errance*), self and other, and humans and nature. Translation of Maunick's poetry into English does it violence because of the panoply of meanings that he taps and the ways in which he combines concrete and abstract imagery.

Poems 6, 7, and 8 of *Saut* (Maunick 1985:36–38) resurrect Maunick's childhood memories of Port-Louis. He remembers the vistas, gardens, and sea, along with the comfort of friends and the pain of departure. Port-Louis is the symbol of youth, home, and stability and is simultaneously the sign of loss. With his childhood friends, Maunick dreamed of reinventing the world. In adulthood, his companions have all gone their separate ways, leaving only the traces of this childhood longing. In poem 7, he writes:

> . . . Port-Louis ma délirante
>   ce délit du partir
> alors que je t'aimais
>   trottoir après trottoir
> qu'avec mes amis d'or
>   nous frappions à ton ciel
> pour une mâne secrète
>   sur nos vies secondaires
> réinventions le monde
>   pour être enfin nous-mêmes
>   (Maunick 1985:37)

[... Port-Louis my rapture
this delirium of leaving
while I loved you
sidewalk after sidewalk
that with my golden friends
we knocked on your sky
for a shadowy secret
on our secondary lives
let us reinvent the world
to at last be ourselves]

Maunick (1989b) explains that personal and national identity are not synonymous. He strives to tap into a "natal identity," which he describes as an identification with one's place of birth—one's origins. Maunick (1989b) elaborates: "Once one has discovered one's personal identity—one's native natal identity—then, if you will, a national identity and a planetary identity follow. That is my writing project. That is my poetic project."

Moving from personal and natal identity to the universal chord of identification with the world involves a leap of faith and a certain disobedience. Although loyalty to natal origins influences links to a universal, or planetary, identity, the universal engulfs individual differences. Nostalgia highlights the tension between personal identity and blending with the universal. Memories echo the paternal voice of conscience that ties the poet to his island roots. In poem 29 of *Saut,* Maunick reflects on these island roots and the dangers of drifting away from them.

... j'ai vécu avant moi
dans des îles sans nom
quelque part sur la mer
avant qu'elles se sabordent
en pleine terre de toi
j'ai suivi leur dérive
en chantant des soleils
sonores et bleus d'iris
mémoire mon beau jardin
ma désobéissance
(Maunick 1985:59)

[... I have, myself, lived before
in the islands without name
somewhere on the sea
before they flooded
fully onto your land

I survived their drifting
in singing of sonorous suns
and iris blues
memory my beautiful garden
my disobedience]

Although Maunick's interview emphasizes that being a poet should not be limited to writing about "beautiful flowers and nature," he constantly draws upon natural images of the beauty of Mauritius to link personal identity with its universal stream. This link emerges, not only through the metaphors, figures, and images that Maunick employs, but also in his stylistic manipulation of French with a creolized resonance. In this regard, one of Maunick's most challenging short pieces is poem 14 in *Saut* (Maunick 1985:44). Here he introduces the perplexing image-analogy of the *paille-en-queue*, a tropical aquatic bird with a tail that looks like straw.[6] This poem contains Maunick's characteristically layered flashes of images and reduplicated metaphors, invoking his nostalgia and longing for natal identity. Maunick compares the shape of the straw-tailed bird with the deep flowing rivers and waterfalls of Mauritius. But the straw-tail also refers to the errant immigrant whose journeys have led him away from his native land

... Gorges de la Rivière Noire
retour à mes cascades
mes lumières d'origine
errance d'écume en vert
à essouffler le temps
tant est folle la durée
du vol d'un seul oiseau
son nom imite l'image
fougère de tout son corps
il s'appelle paille-en-queue
(Maunick 1985:44)

[... Mouths of the Black River
return to my cascades
my sparks of origin
tracings of green foam
have blow away time
so wild is the length
of the flight of a single bird
its name imitates
the ferny image of its whole body
it's called *paille-en-queue* (straw tail)]

This poem resembles Tiémélé's "L'Âme des feuilles." In both poems the bird flying toward other horizons represents the writer in exile. In contrast to Tiémélé's poem, which is written from the vantage point of Europe, from where the bird migrates as winter approaches, Maunick's poem is vividly tropical. The bird's flight path parallels the river, and the images of both are blended together. Time (*la durée*) circumscribes the straw-tailed bird's flight and creates the sense of distance between the bird and its native land. The bird's error in flying too far away for too long is epitomized by its name, an image that suggests that its ferny tail interferes with long journeys. While the fernlike river pours into the sea and rejoins the universal, the straw-tailed bird is adapted to its homeland and will always appear distinctive and odd, no matter where it flies.

Maunick expresses his political engagement and sense of revolution ("the tree of revolt") most vividly in *Mandéla, mort et vif* (1987). The long poem, written five years before Mandela's release from Robben Island, portrays him as a world leader and denounces his imprisonment. Maunick regards Mandela as a signifier for all human suffering. Although, in Maunick's poem, Mandela is doomed to die brutally at the hands of his oppressors, he is destined to live in memory as a hero. When Maunick wrote his poem, he could not have foreseen the dramatic political changes in South Africa leading to Nelson Mandela's presidency in 1994. These events are less relevant to the poem than Mandela's years of imprisonment and oppressive suffering in a political system that Maunick abhors. Maunick (1987:25) speaks of the urgency of his mission at an hour of turbulence (*à cette heure bourrasque*). He asserts that the poet can create and save through words: "seule la Parole crée / seule la Parole sauve" (Maunick 1987:30). This notion coincides with Maunick's statement in his 1989 interview: "Thus, all true poetry is for me an engaged poetry." In *Mandéla, mort et vif*, engaged poetry transmutes into enraged poetry.

The narrative trajectory of the poem is circular, beginning and ending with Mandela's imprisonment on Robben Island. Divided into nine books, or stanzas, the poem opens with an African-style praise song, in which Maunick cries out his hero's name and universalizes the spirit of Mandela. It closes by inviting the reader to traverse a mirror of turmoil and touch Mandela's soul. The poet compares Mandela to the Malian hero Soundjata, to Nat Turner, Gandhi, Martin Luther King, and Lumumba. He invokes Mandela's name in the context of atrocities in Hiroshima, Latin America, and Europe. In stanza 2, he writes:

> . . . Mandela je te nomme
> Mandela Soundjata
> Mandela Nat Turner
> Mandela Anne Zinga
> Mandela Mackandal

Mandela Golgotha
Mandela Mahatma
Mandela L'Ouverture
Mandela Malcolm X
Nelson Chaka Chaka
Mandela Hammarskjöld
Mandela Luther King
Mandela Feraoun
Mandela Amilcar
Mandela Treblinka
Mandela Palestine
Mandela Luthuli
Mandela Lumumba
Mandela Varsovie
Mandela Santiago
Nelson Hiroshima
Mandela Azania
Mandela et j'en passe . . .
(Maunick 1987:26)

[. . . Mandela I dub you
Mandela Soundjata
Mandela Nat Turner
Mandela Anne Zinga
Mandela Mackandal
Mandela Golgotha
Mandela Mahatma
Mandela L'Ouverture
Mandela Malcolm X
Nelson Chaka Chaka
Mandela Hammarskjöld
Mandela Luther King
Mandela Feraoun
Mandela Amilcar
Mandela Treblinka
Mandela Palestine
Mandela Luthuli
Mandela Lumumba
Mandela Varsovie
Mandela Santiago
Nelson Hiroshima
Mandela Azania
Mandela and so forth . . .]

This evocation reminds the reader of both the history of the events in question and the great figures marshaled by the poets of the négritude movement. Mandela is dubbed a "twentieth-century Parsifal," a Round Table knight in quest of the Holy Grail, an "illusory Lancelot," imprisoned on an island.

Familiar island imagery, central to Maunick's writings about identity, is now pressed into the service of politics. The island is no longer a tranquil abode but is, instead, a place where the "blight of solitude" (*la nielle de solitude*) spreads. In stanza 3, storms of discontent and violence loom offshore, along with the specter of Mandela's own death.

> Robben la Carcérale
> où grisonne Galaad
> où l'aube n'est plus qu'orage
> la main noire plus que poing
> Détournement hideux
> d'un coeur en poudrière.
> (Maunick 1987:27)

> [Robben the Prison
> Where Galahad turns gray
> where dawn is never more than a storm
> the black hand more than a fist
> hideous Corruption
> of a heart in a tinder box.]

In this poem, memories of childhood on a tranquil island now become the scars of torture produced by the racism and massacres of Soweto. Maunick's approach to Soweto differs from that of Dakeyo in his poem *Soweto: Soleils fusillés* (1977).[7] Dakeyo describes the conditions of "sordid townships" shrouded in death, while Maunick envisages these townships as part of the storm threatening the imprisoned solitude of the island. Economic oppression is alluded to by "the reading of the surf / where salt glistens like diamonds" (Maunick 1987:29), and by a "carnivorous hatred / with a diamond-studded heart" (Maunick 1987: 31).

Essential to Maunick's perspective on universalism, the image of the tree appears in homologation with Mandela—the strong tree (Maunick 1987:28). Birds in the trees represent both freedom and an ominous threat. The birds of the third millennium (*les oiseaux du troisième millénaire*) have lost their song but forecast better times to come (Maunick 1987:28), while in stanza 8 an ominous bird (*un oiseau pire augure*) invents tricks to wake us from a tranquil sleep and warns of atrocities to come.

. . . un oiseau pire augure
invente des manèges
sur la place des sommeils
et nous dormons tranquilles
bercés par le flon flon
du malheur bien masqué
le Cap c'est tellement loin
notre Bonne Espérance
elle-même si fragile
Un oiseau pire augure
nous plonge avec son vol
au coeur de nos miroirs
(Maunick 1987:32)

[. . . a bird the worst omen
invents tricks
in the place of sleepers
and we all sleep tranquilly
rocked by the refrain
of well-masked misfortune
the Cape is so far away
our Good Hope
itself so fragile
A bird the worst omen
casts us with its flight
into the heart of mirrors]

At the end of stanzas 4 and 5, and in line 11 of stanza 9, Maunick plays upon the term "black South Africa" (*au noir sud de l'Afrique*), which is hyphenated as *au noir-sud de l'Afrique* in stanza 9. Several meanings are possible simultaneously: "in black South Africa," "in the shadows of South Africa," "in the darkest South Africa," and "for the black man of South Africa." This wordplay highlights the tragic political situation and reinforces Mandela's status as the signifier for suffering.

On te dit d'oublier
la vieille cargaison
d'écrire dans la soie vive
d'une époque planétaire
tandis que la poussière
s'épaissit en linceul
à chaque corps cisaillé
au noir sud de l'Afrique . . .
(Maunick 1987:28)

[They say to forget
the old cargo
to write in living silk
of a planetary epoch
while the dust
grows heavy on the shroud
of each scissored body
of black south Africa . . .]

Si demain n'appartient
qu'aux enfants de colère
alors piétine les mots
foulaison de vin fou
et que la mort titube
au noir sud de l'Afrique . . .
(Maunick 1987:29)

[If tomorrow belongs only
to the children of anger
thus tramps on words
the pressing of mad wine
and that death staggers
in black south Africa . . .]

Death stalks black South Africa like a shadow. The specter of revolution and the arm of repression are both represented in the phrase "*au noir sud de l'Afrique.*" In stanza 9, the death of the hero is imminent as the storm approaches the "man-totem," threatening to cut him down in his tracks. The man and the nation are inextricably linked when "*noir*" is interpreted as both an adjective meaning "black," and a noun, translated as "the black man." This label refers to Mandela himself and to all black South Africans.[8]

Dehors l'orage rampe
descend jusqu'aux racines
pour abattre l'Homme-totem
au noir-sud de l'Afrique
(Maunick 1987:33)

[Outside the storm brews
descends to the roots
to cut down the Man-totem
of black South Africa]

The metaphors of suffering and blackness are reinforced by Maunick's recurrent references to the power of words in stanzas 1, 2, and 6, and in his image of the mirror. The poet invites the reader to cross the mirror, separating personal suffering (one's own and Mandela's) from social, economic, and political oppression. He invites the reader to forget childhood misfortunes and sores (*nos délicieux bobos*) and to consider the exploitation of millions of people as epitomized by the fate of a single man.

In conclusion, the poet introduces an image drawn from nature—that of blighted wheat. Solitude and imprisonment are the blights and emblems of Mandela's condition in black South Africa. Maunick calls upon the reader to traverse the mirrors to touch Nelson Mandela and help him to realize the dreams of all of those who have suffered.

Traversons les miroirs
pour le toucher du doigt
là où s'élargit
la nielle de solitude
de ce blé ensilé
en lieu de forclusion
pour que jamais ne soit
panifiée la promesse
d'un peuple aux reins guéris
de cambrures sacrilèges
Traversons les miroirs
jusqu'à toucher Nelson . . .
(Maunick 1987:33)

[Let us traverse the mirrors
to touch his finger
there where this blight
of solitude spreads
from this wheat in silo
in place of foreclosure
that never will the promise
be turned into bread
of a people with backs healed
of sacrilegious curvings
Let us traverse the mirrors
to touch Nelson . . .]

Maunick is a master of metaphor, innuendo, and multiple codes. Marie-Christine Rochmann (1989:315) refers to his manipulation of analogy as "cratylism," based on Plato's characterization of Cratylis, the figure who mediates between words and things. Maunick piles image upon image, creating an aesthetic overcoding in which redundancy, repetition, and rewoven metaphors generate aural and visual effects.[9] Metaphors of nature are blended with descriptions of social and industrial processes. These images appear as disjointed flashes, evocations of conditions and emotions. This "piling up" process gives Maunick's poetry its rich, creolized character. He bends French to his will, playing on different grammatical forms—nouns for adjectives, verbs for nouns—creating an active mélange of meanings, imagery, and sound. Unlike the poets of protest of the antinégritude movement, Maunick shies away from direct description of rebellion in favor of the image-flash in an infinite progression of mirrorlike moves that lead the reader from personal identification to social commentary. This image-flash technique juxtaposes ephemeral images with stable icons around which a narrative of universalism is developed.

Hence, Mandela's plight is not confined to black South Africa (*au noir sud de l'Afrique*). Instead, Mandela represents the human condition and the universals of struggle, suffering, and death. Maunick's point of departure is the passion for the universal, which involves both a creolized self-identification and an extension beyond the self to the poetics of politics. Rather than viewing the affirmation of black identity as a poetic point of departure, Maunick begins with a multifaceted identity that looks toward, and back to, Africa. He reaffirms the value of universalism as a poetic strategy and ideology.

Bolya Baenga: Africa Japanese-style

Born in Kinshasa in 1957, Bolya Baenga is a novelist, essayist, political commentator, and journalist. His first novel, *Cannibale* (1986), published by Pierre-Marcel Favre, in Lausanne, Switzerland, won the Grand Prix Littéraire de l'Afrique Noire. In 1991, Bolya published a collection of essays, entitled *L'Afrique en kimono: Repenser le développement* (1991a), on modernization and the Japanese example for Africa, with Éditions Nouvelles du Sud, which he followed by a sequel, *L'Afrique à la Japonaise: Et si l'Afrique était mal mariée,* published by Éditions Nouvelles du Sud in 1994. Bolya has collaborated actively with Paul Dakeyo in his editorial work for Éditions Silex and Éditions Nouvelles du Sud. (See fig. 21.) Since his two critical essays on African modernization, Bolya has returned to a novel project on African matriarchy. He is a self-confident, opinionated, and assertive cultural spokesperson. In the context of universalism, Bolya focuses on problems of modernization and development as worldwide challenges. He argues that the cultural integrity of non-Western nations can be maintained while these countries play a significant role in international economic competition. For

Fig. 21. Bolya Baenga (right) with Paul Dakeyo, Paris, October 1, 1991. Photograph by Bennetta Jules-Rosette.

this reason, he is fascinated by the early Madagascan nationalism of Mpitandrina Ravelojoana (1879–1956), the Meiji revolution in Japan (1868–1912), and the political economy of African nations such as Zaire and Tanzania. Bolya also uses the novel for purposes of political commentary. *Cannibale* recounts a fable about neocolonial cruelty, torture, and corruption, seen through the eyes of the twins Azanga and Aminata, who avenge their mother's murder at the hands of military forces. In *L'Afrique en kimono* (1991a), published by Éditions Nouvelles du Sud, Bolya attacks what he terms Japan's role as a "narcissistic wound" in the side of the West. He argues that the West will never understand or accept the Japanese success story because it overturns the colonial model in which Western cultural imperialism and economic development must go hand-in-hand. According to Bolya, universalism involves conceding that each culture can operate along its own parameters while succeeding in the world economy.

> It is necessary to insist on the fact that Japan, in outclassing all of the European countries, inventors of modernity, has become more Western than the West. And in a certain way, it has even become the new repository of Western industrial civilization. It is not "the logic of war," but the war of logic. Consequently, the English, the Portuguese, our friends the Belgians . . . must become even more Western if they want—one day—to equal the fantastic performance of Japan.

> If not, we must concede—in the name of the Universal—that these European countries must become more Japanese [*se japoniser*] and, consequently, abandon at the gates of the twenty-first century their Western identity that prohibits and creates an obstacle to their entrance to the third millennium. (Bolya 1991a:29)

For Bolya, the concept of the universal is paradoxical. On the one hand, he argues that universal culture has been used as an synonym for Western culture. On the other hand, he contends that this reasoning is illogical and incorrect. If followed to its conclusion, it suggests that any economically successful nation should impose its culture worldwide. Bolya criticizes cultural imperialism and promotes the separation of culture and political economy. He refers to this separation as "integral universalism." According to Bolya (1991:29): "What is important from now on is the intransigent defense of integral universalism. All the rest consists only of African-style tribal wars." Integral universalism allows each culture to develop according to its own internal dynamics. At the same time, every society and culture can borrow elements from other cultures and reject ideas and values that are in conflict with its own. This process of selection strengthens the culture of origin and fosters continued economic development in a global context. Hence, Bolya argues that a global discourse and set of strategies are necessary for a nation to be competitive in the modern world. Integral universalism incorporates diverse cultures in a global political and economic dialogue.

Bolya also conceives of this process with regard to his own identity. In a 1991 interview, Bolya states: "How can I, Bolya—born in Kinshasa in 1957—adhere at the same time to a totally Western and a totally African reasoning? And while remaining African, if I want to play at being occidental, and even be a Westerner. . . . I am occasionally very Western in any case . . . not occasionally, often!" (Bolya 1991a). Bolya directly connects the idea of integral universalism to his identity as an African writer in France. He demonstrates how he is able to communicate in Western and African styles and to assume different identities, depending upon the context. He contends that entire nation-states can also engage in this type of selective role-playing.

Mpitandrina Ravelojaona (1879–1956) was a Protestant pastor and statesman in Madagascar. Inspired by Ravelojaona's discovery of the Meiji revolution, Bolya devotes the latter portion of *L'Afrique en kimono* to the reproduction and criticism of Ravelojaona's little-known writings. He explains that the Madagascan politician and critic was more fascinated by the cultural than the political and economic model of Japan after the Meiji revolution (Bolya 1991a:22). Ravelojaona argued for the preservation of a "Madagascan personality" and sense of identity, while embarking on radical economic changes. Bolya speculates about what might have happened across the African continent had this model been adopted during the postcolonial era. The model would necessitate abandoning economic handouts, cumbersome development schemes, and outmoded forms of education and scholarly disinformation. Bolya (15–16) distinguishes his approach from "anti-imperialism, Third-worldism, and identity contractions." Instead, he proposes "to celebrate the Universal" (Bolya 1991a:29). This celebration involves retaining the integrity of African cultures without the constraints of clanism, passive collectivism, and outmoded traditionalism. Bolya (40) decries what he terms "the dogmatism of tradition and the Senghorian regression of négritude." He proposes to replace these values and philosophies by a "new African identity." According to Bolya (40): "It is necessary to forge a new African identity for the twenty-first century and a project that is compatible with the incontestable constraints of modernity, and a dream that integrates the formidable possibilities of a future society of production and information."

Although Bolya is not specific about the precise economic and political strategies to be adopted for the African society of the future, he is emphatic about the division between the colonial and postcolonial generations and their strategies. Taking a moralistic stance, Bolya (1991a:17) warns: "The danger that threatens us is complacency. If we concede in the style of 'the experts of the market' and of 'capitalist messianism'. . . then it will be done to us. And the years 2000 will be the worst years of our history and will be written with our blood. Our tears will submerge the entire continent. We will live the last days of all our hopes and dreams."

Rapid economic take-off and clever strategic planning that preserves cultural integrity and pride are the solutions that Bolya proposes for Africa's economic and political crisis. He remarks (Bolya 1991a:15): "Japan's take-off has been rapid while that of Europe has been slow. . . . If we follow the European model, that is the model that takes a long period, of the builders of cathedrals with Arian steeples, we will simply have time to bury millions who have died of AIDS, malnutrition, and tuberculosis. . . . It is urgent to fight myths, all myths, revolutionary or not."

Bolya's plea against complacency and his description of the urgency of the African crisis resemble both Tiémélé's message in "Le Chemin de la liberté" and Maunick's exhortation about universal justice in *Mandéla, mort et vif.* Although he has written a political essay, Bolya's style is poetic—rich in metaphors, assonance, and images. His message is also more provocative than it is conclusive. He warns readers about the disastrous outcomes of past political errors and suggests a pathway to a brighter future without explaining exactly how to achieve it. His clarion call is summarized in a poetic sentence written early in his essay: "Eternal and universal history that takes form in the night of time: that of the versatility of mankind" (Bolya 1991a:18).

In an interview with me on September 12, 1989, Bolya underscored his position about African philosophies in the postcolonial era. "It is necessary to have the courage to say that négritude was a very good thing on June 30, 1960, but that on July 1, it was false. Because the problems that arose the next day were completely different. . . . Independence is very useful as an ideological combat and a cultural reaffirmation of the 'black man,' but once this objective is attained, it is no longer valid" (Bolya 1989). Bolya's skepticism reflects his era. Too young to participate in the halting liberation struggle in his own country, he witnessed many of the promises of independence evaporate. Although he is more strident and direct in his political commentaries than are Tiémélé and Maunick, Bolya shares with them the dream that Africa's active and unique participation in world cultures will point to a way out of its current social and economic crisis.

Postcolonial Universalism's Promise

These three approaches to universalism emphasize the complexity of the concept in its manifestations as a dream, an ideal, and a set of strategies for contemporary African writers in France. The seeds of the universalism debate were planted by the early négritude writers and the conferences sponsored by Présence Africaine. The positions held by Césaire and Depestre concerning innovation in Afro-Antillian poetry had political and cultural repercussions. The three authors discussed in this chapter take vocal stances against négritude. Tiémélé accepts the content but not the container. Maunick begins from his creolized identity and works outward toward an identification with African and universal cultures. Bolya rejects négritude as passé in favor of a new adventure that idealizes Japan's mixture of cultural traditions and economic success. In terms of style of presentation, Maunick is the most experimental of the writers, demonstrating his bold engagement with creolized expression through deep metaphors and flashy images. Tiémélé's poetry has a Senghorian flair, combining the rhythms and images of an idyllic Africa with mordant social commentary and didactic messages. Bolya's poetic prose reinvigorates the political essay by blending exhortation with documentation, rhythm with repartee, and imagery with exposition.

A narrative of longing and belonging thematically links the writers of the négritude period to the contemporary apostles of the new universalism. Underlying postcolonial universalism is a sense of cultural loss and the urgent need to restore this lack by reaffirming personal identity and participation in a universal culture. Ultimately, the dilemma of universalism versus particularism is impossible to resolve. The concept of universalism is filtered like light through a prism and breaks up into many hues. The fundamental contradiction of universalism for both the early négritude writers and those of the contemporary period results from its status as both an ideal—or a dream—and a practical strategy. The writers invoke and manipulate the term "universalism" in order to achieve cultural acceptance. Their dedication to this ideal does not assure the acceptance of their approach by a literary audience or by cultural outsiders. In the three authors, we see a pattern of early publication with restricted Parisian publishing houses such as Éditions Silex and Éditions Nouvelles du Sud. Of the three authors, Maunick has the broadest international reputation. The other two authors have yet to achieve the international reputations that should be the strategic and logical byproduct of their cultural philosophies. This assertion does not imply that universalism is a strategic literary failure, for it was certainly part and parcel of négritude's literary success.[10] Instead, it is apparent that universalism entails many contradictions that both motivate and frustrate its prophets.

Beyond the discussion of literary strategies lies the larger dream of universalism. This dream is shared by writers associated with both Parisianism and the new universalism. In both cases, the writers reassert their dignity and legitimate presence in a global cultural environment, in particular the European literary milieu in which they live and work. They use and enrich French as their medium of communication. They publish with primarily, although not exclusively, Parisian literary houses, and they participate actively in French intellectual and cultural life. In this context, universalism (along with the universal elements of Parisianism) operates as a cultural code, reinforcing the writers' sense of belonging in a competitive and increasingly multicultural environment. Universalism may be flawed as a literary strategy. To the extent, however, that it is a viable cultural code, the African writers' dream of universalism has become a reality.

EIGHT

Identity Discourses: From Négritude to the New Universalism

> Once again, Négritude consists of neither racism nor vulgar contortions. It is, once again, the totality of values of the civilization of the black world.
>
> —Léopold Senghor, 1977

Almost everyone has something passionate to say about identity. Identity discourses are ways of speaking about one's perceived and desired location in the social world. They are complex and deceptive because they appear to be statements of fact and exhortations to act (Austin 1962:147–60; Larreya 1979:7–13), when they are, in fact, expressions of virtual states (e.g., "wanting-to-be" or "wanting-not-to-be"). Assertions such as "I am a good citizen" or "I am black and proud" are not so much reality claims as they are affirmations, or voicings of a wish. The statement "black is beautiful" expresses a similar wish for black to be beautiful in a social universe where this category is demeaned. These assertions are characteristic of virtual discourses. In his semiotic analysis of Paul Dakeyo's poetry, Yves Dakou (1988:41–42) points out that the poet's 1979 title *J'appartiens au grand jour* (I belong to the great day) is neither an assertion of fact nor a performative utterance, but instead the expression of an unfulfilled wish. Dakou (1988:41) refers to Dakeyo's title as a "transcendental revindication" in which the poet wishes not simply to be like everyone else, but to transcend the entire problem of marginality and belonging by announcing that there will be a new awakening of social equality.

An identity discourse is the enunciation of a cultural narrative. This link between identity discourse and narrative surfaces in Foucault's description of "universal discourse" (Foucault 1966:98–99).[1] According to Foucault, universal discourses rely on the unstated dimensions of social and historical knowledge and collective representations. Rooted in its historical epoch, a universal discourse builds upon two fundamental elements of communication—point of view (or modalities of communication) and content (Cervoni 1987:65–71). Modalities of discourse situate speakers with respect to what is being said. Identity discourses, such as négritude, establish boundaries between their users and audiences by reaffirming the dignity of a group and denying outsiders access to certain ways of speaking.

Two factors are crucial in the relationship of identity discourses to cultural narratives: (1) that the discourse promotes a collective representation of the group in question, and (2) that the discourse furthers the interests of the group. The first factor, collective representation, involves the positive redefinition of a marginal or oppressed group. The second point brings us into the realm of performance by questioning whether identity claims have social and political relevance and force. As already seen, however, identity discourses are affirmations of virtual states and ideals; they are not exhortations to act.[2] A group may abandon an identity discourse when it fails to bring about the desired social and political outcomes. The discourse also comes under fire when its meaning shifts due to historical or political circumstances. This shift takes place when a rupture between the signifier (surface content) and the signified (point of reference) occurs. Négritude discourse, for example, is challenged when the existence of its fundamental signifier (essential blackness) is questioned. In the case of négritude, erasure of the signifier coincides with a shift in collective representations. The claims of négritude as an identity discourse seem outmoded today because the relationship between the signifier and the signified has been ruptured by competing discourses, and the field of historical representation has changed.[3] This rupture results in a new space for what Clifford Geertz (1973:219) has termed ideological discourse that results from "an inability, for lack of usable models, to comprehend the universe of civic rights and responsibilities in which one finds oneself located." Some identity discourses situate this social and political universe by recourse to essentialism.

It is now in vogue to disparage essentialist discourses that reduce identity to biological or psychological traits, to the unconditional interests of a particular group, or to narrow forms of cultural nationalism. Instead, particular identities have given way to universal identifications that laud multiculturalism and diversity as their polyphonic expressions (JanMohamed and Lloyd 1987:5–12). In this period of diversity, however, assertions of particular cultural identities and debates about their boundaries have not disappeared. If anything, they have become more entrenched and polarized. For Franco-African writers, the displacement of the signifiers of essential blackness and black civilization associated with the négritude movement has resulted in new trends, three of which I have isolated as important—revolutionary writing, Parisianism, and universalism. These three trends may be analyzed not only as literary genres but also with respect to the identity discourses that they promote.

Virtual Discourses and African Writing

Identity discourses emerge as conversations among concrete social actors who respond to specific historical situations. To understand négritude as a virtual identity discourse, it is important to return to the initial dialogues. In chapters 1 and 2, I described the historical circumstances surrounding the birth of négritude and the Présence Africaine movement. Aimé Césaire (1967) summed up these dialogues when he affirmed: "We must not forget that négritude was first of all a riposte, and that the word nègre was thrown at us as an insult which we took up as the cloak [*parure*] of our identity. . . . I remember that Senghor and I were in ecstasy over a sentence by Gide, who, in citing a phrase by Hegel, pointed out that there is no antithesis between the particular and the universal, that you need to move toward the universal by deepening the particular."[4] Césaire, thus, defined négritude as an affirmative discourse that provides a wedge of entry for black people into the panoply of world civilization. Lilyan Kesteloot extracted a similar observation from Léopold Senghor:

> How did Aimé Césaire and I launch the word "negritude" in the years 1933–35? Together with a few other black students, we were at the time in the depths of despair. The horizon was closed. There was no reform in the offing, and the colonizers were legitimizing our political and economic dependence by the *tabula rasa* theory. . . . To institute a worthwhile revolution, *our* revolution, we first had to get rid of our borrowed clothing—the clothing of assimilation—and to assert our essential being, namely our negritude. . . . To be really ourselves, we had to embody Negro African culture in twentieth-century realities. To enable our negritude to be, instead of a museum piece, the instrument of liberation, it was necessary to cleanse it of its dross and to include in it the united movement of the contemporary world. (Kesteloot 1974:102–3)

It is not clear whether Senghor is referring to Pan-Africanism, decolonization, or some other form of universalism as "the united movement of the contemporary world." Both Césaire and Senghor develop négritude as an identity discourse that renews the pride of a marginalized group. Yet, Césaire's definition of négritude remains fluid, while Senghor insists on viewing négritude as the totality of black Africa's cultural values. This definition, along with Senghor's use of the anthropology of the 1930s and 1940s to support his cause, has led to the interpretation of his version of négritude as an essentialist discourse.

To counter this image, V. Y. Mudimbe (1988:94) has described Senghor's socialism as the ultimate political goal of his philosophy of négritude.[5] According to Mudimbe, Senghor's claim that economic resourcefulness was the solution to Africa's social and political problems exonerates him from négritude's essentialism. But Senghor's socialism developed considerably later than his definition of négritude and had less cultural impact as African identity discourse.

Senghor's négritude was a profoundly antithetical discourse. It must not be forgotten that he published Sartre's "Orphée noir" as the preface to his anthology of African and Madagascan poetry (Sartre 1948:ix–xliv). Sartre's conception of négritude as the antithesis to racial oppression was completely in line with Senghor's notion of négritude as a reaffirmation of black pride in a colonized context. Using the works of Frobenius as a point of departure in spite of slight disagreements with him, Senghor conceived of négritude in juxtaposition to the cultural essences of European civilizations (e.g., *francité* and *germanité*).[6] Examining négritude as an identity discourse leads to the disrobing of Senghor's fundamental wish for a totalization of black experiences and civilization (Diawara 1990:82–86). Treating the virtual reality of négritude as an assertion requires proof of these universal essences.

Drawing on anthropology, archaeology, and Jungian psychoanalysis, Senghor outlined the fundamental features of négritude and later of africanité—a combination of négritude and arabité—as a blend of mystical and magical cultures, spirituality, intuitiveness, rhythm, and sonority. In his presentation for the 1973 conference on African literature in Yaoundé, Senghor stated:

> I have spoken about thoughtful [literary] criticism, but first of all, it must be temperament to temperament, heart to heart: soul [*âme*], I say *soul,* as do our negro-American brothers.
>
> For ideas do not exist apart from sentiments. There are sentiments born of images and ideas born of sentiments. There are idea-sentiments, which are expressed by forms, colors, and movements: that is to say, symbolic and rhythmic. In the African spirit [*Nigritie*], every work of art, whether it is a novel, a riddle, or a caricature, is always a rhythmic image. (Senghor 1977a:514)

Permeating Senghor's notion of idea-sentiments are two philosophical strands—German idealism and the essentialist arguments of Lévy-Bruhl (1923) concerning primitive mentality. If Senghor could prove that blacks and whites, Africans and Europeans think differently, but in equally creative ways, the battle for black dignity and legitimacy would be won. But Senghor's points were obscured by the nationalism following African independence and by black authors who wanted to assert the cultural and cognitive autonomy of their subgroups through national and regional literatures. Thus, the fundamental signifiers of négritude leading to totalization of the black experience were challenged. In négritude, which is a colonial discourse of confrontation between Africa and Europe, the subject (black civilization or the black "man") and the antisubject (European civilization or the white "man") are conjoined in a constant tension. In the counterdiscourse following négritude, subject and antisubject are torn asunder to create a new balance of power. The cultural narrative shifts from one of belonging to Western civilization to the assertion of unconditional autonomy and belonging to the black world. The notion of unconditional autonomy requires further qualification. The individual's autonomous action is limited by identification with the cultural goals and symbols of a group, or, in Senghor's terms, with the totality of black civilization.[7]

Senghor's challenge to assimilation was to create a presence of difference within a dominant culture without turning his back on Europe. The subtleties of this type of universalism are lost on the critics of négritude. Thus, in their critique of négritude from the perspective of postcolonial writing, Ashcroft, Griffiths, and Tiffin (1989:124) emphasize "the essential flaw of Négritudinist thought, which is that its structure is derivative and replicatory, asserting not its difference, as it would claim, but rather its dependence on the categories and features of the colonizing culture." Of course, négritude may be considered to consist of a broad spectrum of writing, much of which was initially published by Présence Africaine, extending from Cheikh Anta Diop's (1954) inspired documentation of Afrocentrism to Jacques Rabemananjara's critique of négritude's universalism (Rabemananjara 1957:12).[8] A final caveat must be added concerning the nature and efficacy of virtual identity discourses such as négritude. The virtuality of a discourse does not preclude the goals that its proponents champion from being translated into social action. Virtual discourses, however, are seldom actualized in the ideal ways and under the conditions that they are conceived.

Counterdiscourses: Antinégritude and Revolutionary Writing

Antinégritude negates the essentialist theses of négritude. Taking négritude as its point of departure, antinégritude acknowledges racism and oppression as the roots of a universal problem but denounces négritude as its solution. This antidiscourse contrasts with the complementary discourse of revolutionary writing and the contradictory discourses of non-négritude (Parisianism and universalism).[9] Stanislas Adotevi's 1969 speech at the symposium of the Pan-

African Festival in Algiers sounded the death knell of négritude. In his 1969 discourse, discussed in chapter 3, Adotevi argued that négritude is a "political mystification" that has failed to contribute to the development and the unity of the African continent (Adotevi 1969:46). The books by Adotevi (1972), Marcien Towa (1971), and René Depestre (1980) continued the antinégritude debate by challenging essentialism and questioning négritude's political efficacy. All of these works included the term "négritude" in their titles, bidding it farewell, or comparing it with servitude and complacency.[10] Adotevi's 1972 *Négritude et négrologues* elaborates on the criticisms that he introduced in Algiers. He refers to négritude and the anthropological discourses from which it developed as distorting. Depestre's *Bonjour et adieu à la négritude* (1980) dissects the ideological contradictions of négritude and concludes with a praise song to Antillian syncretism, hybridity, and poetic creativity. Marcien Towa's 1971 book, *Léopold Sédar Senghor: Négritude ou servitude?* fueled by the development of national literature in Cameroon, concludes that négritude entails a type of fatalistic servitude leading to powerlessness. Antinégritude's dependency on négritude as its subject matter had the paradoxical effect of incorporating antinégritude discourse into the négritude movement. Thus, contemporary critics of négritude often approach the topic via the discourse of antinégritude, conflating the two perspectives into a single discourse.

Adotevi (1972:45) argues that négritude projects a false and abstract homogeneity onto the black world. According to Adotevi's discourse, homogeneity and unity have never existed as foundations of black identity but result from the myths and fantasies of an antiscientific discourse that cannot be substantiated by sociology, anthropology, or geography. Accordingly, Senghor freely adapted an outmoded anthropology to support négritude's cause. Adotevi (1972:194) refers to this type of anthropology (*discours anthrographe*) as an ideological camouflage that supports colonialism. He characterizes early ethnology as "an intellectual refinement of the ideology of domination and exploitation of colonialism that reveals the narrow and narcissistic face of bourgeois history" (Adotevi 1972:204–5). The anthropological claims of négritude can be refuted by an economic and social history that demonstrates the oppression of black people. Adotevi (1972:54) refers to négritude's essentialist philosophy and the politics issuing from it as a troubling "intellectual misadventure."[11]

Depestre (1980:60–62) joins Adotevi by pointing out that the origins of négritude are rooted in a rereading of anthropological sources, such as Frobenius and Maurice Delafosse (1922), and in French classics from Rimbaud to Proust. According to Depestre, this eclectic bibliography does not necessarily lead to essentialism, although Depestre, like Adotevi, is fundamentally critical of négritude's recourse to anthropology. In addition, for Depestre, there are many négritudes, those of Senghor, Césaire, and the Haitian writer Jean Price-Mars, for example. The specific danger of négritude, according to Depestre (1980:85), lies in the "terrorist and scandalously disaggregating role played in our countries by racial dogma, under its negrophage forms in the most refined guises." This dogma has created, for Depestre, a false dichotomy between disparate African elements and the illusion of an apparently unified, organized, and dominant European civilization. To pulverize this distorted discourse, he introduces the cultural syncretism of the Caribbean, in which the mixtures growing out of a complex cultural history leave no culture pure, isolated, or dominant. Although Depestre (1980:51–52) concedes that the impetus of négritude was constructive, he concludes, like Adotevi, that in the final analysis, it consists of a "mystifying operation" that serves social class interests and has the oppressive consequences of "zombifying" its adherents. These results, asserts Depestre, are completely the opposite of what was intended by négritude's founders, but no matter. Négritude masks the realities of African and African diaspora cultures by ignoring their economic oppression. But in bidding farewell to négritude, Depestre does not propose an alternative philosophy.[12] He merely points to a way out of négritude's dilemmas. Depestre's identity discourse is one of cultural mixture and pluralism, but this pluralism is a reaction against, and adjunct to, négritude.

For different but related reasons, both Adotevi and Depestre denounce négritude as a dangerous moral, philosophical, and political strategy. They challenge the virtual claims of négritude discourse and argue for a new discourse that leads to a program of political action. Their program, however, remains ambiguous. Adotevi's approach is further limited by what Georges Balandier (1963:197–201) and Denis-Constant Martin (1992:52) refer to as the psychopathology of Africanist discourse in which social science masks political interests, modalities of discourse, and personal motivations beneath a seemingly benign academic rhetoric.

Marcien Towa (1971:5–6) begins his treatise on négritude and servitude with an analysis of the ambiguities and contradictions of the term. After a lengthy discussion of négritude in Senghor's prose and poems, Towa concludes that Senghor's reduction of black civilization to emotion, rhythm, and sentiment leaves few practical tools for dealing with the modern world and results in political servitude. Towa (1971:113) states: "The great orchestra of pan-human convergence, announced by President Senghor a few years ago in a conference on freedom and culture, would have as its leader Europe, the white man, while the Negro would be relegated to the rhythm section." As in the cases of Depestre and Adotevi, however, Towa, in his 1971 book, proposes no way out of this subaltern position. Ultimately, antinégritude discourse falls back upon négritude as its premise.

Fanon formulated négritude as an antithetical discourse and replaced it with an action plan. Going beyond the antidiscourses of Depestre, Adotevi, and Towa, Fanon established a counterdiscourse of domination in which the subject (oppressed people) overturned the position of the antisubject (colonizers). In semiotic terms, Fanon's approach resulted in a move from a virtual descriptive discourse to one of actualization.[13] Mudimbe (1988:92–93) argues that Fanon adapted and transformed Sartre's dialectic of négritude by moving from a thesis of oppression and alienation, to an antithesis of négritude as a reaffirmation of identity and power, and finally to a synthesis of political liberation, as well as personal freedom. Fanon's dialectic was a discourse about collective political action *and* personal identity. White masks would be thrown off, baring an essential cultural and personal resilience (Fanon 1967:38–40). This transformation, which Fanon conceived of as neither smooth nor pleasant, entailed violence and psychological upheaval.

In his presentation of "critical Fanonism," Henry Louis Gates (1991:468–70) invokes the Tunisian author Albert Memmi's interpretation of Fanon as a dislocated colonial subject in search of his own multicultural identity.[14] For the purposes of this discussion, I am not concerned with Fanon's biography or the faithfulness of his personal and political activities to the virtualities of his discourse. Instead, I have chosen to position Fanon with respect to négritude and the Présence Africaine movement in order to examine the discursive alternatives that he proposed and the vehemence of his response to certain interpretations of African writing and culture.

For Fanon, the first move in the dialectic from alienation to disalienation in négritude was partial and unsatisfactory (Fanon 1967:38). As an early participant in the Présence Africaine movement, Fanon voiced his discontent with it from the "inside." He begins with an incisive, two-pronged counterdiscourse:

> This historical necessity in which the men of African culture find themselves to racialize their claims and to speak more of African culture than national culture will lead them up a blind alley. Let us take for example the case of the African Cultural Society [i.e., SAC]. This Society had been created by African intellectuals who wished to get to know each other and to compare their experiences and the results of their respective research work. The aim of this Society was therefore to affirm the existence of an African culture, to evaluate this culture on the plane of distinct nations, and to reveal the internal motive forces of each of their national cultures. . . . Now, this Society will very quickly show its inability to shoulder these different tasks, and will limit itself to exhibitionist demonstrations, while the habitual behavior of the members of this Society will be confined to showing Europeans that such a thing as African culture exists. . . . We have shown that such a thing is natural and draws its legitimacy from the lies propagated by

> men of Western culture, but the degradation of the aims of this Society will become more marked with the elaboration of the concept of negritude. (Fanon 1963:214–15)

The subject of this passage is African intellectuals in relationship to the antisubject Europeans who have "propagated lies" about Africa and European civilization. SAC is the institutional outcome of the actions of African intellectuals, while négritude is the philosophical result.

Fanon views SAC's institutional structure as an inadequate tool for populist revolt and the philosophy of négritude as dangerous and distorting. For him, the alternative is nationalist collective action, in which intellectuals, in spite of their inadequacies and bad faith, should participate (Fanon 1963:223–24). But, for Fanon, the fruits of this collective action arise from spontaneous responses to oppression when people cannot tolerate any further injustice. These spontaneous reactions include violence and political revolution. The metaphor of "the knife" recurs in Fanon's descriptions of the necessity of revolution. In describing the frustration and aggression that result from colonialism, Fanon (1963:43) remarks: "As soon as the native begins to pull on his moorings and to cause anxiety to the settler, he is handed over to well-meaning souls who, in cultural congresses, point out to him the specificity and wealth of Western values. . . . But it so happens when the native hears a speech about Western values he pulls out his knife—or at least he makes sure it is within reach."[15] The same knife, or expression of violence, turns against oppressed people. "The native's back is to the wall, the knife at his throat (or, more precisely, the electrode at his genitals): he will have no more call for fancies" (Fanon 1963:58). Here Fanon describes the point at which cultural congresses and discourses affirming identity become useless. Exasperated and without any further recourse, oppressed people turn to violence as a response to dehumanizing conditions. The passage to violence is not a solution for Fanon, but only one of several means to the end of political liberation in the context of universal values. At this point, intellectuals join with others in nation building. Fanon (1963:247) concludes: "If this building up is true, that is to say, if it interprets the manifest will of the people and reveals the eager African peoples, then the building of a nation is of necessity accompanied by the discovery and encouragement of universalizing values."

Although Fanon is emphatic about the strategies for action that he advocates, it is important not to reduce the question of politics in négritude discourse and Fanon's counterdiscourse to a zero degree of political action. For example, Kesteloot (1974:292) cites the "considerable Marxist influence" often attributed to the Présence Africaine movement, while Mudimbe (1988:93) refers to Fanon as a "solid Marxist."[16] Although Fanon identifies oppression and racism as the enemies of social justice, the real agony is suffered by individuals caught between contradictory cultures and oppressive political systems.

The diverse political histories, specific political allegiances, and engaged activities of the members and fellow travelers of the Présence Africaine movement, from leading revolutions to governing their own countries, provide ample data for a book in their own right. My focus here, however, is on the virtual nature of Présence Africaine's discourse and on Fanon's response as a strategic plan for action and a means of actualizing psychological elements of the discourse that he thought were valid. Fanon saw the emergence of nationalism and the psychological aggression arising from colonialism as the major stumbling blocks of négritude. Although Senghor also spoke of psychology, for him African psychology consisted of Jungian archetypal essences, intuitive reasoning, and mysticism. Instead, Fanon referred to the psychopathology of oppressed individuals in contexts of racism and domination.

Although they issue from specific dialogues and debates held at conferences and presented on the printed page, the discourses of négritude and antinégritude are more than a sum total of these dialogues. Antinégritude became grafted onto négritude discourse, creating a totalizing effect in which the criticism became a legacy sustaining the discourse. Fanon's counterdiscourse opened up a new path that involved both collective action and individual liberation. The psychological dimension of Fanon's approach relates directly to the views of new-generation writers such as Paul Dakeyo, for whom revolutionary struggle is a matter of personal choice and pain. In contrast to Fanon, however, some of these new-generation writers advocate political action only in a highly abstract sense. They focus instead on interior psychological transformations as a way of changing the world.

Voices Identifying a New Generation

A new generation of writers on the African continent and in France initiated a critical rupture with négritude and moved away from its antidiscourses. I have argued that Paul Dakeyo foreshadows the work of this new generation. He approaches Africa with a mixture of hope, despair, and longing. He presents a pessimistic idealization of Africa in combat and turmoil and looks toward Africa from a position of exile in France. In chapter 3, I introduced Dakeyo's poetry and analyzed his approach to revolutionary love. Here I will touch upon the aspects of Dakeyo's poetry that relate to a diasporic identity discourse also reflected in the new generation's writings.

In *J'appartiens au grand jour,* Dakeyo transforms a virtual discourse into a painful cry that echoes throughout the section of the poem dedicated to "la

Femme." Here Dakeyo expresses the desire to be the lover of his continent and to achieve an eternal unity with Africa.

Je veux être l'amant
De ma terre
Je veux être l'amant
De la mer
Je veux être eau
Et sable dans le sable clair
De nos plages
Je veux être les mots oubliés
Les mots nus et fraternels
Du passé
Je veux être les mots
De l'amour sans bride
Et le sang allumé du jour.
(Dakeyo 1979:47)

[I want to be the lover
Of my land
I want to be the lover
Of the sea
I want to be water
And sand in clear sand
Of our beaches
I want to be the forgotten words
The naked and fraternal words
Of the past
I want to be the words
Of love without reins
And the ignited blood of the day.]

Dakeyo's section on the woman continues with a plea that she (metonymically Africa) surrender her body to him to complete a union with the lost past and achieve his identity.

FEMME
Donne-moi ton corps
Ton corps-soleil-souffle-sang
Là où commence le jour
Là où commence le silence
Là où commence la parole
(Dakeyo 1979:51)

[WOMAN
Give me your body
Your body-sun-breath-blood
There where day begins
There where silence begins
There where the word begins]

But, in spite of this plea for reunion, the poem ends in pathos. The return to Africa brings only the suffering of an unfulfilled dream.

Leçon est pratique de la leçon
Les maîtres d'hier sont toujours là
Et mes larmes comme de gros galets
Dans les rues de SOWETO jonchées de morts
. . . .
Le poèm s'arrête là
Mon cri n'est pas spéculation
On ne vend pas les morts.
(Dakeyo 1979:109)

[The lesson is the practice of the lesson
Yesterday's masters are still there
And tears like large pebbles
In the streets of SOWETO strewn with corpses
. . . .
The poem ends there
My cry is not a speculation
One does not sell the dead.]

The discourse of *Grand jour* moves from a wish for belonging, to despair. Love is a metaphor for the unfulfilled desire to return to an Africa not yet free. Dakeyo combines a revolutionary spirit with the psychological deception of the postcolonial era. In *La Femme où j'ai mal* (Dakeyo 1989a:46), the deception of the return to Africa is expressed in terms of a broken love affair. This rupture incites an identity crisis and a sense of personal loss.

je sais ma solitude
Mes nuits chargées de silences
et de songes sonores
Mes nuits d'insomnie
et de colère qui traversent

mon chant inachevé

je veux tout simplement me retrouver
(Dakeyo 1989a:46)

[I know my solitude
My nights full of silence
and my sonorous dreams
My nights of insomnia
and of anger that penetrates
my hollow song

I simply want to find myself]

This sense of loss and displacement constitutes Dakeyo's literary and ideological challenge to négritude. Reaffirmation based on nation, ethnicity, and class is not enough. Exiled and alone, the poet is in search of his identity. This sense of loss and displacement is echoed in the works of many new-generation writers. Without announcing it in long philosophical diatribes, they simply take another path to resolve their problems. The rupture ending the colonial period renders the inscription of African identity a catharsis that casts off what Mudimbe (1982:34–35) has referred to as "*l'odeur du père,*" or the West as a singular, paternal, oppressive, rational, and oppositional force. This catharsis, which roughly coincides with négritude's decline, opens up a new space for the literary and cultural construction of fragmented, but infinitely rich, identity discourses. These identity discourses cannot be understood without taking into account the roles of memory and diasporic movement in shaping new cultures (Clifford 1994:302–37). Consequently, there simply can no longer be any zero degree of inscribed identity.

Parisianism and Universalism as Identity Discourses

The postcolonial period has ushered in a sense of deception with the broken promise of modernity and the dreams of African independence. For Dakeyo, Africa is still a signifier in the discourse of lost love. In the throes of agony and loss, Dakeyo is not a nihilist. He believes that Africa will rebound with the dawn of a great day. Other critics, both European and African, are less optimistic (Dumont 1962; Jewsiewicki 1985; Bayart 1992:9–23; Mbembe 1992:1–30; Devisch 1995:593–629). The banality of power and demagogy, the contagion of corruption, and the unfulfilled dreams of an impotent consumerism have prompted a barrage of critiques arising out of the ashes of African independence. For a transitional generation of Euro-African intellectuals, and for many intellectuals and activists remaining in their countries to work through the crisis, hope still reigns. For example, V. Y. Mudimbe (1992a:62) states of the postcolonial critique: "My generation, in 1966, did not want to have to choose between the platitudes of colonialism and the excesses of independence. There was not really a visible rupture between pre- and post-independence moments. We have to weigh the commitments of intellectuals against those of politicians." Mudimbe continues with an exhortation to African intellectuals to save the African continent.[17] This plea is not only an exhortation to cultural and political action but also an effort to recuperate Africa as a signifier in a reaffirming identity discourse. In contrast to Mudimbe, the literary critic Georges Ngal argues that a deep rupture has occurred between the colonial and postcolonial generations of African writers in terms of conceptions of the freedom of the literary subject, the gaze (*le regard*) on African societies, and the tone of the writing (Ngal 1994:94–95). He views this shift in identity discourses as a veritable psychological "explosion" (85–86).

The writings of Parisianism, discussed at length in chapters 5 and 6, emphasize four important identity themes: exclusion, alienation, exile, and madness. In Parisianism, exclusion is the motor of a narrative of longing and belonging and the locus of enunciation that establishes the writer's point of view. In addition, exclusion leads to a sense of psychological alienation not unlike the alienation described by Fanon. Alienation, in turn, intensifies the experience of exile, which leads to destabilization and a schizophrenic existence, portrayed as madness and mindless aggression. These psychological reactions contrast with the strategic revolutionary aggression leading to the disalienation described by Fanon. Parisianism's identity discourse is rooted not so much in nihilism as it is in disillusionment and an inward turn. Deception and disillusionment lead to resignation and to skillful strategies for inclusion in a blocked and closed social environment. Although political re-engagement with Africa is a subtext of Parisianism, it is manifest only through inflections of irony and indirect discourse.

Simon Njami's statement concerning Parisianism as interior writing, mentioned in chapter 6, warrants reiteration. The characters in the novels of Parisianism search for their fragmented identities across the Parisian landscape. The dialectical algorithm of black Paris is not just a simple juxtaposition of dominant and marginal cultures. The quest for exoticism permeates the leisure-time activities and institutions of black Paris. Afro-Antillian and North African Paris have become part of the identity repertoire and media representations of the city.[18] As a literary reflection of black Paris, Parisianism contributes to this media image.

Black Paris is not a unified space within the open city. It is experienced in disjointed, incomplete, and contradictory ways by the writers who live in and portray it. Two sets of semiotic oppositions may, thus, be designated to describe the landscape of black Paris (fig. 22).

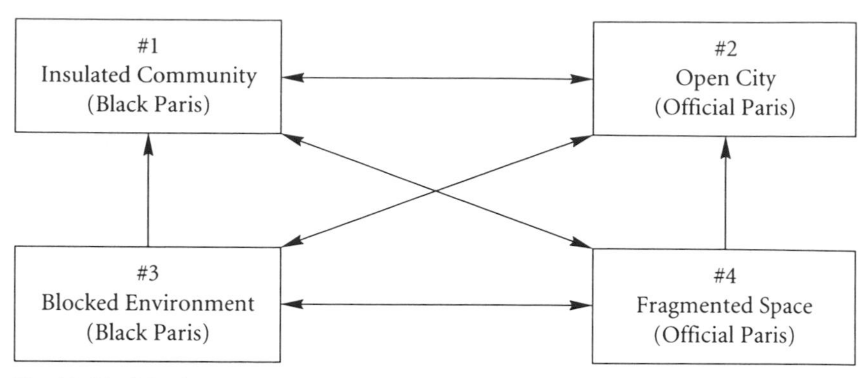

Fig. 22. Black Paris—a semiotic view

The official city is a virtual space that intersects with the insulated community. In spite of its insulation, the existence of the separate community of black Paris is often denied by those who maneuver within its confines as they orient their artistic efforts toward the rest of Paris. Ambivalence and denial by the residents of black Paris lead to ideological fragmentation and blockage. This condition of ideological fragmentation is exacerbated by the social barriers that persist between black Paris and official Paris as virtual spaces.

Within this landscape, experiences of exclusion lead to frustration, anger, and resignation. I have already demonstrated the ways in which the novels of Parisianism deal with these problems, but it is worthwhile to reexamine these strategies in the context of identity discourses. In a revealing excerpt from *African gigolo* (1989a), Njami describes the reactions of his protagonist, Moïse Ndoungué, to the French political scene of the 1980s. Mitterand and Chirac have just begun their famous two-party political cohabitation. Henri-Georges Durand, an art collector who has hired Moïse to help him with appraisals and art deals, asks the Cameroonian what he thinks about the political situation. Njami writes:

> "What do you think about all of this?" asked Durand to break the ice. He tossed to the edge of his desk the newspaper that Moïse had caught him reading. The Cameroonian thought that only the victor could take on the supreme function of government. But his opinions were none of Durand's business.
>
> "I don't give a hoot [*Je m'en contrefiche*]," he responded. "It only concerns the French. I don't vote."
>
> "This will certainly have more repercussions for those who don't vote than for those who vote. Don't you think so?"
>
> "That's their problem." (Njami 1989a:94)

Moïse's identity is in constant mutation as he floats between cultures. He approaches French politics with indifference and negates his attachment to

France, saying, "That's their problem." Haunted by Africa, Moïse is pursued by letters from his mother in Cameroon. Through a series of sexual liaisons, he is drawn to France. His philosopher friend, Étienne, who returns to Cameroon to become a politician, also draws Moïse into moments of activism and reflection, leading the antihero to declare that négritude is not "scientific" enough (Njami 1989a:31). This statement echoes Adotevi's critique of négritude. But, in contrast to Adotevi and the philosophers of négritude, Moïse pretends not to care. Moïse's alienation leads to aggression and murder, but he never examines the motives for his frustration. He does not blame a neocolonial oppressor or the political situation. The nature of his disjointed existence is merely a fact of life. Underlying this alienation is a virtual discourse in which the writer wishes for an ideal world where battles over inclusion and equality would be unnecessary.

In spite of its emphasis on the Parisian landscape, another theme of Parisianism is the discovery of a universal identity with African inflections. Yodi Karone situates his novel *Les Beaux gosses* (Karone 1988b) in the jazz clubs of Abidjan, thereby linking African-American music to Africa. Karone is fascinated by jazz because of its hybridization of African rhythms and European melodies.[19] Eugène Esselé, in *Cannibale amour* (Karone 1988a), searches for his roots in Paris and New York with the tunes of jazz music as a backdrop. Of his own identity, we recall, Karone states: "On the whole, to be Parisian does not mean to be French. I am Cameroonian, but I am also Parisian" (Karone 1991).

Hybridization prevents Parisianism from becoming a trendy reiteration of the virtues of metropolitanism. Parisianism uses the signifiers of modernity and postmodernity—the métro, the computer, the music synthesizer, and *sape*—to develop characters who are masters of a global environment. But there is a price to pay for this mastery. Eugène goes mad during his tricontinental identity quest. The schizophrenia of living in many worlds emerges precisely at the moment when Eugène tries to reconcile his existence of exile in Paris with his search for African roots. There are two ways out of this dilemma—a return to essentialism, which the Parisianists refuse, or nihilism, which they reject as well. This double negation leaves Parisianism in suspended animation as an identity discourse in search of itself.

Calixthe Beyala, like other African women writers of her generation, such as Véronique Tadjo, uses plural narrative voices and discursive stances in her novels.[20] In *Tu t'appeleras Tanga,* Beyala engages in psychological doubling (Bhabha 1987:5–11) when she assumes the voice of Tanga's French cellmate, who believes she becomes the young Cameroonian prostitute. *Le Petit prince de Belleville* (Beyala 1992) and *Maman a un amant* (1993) present Belleville through the narrative voice and eyes of young Mamadou Traoré (Loukoum). Beyala explains that Mamadou's character was inspired by her daily observations of a young African boy at play in Belleville's public park. Using the televisual and roving environmental gazes, Beyala establishes Traoré's alienation and sense of wonderment. Young Loukoum deals with the French school system during the day and watches his parents in their encounters with immigration officials, public assistance, and the social security office. In the evening, he watches television with his father and develops an imaginary rapport with public officials and movie stars. Abdou Traoré, Loukoum's father, adds another narrative voice to the story. Loukoum reads excerpts from his father's letters and journals and learns that his televisual omnipotence is limited by the label "immigrant."

Abdou Traoré writes in his journal: "Who am I? An immigrant. An open mouth. A passing breath of air. I have no sense of direction. I limp in my infirmity with the insolence of a defeated body" (Beyala 1992:169).

In the end, Abdou, imprisoned for welfare fraud, goes mad in his cell. But Loukoum has another fate. In spite of his family's suffering, Loukoum is carefree and curious, empowered by the mass media and his excursions into Belleville. His fantasies allow him to escape the hopeless resignation of his father's generation. By using multiple narrative voices, Beyala engineers her protagonist's escape and rescues Parisianism from its message of global disillusionment.

In her interviews and in her long essay *Lettre d'une africaine à ses soeurs occidentales* (Beyala 1995:20–22), Beyala voices her views on writing as an African woman. During her interview with me, a transcription of which follows chapter 6, Beyala (1990a) qualifies this: "If one asks me to speak about Africa, I can't talk about the Africa of traditions, so-called beauty, lyricism, and pastoralism. I was born in a bidonville. That was my world. For me, that's Africa. For many, Africa is the world of air-conditioned cars, beautiful clothes and *boubous*. Not for me. I saw those people pass by at a distance. For me, Africa is also the Africa of tomorrow where cultures mix and blend." This openness to the new Africa does not prevent Beyala from reappropriating aspects of the term "négritude" in her concept of "feminitude" as a way of situating her writing as a woman. Beyala's feminism moves away from contestatory essentialism and mutes the signifier of "woman" in a hybrid discourse. Whether or not one agrees with her position, Beyala's feminitude is a bold attempt at deconstructing received ideologies about gender relations.

The Parisianists skirt the question of universalism. They describe universal human problems such as dislocation and loss. Africa remains the unstated predicate of what is lost. The resolution of the dialectic, however, is not Sartre's humanistic ideal of a "society without races." The new-generation Parisianist writers are too skeptical for that solution. Instead, the dialectic ends with an existential reprise. The very fact of existing in the metropole, whether in alienation or resignation, is an assertion of African presence and a prognosis for the future of human relations.

In contrast, the writers of the new universalism are not satisfied with this approach to identity discourse. They go further by carving out a niche for Africa in the world of ideas and politics. But what, after all, is Africa? It is, among other things, the consequence of the relations between the colonizer and the colonized, the oppressor and the oppressed, that results in human suffering and compassion. This consciousness of Africa leads to a conclusion that differs somewhat from the rainbow effect of Simon Njami's ethnicolor movement (Njami and Tilliette 1987:8–9). The new universalism begins with the premise that intercultural communication and cultural mixtures, although they may issue from asymmetrical power relations, are a reality. Négritude plays a role in new universalism as a point of divergence.

Jean-Baptiste Tiémélé (1989) described négritude as a faulty foundation for political engagement, "a good philosophy, which is enveloped in a paper that's not of high quality." Later, Tiémélé (1990) discussed identity as an imaginary construction: "Identity has an imaginary side. . . . We all bathe in the same universe with different personal elements. In this halo of values, differences appear as transparent realities." This halo of values is reflected in Tiémélé's poetry, which ranges from the sonorous, Senghorian pieces of his 1969 collection *Chansons païennes,* with lyrical explorations of an idealized Africa, to laments of loss in *Aoyu suivi de Yaley* (1987). For Tiémélé, Africa must remain a signifier in black writing so that one has something special to bring to universal culture. But this special message is part of a humanistic blending with the universal.

Edouard Maunick takes a different tack in approaching the problem of universalism. He believes that the blending of universal elements takes place within the self and moves outward toward humanity. His hybrid cultural heritage provides the point of departure for an identity that blends with a "universal culture." Therefore, Maunick emphasizes the importance of creolization as a cultural strategy and a style of writing. It is interesting that Dakeyo dedicates one of the poems in *Grand jour* to Maunick (Dakeyo 1979:85–97). Here Dakeyo figuratively depicts a longing for the sun, waves, and splendor of the Indian Ocean that heighten the cold solitude of European exile. Maunick's personalization of the passion for the universal, however, differs from Dakeyo's longing and deception in exile. Using the metaphor of the tree of life, Maunick connects the roots of his childhood to a universal tree. "I am the tree that grows, that is, that destroys a little bit of space on earth where it exists. . . . Because I have a right to a place, and each human being has a right to be a tree—the tree that he is—and to grow in everyday life" (Maunick 1989b).

In his poem *Saut dans l'arc-en-ciel,* Maunick proposes creolization as a way of recognizing cultural difference and reappropriating it to the service of a universal discourse.

> regardez-le danser cet homme polychrome / sa nuque syncopée tatoue l'air et le vent des signes insulaires / devant derrière son ILE / divan dérièr so lile / sur les côtés mon ILE / si lé koté mo lile / en bas en haut notre ILE / an ba la ho nou lile / créolisant Rimbaud / paganisant les dieux / regardez-le danser / son corps est point du jour
> (Maunick 1985:21)

> [look at him dance this polychrome man / his syncopated neck tattoos the air and the wind with insular signs / in front of behind his ISLAND / divan dérièr so lile / on the coasts of my ISLAND / si lé koté mo lile / from the bottom to the top of our ISLAND / an ba lo ho nou lile / creolizing Rimbaud / paganizing the gods / look at him dance / his body pointed to the day]

Leaping across barriers of language, culture, and aesthetic form, Maunick's poetry is an exercise in the new universalism. Using the image-flash as a rhetorical tool, he turns the message of universalism outward toward a politics of liberation in *Mandéla* (1987) and inward toward a poetics of self-discovery and creolization in *Saut dans l'arc-en-ciel* (1985).

Bolya's essays, which constitute my third example of new universalist writings and identity discourse, appear on the surface to be quite distant from the poetry of universalism. Bolya, however, shares as a common theme with the other universalists the interrogation of African identity and modernity in the context of world geopolitics. In 1991 Bolya characterized his reasoning as at once "totally Western" and "totally African" (Bolya 1991b). According to Bolya, at the end of the twentieth century, we have run out of time to deal with the African crisis. It's now or never. For him, Japan provides the only non-Western model of modernity that has worked. He calls for an "essential universalism" (*un universalisme intégral*) that bypasses the deceptions of European colonialism and places Africa on the paths of modernity and postmodernity (Bolya 1994:12). Japan fascinates Bolya because of its refusal to do away with cultural traditions while producing a postindustrial economic miracle, which he terms Japan's "revolutionary capitalism" (Bolya 1994:143–44). With regard to identity, he believes that African nations should reject the project of incorporating European civilization and culture. Bolya (1994:21) asserts: "We know henceforth, at the end of this postcommunist century, that with respect to development, Africa, like the rest of Eastern Europe, has more to learn from Asia than from the Old Continent: Europe. We also know that in spite of the cultural crusades of the rearguard and the unbridled identitary narcissism of the 'development experts' of the great 'civilized nations,' as they like to present themselves, the 'war of paradigms' (Kuhn) is over for once and for all."

Although Bolya's plea for an essentialist universalism is more an exhortation than a demonstration of concrete strategies for African development, his suggestion for a reinvigorated collective identity discourse is in tune with the new universalism. Rather than remaining sequestered by the iron cage of personal identity, Bolya pushes for a collective representation of cultures in which African nations reaffirm their own autonomy while participating in the global economic changes instigated by late twentieth-century capitalism. Less idealistic than négritude and more strategically pragmatic than Parisianism, Bolya's universalist approach challenges African nations and intellectuals to adopt collective identity discourses that will serve their economic and cultural interests at the end of the twentieth century.

The poets and essayists of the new universalism assert that the balance of power, knowledge, and discourse is no longer just between Africa and Europe, but between Africa and the rest of the world. Identity ceases to be a reaffirmation of blackness or négritude vis-à-vis Europe, but is, instead, a process of cultural mixture and political action that reveals Africa's plural voices to the world. The Parisianists and the universalists adopt contrasting strategies, but they agree on the fundamental importance of cultural inclusion and political equality. Using Marcien Towa's metaphor of the world orchestra, we can say that Njami and Karone believe that postmodern, diasporic personalities will lead the band. Beyala sees African women of the new generation as the orchestra's leaders, while Tiémélé, Maunick, and Bolya view a creolized and forward-looking Africa as the impresario. To extend the metaphor further, none of these authors sees Africa as picking up the rhythm section of the band. They conceive of a world in which African identity discourses, in all of their complexity, contribute to shaping global political, social, economic, and aesthetic dialogues.

Cultural Displacement and African Writing

The postcolonial critique of Africa's political and economic decline destabilized négritude's signifier of essential blackness. Even more destabilizing was the social fact of south-to-north migration, establishing sizable, permanent diasporic communities in metropolitan European capitals such as Paris, London, and Brussels. With Africa as only a phantom point of reference in the repertoire of their cultural imaginations, the writers of the new diasporic generation could hardly embrace négritude's sense of cultural certainty.

In a parabolic phrase, the postmodern filmmaker and critic Trinh T. Minh-ha (1989:22) states: "Writing necessarily refers to writing."[21] She describes the mirror effect that writing creates for authors in illusory relationships to their subjects and to themselves. Pushing Minh-ha's statement further, writing refers to the act of writing and to the authors' processes of identity construction in social and historical context. Writing also consists of the concatenation of discourses labeled as "literature." In this chapter, I have emphasized the ways in which the five identity discourses of négritude, antinégritude, revolutionary writing, Parisianism, and new universalism evolved from conversations and dialogues into public discourses defining specific periods and cultural spaces for African literature. The market for African writing in France plays a role in this process. Négritude was initially evolved within the institutional structure of the Présence Africaine publishing house and SAC. It moved outward to become the defining discourse of a generation, and to absorb, like a greedy amoeba, the criticisms and counterdiscourses that surrounded it. Négritude also became a market phenomenon, and the mere invocation of the term, for over a decade, practically assured the publication of African writers' works in and beyond the venues developed for African literature. (See figs. 23 and 24.) Then, suddenly, the discourse died. It was neither relevant nor marketable.

I have delineated the semiological and sociological reasons for the move away from négritude. But this shift of paradigms and styles did not mean that négritude's legacy was forgotten. Among revolutionary writers, négritude lives as an antithesis to be refuted. The calculated amnesia concerning négritude among Parisianists of the new generation masks a subtext that strives to erase négritude's primary signifier (essential blackness) through allusion and innuendo. The new universalists restore and then dissolve the essential signifier by placing it in a new envelope, creolizing it, or Nipponizing it. Indeed, the fundamental signifier of négritude has been partially erased, but its traces survive in the discourses of the new generation.[22] What do these new literary trends signify in terms of the political action and virtual identity discourses? On the one hand, they contribute to the formation and rationalization of new political movements, such as the militantly integrationist SOS-Racisme and Sans Papiers movements, through which new immigrants have challenged Charles Pasqua's laws. On the other hand, they spill over into cultural movements and aesthetic expressions, including the new cultural criticism, hybridized art, *banlieue* cinema, and world music (Araeen 1989:3–14; Gaudibert 1991). Whether these new trends represent an empty wedding of costume and capital or a dead end is impossible to predict.

Debates about francophonie in the French mass media have kept African literature alive as a cultural product and a market commodity during the 1980s and 1990s (Bouraoui 1995:83–89). Since the era of négritude, however, no dominant philosophy has developed to unify the multiple discourses of African writing. This discursive fragmentation may be a positive sign. At the very least, it is typical of the postmodern era. The spring 1996 issue of *Revue Noire*, France's lead-

Fig. 23. Display window of the Présence Africaine bookstore, rue des Écoles, July 1991. Photograph by Bennetta Jules-Rosette

Fig. 24. Display window of a bookstore in the twelfth arrondissement of Paris shortly after the publication of Bolya Baenga's *L'Afrique en Kimono,* July 1991. Photograph by Bennetta Jules-Rosette.

ing contemporary African art magazine, devotes its exposé on African art and literature in Paris to a panegyric on trendy Franco-African fashions and hip-hop music. In the cinders of négritude and Pan-Africanism, the mass media and the market have supplanted totalizing philosophy as the unifying discourse for African writing (Diawara 1992:285–91). At this juncture, perhaps one might reinterpret Minh-ha's parable as meaning that "writing" refers to "good writing." And good writing, in the African context, implies a combination of discourses that are philosophically reaffirming, but (post)modern; inclusive, yet contestatory; aesthetically aware while politically forceful. For a brief historical moment, négritude achieved these objectives. It is now up to the new generation of African writers to locate its place in the postmodern symphony of world literature.

CONCLUSION

Particularism and Universalism in African Writing

> Postcolonial intellectuals in Africa . . . are almost entirely dependent for their support on two institutions: the African university—an institution whose life is overwhelmingly constituted as Western—and the Euro-American publisher and reader.
>
> —Kwame Anthony Appiah, 1992

As this book draws to a close, the fiftieth anniversary of the founding of the *Présence Africaine* journal has recently been observed. This is an appropriate time to reflect upon the past half century of African writing in France. Contemporary African literature was born with decolonization movements of the 1950s. But the relationship between literature and society is often indirect. The contrasting trajectories of francophone and anglophone African literatures demonstrate that social conditions of oppression do not automatically result in comparable literatures of protest. One of the major themes of this book has revolved around an exploration of particularism and universalism in African writing. What factors have contributed to the emergence of a distinctive African literature in French? What characteristics qualify these literary productions to enter the category of universal literature?

On the one hand, these questions might be answered with respect to the authors themselves. Did they intend to produce a universal literature? Did they plan to create a distinctively African form of expression? In organizing the journal *Présence Africaine,* Alioune Diop voiced both objectives. Diop believed that during the initial stages, African literature required the support of a social and intellectual movement. As emphasized in chapter 1, the three reasons for establishing the journal that Diop (1947:7–8) cites in his essay "Niam n'goura ou les raisons d'être de *Présence Africaine*" are: (1) publishing works by experts on African culture; (2) promoting the development of African literature through novels, short stories, and theater; and (3) integrating Africa and "the black man" into Western "civilization." Diop viewed the second objective as the most important. Therefore, one can undeniably argue that, from his point of view as a publisher, Diop expressed the unequivocal intention of transforming African cultures through literature by moving from their particular literary manifestations (i.e., indigenous forms of expression) to the universal level—in his terms, "Western civilization."[1]

Several pragmatic and philosophical problems surround Diop's project. First, how did he define "African"? He certainly did not mean works written in African languages and dialects, or works that would be culturally or ideologically inaccessible to a Western audience. Instead, Diop wished to create a bridge between Africa and the West and a source for translating one set of ideas and cultures into another. Second, what exactly did Diop intend by the term "Western civilization"? Here he referred in large part to French culture and literature. His immediate objectives were to make the works of African authors more visible and insert them into the French literary market. The *Présence Africaine* journal and the publishing house were the first tools of insertion, but they were not enough. Merely publishing pieces by African authors did not result in an African presence on the French literary scene. It was necessary to initiate a larger project of cultural renewal in which African writers could express their views, learn their craft, and engage in dialogues with the European intellectuals from whom they sought support. Through this project of cultural transformation, or "reworlding," including the Présence Africaine publishing house, the journal, the Société Africaine de Culture (SAC), and a series of conferences held over two decades, Diop energetically opened up a space for African writing and cultures in France. His strategies of assimilation, however, risked undermining the cultural space that he wished to create for African literature and values.

Culture is a system of signification of which writing is one of the most formal and profound manifestations. Surrounding literature are a host of social, political, and economic conditions and activities that constitute its production environment. Literature develops both in opposition to, and as a reflection of, these conditions. In her analysis of the sociology of culture and literature, Wendy Griswold (1987:4–16) identifies the intentions of authors and the circumstances of reception and comprehension as primary sources for assessing the relationship between literature and society. A major problem with the model of intention, production, and reception stems from the ambiguity of the notion of authorial intentionality. Authors often construct their "intentions" retrospectively, based on the reception of their works, or, alternatively, they deny being able to verbalize their intentions at all. Andy Warhol's famous statement that he agreed with everything his critics had to say about his art is an extreme example of this reconstructed intentionality geared toward the commercial market. In Diop's case, the ideological reasons for publishing African literary works were formulated *before* the works were published, but the mechanisms of reception surrounding the publication and diffusion of these works could not be assessed and explained until after the fact.

This complex, dialectical relationship between literary goals and reception makes the Présence Africaine publishing house an ideal cultural point of departure for examining African literature on the Parisian landscape. In spite of its notoriety and successes, Présence Africaine is not the end of the story. The Présence Africaine publishing house has risen, fallen, and still survives as one of the major outlets for African writing in France. As the first important outlet, the journal and the publishing house are touchstones for the successes or failures of later endeavors.

The Role of Présence Africaine in Retrospect

Arising out of the background of international Pan-Africanism, the Présence Africaine project assumed an avowedly cultural and literary cast that was, nonetheless, fraught with political implications. A long, classical history of debates about the purity, clarity, and logic of the French language cannot be overlooked as a background factor in the development of Présence Africaine (Bouraoui 1995:11–13). The French language became the vehicle and contested terrain for the operation of Présence Africaine's publishing activities. More pertinent to this discussion, however, are the developments in ethnology and, later, sociology during the early twentieth century that challenged the definition and boundaries of Western, in particular French, "civilization." In chapters 1 and 2, I argued that new developments in ethnology, including Marcel Griaule's Dakar-Djibouti expedition (1931–33), offered fertile terrain for the growth of Présence Africaine. More precisely, Griaule's anthropological collaborations with indigenous research subjects in West Africa and Abyssinia initiated a decentering of ethnographic discourse that called into question the dominance of French cultural paradigms (Jules-Rosette 1994:160–62). Présence Africaine turned this technique of intellectual collaboration on its head by appropriating the findings of anthropology and sociology to support the identity discourses of négritude, cultural Pan-Africanism, and a new Africanist anthropology. This discursive reversal sustained the ideas developed by Diop, Senghor, and Césaire, among others, that black civilization was an autonomous and worthy source of ideas, cultural models, and renewed pride. French anthropology was, thus, transformed into the handmaiden rather than the motivating source of a revitalized identity discourse. This objective was achieved through the early issues of the journal and the 1956 and 1959 Congresses of Black Writers and Artists and by a number of books published by Présence Africaine during the 1960s and 1970s.

A series of conferences (Dakar, 1966; Algiers, 1969; and Yaoundé, 1973) broached heated discussions on postcolonial art and literature in which the early models of Présence Africaine were challenged. (See appendix 1.) Temporarily obscured by negative debates of antinégritude in the late 1960s and early 1970s, the influence of Présence Africaine reemerged with a new force and different meaning as national literatures began to appear across the African continent (Mbabuike 1995:482–95). Présence Africaine transformed the battle of political liberation into one of cultural legitimacy in the literary marketplace. In the English-speaking world, W. E. B. Du Bois, Kwame Nkrumah, George Padmore, Ras T. Makonnen, and other Pan-Africanists had opened up a parallel contested terrain, which, although it contained literary products and manifestoes, was defined primarily by political action. A genuine interest in the comparison of these two sources of political and cultural change did not emerge until later in the postcolonial era.[2]

Reconfiguring African Literature

Rooted in Présence Africaine's protest against decolonization, a new revolutionary literature arose. As already emphasized, Frantz Fanon was the prime mover of the new revolutionary writing, voicing its early glimmerings at the 1956 and 1959 Congresses of Black Writers and Artists in Paris and Rome. In "Racisme et Culture," presented at the 1956 congress, Fanon argued that racism carries with it a social and political disease that results in the systematic oppression of all people. Fanon contended that racism cannot be fought with rational arguments. According to Fanon (1963:41), "the natives' challenge to the colonial world is not a rational confrontation of points of view. It is not a treatise on the universal, but the untidy affirmation of an original idea propounded as an absolute." The responses to racism include radical protest and violence, both of which Fanon saw as inevitable parts of the liberation process and the revolutionary discourse of counternégritude.

Part of Fanon's disagreement with the Présence Africaine movement concerned the limitations of négritude and Diop and Senghor's brands of universalism. Fanon (1963:216) stated: "Négritude therefore finds its first limitation in the phenomena which take account of the formation of this historical character of men. Negro and African-Negro culture broke up into different entities because the men who wished to incarnate these cultures realized that every culture is first and foremost national, and that the problems which kept Richard Wright or Langston Hughes on alert were fundamentally different from those which might confront Leopold Senghor or Jomo Kenyatta." This statement, originally presented in Fanon's paper for the 1959 Congress of Black Writers and Artists, alludes to the debates of the 1956 congress. The differences between African and black American intellectuals at the congress suggested that there was no singular philosophy or literature of protest. More important for Fanon, these differences underscored the influence of national cultures and what he termed "national consciousness" on ideologies and strategies of protest. For Fanon, populist strategies of protest were spontaneous byproducts of the colonial and national environments in which oppression developed. Although commonalities existed across these environments, the responses depended upon strategies of protest devised in each national context.

The argument concerning national culture and consciousness instigated Fanon's profound ideological rupture with Présence Africaine. Fanon (1963:206) opened his essay on national culture with a quote from Sékou Touré, first president of Guinea: "To take part in the African revolution it is not enough to write a revolutionary song; you must fashion the revolution with the people." Fanon believed that African writers should be organic intellectuals and that African literature should take a leading role in shaping the popularly accepted tenets for revolutionary action. In contrast, Alioune Diop argued that social and political change issued from an alliance between the assimilated Westernized elite and the African masses. For Diop, this elite leadership was not perfect. The successful Westernized intellectual risked being seduced by the accolades of European critics, thereby losing touch with "the people." The alienated intellectual would then no longer be an effective leader in the battle against cultural and political domination. In spite of the specter of alienation, however, Diop conceived of cultural leadership as the elite's responsibility. This "top-down" model of change was antithetical to Fanon's notion of collective revolutionary action. Fanon was critical of what he considered the "bad faith" of European-trained African intellectuals who abandoned revolutionary causes and ceased to support the welfare of their people. He was not above citing the names of those whom he believed to be the most egregious offenders.[3]

Revolutionary writing's rupture with Présence Africaine is part of an age-old debate about the social and political relevance of art. Is art for art's sake possible in contexts of political turmoil? Can and should aesthetics and political relevance be separated in African art and writing? Although Diop never championed the pure aesthetics of an "art for art's sake," he saw literature as a mediation between Africa and the West—a bridge across which African intellectuals could convey the experiences of their people. In contrast, Fanon was less concerned with literature as cultural mediation than he was with writing as a strategic revolutionary practice, which he believed could both incite and justify political action. These differences reached a critical turning point with the decline of négritude, signaled by the 1969 Algiers festival. But more than négritude and its identity discourses were at stake. The underlying and recurrent conflict centered around the role of African intellectuals, in particular those returning from long sojourns in Europe, in nation building and fostering national consciousness and literatures at home. As is evident in retrospect, the development of these national literatures took place in part as a reaction against the mediating influences of the European models that Diop and Senghor held to be sacred. Nevertheless, as my analysis of Ivoirian literature in chapter 4 emphasizes, writers and intellectuals were caught in the economic and political double bind of neocolonialism, which stifled the literary market in Africa.

The development of national literatures in Africa, whether revolutionary or not, constitutes the focus of a sequel to this volume. Because I have focused on African writing in France, I have chosen examples of the revolutionary approach as it evolved there, both thematically and commercially, during the late 1960s and 1970s. To exemplify this development, I selected the poet and publisher Paul Dakeyo, whose writings and publication activities offer a bridge from revolutionary writing to the two major currents in contemporary French-African writing—Parisianism and the new universalism. Taking as his point of departure the concept of oppression so clearly delineated by Fanon, Dakeyo reconfigures "revolution" as a response to thwarted desires. Dakeyo's three-part dialectic involves oppression, alienation, and acceptance and belonging or, in personal terms, hatred, deception, and love.[4] Narratives of longing and belonging transmute his revolutionary discourse into a personal challenge. The acceptance of the alienated individual resolves intergroup conflict by a movement from cultural particularism toward universalism. These conflicts and problems, however, are experienced by an individual as emotional and psychological crises. Revolution and change are not just abstract social processes. Change is personified, individualized, and personalized. The two axes of the universal (collective) and the particular (personal) converge to create revolutionary change.

The ideological link that Dakeyo creates between old and new forms of African writing enhances his role as an entrepreneur. By publishing the poems, novels, and critical essays of the new generation, Dakeyo engages in his brand of revolutionary action. Both Alioune Diop and Paul Dakeyo are culture brokers who view literary inclusion as one of the goals of universal cultural change. For Diop, this inclusion was originally part of the decolonization process and the political uplifting of the African masses. But for Dakeyo, literary inclusion must also lead to an affirmation of political belonging to "the great day."

The Parisianists—or the members of the "intimate generation"—adopt a contrasting approach to African writing in France. These writers situate their works in Paris and other European metropoles and focus on the problems of alienation, integration, and assimilation confronting Africans in Europe. Critics (Magnier 1990:102–7; Omerod and Volet 1994:43–45; Nkashama 1994:58–63) differ about the position of these writers in "African literature."[5] Only recently have they been included in anthologies of francophone African literature, and they are practically absent from all but the most recent anglophone criticism. Although individual titles often sell very well, the French reading public and some publishers approach the works of the intimate generation with skepticism and disdain. Parisianism does not comply with perceived notions and accepted stereotypes of "African literature." The antiheroes are uprooted, displaced, and even disagreeable persons—often troubled women, abandoned children, or unsavory characters. In turmoil about their African identity, they are frantically in search of cultural roots, self-definition, and elusive acceptance.[6]

The novel is the most appropriate vehicle for the literary explorations of Parisianism because it permits the development of narratives of transformation that reflect the identity discourses, crises, and soul searching of the protagonists. Karone's Eugène Esselé in *A la Recherche du cannibale amour* (1988a), Njami's Moïse Ndoungué in *African gigolo* (1989a), and Beyala's Abdou Traoré and Loukoum in *Le Petit prince de Belleville* (1992) are caught in identity crises and personal searches that cross-cut a variety of Parisian environments. Going beyond the personalization of pain in the poetry of revolutionary love, the Parisianists delineate the detrimental effects of marginalization, racism, and exclusion on the psychological development of their fictional characters. They present imperfect resolutions of these personal crises with narratives that are rooted in quotidian experience. The verisimilitude of their narratives occasionally results in the critical response that they are "clichés." In fact, these novels are replete with social realism and ethnographic details on aspects of the Parisian landscape that many French observers would prefer to avoid. They bring to light the social consequences of the Euro-African diaspora, the attendant processes of cultural blending, and the burdens of political rejection and exclusion.

The writings of the intimate generation are not exactly what Alioune Diop had in mind when he began to promote a new standard for African literature in France. Nevertheless, the works of these authors can be found in the Présence Africaine bookstore, even if they do not figure on the publication list. In this regard, two important sociological developments are worthy of summary. First, as discussed in chapters 5 and 6, the changing immigration patterns in France resulting in a south-north movement of tremendous proportions created the new environment of black Paris with African families, second- and third-generation offspring, and a host of new networks and institutions not yet present in the 1950s. This environment constitutes the new generation's literary landscape. Although it contains various social, nostalgic, and imaginary links to Africa, this environment exists as a self-contained part of the French and, in particular, the Parisian landscape and as a social and symbolic point of reference for the writers. Second, French literary outlets have opened up, even if on a restricted and ghettoized basis, for African writers. Consequently, the guiding principles established by the Présence Africaine publishing house in 1949 ceased to be a touchstone and singular resource for new generation African writers in France. Although Diop may have foreseen and even wished for this type of literary progress, the inclusion of African literature in the French market resulted in new strategies of commercialization, including francophonie, that have, in some instances, marginalized or harmed the authors. From René Maran to Yambo Ouologuem and Calixthe Beyala, authors have been praised and then bruised and attacked for adapting African narratives to the mainstream market. The collective goals of Présence Africaine for pure (as opposed to hybridized) standards for African literature have been diluted and transformed.[7] African writers of the new generation have restaged the literary drama to reflect their social situations and economic interests.

Restaging the literary drama with respect to Parisianism did not mean abandoning all concerns with universalism. In their interviews, these writers prefer to drop the label "African," substituting "Parisian," "ethnicolor," or simply no qualifier at all. They have chosen universal themes of belonging and inclusion and have positioned themselves, through media and publication outlets, to benefit from literary and commercial opportunities that equal those of any other writers in France.

The new generation of writers also includes the universalists, who, on the surface, have perpetuated the ideals of Présence Africaine. Although these writers begin by treating the themes of African identity, culture, and politics, they reconfigure African problems within a global context. The poems of Jean-Baptiste Tiémélé cover issues as far ranging as nostalgia for Abidjan, lost love, the isolation of immigration, the war in Vietnam, and famine in Latin America. The poet Edouard Maunick links the cultural syncretism and diversity of Mauritius to political problems in South Africa and his own sense of universal identity. In essays and novels, Bolya Baenga analyzes neocolonial corruption and powerlessness in Africa with respect to Japanese models of modernity. The universalists share with the writers of Parisianism an irreverence for essentialist definitions of African psychology, culture, and society. They, too, develop a hybridized version of the African presence on the world scene.

In their analysis of world literatures, Ashcroft, Griffiths, and Tiffin (1989:196) formulate the project of postcolonial writing as an effort "to interrogate European discourse and discursive strategies from its [postcolonial writing's] position within and between two worlds." Alioune Diop began this process of interrogation by using négritude as a motivating identity discourse and the Présence Africaine publishing house as a strategic base. Revolutionary writing reversed the terms of this discourse, and the Parisianists and universalists transformed the discourse altogether. The new generation has questioned the fundamental unity and homogeneity of African identity while simultaneously expanding the opportunities for the distribution and commercialization of African writing in France. Going beyond a single counterdiscourse, the new generation has broadened the array of possibilities for African literary expression in France.

The Political Economy of African Writing

As an anecdotal example, Alioune Diop presents the case of an African writer who receives an international prize. His fame and reputation soar. He is also seduced by the Western audience and those who have awarded him the prize. Diop (1987:51) concludes: "This is human but he also risks moving away from his own people and culture because his work will be neither awaited nor heard by black opinion." Once again, Diop develops a binary opposition between Africa and the West, between the culturally pure and the hybrid, the authentic and the inauthentic. Diop's allegory masks the political economy of African literature.

During its early years, the Présence Africaine publishing house served as the only French outlet for many African writers, intellectuals, and students who did not have access to European publishers. It functioned as a clearing house for the exchange of ideas between French and African intellectuals. From the ranks of these writers rose such literary giants as Césaire and Senghor. Others, such as David Diop and Paulin Joachim, began literary and journalistic careers that were launched by Présence Africaine. Still others, like Richard Wright and Gwendolyn Brooks, were introduced from the United States to a French audience (Walker 1988; Gilroy 1993:146–86). But as the years wore on, Présence Africaine experienced financial and organizational difficulties. Manuscripts were held for five years or more before authors received a minimal response, and then the answer was often no. The publishing house was slow in adapting to new computerized techniques of publication, inventorying, and business organization. As late as 1990, Présence Africaine's correspondence, accounts, and inventories were still done by hand. Moreover, the Afrocentric European market that Diop had hoped to create was fragile, and its heyday was short-lived. Présence Africaine, nevertheless, retained loyal supporters among French, African, and other international intellectuals. A new interest in minority discourse in the United States led scholars to review the contribution of Présence Africaine, often in idealized historical terms rather than with respect to the pragmatic challenges of the increasingly competitive French publishing scene.

In chapter 4, I discussed the problems faced by writers on the African continent in their attempts to publish and circulate works on an international scale. The Pan-African organizational and publication efforts promoted by Présence Africaine in the 1960s and early 1970s never came to fruition and splintered off into the hands of numerous national, regional, and local cultural groups in Africa. Limited local resources for publication and the neocolonial control and increasing centralization of the publication industry, particularly since the 1980s, led authors to adopt a variety of survival strategies. Self-publication became one of the most viable options. In some cases, self-publication gave authors enough visibility to attract French and other international publishing houses. In other instances, self-publication became an outlet for the local and grass-roots circulation of their works, or simply a dead end. Although it has resulted in potential benefits and rewards for writers, one of the risks of self-publication is the stigma that authors could not be published elsewhere. This stigma relates to what Jean Baudrillard (1968:270–74) terms the problem of "standing" in a consumer society. Foreign publishers have the highest "standing" or prestige, followed by local outlets. According to the "code of standing," self-publishers lose status by attempting to reproduce and distribute their own works. Power then falls into the hegemonic networks of global economic control.

Censorship is another problem faced on the African continent, but supposedly attenuated in Europe. Ivoirian authors such as Jean-Marie Adiaffi Ade claim that they were victims of censorship, although of a subtle variety, by European presses that required them to cut manuscripts for supposed problems of space and reproduction, when censoring politically sensitive parts of the manuscript was really the issue. Another indirect form of censorship on the European market results from consumer demand. Authors are encouraged to write in a certain style and to emphasize particular points of view in order to meet consumer demand. Smaller publishing houses such as Éditions L'Harmattan and Karthala, in Paris, have developed ranking systems for more commercially viable pieces, academic books, and the works of lesser-known African authors. Books of lesser-known authors are printed in limited quantities of 1,000 to 1,500 books, which are stockpiled and disappear from view when they do not sell quickly.[8] The Ivoirian author Jérôme Carlos referred to this process as "writing books to put in our desk drawers."

Yet, there have been changes in the French publication industry for African literature since the founding of the *Présence Africaine* journal in 1947. With electronic communications, computer-assisted technologies, and laser disks, books can, in theory, be produced more rapidly and more efficiently than ever. Books that are not printed or that are censored may be distributed by the Internet, in spite of the legal problems posed. Books, as well, may be entirely conceived as electronic communications distributed exclusively over the Internet or on disks. Nevertheless, many African publishers still send books to Europe to be printed, and economic control of technological resources remains in developed nations. Increasingly, publishing houses are being bought up by larger and larger information and media conglomerates. This situation leaves African publishers, and publishers of books on African topics, on the margins.

Financial and cultural capital determine who is included and who is excluded in the political economy of techno-publication.[9] Although newer French and African publishers, such as Éditions L'Harmattan, Karthala, Éditions Nouvelles du Sud, and Revue Noire Publications, have joined Présence Africaine in the field of African-oriented publishing, and in spite of occasional literary prizes, African works remain ghettoized in major French publishing houses. Problems of staffing, technological upgrading, and limitations in publishing and distribution capacity prevent the smaller publishing houses from taking on more of the burden of African literature than they already have. In turn, these publishers complain about the mixed quality and low commercial viability of many of the manuscripts they receive. A policy of tossing manuscripts arriving without recommendation into the dust bin is one of the more radical solutions to the oversubscription problem. The situation is no better in the United States, where works of the new generation of Franco-African writers are translated and published sporadically, with considerable time lags and mostly by academic presses. African writing in French is a specialty market, and the political economy of African writing determines the success of writers' careers.

Writers' Careers

Writing, like art, music, and other forms of cultural expression, is conducted within the purview of cultural, social, and material circumstances (Waterman 1990:7). Only a few of the African writers discussed in this volume have been able to survive on purely literary careers. Four major alternative career routes are available to them: (1) university academic careers; (2) journalism and related cultural pursuits; (3) work unrelated to writing, such as diplomacy or employment by an international agency; and (4) full-time writing on long-term contracts provided by major publishing houses. Mixed writing careers, exemplified by the first three alternatives, result in sporadic and varied qualities and types of writing. The fourth alternative requires the consistent publication of books that are controlled by the demands, desires, and whims of established publishing houses and the commercial market. Elsewhere (Jules-Rosette 1984:226–30), I have referred to the fourth alternative as responding to perceived consumer demand.[10]

On the African continent, combining writing with a university career is a precarious endeavor. Universities are often in turmoil or closed, and pay for faculty is low. In addition, working from an African university base does not assure development of an international reputation or a broad audience for the author's works. The "francophonie" circuit helps African writers enter the international market by giving them publicity through conferences and festivals outside of Africa, notably in France. These festivals—including the Festival International des Francophonies in Limoges, the Festival d'Avignon, the Théatre International de la Langue Française in Paris, the Carthage Film Festival, and the FESPACO international film festival in Ouagadougou, Burkina Faso—provide writers with an opportunity to contact publishers, distribute their works, and keep up with current literary trends and cultural debates. In some cases, the festivals assume the role of a good international publishing house by offering publicity, increased sales opportunities, and monetary prizes to authors. Some writers, both in Africa and France, remain almost exclusively within the francophonie circuit.[11] Restriction to this circuit is a byproduct of the media coverage of works by African writers and of a labeling process that resembles the classification of "race records" in the U.S. recording industry of the 1930s and 1940s. Although it is not necessary to leave the francophonie circuit in order to achieve success, writers who have long-term contracts with major French publishing houses seldom restrict themselves to this festival circuit and occasionally disparage it. Writers and artists such as Werewere Liking, Suzanne Tanella Boni, and Maurice Bandaman, who are based on the African continent, have successfully used the francophonie circuit to promote their works internationally. The festival circuit is one route to international visibility by virtue of the literary and creative prizes it offers.

African writers with university connections in France have a different relationship to French publishing houses. As academics, they have direct access to university and research presses and to the smaller African-oriented publishing houses such as Éditions L'Harmattan and Karthala. Depending on their status and contacts, they establish regular contractual arrangements with the larger French publishing houses. In this case, French and European literary prizes, such as the Prix Goncourt, the Prix Renaudot, and lesser regional prizes, play an important role in furthering the literary careers of authors. For short periods, the fact that an African or Antillian author, such as Calixthe Beyala or the Martinican author Patrick Chamoiseau, has won a prize opens up the publication market for other African writers by creating a commercial basis of acceptability and popularity for African-oriented writing.

Authors pushed by choice and daily exigencies into combinatorial careers are often able to press these careers into the service of writing. Edouard Maunick has pursued a tripartite career of diplomacy, journalism, and university teaching. While working for the international educational division of UNESCO, he continued to write poetry and to anthologize the works of other writers whose manuscripts were submitted to his office. His epic poem *Mandéla* clearly voiced his political commitments in literary form. Maunick's position as ambassador from his country to the new South African government was furthered by his public literary commitment to Nelson Mandela. Novelists such as Simon Njami have been successful in pursuing innovative journalistic careers in concert with their creative and expository writing. Njami's editorial role at *Revue Noire* has made a significant impact on the presentation and circulation of contemporary African art in France.[12] *Revue Noire* links Njami to the festival circuit as an entrepreneur and promoter of African art while he maintains long-term literary contracts with major French publishing houses (Gallimard, Le Seuil, and Seghers). Werewere Liking offers another example of an active combinatorial career. She uses her literary works to support her theatrical performances, and vice versa, while remaining largely in the francophonie circuit when she is in France.

Among the new generation of African writers in France, Calixthe Beyala is one of the few examples of an author able to pursue a purely literary career. Long-term publication contracts with Librairie Stock and Albin Michel, effective media promotion of her work, and winning the 1996 Grand Prix of the Académie Française have allowed Beyala to survive almost exclusively on her royalties, lectures, and literary appearances. Successful pursuit of this type of career requires the rapid and regular publication of at least one book per year and numerous promotional appearances. Beyala's active and successful literary career demonstrates that a new-generation African writer can thrive uniquely as an artist. Her themes, topics, and intensive production schedule, however, have inevitably been influenced by the demands of the publication houses with which she is associated.

The intertwining influences of mass media and public opinion influence the career trajectories and visibility of African writers in France. Commercial demand affects their public identities. Some of the writers go to great lengths to develop themselves as public media personalities in order to attract attention to their works. The new-generation writers who denounce the label "African" do so, in part, because they are able to break away from this label in the commercial arena. Commercial influences do not determine literary identity, but positive market forces can enable African writers to have greater degrees of freedom in carving out a public space. If we concede that perpetuation of the label "francophonie" is a media construction, then it is clear that the dual forces of media and the market must be taken into account when we assess the future of African writing in France.

Agendas for the Future

"Globalization" is a hotly contested term. Many sociologists and other scholars of society want to do away with it.[13] But the fact remains that global networks of communication and exchange have the potential of linking authors and literary publics around the world. In spite of these new technological developments, which could lead to a changing concept of what is "universal" in literature, local markets, language barriers, and cultural particularism persist. With regard to African literature, this particularism is reinforced by European domination of publication resources and technologies. I have described this domination in terms of the "green beans" export problem. Technological domination goes hand-in-hand with ideological control and the manipulation of media to shape public receptivity to literature. What is universal is defined by a Western canon that includes only a highly selective representation of African literature. Thus, the exclusion of certain types of writing from the "worlding" of the literary mainstream results in an artificial and forced particularism (Spivak 1985:262–63).

By emphasizing common elements of cultural, regional, ethnic, and biographical identity, writers generate their own forms of particularism. Using Paris as their literary landscape, the Parisianists reconfigure their visions of Africa while simultaneously creating a new closed environment for their works. This environment is accompanied by a unique style that sets them apart from others. Although the aesthetic and ideological closure of Parisianism is particularistic, its underlying universalistic message supports the social, political, and cultural acceptance of Africans, other immigrants, and marginal people. Hence, in Parisianism, universalism is actually the goal of the assertion of a particularistic identity discourse.

Granted, all literature that deals with fundamental human problems and struggles has universalistic components. Nevertheless, I have identified two trends in Franco-African literature as essentially universalistic: (1) the early efforts of Présence Africaine to define black inclusion in global terms, and (2) the writings of more recent essayists and poets (e.g., Maunick, Tiémélé, and Bolya) who situate African problems in a world context. The paradox once again arises that these two types of universalistic writing are based on the particularism of African inflections. In the first instance, the writers attempt to define a spirit, soul, or style that is fundamentally "African" (e.g., négritude). In the second case, the authors take Africa, or specific aspects of African cultures, as a point of departure for redefining universal psychological, social, and political problems (e.g., alienation, immigration, political oppression, and economic inequality). This intertwining of universal and particular values makes it all the more difficult to determine what is "African" about the new generation of African literature in

France. Therefore, in the end, in spite of literary and semiotic classifications, what is "African" is left up to the authors' own self-assertions and to the forces of the media and the literary marketplace.[14]

Agendas for the future of African writing may be approached on the political, economic, and aesthetic levels. Négritude's solution to the problem of universalism in African literature was political and cultural. Although the Présence Africaine publishing house created a new space for African writing in France, the content of many of the early works revolved around an identity discourse of anthropological essentialism, which provided an ideological justification for these publications. Events over the past fifty years, including, but certainly not limited to, the independence of African nations and south-north migration, have transformed the political terms of the universalism debate. In the wake of Africa's false starts, economic crises, and the broken promise of African modernity, new challenges face African writers (Sandbrook 1993:21–29). Not the least of these challenges is an ambivalence about the international marketplace for African literature. Although the authors' purported target audiences for certain works may be primarily African, the loci of publication and distribution are still primarily European or international.[15] This schizophrenia of the marketplace, in which a book produced in, and targeted toward, Africa may be printed in Hong Kong, bound in Africa, and sold in Europe or North America, affects the writers' strategic moves from creation to distribution in a global context. The phenomenon of globalization adds a new dimension to the definition of universalism.

With regard to aesthetics, the meeting of the universal and the particular in African literature is also fraught with ambivalence. In an article on Werewere Liking, the literary critic Anne Adams (1993:154) states: "Therefore, 'classic' forms of artistic expression that are bound by formal constraints and which might have suited the artistic impulse of an earlier generation (apologies to négritude) do not fit the neurosis of today's situation." A new aesthetic trend emphasizes breaking down barriers of language, genre, and style. The Cameroonian authors Werewere Liking and Calixthe Beyala, both of whom live and work outside of their natal country, refer to this new tendency as "madness" or "lunatic writing." Abdel Kebir Khatibi (1990:10–12), a Moroccan author, introduces two related aesthetic notions: diglossia (or bilingual passion) and *unicité,* or intercultural "oneness" of the *bilingue* in writing. Diglossia, involving shifting between languages and aesthetic codes, begins with an intercultural encounter as the point of departure for writing. Accordingly, dominant literary languages, such as French or English, are enriched by their encounters with other languages and the attendant cultural presuppositions. The fruits of these encounters is unicité, a new whole, born of intercultural contact. Unicité has the potential to create new literary standards (Bouraoui 1995:67). As a result, African literature would no longer be classified as a category apart, or an adjunct of francophonie, but would be included in the international panorama of world literature.

In spite of these laudable aims of inclusion and oneness, publishers, the literary market, and the reading public remain final arbiters of the works that are accepted as African, French, and/or world literature. There is a sense in which all great literature has the capacity to be universal. As Hédi Bouraoui (1995:68) points out, Dante is not merely an Italian author; Shakespeare, English; or Molière, French. But great literature is born of social and cultural contexts in which many lesser forms of literary expression compete. The intercultural critic's task, then, becomes to justify how and why many writers, and not just the exceptional authors, should have a chance to participate in world literature, or at least to be competitive on the global scene.

Seven mechanisms may be used to open this global literary scene to more diversity.

1. Development of new marketing and exchange networks. The centralization of marketing and publication resources in the West, or the so-called developed countries, needs to be diffused. Literary copublications are one step in this direction. This step, however, is blocked by the increasing control of African publishing houses by international conglomerates. Self-publication is another solution to this problem, but it is not an adequate strategy for most long-term, professional writers.

2. Reinforcing south-north support networks for writers. Increased communication among writers and between writers and publishers across the south-north divide would contribute to a change in critical standards, innovations in literature, and the opening up of new publication possibilities.

3. New criteria of literary and genre classification. Authors such as Beyala, Khatibi, Liking, and Tadjo have demonstrated the importance of breaking down genre and aesthetic stereotypes for intercultural writers. The dissolution of stereotypical classifications, however, does not come from the writers alone. Their experiments may fail, but the market and audiences for innovative writing need to expand. This expansion is, in part, a byproduct of the media coverage of experimental works and the willingness of publishers to take risks with new works.

4. Internationalization of local literary markets. Mechanisms already exist through publishers, wholesalers, and bookstores for the north-south exchange of books, and the importation into Africa of books published in Europe. These networks need to be strengthened and expanded so that rich local markets can develop to benefit from the exchange and the interaction with a variety of literary models. The music industry has experienced more success than the publishing industry with this type of importation.

5. Increasing cultural permeability in international literary markets. The reverse process of exporting local works to international markets would strengthen the web of international literary communication. It would also give unknown or "popular" writers and artists more access to international reading publics and markets. In this case, both informed literary critics and publishers play an important role in the transfer of local works to the international scene. Journals, reviews, and anthologies marketed internationally serve as important mechanisms for this diffusion.

6. Stable institutional frameworks for multicultural writing. International festivals, summits, and conferences are part of the new institutional framework for multicultural writing. These events, however, are sporadic and may be short-lived. New writers and artists launched by festivals and conferences may have no further public contact until the next event occurs. Part of the problem with the early conferences staged by Présence Africaine was the fragility of a sustained intellectual framework that might follow up on results between conferences. Universities and other educational institutions can strengthen these literary networks, along with the writers and publishers themselves.

7. Translation projects. As African writing universalizes and enters the global market, translation projects play an important role. To a certain extent, the translation endeavor has always been part of the activities of *Présence Africaine,* in which some articles and conference proceedings were translated from French into English. *Revue Noire* uses a bilingual French-English format. In both of these cases, African languages are left on the margins. A larger vision of the translation enterprise and more subsidy for it from agencies and publishing houses would enrich African writings and make them more internationally accessible.

Growing out of the legacy of Présence Africaine in France, these seven new developments are now within the reach of writers and publishers and their audiences. The literary challenges discussed here, however, entail more than a shift in intellectual paradigms and philosophies. Social and economic changes play an important part in transforming the literary marketplace. The contemporary music industry has demonstrated how various local and popular forms of artistic expression, from rap music to reggae, can be incorporated rapidly into "world music" or "world beat" (Lipsitz 1994:51–58). The canons and institutional structures maintaining literature and the plastic arts change much more slowly. It is now time for a regeneration of African and intercultural literatures that builds upon the traditions and conventions of the past while structuring a more culturally and aesthetically open future.

APPENDIX ONE

Chronology of Key Events

The following chronology summarizes some of the key events that have influenced African writing in France.

1931–33 Marcel Griaule mounts the Dakar-Djibouti Mission, an expedition that transforms anthropological research methods. He returns to France with 3,500 African objects for the Musée de l'Homme.

1945 The Fifth Pan-African Congress is held in Manchester, England. Participants include W. E. B. Du Bois, Jomo Kenyatta, Kwame Nkrumah, Ras T. Makonnen, and a host of local organizers. Plans are made for decolonization in anglophone Africa.

1947 Alioune Diop founds the journal *Présence Africaine* with editorial and patronage committees consisting of African, Antillian, African-American, and French intellectuals.

1949 The Présence Africaine publishing house (Éditions Présence Africaine) is established by Alioune Diop and his colleagues in Paris. Placide Tempels's *La Philosophie bantoue* (1949) is the first book published by Éditions Présence Africaine.

1954 Vietnamese victory at Dien Bien Phu on May 7 results in French withdrawal from Indochina. The country is temporarily divided by a peace accord signed in Geneva on July 21.

The United States Supreme Court rules to end school segregation in public schools in the case of *Brown v. Board of Education,* on May 17.

1955 The Afro-Asiatic Conference is held in Bandoeng, Indonesia, April 18–24. The terms of decolonization are debated once again.

A unanimous U.S. Supreme Court decision orders desegregation of public facilities "with all deliberate speed," on May 31.

The journal *Présence Africaine* sponsors a debate in Paris on national poetry on July 9. Aimé Césaire, David Diop, René Depestre (in absentia), and others hammer out the criteria for national poetry and the contributions of black aesthetics.

Rosa Parks is arrested on December 5 for desegregating a Montgomery, Alabama, bus, and a new era is launched in the U.S. civil rights movement.

1956 The Présence Africaine committee organizes the First Congress of Black Writers and Artists, held at the Sorbonne, September 19–22. The congress launches two decades of debates on African art, culture, and politics.

Alioune Diop and his supporters establish the Société Africaine de Culture (SAC) to promote the cultural and research activities of black intellectuals. Dr. Jean Price-Mars of Haiti becomes the first president of SAC.

1958 Guinea is the first francophone African nation to become independent. France negotiates the terms for the end of the colonial era in Africa.

1959 Présence Africaine and the Société Africaine de Culture sponsor the Second Congress of Black Writers and Artists in Rome from March 26 to April 1. Loyal supporters return to plan the cultural agenda for postcolonial Africa.

Bernard B. Dadié publishes *Un Négre à Paris* and establishes the foundations for the Parisianism genre of African writing.

1960 Benin (Dahomey), Burkina Faso (Upper Volta), Cameroon, Central African Republic, Chad, Congo, Côte d'Ivoire, Gabon, Mali, Niger, Senegal, and Togo declare their independence. Nation building begins.

1962 Algerians vote independence from France following a series of bloody struggles throughout the 1950s.

1966 With the support of UNESCO, the Société Africaine de Culture organizes the First World Festival of Black Arts, convening in Dakar, Senegal, April 1–24.

1968 Yambo Ouologuem wins the Prix Renaudot for his novel *Le Devoir de violence,* criticizing corruption and injustice in Africa.

1969 The Pan-African Cultural Festival takes place in Algiers from July 21 to August 1. The death of négritude is announced.

Léopold Senghor is elected to the Academy of Moral and Political Sciences of the Institute of France as a foreign member.

1972 Stanislas Adotevi publishes *Négritude et négrologues,* a poignant critique of négritude. He launches the antinégritude movement.

1973 The Société Africaine de Culture organizes the Colloquium on Literary Criticism held in Yaoundé, Cameroon, April 16–20. Participants map out the terrain of African writing and speculate on the future of national literatures.

1975 Former Catholic priest Denis Pryen establishes Éditions L'Harmattan in Paris and broadens the market for African and Third World literature.

The Second World Black and African festival of Arts and Culture (FESTAC) is held in Lagos, Nigeria. FESTAC prolongs the tradition established by the Société Africaine de Culture and the Pan-African Cultural Festival of Algiers. It also manifests the emergence of new ideologies of black consciousness worldwide.

1980 René Depestre publishes *Bonjour et adieu à la négritude* with Éditions Robert Laffont in Paris. He refuels the antinégritude debate.

Robert Ageneau breaks away from Éditions L'Harmattan and establishes Éditions Karthala with a focus on African scholarly texts and literature.

Paul Dakeyo and a group of African poets found Éditions Silex to promote the diffusion of African literature in France and Africa.

1982 The French national census systematically counts African immigrants in France for the first time.

1983 Creation of the Haut Conseil de Francophonie to assess and oversee the status of francophone literature and the media in France and worldwide.

1990 The French national census further aggregates African populations in France by nationality and citizenship. These statistics stimulate a heated national debate on immigration.

1991 The first issue of *Revue Noire*, a new-generation, multicultural art magazine, is published in the spring.

1992 The Haut Conseil à l'Intégration is established by President François Mitterand to make recommendations on immigration issues in France.

1993 Interior Minister Charles Pasqua is the architect of Law #93-933 of July 22, requiring second-generation immigrants to petition for French citizenship. The French national debate over immigration escalates.

1996 Cameroonian writer Calixthe Beyala receives the Grand Prix Littéraire of the Académie Française for her novel *Les Honneurs perdus* and places Parisianism on the French literary map.

APPENDIX TWO

Immigration Statistics

These comparative population figures are based on raw data collected from the 1982 and 1990 French census reports (Institut National de la Statistique et des Études Économiques 1982, 1990).

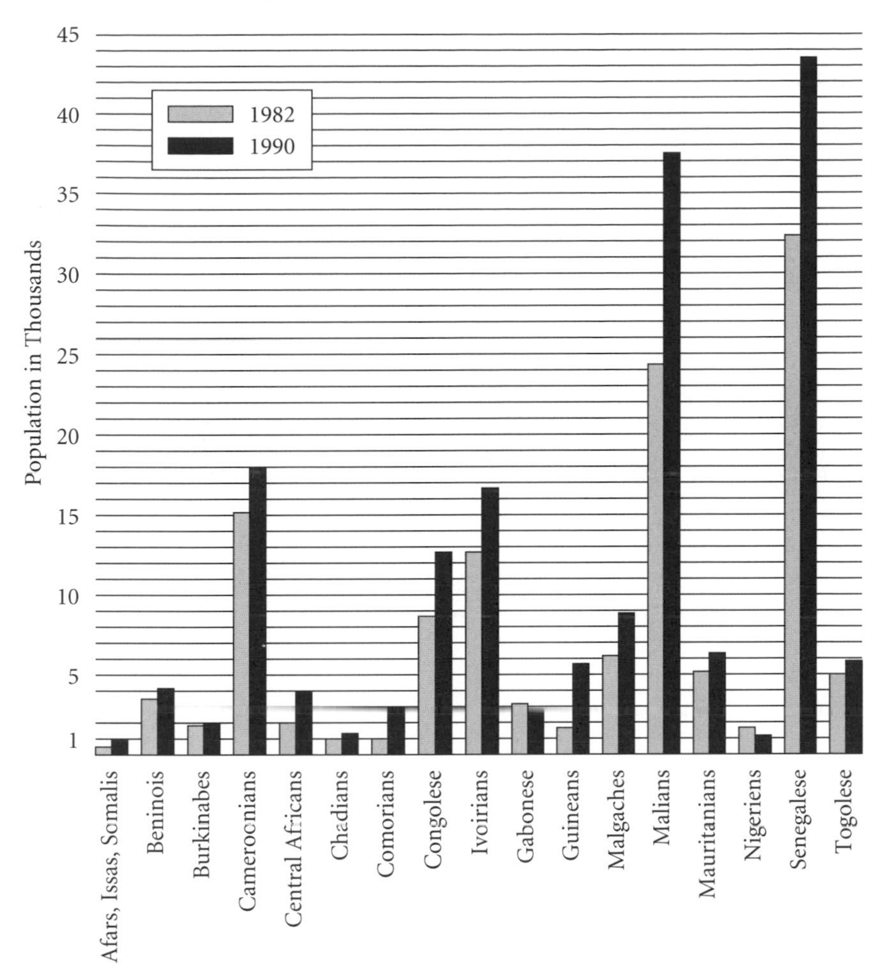

Fig. A-1. African Populations from Former French Colonies Living in France, 1982–90. The total population from formerly French African countries living in France has increased dramatically over the last thirty years. Demographic estimates by INSÉÉ show a steady rise in immigration over the past decade.

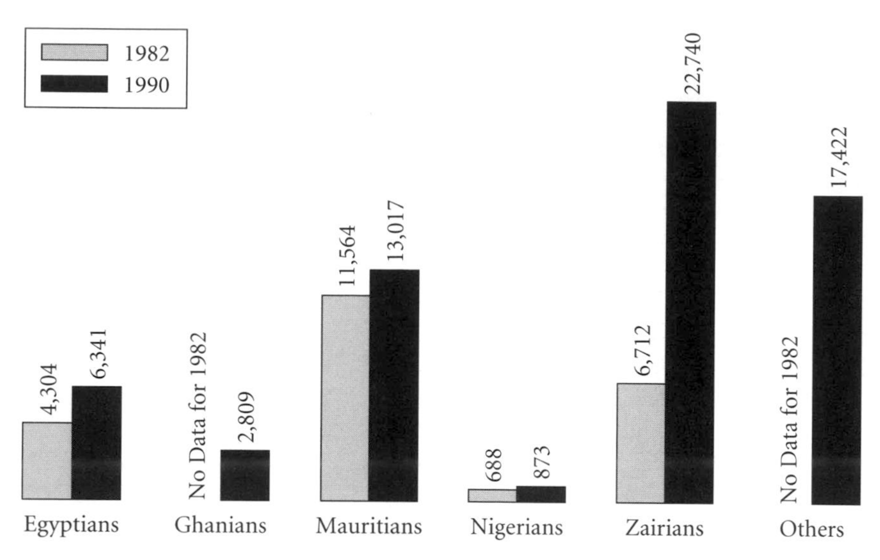

Fig. A-2. Other African Populations Living in France, 1982–90. A notable increase has occurred among other African populations from countries outside of the French community who are residing in France.

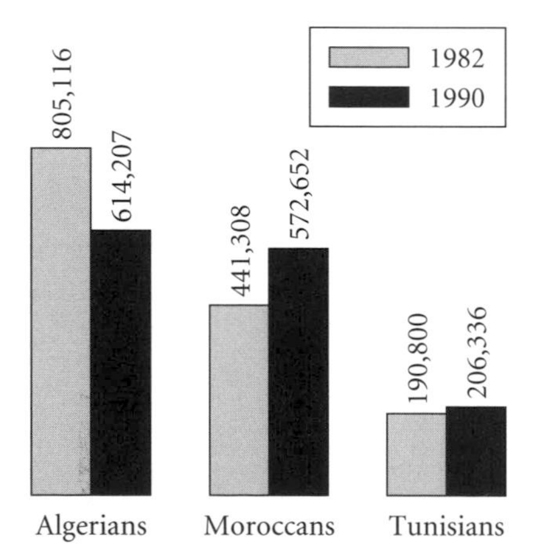

Fig. A-3. North African Populations Living in France, 1982–90. Maghrebi populations in France have increased steadily over the past decade, although, for political reasons, there has been a decline in the number of Algerians residing in France.

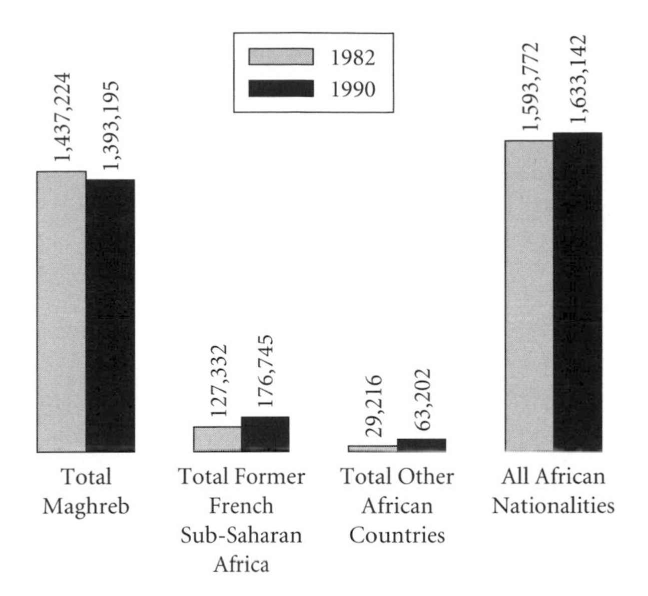

Fig. A-4. North African and Sub-Saharan African Populations Living in France, 1982–90. Comparative statistics show an overall increase in all African populations in France, except the Maghrebi population. The Maghrebi decline results from a drop in Algerian immigration.

NOTES

Introduction

1. In *Black Writers in French,* Lilyan Kesteloot (1974:75–79) devotes a chapter to René Maran, whose novel *Batouala, véritable roman nègre* (Batouala: A true black novel) describes his experiences as a West Indian colonial administrator in the Ubangi-Shari territory of Central Africa. Adopted as a founding father by the négritude movement, Maran denied this role.

2. "Congo" presents an idyllic view of life along the Congo River, complete with beating drums, palm trees, and canoes. "Le Kaya-Magan" praises the traditional African chieftain and hero, whose spirit liberates Africa. Both poems appear in Senghor 1948:168–71 and in Senghor 1956:11–13.

3. In *Un Nègre à Paris,* Dadié (1959) uses the format of an epistolary novel to reinforce the verisimilitude and sincerity of Tanhoé Bertin's observations. Brench (1967:87) compares Dadié's novel to Montesquieu's *Lettres persanes.*

4. The use of aerial photography is described as a rapid research technique for collecting ethnological, botanical, geological, and geographic data and as a tool for colonial administration and control (Griaule 1937:469–74).

5. Paul Rivet and Georges-Henri Rivière describe in detail their plans for reorganizing and remodeling the museum at Trocadéro in a bulletin produced for the museum and administrative officials; see Rivet and Rivière 1931:3–11 and Rivière 1949:206–26. By 1932, the museum was ready to receive the objects from Marcel Griaule's expedition, listed variously by sources as 3,500 to 3,600 pieces. See Rivet and Rivière 1933:3–6; Jamin 1982:72.

6. Paul Niger's "Je n'aime pas l'Afrique" is widely cited as a precursor of revolutionary writing (Markovitz 1969:58; Kesteloot 1974:279). The poem, however, might more effec-

tively be interpreted as expressing Niger's disillusionment with the narratives of longing and belonging. He found an Africa that he did not long for and with which he could not identify. "Je n'aime pas l'Afrique" was published in Senghor 1948:93–100 and reprinted with an English translation in Jones 1971:82–83.

7. Nkashama (1993:17) states that the quality of African publications depends in large part on the publishers' commercial and ideological concerns. He argues that during the postcolonial era, négritude ceased to be a commercially viable approach for African writers.

8. Nkashama (1993:17) asserts that "there has not existed in France, outside of Présence Africaine, a publishing house that is interested exclusively in Africa." Éditions Karthala, founded in 1980, publishes books on Africa with a comparative focus. These works, however, tend to be scholarly texts and travel guides with a limited literary collection. Présence Africaine was the first publishing house to launch and encourage African authors on a consistent basis. For further discussion of the role of Présence Africaine in the French publication industry between 1953 and 1968, see also Kouamé 1991 and Mel 1995.

Chapter 1: An Uneasy Collaboration

1. I presented a much shorter version of this chapter at an invitational session of the American Ethnological Society in Chicago on November 21, 1991. There I documented the ways in which Paul Rivet and Georges-Henri Rivière modified the synthetic anthropology of Pierre Paul Broca and Armand de Quatrefages de Bréau as the Musée d'Éthnographie evolved into the new Musée de l'Homme in 1937.

2. Denise Ferembach (1980:4) presents this original quote by Broca. From this statement, it is clear that Broca viewed his cabinet of anthropometric instruments as a major innovation for advancing research and teaching in the anthropology of his day. See also Broca 1875.

3. Lévy-Bruhl (1923) proposed a total anthropology in which the "primitive mentality" would be studied by examining the cultures in which it arose. Lévy-Bruhl believed that this mentality revealed emotional, prelogical thinking that was largely devoid of abstract ideas. The very assertion, however, that a primitive mentality and imagination existed signaled the birth of a new anthropological paradigm.

4. Arroyo (1982) presents a sympathetic and detailed description of Brown's rise to fame and sad demise. During the late 1920s and 1930s, Brown enjoyed his heyday boxing under the management of an American fight promoter, David Lumiansky, in Paris, Brussels, and Madrid. Brown became a member of Parisian café society and was a flamboyant figure. Meunier (1992) recounts the story of Jack Johnson, who rose to fame and, for a short time, became part of Parisian café society a decade earlier than Brown. Guillaume Apollinaire, Blaise Cendrars, André Breton, and other surrealists were boxing fans, viewing boxing as a genuine expression of the exotic and of primitive poetics. Arroyo (1982:92) provides the most detailed account available of the 1931 Brown-Simendé match. See also Jamin 1982:69–100.

5. Griaule (1931a:4) states: "Al Brown will have known how to put his fists to the service of this cause of universal interest: to make possible between colonizers and colonized

people, thanks to a better knowledge of the mentalities of the latter, a more fruitful collaboration, exercised according to a less brutal and at the same time a more rational plan." According to Jean Jamin (1982:71), Griaule also sent this text, which was part of the original program for the boxing match held at the Cirque d'Hiver on April 15, 1931, to the newspaper *Paris-Soir* and other French newspapers as a press release.

6. The letter that Michel Leiris wrote to Georges-Henri Rivière on October 16, 1931, is still in the closed files of the Musée de l'Homme. Although the letter (Leiris 1931) may be read in the archives by researchers, direct quotation is not permitted. In the letter, which is personal, Leiris asks about a number of colleagues and friends in Paris and inquires about the activities of David Lumiansky and Al Brown.

7. In scaffolding the philosophy of négritude, Senghor drew an emphasis on African cultural unity from Leo Frobenius and a concern with the integrity of African religions and symbolic systems from Marcel Griaule (Senghor 1987:vi). In an adaptation of German idealist philosophy, Senghor attempted to capture cultural essences by using the concepts of négritude, *francité,* and *germanité.* In 1979, an entire conference was sponsored in Dakar on the relationship between négritude and *germanité.* (See Association des Germanistes de l'Enseignement Supérieur 1983.) See also Senghor, "Négritude et Germanité" (Senghor 1977b:11–17).

8. Over the years, Césaire, Senghor, and other participants in the early négritude movement have presented numerous lectures on the topic. One of their primary concerns was to defend the concept of négritude against charges that it constituted racism in reverse and to show that the term originated with the sense of marginalization shared by African and Antillian students in Paris during the 1930s (Markovitz 1969:50–54). When Césaire presented a lecture of this kind, he also presided over an open question-answer session on his work at the Maison Helvétique in Paris. The tape recording of this session, from which I quote, was provided courtesy of the anthropologist Serge Tornay, a participant in these discussions.

9. Here I quote the English translation of Diop's "Itinéraire" reproduced in the Présence Africaine catalog (Diop 1987:48–52). It is interesting that the publishing house continues to reproduce this statement as an explanation of its original mission.

10. An extended version of this lecture is included in Njami 1993, from which I quote. Njami views the anthropometric vision in French ethnology as static and does not concern himself with changes in ethnology or debates in contemporary anthropology. Note that V. Y. Mudimbe (1988:75–76) takes a similar stance when he criticizes evolutionary and functionalist trends in British and French anthropology.

11. James Clifford (1988:117–51) argues strongly in favor of surrealism's humanizing and liberalizing effects on French ethnology. The birth of so-called "ethnographic surrealism" was exemplified by the works of Leiris, Griaule, and others, and by the emergence of Rivet and Rivière's remodeled dream museum. Although I do not disagree with this argument, my emphasis is on ethnology's dialogue with black Paris in general, and the Présence Africaine movement in particular. While surrealism challenged scientism, Présence Africaine attacked scientism, naive exoticism, and the stereotypical tendencies of the anthropometric vision. In this respect, the Présence Africaine movement, which

was not immune to the influences of surrealism, may, nonetheless, have moved French anthropological paradigms toward a more fundamentally humanistic vision.

Chapter 2: Antithetical Africa

1. I presented an earlier version of this chapter, focusing on the First Congress of Black Writers and Artists in 1956, at the African-Americans and Europe Conference organized by Michel Fabre at the Université de Paris III, February 5–9, 1992 (Jules-Rosette 1992a). The present discussion explores in greater depth the implications of the conferences sponsored by Présence Africaine in Europe and Africa between 1956 and 1973.

2. Two special editions of the journal *Présence Africaine* were devoted to the 1956 Congress of Black Writers and Artists. *Présence Africaine,* 2d ser., 8–9–10, special issue (June–Nov. 1956) contains a summary of the congress and includes the papers and debates actually presented at that time. *Présence Africaine,* 2d ser., 14–15, special issue (June–Sept. 1957) summarizes the papers that were not presented and several additional commentaries. These special issues contain introductions signed by *Présence Africaine* but clearly written under the direction of Alioune Diop. (See also Mouralis 1984:426–32.) Interesting discrepancies emerge between the oral histories of the congress and the written summaries of its proceedings. These discrepancies provide the basis for a discussion of the ideological cleavages emerging at the congress and the effects of these disputes on subsequent encounters among black writers and artists in Europe and Africa.

3. In the case of competing narratives about Africa, the continent and its images operate as subjects and antisubjects. Thus, idyllic Africa is destroyed by its antisubject—Africa in combat. Both narrative subjects may exist simultaneously in discourses about changing Africa (Greimas and Courtés 1986:14–16).

4. This statement combines Sartre's commitment to political liberation with the ideal of an idyllic and untouched Africa. The original statement in French appears in Sartre 1947:28–29.

5. While interviewees associated with Présence Africaine, with whom I discussed these problems (Christiane Diop, Jacques Rabemananjara, and Paulin Joachim), were not reluctant to reveal the political fears of the time, they vehemently denied that the 1956 congress was a political event.

6. Miller and Watts (1992) have argued that Présence Africaine selected conservative black American participants to attend the conference under political pressure. In my interviews with conference organizers, I did not find evidence for their claim.

7. An account of the influence of the Bandoeng conference on African students in France during the 1950s is contained in Diané 1990:98–99. Immediately following Bandoeng, the Fédération des Étudiants d'Afrique Noire en France (FÉANF) mobilized informational campaigns to urge the populations of various African countries to express their solidarity with the Algerian independence struggle. FÉANF also formed an anticolonialist committee as an offshoot of the Bandoeng deliberations. The FÉANF students figured among the observers at the 1956 congress, and several subsequently held political offices in their home countries.

8. Howlett (1958:114) contrasts the laudatory reviews of the 1956 congress by the left and liberal French press with the severe criticisms issuing from the conservative press. The

former framed the congress as the intellectual wing of an emerging struggle against colonialism. Mouralis (1984:425) summarizes the liberal and left press coverage but, for some reason, omits the conservative criticisms that branded the 1956 congress participants as dangerous political agitators. A more thorough and balanced summary of the press coverage from all political perspectives is provided by Mel (1995:165–66).

9. In a message entitled "Crise de la culture noire," contained in the congress proceedings, Madeleine Rousseau (1957:331–35), an independent French scholar and long-term supporter of Présence Africaine, quoted Richard Wright's comment concerning technology. She argued that the "African artistic spirit" will revive Western humanism. Rousseau's view relies upon Senghor's theory of négritude as a catalyst for renewing European cultures.

10. For Césaire's full argument, see Césaire 1956b:190–205.

11. For Fanon's text on colonialism and its psychological effects, see Fanon 1956.

12. Ed Clark, a black American painter who frequented the Tournon during the 1950s, informed me in a personal communication that he often had to fend off requests by government agents that he report on the activities of his colleagues.

13. Evidence from both interview and archival sources points to genuine differences in the ways in which U.S. and African delegates viewed their respective political circumstances. Some of the U.S. delegates created a negative impression at the congress (Rabemananjara 1988).

14. Baldwin's biographer, Simon Njami (1991b:132), asserts that the 1956 congress marked the birth of Baldwin's mature awareness of Africa in relationship to racial problems in the United States. Nevertheless, Baldwin continued to view African issues from a cautious distance.

15. Mouralis (1984:431–32) mentions Dia's summary of the significance of the congress as an ideological model for decolonization. Nevertheless, he overlooks Dia's brilliant congress communication outlining the economic hurdles that independent African nations would face as they entered a period of social, cultural, and political liberation (Dia 1957:58–72).

16. Although African and Antillian poets and critics participated in various French debates about national literature, it was not until the 1973 SAC-sponsored conference in Yaoundé, Cameroon, that an effort was made to develop systematic criteria for African literary criticism (Société Africaine de Culture 1977:538–44).

17. These objectives are outlined in *Présence Africaine* 1959:9–12.

18. Mulago (1959:190) advocates an "incarnated" and "engaged" Christianity in which the theologian returns to uncover African traditions and graft aspects of them onto Christianity. Mulago's approach set a precedent for new developments in African theology.

19. In his communication at the 1966 festival symposium, Engelbert Mveng, director of cultural affairs in Cameroon and professor at Université Fédérale at Yaoundé in Cameroon, succinctly outlined the festival's objectives seen from his perspective. Mveng (1968:27) stated: "The promotion of art and research in the domain of art in Africa would have much more chance of success if through the Société Africaine de Culture and in the framework of its Arts Commission we could manage to coordinate the efforts, on one side, of all the artists and craftworkers throughout Africa, and on the other, of all the research-workers and specialists of African Art in all African countries and the whole world. Our

heart-felt wish is that the Dakar Festival should be the point of departure of such an organisation." This goal harks back to Senghor's proposal for developing Africanism, or research on African civilizations, with a cultural and political search for identity. In an interview with Frédéric Grah Mel (1995:282), Mveng recalls the excitement surrounding the Dakar festival and Senghor's role in continuing to promote his theories of négritude and Africanism. The Dakar festival symposium was heavily weighted toward developing an academic framework for Africanism at the expense of some of its political implications.

20. In a 1991 personal communication with me, the anthropologist and filmmaker Jean Rouch criticized the 1966 cinema resolutions and expressed the view that the resolutions from the 1969 Festival of Algiers were a potential threat to aesthetic freedom in African cinema.

21. The fifty-nine papers presented in Algiers took the form of political manifestoes. Some documents from countries engaged in liberation struggles were actually tracts pleading for support. The communications were hastily prepared and characterized by a tone of urgency. These presentations have not been published.

22. The papers presented at the Algiers Festival symposium (Musée de l'Homme 1969) contrast markedly with the moderate and measured academic presentations of the 1966 Dakar festival. The style of the Algiers papers reflects impatience with previous knowledge frameworks and an effort to advance the cause of integrating research with political action. This format of presentation marks a clear break with the more literary and scholarly style characteristic of the European congresses sponsored by Présence Africaine and reflects a strategic approach to political action.

23. Bjornson (1991:174–75) describes Diop's influence on the founding of *Abbia* and on the Cameroonian literary scene in the 1960s.

24. The framework of national literature was introduced as early as the 1956 congress and became a point of future discussion and debate for the activities of Présence Africaine (Mouralis 1984:465–67).

Chapter 3: Revolutionary Writing

1. Bhabha (1984:125–33) and JanMohamed (1985:78–106) present competing theories of colonial discourse. Bhabha is concerned with the ambivalence of colonial discourses as coproductions of the colonizer and the colonized. JanMohamed argues that a discourse representing the Manichean character of the colonial situation from the perspective of the oppressed is no longer colonial. In contrast, I contend that if a discourse, such as négritude, presupposes the colonial encounter as a reason for its existence, it remains within the colonial paradigm.

2. Minh-ha (1989:13–15) uses Rabemananjara's article, along with Aimé Césaire's poetry, to illustrate the problems of political engagement and art in general terms. I am concerned with situating these comments on African writing within the social context of the négritude movement and the subsequent emergence of revolutionary writing.

3. The 1988 interview I conducted with Jacques Rabemananjara, presented following chapter 1, explores the relationship between political commitment and art, and illustrates his view that popular political leadership can issue from an elite cadre.

4. Fanon (1963:240) is clear about the political content of a revolutionary national literature, but does not define its format and aesthetic criteria.

5. "Reworlding" refers to the loss of cultural authority of one literary tradition in the face of a new perspective (Spivak 1985:262–80; Chambers 1996:50–54). This shift in the axis of power occurs not only across literatures and cultures but also across generations.

6. Fanon's approach in his essays on racism and national culture and in *Peau noire, masques blancs* (1952) established the importance of a psychological interpretation to race and culture. In modified form, this psychological perspective became a resource for the African writers of the Parisianism school during the 1980s.

7. For convenience of reference, the 1963 English translation of Fanon's *Les Damnés de la terre* (1961) (The wretched of the earth) by Constance Farrington has been used in most instances in this chapter. Although this translation is widely known, it occasionally misses some of the nuances and power of Fanon's writing.

8. Depestre's 1969 "Fondements socio-culturels de notre identité," presented at the Pan-African Cultural Festival in Algiers, has already been discussed in chapter 2. One of the constant themes in Depestre's 1969 and 1978 publications and in his 1980 book on négritude is the search for a balance between the cultural ideal of a deracialized society and its social expression in the Cuban case. Depestre believed that he was participating in the building of a new utopian and integrated society in which philosophies such as négritude would be outmoded.

9. Dakeyo's approach to revolutionary love forecasts aspects of the intimate generation's writing in the 1980s. Works by Simon Njami (1989a), Abdelkebir Khatibi (1990), and others use love as a register for expressing social protest and for providing a commentary on problems of integration and assimilation in French society. The translations of Dakeyo's poetry provided here are my own.

10. Between 1989 and 1992, I interviewed Paul Dakeyo several times in Paris and West Africa.

Chapter 4: Green Beans and Books

1. Walter Rodney's classic work, *How Europe Underdeveloped Africa* (1972), provides an analysis of the roots of neocolonialism in the economic and technological dependence of Africa on the West (Rodney 1972:32–36). Although Rodney does not deal explicitly with neocolonialism in the cultural sphere, his analysis can be expanded to examine the worlds of art and literature, as well as high technology. According to Rodney (1972:36): "Any diagnosis of underdevelopment in Africa will reveal not just low per capita income and protein deficiencies, but also the gentlemen who dance in Abidjan, Accra, and Kinshasa when music is played in Paris, London, and New York."

2. I audiotaped and videotaped the Municipal Club debate held at Deux Plateaux on July 30, 1992. The statements by Paul Dakeyo and Jean-Marie Adiaffi Ade and the audience responses are quoted from the audiotape recording.

3. The censorship issue arose repeatedly in my discussions with other Ivoirian authors, such as Bernard Dadié and Jérôme Carlos. Dadié traced the roots of censorship to the colonial era and Carlos emphasized its debilitating effects on contemporary cultural production.

4. The anthology of Ivoirian poetry was ultimately published by Dakeyo and Éditions Nouvelles du Sud in 1994 under the title *Portrait des siècles meutris: Anthologie de la poésie de Côte d'Ivoire* (Bandaman, Ahizi, Anouma, and Zongo 1994).

5. See Hatier 1993. This catalog lists fifty-three titles that were available in 1993 in the Hatier Monde Noir Poche Series, including classic works of francophone African literature, a few translations from anglophone African literature, and a handful of titles by new authors. See also Désalmand 1991: 6–18.

6. The political unrest that began just prior to the 1992 death of Félix Houphouët-Boigny, first president of Côte d'Ivoire, continued through 1995. The national elections held on October 22, 1995, were surrounded by a climate of imminent violence and tension. See Sotinel 1995.

7. Initiated in 1983, the Festival International des Francophonies, directed by Monique Blin, provides an opportunity for African and other francophone authors and artists to meet, discuss their works, and have their theatrical pieces performed. Since 1988, the festival's "Maison des Auteurs" has housed fifty resident writers and artists who spend short sabbatical periods after the festival to work on their writing and theatrical projects. The Limoges festival is particularly helpful to new African writers and authors seeking to break into European publishing. See Festival International des Francophonies 1995.

8. During the 1990s, L'Harmattan grew from a small publishing house producing approximately 40 titles a year, to a much larger and more lucrative operation. By 1990, L'Harmattan was receiving close to 3,000 manuscripts a year, and publishing a total of 400 to 500 (Desjeux 1995:9). Note that these figures are estimates. Among these are several new editions of high-quality and interesting books printed in small quantities or stockpiled by other publishers. By paying close attention to the African market, L'Harmattan is able to promote African-oriented titles that larger publishers often ignore.

9. In *L'Harmattan, 1975–1995,* an authors' listing and catalog commemorating twenty years of L'Harmattan's publications, Bandaman is described as a prizewinning new author whose career should be watched (Éditions L'Harmattan 1995:49).

10. Sophie Ruppert (1991:156–57) found that of the 1,860 books listed in L'Harmattan's 1990 catalog, 634 (or 34.64 percent) were about sub-Saharan Africa and another 41 (2.7 percent) dealt with immigration issues. During the 1990s, L'Harmattan's publication rate steadily increased, with the largest percentage of volumes still devoted to sub-Saharan Africa.

11. Speaking from memory, Armelle Riché states that L'Harmattan had published over 500 titles on Africa by 1992. This figure appears to be a total rather than an annual estimate, if we compare it with Sophie Ruppert's total of 634 volumes on sub-Saharan Africa, 501 of which appeared in the 1990 catalog (Ruppert 1991:156).

12. Karin Barber (1987:1–78) and Wendy Griswold (1987:1–35) analyze popular or "street" literature in Kenya and Nigeria, respectively. Barber (1987:48–53) claims that the *Ontisha* (tabloid) market literature of Kenya, consisting of pulp fiction and pamphlets about daily life, has a broad popular appeal among schoolchildren, traders, and the local proletariat. It is also beginning to sell in England. Some tabloid authors have been able to cross over into more stable and lucrative literary careers. Griswold (1987:28–33) notes

that Nigerian popular literature has a similar broad local appeal, but she does not discuss its reception outside of Nigeria.

13. Ashcroft, Griffiths, and Tiffin (1989:7–8) argue that postcolonial literatures are characterized by a break away from the constraining and dominating aspects of imperial languages. Even when this break is successful, however, works may still become ghettoized by labels. In a 1992 interview with me, the literary critic Bernard Magnier claimed that the audience for francophone African literature is so limited that it becomes saturated quickly, and new works simply do not sell well in France.

14. In the French context, world literature starts at home with the state-approved lists of great literature for the baccalaureate exam and with the approval of the Académie Française and numerous regional academies. The participation of African writers in international markets does not assure them a place on this roster of world literature.

15. Some of the encounters and debates at the twelfth Festival International des Francophonies in Limoges offered African writers the chance to challenge labels, hone themes, and publicize their works. The topic "Écrivains africains: La Génération intime," for example, prompted a heated discussion of political commitment, art, and aesthetics for the postnégritude generation of African writers. Although most of them rejected the label of the "intimate generation," they acknowledged that new trends and literary themes, and styles distinguished them from their predecessors.

Chapter 5: The African Writers' Parisian Landscape

1. The term "black" in France is used to refer to second-generation sons and daughters of African and Antillian migrants born in France. Their culture is the topic of much of the writing of Parisianism (Magnier 1990:102–7).

2. These figures are quoted from the 1982 French census annex and 1990 French census report (Institut National de la Statistique et des Études Économiques 1982, 1990). In an article reacting to the 1990 census, former French president Valéry Giscard d'Estaing (1991) reviewed the consequences of what he saw, from a conservative perspective, as an alarming rate of non-European migration and naturalization in France. He was severely criticized by representatives of the political left for labeling immigration as invasion.

3. Teshome Gabriel (1989:59–60) analyzes the representation of popular memory along three axes: (1) the constitution of the subject, (2) the hierarchical ordering of images, and (3) the use of collective social space. These axes may be adapted to the examination of memory construction in black Paris, along with Gabriel's concept of ruins, or the collective memories attached to literary and filmic landscapes (Gabriel 1993:214–15).

4. The concept of double-rootedness is well established, although controversial, in studies of African migration. Philip Mayer (1971:8–19) first used the term in his classic study of Xhosa migration in South Africa. Mayer's conclusions of double-rootedness were challenged by Bernard Magubane (1973), who argued that this classification is a false typology that masks the common conditions of socioeconomic deprivation shared by all categories of new urban migrants in South Africa. De Rudder, Taboada-Leonetti, and Vourc'h (1990) have emphasized that the cultural orientation of double-rootedness is a response to the social and economic obstacles faced by second-generation immigrants in France.

5. The three Cameroonian novelists highlighted in this chapter are part of the school of Parisianism, in which Paris constitutes the environment for their writing, the source of its literary inspiration, and the resource for its audience. Parisianism contains elements of universalism in its assertion of the presence and worth of African literature on the European scene. The school of Parisianism and the works of its authors are analyzed in greater detail in chapters 6 and 8, and in the conclusion.

6. Jean-Paul Sartre (1976:256–57) argues that the totalizing gaze situates the individual within the group via a relationship to the landscape. Using Paris as an example, Sartre (1976:257) states: "And through the medium of the city, there are given the millions of people who are in the city, and whose completely invisible presence makes of everyone *both* a polyvalent isolation (with millions of facets), and an integrated member of the city (the '*vieux Parisien*' the '*Parisien de Paris,*' etc.)." Identity is achieved through both self-designation (the "interiorization of signification," in Sartre's terms) and interaction with others, which are both totalizing processes. For an analysis of the phenomenology of the gaze, see also Husserl (1964:38–40).

7. The Place de la République in the eleventh arrondissement and boulevard Barbès-Rochechouart in the eighteenth arrondissement are locations where African *sapeurs* congregate. See Gandoulou 1989:18–22 for a detailed discussion of *sapeurs.*

8. In *The Semiotics of Passion,* A. J. Greimas and Jacques Fontanille (1993:90–91) describe the process of "potentialization" in which the narrative subject, ready to act, fantasizes about the outcomes of action, which may be blocked: "With all modalizations in place, the imaginary path they open can be seen in terms of, and in the form of, the existential trajectory. This allows us to understand, among other things, why passion often appears in the narrative unfolding as a shying away from performance: once he has been manipulated or persuaded or made capable, the impassioned subject takes refuge, or finds himself carried away into his imaginary, before renouncing action or, instead, rushing into it. This is how fear works, for example, or as we shall see, jealousy."

9. The gaze of alienation in *African gigolo* resembles Eugène Esselé's gaze of loss in *A la Recherche du cannibale amour.* In both cases, the second-level gaze is directed toward a written text. In contrast, the alienated televisual gaze in Beyala's *Le Petit prince de Belleville* inspires the protagonist, Loukoum, to act by writing letters to his girlfriend, Lolita, and to François Mitterand.

10. In the manner of Roland Barthes, in his discussion of the reality effect, or the creation of a sense of verisimilitude in narrative (Barthes 1975:270–72), I am suggesting that an actual sequence of displacement is not necessary to describe the dislocation of the literary or artistic subject. Rather, the logic of displacement is conveyed through the reality effect of specific visual or literary signs. In the case of the African writers and artists discussed here, displacement is both a theme of their works and a condition under which they live.

11. Baudrillard (1981:50–56) analyzes the reflexive character of television as a mirror and a system of control (*un système panoptique*). He demonstrates the way in which everyday reality is created as a copy of televisual reality. He refers to this televisual coding process as media's micromolecular code. For Baudrillard, politics, social life, and culture

may be viewed as simulations of their mediated copies. Beyala uses a similar idea of televisual simulation when she describes how young Loukoum models his life both in imitation of and rebellion against the televised image of French culture.

12. Jean-Marie Volet (1993:312) states: "Misery and economic difficulties are always in the background of Beyala's literary universe." He documents his thesis across four of her novels, arguing that the portrayal of suffering is a thematic and narrative key to Beyala's writing. Richard Bjornson (1991:417) argues that the suffering portrayed by Beyala, particularly in her first novel, *C'est le soleil qui m'a brûlée* (1987), is caused by men who "are portrayed as having produced this ugliness by the selfish pursuit of their own gratification."

13. Some critics believe that Parisianism lacks psychological depth because of its emphasis on the social and cultural environment of the literary characters (Madeleine Mukambamano, personal communication, July 26, 1991). The ethnographic style fostered by the environmental gaze, however, gives Parisianism its distinctive flavor and, according to the authors, lends it psychological depth.

14. It is noteworthy that Désir's plea for direct political action was published in France's major news organ, *Le Monde,* with a potential for stimulating dialogues across the boundaries of black and official Paris. In her open letter to Harlem Désir, Julia Kristeva (1993:49–64) responds that a more universalistic, historical view of French citizenship should relegate expressions of cultural difference to private concerns. While it is implicit in some of the African writings analyzed here, this debate has far-reaching social and political consequences.

15. The underlying philosophical basis of Parisianism is a claim for cultural recognition while preserving uniqueness. As will be seen later, this idea converges with the claims of the poets and essayists of universalism.

Chapter 6: Parisianism

1. The critical literature on Parisianism is relatively new, and the verdicts that it renders are mixed. Two important collections (Ngandu Nkashama 1994; Omerod and Volet 1994) contain brief biographies of the authors and summaries of their works in the context of contemporary African literature. Cévaër (1994) presents biographies and edited interviews with contemporary African writers, including the three major authors of Parisianism: Beyala, Karone, and Njami. None of these works ventures an in-depth, critical analysis of Parisianism. Coulon (1997) presents an annotated bibliography of selected works of Parisianists in the context of African literature. More works of criticism will probably appear after several anthologies of the literature are in circulation. Magnier (1990:102–7) lays the foundation for this criticism in a brief article on "new wave" African writers by referring to them as *beurs noirs.*

2. Pius Ngandu Nkashama (1994:58–63) devotes more space to Beyala than he does to any other representative of Parisianism. It is important to note that Beyala's first three novels are set in Cameroon, and she is considered in some critical literature as a Cameroonian national writer (Bjornson 1991:416–20). Jean-Marie Volet addresses her work in both the Cameroonian and the French contexts (Volet 1993:309–14; Omerod and Volet 1994:43–45).

3. Njami's *Cercueil et cie* (1985) was translated into English by Marlene Raderman and published by Black Lizard (Berkeley, California) in 1987 as *Coffin and Co.* Four of Beyala's works have been translated into English. Of the new-generation writers, Njami has been the most consistently concerned with integrating African-American issues and characters into his works. Although Guy Maçou's *Voyage au bout de la négritude* (1994) is not technically an example of Parisianism, it shares several stylistic affinities with this approach. Note that the term "négritude" is relegated, in this work, to the description of an African-American's search for cultural roots.

4. My first interviews with the Parisianists were conducted in 1989, following a preliminary study of the Présence Africaine publishing house (Jules-Rosette 1992b). These interviews addressed issues of language, style, audience reception, publication, and the social engagement of the authors. My objective was to develop a point of departure for the critical analysis of these works rather than a comprehensive anthology.

5. In chapter 1, I pointed out that Paulin Joachim (1988) referred to the journal *Présence Africaine* as "a sort of bible that circulated in all of the African hands, everyone's hands in Africa." He viewed the journal as a foundational point of departure for African writing. Njami iconoclastically challenges this perspective by emphasizing the notion that writers are the individual witnesses of their histories and eras.

6. The theme of insanity also appears on Beyala's *Tu t'appeleras Tanga* (1988:181–201) and *Le Petit prince de Belleville* (1922:245–51). Madness is a capitulation to the external forces that create cultural difference and is one of the tragedies of assimilation.

7. Jacques Fontanille (1989:46–49) distinguishes the categories of observer and spectator from the witness. The observer focuses the narrative and the spectator advances the action by relating the story. The witness, in contrast, both observes and participates in the narrative by developing an internal monologue that shapes the plot. Njami, Karone, and Beyala use internal monologues to present the perspectives of their protagonists and to witness the reactions of French characters.

8. Karone's narrative of the search for inspiration through a return to Africa might be interpreted as a metaphor for the ideals and the deceptions of négritude. See Karone 1988a:167–82.

9. In *Love in Two Languages,* Abdelkebir Khatibi (1990) explores the dimensions of power, desire, and identity associated with bilingualism. Using an erotic ideal as a vehicle for his journey across cultures, he seeks the utopian moment in which shared experiences erase the barriers of linguistic domination.

10. The problem of language in French-African writing has been addressed from several perspectives. In an interview with me on July 17, 1991, the Malian writer Doumbi Fakoly argued for a continental African language, ancient Egyptian, that would unify the continent and free writers from foreign linguistic domination. His unusual viewpoint has met with considerable criticism from writers of the Parisianism school.

11. Baudrillard (1995:196–202) characterizes indifference as the psychological plague of the postmodern era. Aggression (*la haine*) emanates from indifference and exhaustion when marginal groups experience exclusion in Western societies. Baudrillard (1995:202) concludes: "Their resentment may be impotent, but, in the end their virtual extermina-

tion, a passion for revenge, infiltrates and dislocates the Western world, as a phantom of the excluded begins to haunt our conventional societies."

12. The definition of integration provided by France's Haut Conseil à l'Intégration (1993:34–36) is made in terms of legal conformity. In contrast, the new-wave African writers define integration with respect to psychological adjustment and access to markets for distributing their works.

Chapter 7: Universalism

1. Clifford (1988:179) argues that Césaire's use of the verb *marronner* defies translation. He cites the English infinitive "to maroon" as the only possible equivalent. Nevertheless, the English verb does not carry with it the connotation of escape from slavery but, instead, merely refers to abandonment. Césaire's wordplay refers not only to the escaped slaves of the Caribbean, but also to the act of abandoning dominant European cultures. In the debate on national poetry, Césaire challenges Depestre to integrate the Caribbean experience into a new and universal vision of poetic creativity.

2. In his response, Depestre continued his play on the verb *marronner* by adding a section entitled "Rions, buvons, marronnons," taken from the last line of Césaire's 1955 poem "Le Verbe marronner." He proposed a dialectic that unites literary creativity and tradition. Thus, Depestre used his attempts at "*marronnage*" to combine stylistic innovation with a fundamental sense of Haitian identity and traditions.

3. In an interview with Françoise Cévaër (1994:144–46), Tiémélé explains that his first collections of poetry were published under self-subsidy agreements with Parisian publishers. This process of self-publication is common in the world of African poetry, both in France and on the African continent. More broadly, the process of self-publication is crucial to the emergence and reputation building of many new writers on the African continent. (See chapter 4.) In Tiémélé's case, however, the Parisian publication networks are at hand, even though he resorted to personal subsidy in order to bring about his early publications.

4. Tiémélé's use of the term *homme noir* in this interview excerpt resembles the usage of the same term developed by Senghor, Alioune Diop, and the négritude poets.

5. Note that all translations of poetry in this chapter are my own. For purposes of this analysis, several poems have been excerpted and translated.

6. Marie-Christine Rochmann (1989:315–33) argues that Edouard Maunick's poetry "exists in the spaces between words and things," linking them by analogy and mimesis rather than convention. Images of birds appear throughout Maunick's poetry, signifying longing, freedom, and oppression. The *paille-en-queue* is a paradoxical image evoking longing for natal identity and escape. The term's literal meaning (straw in the tail), and its placement at the end of the poem, also resemble a humorous punch line.

7. Dakeyo's poems *Soweto: Soleils fusillés* (1977) and *J'appartiens au grand jour* (1979) describe the immediacy of suffering in South Africa. (See chapter 3.) In contrast, Maunick treats Mandela as a universal figure whose suffering epitomizes all human injustice. Maunick uses the method of "cratylism," or image-flashes and analogies, to make Mandela a signifier for all human suffering.

8. In its nominal form, *noir* is used in a way that resembles the term *muntu*, meaning "man" in many Central Bantu languages. As both a noun and an adjective, *noir* refers to the plight of every black man in South Africa. In these usages, Maunick's gifts for metaphor and analogy are apparent.

9. Umberto Eco (1979:268–70) refers to the process of layering image upon image used by Maunick and other poets as "aesthetic overcoding." In Maunick's case, the format of analogical ambiguity reinforces the universalistic message that he conveys. Concrete images of Mandela's solitude, seclusion, and suffering carry with them a universal message.

10. It is important to emphasize that Pius Ngandu Nkashama, whose critical 1992 work *Négritude et poétique* has inspired a rereading of Senghor, argues in his 1993 survey of African literature that négritude was a commercial and literary success for a limited time. The basic problem, as Nkashama (1993:17–18) sees it, was a failure on the part of some African authors to take into account changing commercial trends during the 1960s and 1970s. The new universalism also shows signs of growing as a literary approach. Other authors such as Doumbi Fakoly, whose book on AIDS in Africa (Fakoly 1988) and work on Islam in France (Fakoly 1992) are noteworthy, may be classified as writers in the new universalism genre.

Chapter 8: Identity Discourses

1. In his discussion of general grammar, Foucault (1966:98–100) defines a universal discourse as a series of representations and signs linked to a specific domain of knowledge and constituting the full range of possibilities in that domain. Accordingly, Senghor's definition of négritude as the "totality of values" of the black world can be interpreted as a universal discourse.

2. Explaining the archaeology of knowledge, Foucault (1972:139) qualifies that an archaeology undertakes "a differential analysis of the modalities of discourse." According to Foucault (1972:139), an archaeology "does not await the moment when, on the basis of what they [discourses] were not yet, they became what they are. . . . On the contrary, its problem is to define discourses in their specificity; to show in what way the set of rules they put into operation is irreducible to any other." Conducting an archaeological project with respect to identity discourses, however, introduces the problem of their enunciation, which depends upon the pertinence of the discourse to the group promoting it during a specific historical period. Identity discourses express virtual ideals that are relevant to their times.

3. Négritude is an identity discourse that entails what V. Y. Mudimbe (1991:276) has termed the enunciative "reprise" of an "interrupted tradition." When the meaning of this tradition changes considerably or ceases to be relevant to a group, the discourse is threatened. In addition, négritude may be viewed in the Greimasian sense, as a discourse of confrontation between "black values" and "European civilization" (Greimas 1970:172–78). When the terms of this confrontation shift, the discourse is challenged and changes (Jules-Rosette 1990:30–34).

4. I have quoted from this lecture (Césaire 1967) courtesy of the anthropologist Serge Tornay, who participated in the question-answer session and permitted me to transcribe an audiotape of it.

5. Mudimbe (1988:93) states: "Negritude is 'the warmth' of being, living, and participating in a natural, social, and spiritual harmony. . . . Marxism is, for Senghor, a method." Mudimbe adds that Senghor accepts socialism as a solution to Africa's social and economic problems and views it as completely in tune with négritude's cultural assertion of black pride.

6. In disagreement with Frobenius, Senghor did not believe that African civilizations could be divided along the lines of Ethiopian and Hamitic types (Senghor 1977b:11–13; Senghor 1987:vi–vii). Although he accepted Frobenius's definition of Ethiopian cultures as spiritual and mystical, and incorporated this definition into négritude, Senghor conceived of Africa in terms of a mixture of cultures. His concept of africanité combined what he considered to be the essential elements of North and sub-Saharan African cultures.

7. Sartre (1976:410–12) defines unconditional autonomy in terms of the relationship between the existence of a group (*l'exis*) and praxis. The individual discovers liberty of action, or autonomy, based on the urgent necessity for joining a group. Freedom is a product of the individual participation in collective action. For Senghor, this collective action was rooted in and framed by négritude.

8. Lilyan Kesteloot (1974:318–19) claims that Rabemananjara objected to the essentialism of négritude and instead asserted that unity issued from a common experience of oppression rather than a common culture shared by black people around the world. Note that Senghor alternates between an ethnopsychological definition of black values and the leveling effects of colonialism in constructing his versions of négritude's identity discourse.

9. Using a semiotic square (Greimas and Courtés 1979:29–32) to clarify the polarities of discourse, négritude appears, of course, in opposition to antinégritude. Revolutionary writing is the positive complex term that incorporates and goes beyond both négritude and antinégritude. Thus, I have referred to revolutionary writing as a counterdiscourse. The negative complex term, or complementary pole of the square, consists of Parisianism and the new universalism, which are approaches that reject or criticize all of the other discourses (Schleifer 1987:25–27). The radical negativity of the new generation discourses, however, does not destroy the legacy of négritude, which made them possible. Finally, it is worth noting that the semiotic square refers only to ideal polarities and that, in fact, each identity discourse is open to multiple interpretations.

10. Négritude is the thesis motivating the counterclaims in all three books, and it also furnished the marketing category in which the books were sold (Nkashama 1993:17–18).

11. Adotevi believes that an engaged and objective social science is possible and will resolve the epistemological problems posed by négritude. He states: "Also to proclaim the special character of the social sciences is not to pronounce the impossibility of scientific discourse, but to indicate that to achieve the true value of science, they must not only be an accumulation of knowledge, but also cease to be a hermeneutic and become a practice" (Adotevi 1972:176–77). The social sciences would then, according to Adotevi, necessarily discard the distorting conclusions of négritude and ethnology and would become the basis for a liberating political practice.

12. Although the criticisms by Adotevi, Towa, and Depestre, discussed in chapter 3 and here, chronologically follow those presented by Fanon, the criticisms by the antinégri-

tudinists remain tied to the themes of négritude (Depestre 1980:144–49). Fanon provided a bridge into the counterdiscourse of revolutionary writing that proposed political strategies which differed considerably from those of négritude (Fanon 1963:58–69).

13. Fanon's discourse moves from one in which the modal values are virtual, expressed in the desire of the colonized individual for freedom, to one in which these values are actualized in performance, namely the exhortation to revolution. This move toward actualized values is a semantic operation that changes the relationship of the speaker to the discourse and modifies the content of the discourse (Greimas 1970:179).

14. The argument presented by Gates (1991:457–70) challenges Fanon's position as a global theorist of colonial discourse by examining Fanon's own ambivalent reflections about identity and the contradictions of his revolutionary writing. In contrast, my goal is to situate Fanon's discourse in the chronology and thematic development of diasporic African writing in France.

15. For Fanon, although violence may be a regrettable alternative, it results in the unification of the people in a common struggle. Fanon (1963:93) states: "The armed struggle mobilizes people; that is to say, it throws them in one way and one direction. The mobilization of the masses when it arises out of a war of liberation, introduces into each man's consciousness the ideas of a common cause, of a national destiny, and of a collective history."

16. This discussion is not intended to minimize the political commitments and activities of the Présence Africaine movement and its fellow travelers. Nevertheless, in contrast with the discussion by Kesteloot (1974:292), my interpretation of political action does not refer to partisanship, but to the broader consequences of négritude and its counterdiscourses in offering alternative strategies for political action.

17. This ideal of saving Africa from self-destruction by developing more viable theoretical discourses and political practices also emerges in Mudimbe's earlier work (Mudimbe 1973:10).

18. These media representations are documented in the *Guide Actuel du Paris Mondial* (Équipe du Guide Paris Mondial 1992:37–56). Recent developments such as *beur* and *banlieue* cinema have also brought the marginalization of urban immigrants in France into public view (Bloom 1995:1–6).

19. Karone (1988a, 1988b) and Njami (1985, 1991b) use African-American personages and music to underscore the displacement of their diasporic characters in Europe. They offer a new look at African-American culture from the vantage point of the European diaspora. The link that they suggest between Africans in Europe and the African-American situation is not based on cultural essences but, instead, on similar contexts of exclusion and marginality.

20. Beyala's *Tu t'appelera Tanga* (1988) is written with the multiple voices of Tanga and Anna-Claude, who communicate across a cultural chasm. *Le petit prince de Belleville* (1992) and *Mama a un amant* (1993) use the two male voices, of Mamadou and Abdou Traoré, to present contrasting generational views of the immigration experience. In *A Vol d'oiseau,* Tadjo (1986) alternates among the voices of several women, a young boy, a male beggar, and a neutral omniscient voice. These changes in voice, modality, and register

reflect the identity searches and discourses of contemporary African women. Mudimbe-Boyi (1993:75) refers to these narrative strategies as women writers' resistance against "oppression, invisibility, erasure, and stereotyping."

21. Minh-ha's notion of "writing" is part of an identity discourse in which she describes Third World women's writing as a fragmented cultural expression in search of affirming itself (Minh-ha 1989:22–28). This type of women's writing, or *femmage*, breaks the semantic and syntactic rules of established discursive canons in order to create a new aesthetic and political space for women writers. Minh-ha's approach to writing echoes the multiple shifts in narrative voice that are part of the identity discourses of African women writers of the new generation.

22. Bolya's exhortation to remove the masks of négritude and failed African development (Bolya 1994:20) suggests that négritude is still a master paradigm to which the new writers are responding. The apparent erasure of the term "négritude" from their identity discourses does not mean that the basic questions posed by the philosophers and writers of négritude have been answered.

Conclusion

1. Alioune Diop and the Présence Africaine authors focused on broadening the concept of "civilization" that is so deeply rooted in French pedagogy and cultural discourse (Diop 1987:49–50). See chapters 1 and 2 for my discussion of the importance of essentialist notions of black civilization and Africanity for the négritude movement. Simon Njami (1996:9) refers to this notion of black civilization as "the illusory vision of a unified Black world."

2. Much of the critical writing on négritude approaches the topic from a purely literary perspective (Nkashama 1992:9–12). Recent essays (Appiah 1992:137–57; Njami 1996:7–9) have situated the outcomes of literary, cultural, and political Pan-Africanism in a larger postcolonial context.

3. Fanon was outraged by Jacques Rabemananjara's official opposition to Algeria in his role as the Madagascan representative to the United Nations General Assembly. He made his criticisms public and included them in his 1959 address to the Congress of Black Writers and Artists in Rome (Fanon 1963:235). This episode is discussed at greater length in chapter 3.

4. Dakeyo's 1977 epic poem *Soweto: Soleils fusillés* establishes his commitment to revolutionary action and change. In *J'appartiens au grand jour* (1979), he expresses optimism about the arrival of a new day in which oppressed people will experience freedom and joy. *La Femme où j'ai mal* (1989) personalizes his message about deception with political change by using the autobiographical metaphor of lost love. This personalization of revolutionary action links Dakeyo to the old generation of decolonization writers and to the new generation of Parisianism.

5. Parisianism calls into question the specifically African content of the new African literature in France. In his discussion of the *beur* literature of second-generation North African writers in France, Alec Hargreaves (1991:36–87) has emphasized the markers of identity found in autobiography and fiction. Markers are traces of cultural identification that

are often implicit. Critics attempting to provide syntheses and compilations of the new generation's work are often confronted by the problem that the writers' sources of cultural identification are muted or hidden (Magnier 1990:102–7; Nkashama 1994:11–14).

6. In addition to discussing the three major authors of Parisianism—Yodi Karone, Simon Njami, and Calixthe Beyala—I have also touched upon the works of the Cameroonian writer Blaise N'Djehoya, whose narratives take as their focus problems of immigration and assimilation in France. Other new writers, such as Jean-Jacques Nkollo (1990, 1992), are also beginning to emerge in this literary school through both the francophonie circuit and smaller French publishing houses.

7. In "Niam n'goura" (1947:7–9), Alioune Diop emphasizes the importance of diversity in African literature, but he also underscores the necessity for African intellectuals to return to their cultural roots. Without an attachment to these roots, according to Diop (1947:8), writers have no source of ethical commitment (*souci éthique*).

8. The problems of declining sales and stockpiling of literary works constituted a recurrent theme of my interviews with the representatives of French publishing houses such as Éditions L'Harmattan, Karthala, and Hatier. They used nonfiction and educational books geared toward a popular audience to support the limited publication of specialized African fiction titles.

9. Walter Rodney (1972:35–36) argues that technological centralization perpetuates a cycle of neocolonial political and cultural dependency in Africa. Following his argument, African literature is included in the Western market only as long as it is economically profitable. This argument, of course, is attenuated by the fact that political and social pressures for the inclusion of alternative literatures also affect the publication market. The prevalence of self-publication in Côte d'Ivoire, discussed in chapter 4, nevertheless sustains Rodney's thesis that local African literatures remain marginal on the world market.

10. In spite of marketing surveys, consumer demand is often difficult to assess. Therefore, I have referred to "perceived consumer demand" in the art world as a means by which writers and artists target their works toward diverse commercial publics (Jules-Rosette 1984:194–216). In some cases, perceived consumer demand may influence the quality, themes, and styles of work that an artist produces.

11. The literary critic Françoise Naudillon argues that the francophonie circuit is largely a product of the mass media. In a 1995 article, Naudillon traces Césaire's radio and television appearances and media coverage of his works as indicators of their public reception (Naudillon 1995:243–50). She argues that, by virtue of media coverage, a writer may be transformed from a regional author into a universally recognized artist. Festivals and media coverage play important roles in this transformation.

12. *Revue Noire,* now in its twenty-third issue after seven years of circulation, is a major outlet for contemporary African and Afro-Antillian writing and art. The magazine has now expanded into music and video production. It provides an important outlet for the distribution of works of new African writers.

13. The French sociologist Michel Maffesoli points out that tendencies toward globalization in contemporary society are counterbalanced by a new tribalization in which groups based on ethnicity, leisure, and personal and political interests form with a new

force and commitment (Maffesoli 1988:93–101; Maffesoli 1992:70–74). This new particularism in social relations uses international communication networks and advanced technologies to reinforce the solidarity and identity of small groups.

14. This assertion should be qualified by an understanding that a complex dialectic operates between literature and the marketplace. New literary developments are not necessarily market driven, but their survival depends upon reaching a large public. The media and the policies of publishing houses influence and shape the reception of literary innovations.

15. Rodney (1972:34) asserts that "African economies are integrated into the very structure of the developed capitalist economies." His observation also applies to literary markets, which now depend upon a worldwide system of production and distribution in which contemporary African literature and art continue to be at a disadvantage.

REFERENCES

Adams, Anne. 1993. "To Write in a New Language: Werewere Liking's Adaptation of Ritual to the Novel." *Callaloo* 16, no. 1 (Winter): 153–68.

Adi, Hakim, and Marika Sherwood. 1995. *The 1945 Manchester Pan African Congress Revisited.* London: New Beacon Books.

Adiaffi Ade, Jean-Marie. 1980. *La Carte d'identité.* Abidjan, Côte d'Ivoire: Éditions CÉDA.

———. 1992. *Silence, on développe.* Ivry-sur-Seine: Éditions Nouvelles du Sud.

Adotevi, Stanislas Spero. 1969. "Discours de S.E.M. Stanislas Adotevi, Commissaire Géneral à la Culture et à la jeunesse du Dahomey." Paper given at Organizing Cultural Symposium, First Panafrican Cultural Festival, Algiers. File GN 460-A315-F41-M10. Musée de l'Homme, Paris.

———. 1972. *Négritude et négrologues.* Paris: Union Générale d'Éditions.

———. 1973. "Le Musée, Inversion de la vie." *Chroniques de l'art vivant* 35 (Jan.): 10–11. Special issue: "Le Musée en question."

Agblémagnon, N'Sougan F. 1959. "Les Responsabilités du sociologue africain." *Présence Africaine,* 2d ser., 27–28, special issue (Aug.–Nov.): 206–14.

Amselle, Jean-Loup. 1996. *Vers un multiculturalisme français: L'Empire de la coutume.* Paris: Aubier.

Appiah, Kwame Anthony. 1992. *In My Father's House: Africa in the Philosophy of Culture.* New York: Oxford University Press.

Araeen, Rasheed. 1989. "Our Bauhaus, Others' Mud House." *Third Text* 6 (Spring): 3–14.

Arnold, A. James. 1981. *Modernism and Negritude: The Poetry and Poetics of Aimé Césaire.* Cambridge, Mass.: Harvard University Press.

Arroyo, Eduardo. 1982. *"Panama" Al Brown, 1902–1951.* Paris: Éditions Jean-Claude Lattès.

Ashcroft, Bill, Gareth Griffiths, and Helen Tiffin. 1989. *The Empire Writes Back: Theory and Practice in Post-Colonial Literatures.* London: Routledge.

Association des Germanistes de l'Enseignement Supérieur. 1983. *Négritude et Germanité: Douzième Congrès de l'Association des Germanistes de l'Enseignement Supérieur.* Dakar, Senegal: Nouvelles Éditions Africaines.

Austin, J. L. 1962. *How to Do Things with Words.* London: Oxford University Press.

Bâ, Sylvia Washington. 1973. *The Concept of Negritude in the Poetry of Léopold Sédar Senghor.* Princeton: Princeton University Press.

Balandier, Georges. 1947. "Le Noir est un homme." *Présence Africaine,* 1st ser. (Nov.–Dec.): 31–36.

———. 1955. *Sociologie actuelle de l'Afrique noire.* Paris: Presses Universitaires de France.

———. 1963. "L'Africanisme face aux problèmes de l'anthropologie et de la sociologie politique." *Présence Africaine,* 2d ser., 46: 197–201.

Baldwin, James. 1957. "Princes and Powers." *Encounter* (Jan.).

———. 1972. *No Name in the Street.* New York: Dial Press.

Bandaman, Maurice. 1986. *Une Femme pour un médaille.* Abidjan, Côte d'Ivoire: Éditions CÉDA.

———. 1991. *Le Sang de la république.* Abidjan, Côte d'Ivoire: I.P.C./Maurice Bandaman.

———. 1992. Interview with Bennetta Jules-Rosette, Abidjan, Côte d'Ivoire, Aug. 9.

———. 1993. *Le Fils de-la-femme-mâle.* Paris: Éditions L'Harmattan.

Bandaman, Maurice, Paul Ahizi, Joseph Anouma, and Daniel Zongo, eds. 1994. *Portrait des siècles meurtris: Anthologie de la Poésie de Côte d'Ivoire.* Ivry-sur-Seine: Éditions Nouvelles du Sud.

Bankara, Félix. 1988. *Black Micmacs.* Paris: Éditions Robert Laffont.

Barber, Benjamin. 1995. "Face à la retribalisation du monde." *Esprit* 212, no. 6 (June): 132–44.

Barber, Karin. 1987. "Popular Arts in Africa." *African Studies Review* 30, no. 3 (Sept.): 1–78.

Barthes, Roland. 1975. "An Introduction to the Structural Analysis of Narrative." *New Literary History* 6, no. 2:237–72.

Battestini, M., S. Battestini, and Roger Mercier. 1964. *Bernard Dadié: Ecrivain africaine.* Paris: Éditions Fernand Nathan.

Baudrillard, Jean. 1968. *Le Système des objets.* Paris: Éditions Gallimard.

———. 1972. *Pour une critique de l'économie politique du signe.* Paris: Éditions Gallimard.

———. 1981. *Simulacres et simulation.* Paris: Éditions Galilée.

———. 1995. *Le Crime parfait.* Paris: Éditions Galilée.

Bayart, Jean-François. 1992. "Introduction." In *Le Politique par le bas en Afrique noire,* ed. Jean-François Bayart, Achille Mbembe, and Comi Toulabor, pp. 9–23. Paris: Éditions Karthala.

Bekombo, Manga. 1988. Interview with Bennetta Jules-Rosette, Paris, July 12.

Benbelaid, Farida. 1993. Interview with Bennetta Jules-Rosette, Paris, Aug. 13.

Beyala, Calixthe. 1987. *C'est le soleil qui m'a brûlée.* Paris: Éditions Stock.

———. 1988. *Tu t'appeleras Tanga.* Paris: Éditions Stock.

———. 1990a. Interview with Bennetta Jules-Rosette, Paris, July 27.

———. 1990b. *Seul le diable le savait.* Paris: Le Pré aux Clercs.

———. 1992. *Le Petit prince de Belleville.* Paris: Éditions Albin Michel.
———. 1993. *Maman a un amant.* Paris: Éditions Albin Michel.
———. 1994. *Assèze l'africaine.* Paris: Éditions Albin Michel.
———. 1995. *Lettre d'une africaine à ses soeurs occidentales.* Paris: Éditions Spengler.
———. 1996. *Les Honneurs perdus.* Paris: Albin Michel.
Bhabha, Homi K. 1984. "Of Mimicry and Man: The Ambivalence of Colonial Discourse." *October* 28:125–33.
———. 1987. "Interrogating Identity." *ICA Documents* 6:5–11.
Bjornson, Richard. 1991. *The African Quest for Freedom and Identity.* Bloomington: Indiana University Press.
———. 1992. "Alienation and Disalienation: Themes of Yesterday, Promises of Tomorrow." In *The Surreptitious Speech:* Présence Africaine *and the Politics of Otherness, 1947–1987,* ed. V. Y. Mudimbe, pp. 147–56. Chicago: University of Chicago Press.
Bloom, Peter. 1995. "Locating *Beur* Cinema: Social Activism, Immigration Politics, and the Naming of a Social Movement." Paper presented at the Tenth Triennial Symposium on African Art, New York University, Apr. 19–23.
Bolya, Baenga. 1986. *Cannibale.* Lausanne: Pierre-Marcel Favre.
———. 1989. Interview with Bennetta Jules-Rosette, Paris, Sept. 12.
———. 1991a. *L'Afrique en kimono: Repenser le développement.* Ivry-sur-Seine: Éditions Nouvelles du Sud.
———. 1991b. Interview with Bennetta Jules-Rosette, Paris, July 23.
———. 1994. *L'Afrique à la japonaise: Et si l'Afrique était mal mariée?* Ivry-sur-Seine: Éditions Nouvelles du Sud.
Boni, Suzanne Tanella. 1984. *Labyrinthe.* Paris: Akpagnon.
———. 1990. *Une Vie de crabe.* Dakar, Senegal: Nouvelles Éditions Africaines.
———. 1991. *De l'autre côté du soleil.* Dakar, Senegal: Nouvelles Éditions Africaines.
———. 1992a. *La Fugue d'ozone.* Dakar, Senegal: Nouvelles Éditions Africaines.
———. 1992b. Interview with Bennetta Jules-Rosette, Abidjan, Côte d'Ivoire, July 26.
Boudimbou, Guy. 1991. *Habitat et modes de vie des immigrés africains en France.* Paris: Éditions L'Harmattan.
Bouraoui, Hédi. 1995. *La Francophonie à l'estomac.* Ivry-sur-Seine: Éditions Nouvelles du Sud.
Brench, A. C. 1967. *The Novelists' Inheritance in French Africa: Writers from Senegal to Cameroon.* London: Oxford University Press.
Brière, Eloise. 1988. "In Search of Cultural Equivalences: Translations of Camara Laye's *L'Enfant noir.*" *Translation Review* 27:34–39.
Broca, Pierre Paul. 1864. "On the Phenomena of Hybridity in Genus Homo." Trans. C. Carter Blake. London: Anthropological Society.
———. 1875. *Instructions craniologiques et craniométriques de la société d'anthropologie de Paris.* Paris: G. Masson.
———. 1876. *Le Programme de l'anthropologie.* Paris: Imprimerie Cusset.
Campbell, James. 1991. *Talking at the Gates: A Life of James Baldwin.* New York: Viking.
Carlos, Jérôme Tovignon. 1973. *Cri de la liberté.* Cotonou, Benin: Éditions A.B.M.

———. 1990. *Fleur du désert*. Abidjan, Côte d'Ivoire: Éditions CÉDA.

———. 1992. Interview with Bennetta Jules-Rosette, Abidjan, Côte d'Ivoire, Aug. 7.

Cendrars, Blaise. 1921. *Anthologie nègre*. Paris: Buchet-Chastel.

Cervoni, Jean. 1987. *L'Énonciation*. Paris: Presses Universitaires de France.

Césaire, Aimé. 1955a. "Réponse à Depestre poète haitien." *Présence Africaine*, 2d ser., 1–2 (Apr.–July): 113–15.

———. 1955b. "Sur la poésie nationale." *Présence Africaine*, 2d ser., 4 (Oct.–Nov.): 113–15.

———. 1956a. *Cahier d'un retour au pays natal*. Paris: Présence Africaine. This collection originally appeared in the Parisian review *Volontés* 201 (1939). It was first published in book form by Bordas (Paris, 1947).

———. 1956b. "Culture et colonisation." *Présence Africaine*, 2d ser., 8–9–10, special issue (June–Nov.): 190–205.

———. 1960. *Ferrements*. Paris: Éditions du Seuil.

———. 1966. *Une Saison au Congo*. Paris: Éditions du Seuil.

———. 1967. "Entretien et débat." Transcribed from audiotape of presentation at La Maison Helvétique, Paris; tape courtesy of Serge Tornay.

———. 1983. "Afrique." Trans. Clayton Eshleman and Annette Smith. In *Aimé Césaire: The Collected Poetry*, ed. Eshleman and Smith, pp. 346–47. Berkeley: University of California Press.

Cévaër, Françoise. 1991. "African Literatures Take the Offensive." *Research in African Literatures* 22, no. (Spring): 101–6.

———. 1994. *Ces Écrivains africains qui font L'Afrique*. Ivry-sur-Seine: Éditions Nouvelles du Sud.

Chambers, Iain. 1996. "Signs of Silence, Lines of Listening." In *The Post-Colonial Question*, ed. Iain Chambers and Lidia Curti, pp. 47–62. London: Routledge.

Clark, Ed. 1993. Personal communication, San Diego, Calif., May 13.

Clifford, James. 1983. "Power and Dialogue in Ethnography: Marcel Griaule's Initiation." In *Observers Observed: Essays on Ethnographic Fieldwork*, ed. George W. Stocking, pp. 121–56. Madison: University of Wisconsin Press.

———. 1986. "Introduction." In *Writing Culture: The Poetics and Politics of Ethnography*, ed. James Clifford and George E. Marcus, pp. 1–26. Berkeley: University of California Press.

———. 1988. *The Predicament of Culture: Twentieth-Century Ethnography, Literature, and Art*. Cambridge, Mass.: Harvard University Press.

———. 1989. "Notes on Theory and Travel." *Inscriptions* 5:177–88. Special issue: "Traveling Theories, Traveling Theorists."

———. 1994. "Diasporas." *Cultural Anthropology* 9, no. 3:304–38.

Comaroff, John, and Jean Comaroff. 1992. *Ethnography and the Historical Imagination*. Boulder, Colo.: Westview Press.

Connickx, Claude. 1993. Interview with Bennetta Jules-Rosette, Paris, July 22.

Cook, Mercer. 1957. "Les Relations raciales aux États-Unis vues par les voyageurs français depuis la deuxième guerre mondiale." *Présence Africaine*, 2d ser., 14–15, special issue (June–Sept.): 119–28.

Corbett, James. 1994. *Through French Windows: An Introduction to France in the Nineties.* Ann Arbor: University of Michigan Press.

Costa-Lascoux, Jacqueline. 1994. "La Nationalité par la naissance et par le choix." *Hommes et migrations* 1178 (July): 18–22.

Coulon, Virginie. 1997. *Notre librairie* 129 (Jan.–Mar.). Issue title: "1,500 nouveaux titres de littérature d'Afrique noire: 1988–1996."

Dadié, Bernard B. 1947. "L'Aveu." *Présence Africaine* 1, (Nov.–Dec.): 78–80.

———. 1956. *Climbié.* Paris: Éditions Seghers.

———. 1957. "Le Rôle de la légende dans la culture populaire des noirs d'Afrique." *Présence Africaine,* 2d ser., 14–15, special issue (June–Sept.): 165–74.

———. 1959. *Un Nègre à Paris.* Paris: Présence Africaine. Published in English as *An African in Paris,* trans. Karen C. Hatch (Urbana: University of Illinois Press, 1994).

———. 1964. *Un Patron de New York.* Paris: Présence Africaine. Published in English as *One Way,* trans. Jo Patterson (Urbana: University of Illinois Press, 1994).

———. 1966. *Légendes et poèmes.* Paris: Éditions Seghers.

———. 1970. *Béatrice du Congo.* Paris: Présence Africaine.

———. 1978. "Lettre au grand frère Alioune Diop." In *Hommage à Alioune Diop,* ed. Les Amis Italiens de Présence Africaine, pp. 307–11. Rome: Présence Africaine et les Amis Italiens de Présence Africaine.

———. 1992. Interview with Bennetta Jules-Rosette, Abidjan, Côte d'Ivoire, Aug. 10.

Dakeyo, Paul. 1973. *Les Barbelés du matin.* Paris: Éditions Saint-Germain-des-Prés.

———. 1976a. *Chant d'accusation.* Paris: Éditions Saint-Germain-des-Prés.

———. 1976b. *Le Cri pluriel.* Paris: Éditions Saint-Germain-des-Prés.

———. 1977. *Soweto: Soleils fusillés.* Paris: Droit et Liberté.

———. 1979. *J'appartiens au grand jour.* Paris: Éditions Saint-Germain-des-Prés.

———. 1989a. *La Femme où j'ai mal.* Paris: Éditions Silex.

———. 1989b. Interview with Bennetta Jules-Rosette, Paris, Sept. 11.

———. 1992. "The African Publication in Question: The Examples of Silex and Nouvelles du Sud." Speech presented at the Municipal Club of Deux Plateaux, Abidjan, Côte d'Ivoire, July 30. Transcribed from author's audiotape.

———. 1994. *Les Ombres de la nuit.* Ivry-sur-Seine: Éditions Nouvelles du Sud.

Dakou, Yves. 1988. "'La Quête identitaire' dans j'appartiens au grand jour de Paul Dakeyo: Approche sémiolinguistique." Ph.D. diss., Université de Toulouse, Le Mirail, 1988.

Davis, John A. 1957. "The Participation of the Negro in the Democratic Process in the United States." *Présence Africaine,* n.s., 14–15 (June–Sept.): 129–47.

Delafosse, Maurice. 1922. *L'Âme nègre.* Paris: Payot.

Depestre, René. 1955. "Réponse à Aimé Césaire: Introduction à un art poétique haïtien." *Présence Africaine,* 2d ser., 4 (Oct.–Nov.): 42–62.

———. 1969. "Les Fondamentes socio-culturels de notre identité." Paper given at Organizing Cultural Symposium, First Panafrican Cultural Festival, Algiers. File GN 460-A315-F41-M26. Musée de l'Homme, Paris.

———. 1978. "Lettre à Alioune Diop." In *Hommage à Alioune Diop,* ed. Les Amis Italiens de Présence Africaine, pp. 59–62. Rome: Présence Africaine et les Amis Italiens de Présence Africaine.

———. 1980. *Bonjour et adieu à la négritude.* Paris: Éditions Robert Laffont.

de Rudder, Véronique, I. Taboada-Leonetti, and F. Vourc'h. 1990. "Immigrés et Français: Stratégies d'insertion, représentations et attitudes." Paris: Rapport du Centre National de la Recherche Scientifique. Scientific report.

Désalmand, Paul. 1991. *25 Romans clés de la littérature négro-africaine.* Paris: Hatier.

Désir, Harlem. 1990. "Militer: Un point de vue du président de SOS-Racisme." *Le Monde,* July 29–30, pp. 1–2.

Desjeux, Dominique. 1995. "Vingt ans d'édition à L'Harmattan, 1975–1995." In *L'Harmattan, 1975–1995: Vingt ans d'édition,* ed. L'Harmattan, pp. 5–10. Paris: Éditions L'Harmattan.

Desportes, Gérard. 1996. "Après l'évacuation, l'émotion et la colère." *Libération,* Aug. 24–25, p. 4.

Devisch, René. 1995. "Frenzy, Violence, and Ethical Renewal in Kinshasa." *Public Culture* 7, no. 3:593–629.

Dewitte, Philippe. 1987. "Le Regard des français." In *Ethnicolor,* ed. Simon Njami and Bruno Tilliette, pp. 13–21. Paris: Éditions Autrement.

Dia, Mamadou. 1957. "Économie et culture devant les élites africaines." *Présence Africaine,* 2d ser., 14–15, special issue (June–Sept.): 58–72.

Diané, Charles. 1990. *La FÉANF et les grandes heures du mouvement syndical étudiant noir.* Vol. 5. Paris: Éditions Chaka.

Dias, Nélia. 1991. *Le Musée d'ethnographie du Trocadéro (1878–1908): Anthropologie et muséologie en France.* Paris: Éditions du CNRS.

Diawara, Manthia. 1990. "Reading Africa through Foucault: V. Y. Mudimbe's Reaffirmation of the Subject." *October* 55 (Winter): 79–92.

———. 1992. "Afro-Kitsch." In *Black Popular Culture,* ed. Gina Dent, pp. 285–91. Seattle: Bay Press.

Diop, Alioune. 1947. "Niam n'goura ou les raisons d'être de *Présence Africaine.*" *Présence Africaine,* 1st ser. (Nov.–Dec.): 7–14.

———. 1949a. "Malentendus." *Présence Africaine,* 1st ser., 6 (1st trimester): 3–8.

———. 1949b. "'Orphée noir' de J.-P. Sartre." *Présence Africaine,* 1st ser., 6 (1st trimester): 154–55.

———. 1957. "Nos Tâches." Présence Africaine, 2d ser., 14–15 (June–Sept.): 3–6. Special issue: "Contributions au premier congrès des écrivains et artistes noirs," written by Alioune Diop on behalf of Présence Africaine.

———. 1959. "Le Sens de ce Congrès: Discours d'ouverture, Rome, 26 mars–1 avril, 1959." *Présence Africaine,* 2d ser., 24–25, special issue (Feb.–May): 40–48.

———. 1977. "Message de M. Alioune Diop, Secrétaire Général de la Société Africaine de Culture." In *Le Critique africain et son peuple comme producteur de civilisation: Colloque de Yaoundé, 16–20 avril, 1973,* ed. Société Africaine de Culture, pp. 528–32. Paris: Présence Africaine.

———. 1987. "Itinéraire." In *Catalogue 1987: Présence Africaine,* pp. 43–52. Paris: Présence Africaine. Originally published in *Présence Africaine* 92, no. 4 (1974).

Diop, Boubacar Boris. 1990. *Les Tambours de la mémoire.* Paris: Éditions L'Harmattan.

Diop, Cheikh Anta. 1954. *Nations nègres et culture.* Paris: Présence Africaine.

Diop, Christiane Yandé. 1988. Interview with Bennetta Jules-Rosette, Paris, July 12.

Diop, David. 1955. "Un Enfant noir." *Présence Africaine,* 2d ser., 4 (Oct.–Nov.): 63.

———. 1956. "Contribution au débat sur la poésie nationale." *Présence Africaine,* 2d ser., 6 (Feb.–Mar.): 113–15.

Djungu-Simba, Kamatenda. 1988. *Cité 15.* Paris: Éditions L'Harmattan.

Duchet, Michèle. 1971. *Anthropologie et histoire au siècle des lumières.* Paris: François Maspero.

Dumont, René. 1962. *L'Afrique noire est mal partie.* Paris: Éditions du Seuil.

Eco, Umberto. 1979. *A Theory of Semiotics.* Bloomington: Indiana University Press.

Éditions Karthala. 1990. *Karthala en bref, 1980–1990.* Paris: Éditions Karthala. Publicity brochure, November.

Éditions L'Harmattan. 1995. *L'Harmattan, 1975–1995: Vingt ans d'édition.* Intro. Dominique Desjeux. Paris: Éditions L'Harmattan.

Équipe du Guide Paris Mondial. 1992. *Guide actuel du Paris mondial.* Paris: Éditions du Seuil.

Eshleman, Clayton, and Annette Smith, eds. 1983. *Aimé Césaire: The Collected Poetry.* Trans. Eshleman and Smith. Berkeley: University of California Press.

Ewens, Graeme. 1991. *Africa O-ye!: A Celebration of African Music.* London: Sango Publications.

Fabian, Johannes. 1996. *Remembering the Present: Painting and Popular History in Zaire.* Berkeley: University of California Press.

Fabre, Michel. 1985. *La Rive noire: De Harlem à la Seine.* Paris: Éditions Lieu Commun, 1985. Published in English as *From Harlem to Paris: Black Writers in France, 1840–1980* (Urbana: University of Illinois Press, 1991).

Fagg, William. 1968. "Tribality." In *First World Festival of Negro Arts: Colloquium on Negro Culture,* ed. Société Africaine de Culture, pp. 107–19. Paris: Présence Africaine. First presented in French as a paper, "Tribalité," at the First World Festival of Negro Arts, Colloquium on Negro Art, Dakar, Senegal, 1966. File GN 460-A315-F41-M68, Musée de l'Homme, Paris.

Fainzang, Sylvie, and Odile Journet. 1988. *La Femme de mon marie: Anthropologie du mariage polygamique en Afrique et en France.* Paris: Éditions L'Harmattan.

Fakoly, Doumbi. 1988. *Certificat de contrôle anti-sida.* Paris: Publisud.

———. 1991. Interview with Bennetta Jules-Rosette, Paris, July 17.

———. 1992. *Bilal le prophète.* Ottawa, Canada: Éditions Panafrica Plus.

Fanon, Frantz. 1952. *Peau noire, masques blancs.* Paris: Éditions du Seuil.

———. 1956. "Racisme et Culture." *Présence Africaine,* 2d ser., 8–9–10, special issue (June–Nov.): 122–31. Reprinted in Fanon 1969:33–45.

———. 1961. *Les Damnés de la terre.* Paris: François Maspero.

———. 1963. *The Wretched of the Earth.* Trans. Constance Farrington. New York: Grove Weidenfeld.

———. 1967. *Black Skin, White Masks.* Trans. Charles Lam Markmann. New York: Grove Weidenfeld.

———. 1969. *Pour la révolution africaine.* Paris: François Maspero.

Ferembach, Denise. 1980. "Paul Broca—l'homme—l'anthropologue." Paper presented at the Colloque International du CNRS, "Les Processus de l'Hominisation," Paris, June 16–20. File B-3830, Musée de l'Homme, Paris.

Festival International des Francophonies. 1995. *La Maison des auteurs: 50 écrivains en résidence, 1988/1995.* Limoges: Festival International des Francophonies, 1995.

Fontanille, Jacques. 1989. *Les Espaces subjectifs: Introduction à la sémiotique de l'observateur.* Paris: Hachette.

Foucault, Michel. 1966. *Les Mots et les choses: Une archéologie des sciences humaines.* Paris: Éditions Gallimard.

———. 1972. *The Archaeology of Knowledge and the Discourse on Knowing.* Trans. A. M. Sheridan Smith. New York: Harper and Row. Originally published as *L'Archéologie du savoir* (Paris: Éditions Gallimard, 1969).

Frobenius, Leo. 1936. *Histoire de la civilisation africaine.* Paris: Éditions Gallimard.

Frutkin, Susan. 1973. *Aimé Césaire: Black Between Two Worlds.* Miami: Center for Advanced International Studies, University of Miami.

Gabriel, Teshome. 1989. "Third Cinema as a Guardian of Popular Memory: Towards a Third Aesthetics." In *Questions of a Third Cinema,* ed. Jim Pines and Paul Willemen, pp. 53–58. London: BFI Publishing.

———. 1993. "Ruin and the Other: Towards a Language of Memory." In *Otherness and the Media,* ed. Hamid Naficy and Teshome H. Gabriel, pp. 211–19. Chur, Switzerland: Harwood Academic Publishers.

Gandoulou, Justin-Daniel. 1989. *Au Coeur de la sape: Moeurs et aventures de Congolais à Paris.* Paris: Éditions L'Harmattan.

Gates, Henry Louis, Jr., ed. 1985. *"Race," Writing, and Difference.* Chicago: University of Chicago Press.

———. 1991. "Critical Fanonism." *Critical Inquiry* 17 (Spring): 457–70.

Gaudibert, Pierre. 1991. *Art africain contemporain.* Paris: Diagonales.

Geertz, Clifford. 1973. "Ideology as a Cultural System." In Geertz, *The Interpretation of Cultures,* pp. 193–229. New York: Basic Books.

Gilroy, Paul. 1993. *The Black Atlantic: Modernity and Double Consciousness.* Cambridge, Mass.: Harvard University Press.

Giscard d'Estaing, Valéry. 1991. "Immigration ou invasion?" *Figaro Magazine,* Sept. 21, pp. 48–56.

Greimas, Algirdas Julien. 1970. *Du Sens: Essais sémiotiques.* Paris: Éditions de Seuil.

———. 1983a. *Du Sens II: Essais sémiotiques.* Paris: Éditions de Seuil.

———. 1983b. *Structural Semantics: An Attempt at Method.* Trans. Daniele McDowell, Ronald Schleifer, and Alan Velie. Lincoln: University of Nebraska Press, 1983. Originally published as *Sémantique structurale: Recherche de méthode* (Paris: Libraire Larousse, 1966).

Greimas, A. J., and Joseph Courtés. 1979. *Sémiotique: Dictionnaire raisonné de la théorie du langage.* Paris: Librairie Hachette.

———. 1986. *Sémiotique: Dictionnaire raisonné de la théorie du langage, Tome 2.* Paris: Librairie Hachette.

Greimas, Algirdas Julien, and Jacques Fontanille. 1993. *The Semiotics of Passions: From States of Affairs to States of Feelings.* Trans. Paul Perron and Frank Collins. Minneapolis: University of Minnesota Press. Originally published as *Sémiotique des passions: Des états des choses aux états d'âme* (Paris: Éditions du Seuil, 1991).

Griaule, Marcel. 1931a. *Al Brown et la mission Dakar-Djibouti.* Photothèque file C-80-611-493. Musée de l'Homme, Paris. Publicity brochure.

———. 1931b. *Instructions sommaires pour les collecteurs d'objets ethnographiques.* Paris: Musée d'ethnographie du Trocadéro et mission Dakar-Djibouti. Brochure by Griaule with participation of Michel Leiris.

———. 1932. "Mission Dakar-Djibouti, Rapport Général." File DT 350.g.Zg.ex. 4.m. Musée de l'Homme, Paris.

———. 1933. "Introduction méthodologique." *Minotaure* 2:7–12. Special issue: "Mission Dakar-Djibouti, 1931–1933."

———. 1937. "L'Emploi de la photographie aérienne et la recherche scientifique." *L'Anthropologie* 47:469–74.

———. 1947. "L'Inconnue noire." *Présence Africaine,* 1st ser., 1 (Nov.–Dec.): 21–27.

———. 1948a. "L'Action sociologique en Afrique noire." *Présence Africaine,* 1st ser., 3, 1st trimester (Jan.): 388–91.

———. 1948b. *Dieu d'eau: Entretiens avec Ogotemmêli.* Paris: Chêne.

Griswold, Wendy. 1987. "A Methodological Framework for the Sociology of Culture." *Sociological Methodology* 17:1–35.

Hall, Stuart. 1981. "The Whites of Their Eyes: Racist Ideologies and the Media." In *Silver Linings,* ed. George Bridges and Rosalind Bruat, pp. 53–67. London: Lawrence and Wishart.

Hargreaves, Alec G. 1991. *Voices from the North African Immigrant Community in France: Immigration and Identity in Beur Fiction.* Oxford: Berg.

Hatch, Karen C. 1994. "Translator's Introduction." In Bernard Binlin Dadié, *An African in Paris,* trans. Hatch, pp. v–xxvi. Urbana: University of Illinois Press.

Hatier. 1993. *Hatier international: Afrique, Océan Indien.* Catalog for 1993–94.

Haut Conseil à l'Intégration. 1992. "Conditions juridiques et culturelles de l'intégration." File D.31–651. Institut des Études Démographiques, Paris.

———. 1993. *L'intégration à la française.* Paris: Éditions 10/18.

Hazoumé, Paul. 1957. "L'Humanisme occidental et l'humanisme africaine." *Présence Africaine,* 2d ser., 14–15, special issue (June–Sept.): 29–45.

Himes, Chester. 1965. *Cotton Comes to Harlem.* New York: Vintage Books.

Howlett, Jacques. 1947. "Absence et présence." *Présence Africaine,* 1st ser., 1 (Nov.–Dec.): 50–55.

———. 1958. "Le Premier congrès des écrivains et artistes et la presse internationale." *Présence Africaine,* 2d ser., 20 (June–July): 111–17.

———. 1977. *Présence Africaine: Index alphabétique des auteurs et des matières, 1947–1976.* Paris: Présence Africaine.

Hughes, Langston. 1968. "Black Writers in a Troubled World." In *First World Festival of Negro Arts: Colloquium on Negro Culture,* ed. Société Africaine de Culture, pp. 505–10. Paris: Présence Africaine.

Humbolt, Catherine. 1991. "Immigrés et minorités ethniques à la télévision française: Intégration ou rejet?" *Le Monde*, Dec. 1, pp. 17–18.

Husserl, Edmund. 1964. *The Idea of Phenomenology.* The Hague: Martinus Nijhoff.

Institut National de la Statistique et des Études Économiques (INSÉE). 1982. *Recensement général de la population de 1982: France métropolitaine.* Paris: INSÉE.

———. 1990. *Recensement de la population de 1990, nationalités: Résultats du sondage au quart.* Paris: INSÉE.

Irele, Abiola. 1981. *The African Experience in Literature and Ideology.* Bloomington: Indiana University Press.

Ivy, James W. 1956. "The National Association for the Advancement of Colored People as an Instrument of Social Change." *Présence Africaine*, 2d ser., 8–9–10, special issue (June–Nov.): 330–35.

Jamin, Jean. 1979. "Naissance de l'observation anthropologique." *Cahiers internationaux de sociologie* 67:313–35.

———. 1982. "Objets trouvés des paradis perdus: A propos de la mission Dakar-Djibouti." In *Collections Passion*, pp. 69–100. Neuchâtel: Musée d'Ethnographie.

———. 1984. "Aux origines du Musée de l'Homme: La Mission ethnographique et linguistique Dakar-Djibouti." *Cahiers ethnologiques de Bordeaux*, n.s., 5: 9–71.

JanMohamed, Abdul. 1985. "The Economy of Manichean Allegory: The Function of Racial Difference in Colonialist Literature." In *"Race," Writing, and Difference*, ed. Henry Louis Gates Jr., pp. 78–106. Chicago: University of Chicago Press.

JanMohamed, Abdul, and David Lloyd. 1987. "Introduction: Toward a Theory of Minority Discourse." *Cultural Critique* 6 (Spring): 5–12.

Jewsiewicki, Bogumil. 1985. *Marx, Afrique et occident: Les pratiques africanistes de l'histoire Marxiste.* Monograph No. 19. Toronto: McGill University Centre for Developing-Area Studies.

Joachim, Paulin. 1967. *Éditorial africain.* Strasbourg: Imprimerie des Dernières Nouvelles.

———. 1984. *Oraison pour une re-naissance.* Paris: Éditions Silex.

———. 1988. Interview with Bennetta Jules-Rosette, Paris, July 20.

Jones, Edward A., ed. 1971. *Voices of Négritude: The Expression of Black Experience in the Poetry of Senghor, Césaire and Damas.* Valley Forge, Pa.: Judson Press.

Jules-Rosette, Bennetta. 1981. *Symbols of Change: Urban Transition in a Zambian Community.* Norwood, N.J.: Ablex.

———. 1984. *The Messages of Tourist Art: An African Semiotic System in Comparative Perspective.* New York: Plenum.

———. 1990. *Terminal Signs: Computers and Social Change in Africa.* Berlin: Mouton de Gruyter.

———. 1992a. "Antithetical Africa: Implications of the 1956 Congress of Black Writers and Artists in Paris." Paper presented at the African Americans and Europe Conference, Université de Paris III, Feb. 5–9.

———. 1992b. "Conjugating Cultural Realities: Présence Africaine." In *The Surreptitious Speech:* Présence Africaine *and the Politics of Otherness, 1947–1987*, ed. V. Y. Mudimbe, pp. 14–44. Chicago: University of Chicago Press.

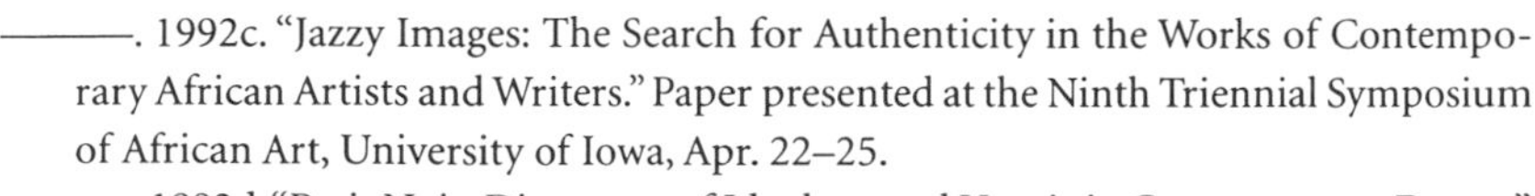

———. 1992c. "Jazzy Images: The Search for Authenticity in the Works of Contemporary African Artists and Writers." Paper presented at the Ninth Triennial Symposium of African Art, University of Iowa, Apr. 22–25.

———. 1992d. "Paris Noir: Discourses of Ideology and Utopia in Contemporary France." Paper presented at the Conference on Ideological Containment and Utopian/Heterotopian Potentials, University of California Humanities Research Institute, Irvine, June 6.

———. 1994. "Decentering Ethnography: Victor Turner's Vision of Anthropology." *Journal of Religion in Africa* 24, no. 2:160–81.

Jules-Rosette, Bennetta, and Denis-Constant Martin. 1997. "Cultures populaires, identités et politique." *Les Cahiers du CERI* 17:1–47.

Karone, Yodi. 1980a. *Le Bal des Caïmans.* Paris: Éditions Karthala.

———. 1980b. *Sacré dernier.* Paris: Éditions Nathan.

———. 1982. *Nègre de paille.* Paris: Éditions Silex.

———. 1988a. *A la Recherche du cannibale amour.* Paris: Éditions Nathan.

———. 1988b. *Les Beaux gosses.* Paris: Publisud.

———. 1991. Interview with Bennetta Jules-Rosette, Paris, July 17.

Kesteloot, Lilyan. 1974. *Black Writers in French: A Literary History of Negritude.* Trans. Ellen Conroy Kennedy. Philadelphia: Temple University Press, 1974. Originally published as *Les Écrivains noir de langue française: Naissance d'une littérature* (Brussels: Éditions de l'Université Libre de Bruxelles, 1963).

Khatibi, Abdelkebir. 1990. *Love in Two Languages.* Trans. Richard Howard. Minneapolis: University of Minnesota Press. Originally published as *Amour bilingue* (Paris: Éditions Fata Morgana, 1983).

Kouamé, Kouamé. 1991. "Aliénation et création romanesque chez les romanciers d'Afrique noire de langue française de 1953 à 1968." Ph.D. diss., Université de Paris VIII.

Krafona, Kwesi. 1986. *The Pan-African Movement: Ghana's Contribution.* London: Afroworld.

Kristeva, Julia. 1993. *Nations without Nationalism.* Trans. Leon S. Roudiez. New York: Columbia University Press. Originally published as *Lettre ouvert à Harlem Désir* (Paris: Éditions Rivages, 1990).

Larreya, Paul. 1979. *Enoncés performatifs présupposition: Eléments de semantique et de pragmatique.* Paris: Nathan.

Laye, Camara. 1953. *L'Enfant noir.* Paris: Libraire Plon.

Leiris, Michel. 1931. "Letter to Georges-Henri Rivière." Photothèque file D-84-2244, Oct. 16. Musée de l'Homme, Paris.

———. 1934. *L'Afrique fantôme: De Dakar-Djibouti, 1931–33.* Paris: Éditions Gallimard, 1934.

Lévy-Bruhl, Lucien. 1923. *L'Âme primitive.* Paris: Presses Universitaires de France.

———. 1930. "Accord et attribution de subventions à Marcel Griaule pour la mission Dakar-Djibouti." Photothèque file C-81-1027-493. Musée de l'Homme, Paris.

Liking, Werewere. 1984. *Une Vision de Kaydara d'Hamadou-Hampate Bâ.* Abidjan, Côte d'Ivoire: Nouvelles Éditions Africaines.

———. 1987. *Statues colons.* Paris: Nouvelles Éditions Africaines and Arhis.

———. 1988. *L'Amour-cent-vie.* Paris: Publisud.

———. 1992a. Interview with Bennetta Jules-Rosette, Abidjan, Côte d'Ivoire, July 28.

———. 1992b. *Un Touareg s'est marié à une Pygmée.* Abidjan, Côte d'Ivoire: Groupe Ki-Yi M'Bock Théâtre and Fondation Afrique en Créations.

Liking, Werewere, and Marie-José Hourantier. 1987. *Spectacles rituels.* Abidjan, Côte d'Ivoire: Nouvelles Éditions Africaines.

Liking, Werewere, Bomou Mamadou, and Binda Ngazolo. 1990. *Singue mura: Considérant que la femme . . .* Abidjan, Côte d'Ivoire: Éditions Eyo Ki-Yi.

Lipsitz, George. 1994. *Dangerous Crossroads: Popular Music, Postmodernism, and the Poetics of Place.* London: Verso.

Little, Kenneth. 1974. *Urbanization as a Social Process.* London: Routledge and Kegan Paul.

Lloyd, Cathie, and Hazel Waters. 1991. "France: One Culture, One People?" *Race and Class* 32, no. 3:49–65.

Lomomba, Emongo. 1989. *L'Instant d'un Soupir.* Paris: Présence Africaine.

MacCannell, Dean. 1989. *The Tourist: A New Theory of the Leisure Class.* 2d ed. New York: Schocken.

MacCannell, Dean, and Juliet Flower MacCannell. 1982. *Time of the Sign: A Semiotic Interpretation of Modern Culture.* Bloomington: Indiana University Press.

Maçou, Guy. 1994. *Voyage au bout de la négritude.* Paris: Éditions L'Harmattan.

Maffesoli, Michel. 1988. *Les Temps des tribus: Le Déclin de l'individualisme dans les sociétés de masse.* Paris: Librairie des Méndiens Klincksieck.

———. 1992. *La Transfiguration du politique: La Tribalisation du monde.* Paris: Bernard Grasset.

Magnier, Bernard. 1990. "Beurs Noirs à Black Babel." *Notre librairie* 103 (Oct.–Dec.): 102–7. Special issue: "Dix ans de littératures, 1980–1990. I. Maghreb–Afrique Noire."

———. 1992. Interview with Bennetta Jules-Rosette, Paris, Dec. 5.

Magubane, Bernard. 1973. "The 'Xhosa' in Town Revisited, Urban Social Anthropology: A Failure of Method and Theory." *American Anthropologist* 75, no. 5 (Oct.): 1701–15.

Mannheim, Karl. 1936. *Ideology and Utopia: An Introduction to the Sociology of Knowledge.* Trans. Louis Wirth and Edward Shils. New York: Harcourt, Brace, and World.

———. 1952. *Essays on the Sociology of Knowledge.* Ed. Paul Kecskemeti. London: Routledge and Kegan Paul.

Maran, René. 1921. *Batouala, véritable roman nègre.* Paris: Albin Michel. Published in English as *Batouala: A True Black Novel,* trans. Barbara Beck and Alexandre Mboukou (Washington, D.C.: Black Orpheus Press, 1972).

Markovitz, Irving Leonard. 1969. *Léopold Sédar Senghor and the Politics of Negritude.* New York: Atheneum.

Martin, Denis-Constant. 1992. "Out of Africa! Should We Be Done with Africanism?" In *The Surreptitious Speech:* Présence Africaine *and the Politics of Otherness, 1947–1987,* ed. V. Y. Mudimbe, pp. 45–56. Chicago: University of Chicago Press.

———. 1994. *Cartes d'identité: Comment dit-on nous en politique.* Paris: Presses de la Fondation Nationale de Sciences Politiques.

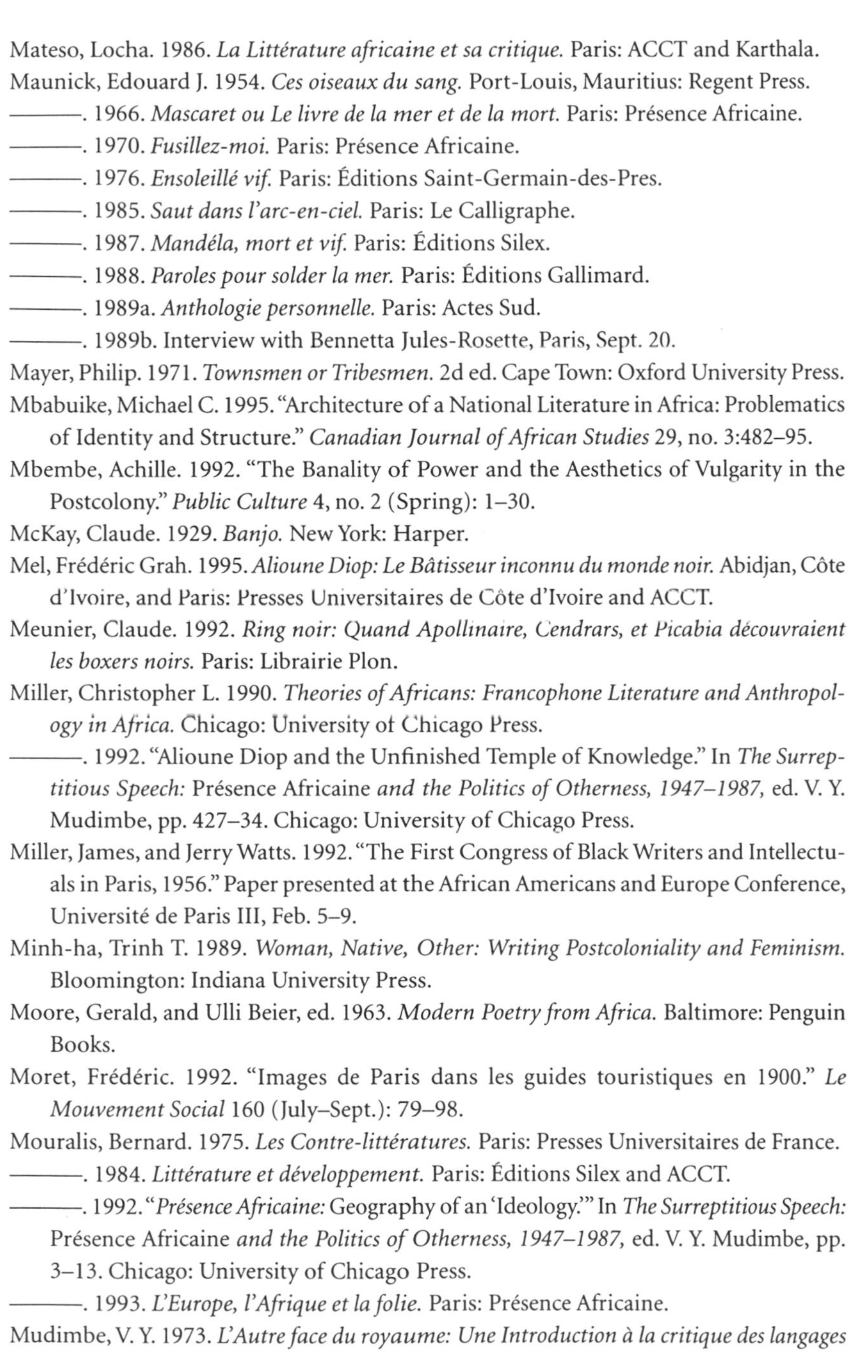

Mateso, Locha. 1986. *La Littérature africaine et sa critique.* Paris: ACCT and Karthala.

Maunick, Edouard J. 1954. *Ces oiseaux du sang.* Port-Louis, Mauritius: Regent Press.

———. 1966. *Mascaret ou Le livre de la mer et de la mort.* Paris: Présence Africaine.

———. 1970. *Fusillez-moi.* Paris: Présence Africaine.

———. 1976. *Ensoleillé vif.* Paris: Éditions Saint-Germain-des-Pres.

———. 1985. *Saut dans l'arc-en-ciel.* Paris: Le Calligraphe.

———. 1987. *Mandéla, mort et vif.* Paris: Éditions Silex.

———. 1988. *Paroles pour solder la mer.* Paris: Éditions Gallimard.

———. 1989a. *Anthologie personnelle.* Paris: Actes Sud.

———. 1989b. Interview with Bennetta Jules-Rosette, Paris, Sept. 20.

Mayer, Philip. 1971. *Townsmen or Tribesmen.* 2d ed. Cape Town: Oxford University Press.

Mbabuike, Michael C. 1995. "Architecture of a National Literature in Africa: Problematics of Identity and Structure." *Canadian Journal of African Studies* 29, no. 3:482–95.

Mbembe, Achille. 1992. "The Banality of Power and the Aesthetics of Vulgarity in the Postcolony." *Public Culture* 4, no. 2 (Spring): 1–30.

McKay, Claude. 1929. *Banjo.* New York: Harper.

Mel, Frédéric Grah. 1995. *Alioune Diop: Le Bâtisseur inconnu du monde noir.* Abidjan, Côte d'Ivoire, and Paris: Presses Universitaires de Côte d'Ivoire and ACCT.

Meunier, Claude. 1992. *Ring noir: Quand Apollinaire, Cendrars, et Picabia découvraient les boxers noirs.* Paris: Librairie Plon.

Miller, Christopher L. 1990. *Theories of Africans: Francophone Literature and Anthropology in Africa.* Chicago: University of Chicago Press.

———. 1992. "Alioune Diop and the Unfinished Temple of Knowledge." In *The Surreptitious Speech:* Présence Africaine *and the Politics of Otherness, 1947–1987,* ed. V. Y. Mudimbe, pp. 427–34. Chicago: University of Chicago Press.

Miller, James, and Jerry Watts. 1992. "The First Congress of Black Writers and Intellectuals in Paris, 1956." Paper presented at the African Americans and Europe Conference, Université de Paris III, Feb. 5–9.

Minh-ha, Trinh T. 1989. *Woman, Native, Other: Writing Postcoloniality and Feminism.* Bloomington: Indiana University Press.

Moore, Gerald, and Ulli Beier, ed. 1963. *Modern Poetry from Africa.* Baltimore: Penguin Books.

Moret, Frédéric. 1992. "Images de Paris dans les guides touristiques en 1900." *Le Mouvement Social* 160 (July–Sept.): 79–98.

Mouralis, Bernard. 1975. *Les Contre-littératures.* Paris: Presses Universitaires de France.

———. 1984. *Littérature et développement.* Paris: Éditions Silex and ACCT.

———. 1992. "*Présence Africaine:* Geography of an 'Ideology.'" In *The Surreptitious Speech:* Présence Africaine *and the Politics of Otherness, 1947–1987,* ed. V. Y. Mudimbe, pp. 3–13. Chicago: University of Chicago Press.

———. 1993. *L'Europe, l'Afrique et la folie.* Paris: Présence Africaine.

Mudimbe, V. Y. 1973. *L'Autre face du royaume: Une Introduction à la critique des langages en folie.* Lausanne: L'Age de Homme.

———. 1982. *L'Odeur du père: Essai sur des limites de la science et de la vie en Afrique noire.* Paris: Présence Africaine.

———. 1988. *The Invention of Africa: Gnosis, Philosophy and the Order of Knowledge.* Bloomington: Indiana University Press.

———. 1991. "'Reprendre': Enunciations and Strategies in Contemporary African Arts." In *Africa Explores: Twentieth-Century African Art,* ed. Susan Vogel, pp. 276–87. New York: Center for African Art.

———. 1992a. "Save the African Continent." *Public Culture* 5, no. 1 (Fall): 61–62.

———. 1992b. *The Surreptitious Speech:* Présence Africaine *and the Politics of Otherness, 1947–1987.* Chicago: University of Chicago Press.

Mudimbe-Boyi, Elisabeth. 1993. "Breaking Silence and Borders: Women Writers from Francophone and Anglophone Africa and the Caribbean." *Callaloo* 16, no. 1 (Winter): 75–76.

Mukambamano, Madeleine. 1991. Personal communication, Paris, July 26.

Mulago, Vincent. 1959. "La Théologie et ses responsabilités." *Présence Africaine,* 2d ser., 27–28, special issue (Aug.–Nov.): 188–205.

Musée de l'Homme. 1969. Collection of papers presented at Organizing Cultural Symposium, First Pan-African Cultural Festival, Algiers. Files GN 460-A315-F41-M1 through M59. Musée de l'Homme, Paris.

Mveng, Engelbert. 1968. "The Function and Significance of Negro Art in the Life and Peoples of Black Africa." In *First World Festival of Negro Arts: Colloquium on Negro Culture,* ed. Société Africaine de Culture, pp. 11–27. Paris: Présence Africaine, 1968. First presented in French as a paper, "La Fonction et la signification de l'art nègre dans la vie des peuples de l'Afrique noire," at the First World Festival of Negro Arts, Colloquium on Negro Art, Dakar, Senegal, 1966. File GN 460-A315-F41-M60, Musée de l'Homme, Paris.

Nantet, Jacques. 1972. *Panorama de la littérature noire d'expression française.* Paris: Librairie Arthème Fayard.

Naudillon, Françoise. 1995. "Aimé Césaire, l'homme universel." *Oeuvres et critiques* 20, no. 1:243–50.

N'Diaye, Jean-Pierre. 1991. Interview with Bennetta Jules-Rosette, Paris, July 30.

N'Djehoya, Blaise. 1988. *Le Nègre Potemkine.* Paris: Éditions Lieu Commun.

N'Djehoya, Blaise, and Massaër Diallo. 1984. *Un Regard noir: Les Français vus par les africains.* Paris: Éditions Autrement.

Ngal, Georges. 1994. *Création et rupture en littérature africaine.* Paris: Éditions L'Harmattan.

Nicollet, Albert. 1992. *Femmes d'Afrique noire en France: La Vie partagée.* Paris: Éditions L'Harmattan.

Niger, Paul. 1948. "Je n'aime pas l'Afrique." In *Anthologie de la nouvelle poésie nègre et malgache de langue française,* ed. Léopold Sédar Senghor, pp. 93–100. Paris: Presses Universitaires de France, 1948. This poem is reprinted with an English translation in *Voices of Négritude: The Expression of Black Experience in the Poetry of Senghor, Césaire and Damas,* ed. Edward A. Jones (Valley Forge, Pa.: Judson Press, 1971), pp. 82–93.

———. 1958. *Les Puissants.* Paris: Éditions du Scorpion.

Njami, Simon. 1985. *Cercueil et cie.* Paris: Éditions Lieu Commun. Published in English as *Coffin and Co.* (Berkeley: Black Lizard Books, 1987).

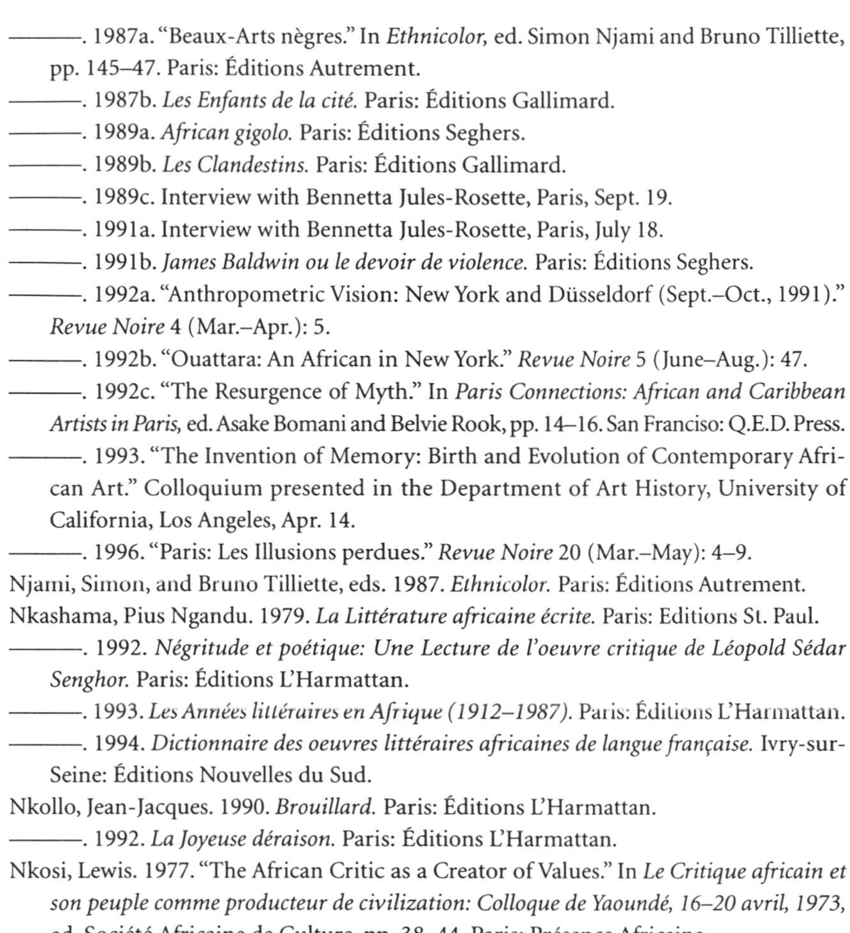

———. 1987a. "Beaux-Arts nègres." In *Ethnicolor,* ed. Simon Njami and Bruno Tilliette, pp. 145–47. Paris: Éditions Autrement.

———. 1987b. *Les Enfants de la cité.* Paris: Éditions Gallimard.

———. 1989a. *African gigolo.* Paris: Éditions Seghers.

———. 1989b. *Les Clandestins.* Paris: Éditions Gallimard.

———. 1989c. Interview with Bennetta Jules-Rosette, Paris, Sept. 19.

———. 1991a. Interview with Bennetta Jules-Rosette, Paris, July 18.

———. 1991b. *James Baldwin ou le devoir de violence.* Paris: Éditions Seghers.

———. 1992a. "Anthropometric Vision: New York and Düsseldorf (Sept.–Oct., 1991)." *Revue Noire* 4 (Mar.–Apr.): 5.

———. 1992b. "Ouattara: An African in New York." *Revue Noire* 5 (June–Aug.): 47.

———. 1992c. "The Resurgence of Myth." In *Paris Connections: African and Caribbean Artists in Paris,* ed. Asake Bomani and Belvie Rook, pp. 14–16. San Franciso: Q.E.D. Press.

———. 1993. "The Invention of Memory: Birth and Evolution of Contemporary African Art." Colloquium presented in the Department of Art History, University of California, Los Angeles, Apr. 14.

———. 1996. "Paris: Les Illusions perdues." *Revue Noire* 20 (Mar.–May): 4–9.

Njami, Simon, and Bruno Tilliette, eds. 1987. *Ethnicolor.* Paris: Éditions Autrement.

Nkashama, Pius Ngandu. 1979. *La Littérature africaine écrite.* Paris: Editions St. Paul.

———. 1992. *Négritude et poétique: Une Lecture de l'oeuvre critique de Léopold Sédar Senghor.* Paris: Éditions L'Harmattan.

———. 1993. *Les Années littéraires en Afrique (1912–1987).* Paris: Éditions L'Harmattan.

———. 1994. *Dictionnaire des oeuvres littéraires africaines de langue française.* Ivry-sur-Seine: Éditions Nouvelles du Sud.

Nkollo, Jean-Jacques. 1990. *Brouillard.* Paris: Éditions L'Harmattan.

———. 1992. *La Joyeuse déraison.* Paris: Éditions L'Harmattan.

Nkosi, Lewis. 1977. "The African Critic as a Creator of Values." In *Le Critique africain et son peuple comme producteur de civilization: Colloque de Yaoundé, 16–20 avril, 1973,* ed. Société Africaine de Culture, pp. 38–44. Paris: Présence Africaine.

Omerod, Beverly, and Jean-Marie Volet. 1994. *Romancières africaines d'expression française: Le Sud du Sahara.* Paris: Éditions L'Harmattan.

Ouologuem, Yambo. 1968. *Le devoir de violence.* Paris: Éditions du Seuil. Published in English as *Bound to Violence,* trans. Ralph Manheim (Oxford: Heinemann International, 1971).

Palmer, Eustace. 1979. *The Growth of the African Novel: Studies in African Literature.* London: Heinemann Educational Books.

Parsons, Talcott. 1960. *Structure and Process in Modern Societies.* New York: Free Press.

Patterson, Jo. 1994. "Translator's Note." In Bernard Binlin Dadié, *One Way,* trans. Patterson, p. xi. Urbana: University of Illinois Press.

Paul, Emmanuel C. 1959. "Tâches et responsabilités de l'ethnologie." *Présence Africaine,* 2d ser., 27–28, special issue (Aug.–Sept.): 237–43.

Prakash, Gyan. 1995. "Introduction." In *After Colonialism: Imperial Histories and Postcolonial Displacements,* ed. Gyan Prakash, pp. 3–17. Princeton: Princeton University Press.

Présence Africaine. 1955. "La Conférence de Bandoeng: Témoignages des africains sur Bandoeng." *Présence Africaine,* 2d. ser., 3 (Aug.–Sept.): 28–44.

———. 1956. "Le Premier congrès international des écrivains et artistes noir (Paris–Sorbonne, 19–22 September, 1956)." *Présence Africaine,* 2d ser., 8–9–10, special issue (June–Nov.): 361–65.

———. 1959. "Notre politique de la culture." *Présence Africaine,* 2d ser., 24–25, special issue (Feb.–May): 5–7.

Quatrefages de Bréau, Armand de. 1877. *L'Espèce humaine.* 2d ed. Paris: Germer Baillière.

———. 1889. "Introduction anthropologique." In *Encyclopédie d'hygiène et de médecine publique,* ed. Jules Rochard, pp. 1–118. Paris: A. Hennuyer.

Rabemananjara, Jacques. 1957. "Le Poète noir et son peuple." *Présence Africaine,* 2d ser., 16 (Oct.–Nov.): 9–25.

———. 1959. "Les Fondements de notre unité tirés de l'époque coloniale." *Présence Africaine,* 2d ser., 24–25, special issue (Feb.–May): 66–81.

———. 1988. Interview with Bennetta Jules-Rosette, Paris, July 12.

Riché, Armelle. 1993. Interview with Bennetta Jules-Rosette, Paris, July 27.

Rivet, Paul. 1931. "L'Anthropologie et les missions." Congrès des Missions Protestantes. Paris: Société des Missions Évangéliques.

Rivet, Paul, and Georges-Henri Rivière. 1931. "La Réorganisation du musée d'ethnographie du Trocadéro." *Bulletin du Musée d'Ethnographie du Trocadéro* 1 (Jan.): 3–11.

———. 1933. "La Mission ethnographique et linguistique Dakar-Djibouti." *Minotaure* 2:3–6.

Rivet, P., P. Lester, and G.-H. Rivière. 1935. "Le Laboratoire d'anthropologie du muséum." *Archives du muséum d'histoire naturelle,* 6th ser., 12:507–31.

Rivière, Georges-Henri. 1949. "The Organization and Functions of the Museums." *Museum* 2, no. 4:206–26.

———. 1968. "My Experience at the Musée d'Ethnologie." *Proceedings of the Royal Anthropological Institute,* 117–22.

Rochmann, Marie-Christine. 1989. "Le Cratylism d'Edouard Maunick." *Travaux de Littérature* 2:315–33.

Rodney, Walter. 1972. *How Europe Underdeveloped Africa.* London: Bogle-L'Ouverture Publications.

Roman, Joël. 1995. "Un Multiculturalisme à la française." *Esprit* 212, no. 6 (June): 145–60.

Rouch, Jean. 1968. "Films Inspired by Africa." In *First World Festival of Negro Arts: Colloquium on Negro Art,* ed. Société Africaine de Culture, pp. 523–37. Paris: Présence Africaine. First presented in French as a paper, "Le Cinéma d'inspiration africaine," at the First World Festival of Negro Arts, Colloquium on Negro Art, Dakar, Senegal, 1966. File GN 460-A315-F41-M85, Musée de l'Homme, Paris.

———. 1991. Personal communication, Paris, Oct. 4.

Rousseau, Madeleine. 1957. "Crise de la culture noire." *Présence Africaine,* 2d ser., 14–15 (June–Sept.): 331–35.

Rowell, Charles. 1989. "An Interview with Edouard Maunick and Selected Poems." *Callaloo* 12, no. 3 (Summer): 491–505.

Ruppert, Sophie. 1991. "L'Harmattan Publishing on the Third World." *Research in African Literature* 22, no. 4 (Winter): 155–59.

Said, Edward W. 1978. *Orientalism.* New York: Random House.

———. 1989. "Representing the Colonized: Anthropology's Interlocutors." *Critical Inquiry* 15, no. 2 (Winter): 205–25.

Sainville, Léonard. 1959. "Le Roman et ses responsabilités." *Présence Africaine,* 2d ser., 27–28, special issue (Aug.–Nov.): 37–50.

Sandbrook, Richard. 1993. *The Politics of Africa's Economic Recovery.* Cambridge: Cambridge University Press.

Sartre, Jean-Paul. 1947. "Présence noire." *Présence Africaine,* 1st ser., 1 (Nov.–Dec.): 28–29.

———. 1948. "Orphée noir." In *Anthologie de la nouvelle poésie nègre et malgache de langue française,* ed. Léopold Sédar Senghor, pp. ix–xliv. Paris: Presses Universitaires de France. Excerpted in *Présence Africaine,* 1st ser., 6, 1st trimester (1949): 9–14.

———. 1976. *Critique of Dialectical Reason.* Trans. Alan Sheridan-Smith. London: NLB. Originally published as *Critique de la raison dialectique* (Paris: Éditions Gallimard, 1960).

Schleifer, Ronald. 1987. *A. J. Greimas and the Nature of Meaning.* Lincoln: University of Nebraska Press.

Schlumberger, Eveline. 1974. "Georges-Henri Rivière: Homme-orchéstrê des musées du 20e siècle." *Connaissance des arts* (Dec.): 100–106.

Senghor, Léopold Sédar. 1948. "Congo." In *Anthologie de la nouvelle poésie nègre et malgache de langue française,* ed. Senghor, pp. 168–70. Paris: Presses Universitaires de France. This poem also appears in Léopold Sédar Senghor, *Éthiopiques* (Paris: Éditions du Seuil, 1956).

———. 1977a. "Discours du Président Léopold Sédar Senghor." In *Le Critique africain et son peuple comme producteur de civilisation: Colloque de Yaoundé, 16–20 avril, 1973,* ed. Société Africaine de Culture, pp. 513–15. Paris: Présence Africaine.

———. 1977b. *Liberté III: Négritude et civilisation de l'universel.* Paris: Éditions du Seuil.

———. 1987. "Préface." In *Ethnologiques: Hommages à Marcel Griaule,* ed. Annie Solange de Ganay, Jean-Paul Lebeuf, and Dominique Zahan, pp. v–vii. Paris: Éditions Hermann.

Seweje, M. A. 1959. "Observations de la Société Africaine de Culture pour le second congrès de Rome." *Présence Africaine,* 2d ser., 27–28, special issue (Aug.–Nov.): 314–20.

Sié, Konaté. 1996. *La Littérature d'enfance et de jeunesse en Côte d'Ivoire: Structures de production et de distribution du livre pour enfants.* Paris: Éditions L'Harmattan.

Société Africaine de Culture (SAC). 1977. "Resolution des Ateliers." In *Le Critique africain et son peuple comme producteur de civilisation: Colloque de Yaoundé, 16–20 avril, 1973,* ed. SAC, pp. 538–44. Paris: Présence Africaine.

Sotinel, Thomas. 1995. "Une Extrême tension entoure l'élection présidentielle ivoirienne." *Le Monde,* Oct. 21, p. 4.

Spivak, Gayatri Chakravorty. 1985. "Three Women's Texts and a Critique of Imperialism." In *"Race," Writing, and Difference,* ed. Henry Louis Gates Jr., pp. 263–80. Chicago: University of Chicago Press.

Stovall, Tyler. 1996. *Paris Noir: African Americans in the City of Light.* New York: Houghton Mifflin.

Tadjo, Véronique. 1983. *Latérite.* Paris: Hatier, 1983.

———. 1986. *A Vol d'oiseau.* Paris: Éditions Fernand Nathan. Republished by Éditions l'Harmattan (Paris, 1992).

———. 1990a. Interview with Bennetta Jules-Rosette, Paris, July 23.

———. 1990b. *La Chanson de la vie.* Paris: Hatier.

———. 1990c. *Le Royaume aveugle.* Paris: Éditions L'Harmattan, 1990.

———. 1993. *Le Seigneur de la danse.* Abidjan, Côte d'Ivoire: N.E.I.

Tempels, Placide. 1949. *La Philosophie bantoue.* Paris: Présence Africaine.

Tiémélé, Jean-Baptiste. 1969. *Chansons païennes.* Honfleur: Pierre Jean Oswald.

———. 1981. *Ce monde qui fume.* Paris: Éditions Saint-Germain-des-Prés.

———. 1983. "Thomas-Alexandre: Pièce en six tableaux." Unpublished six-act play.

———. 1987. *Aoyu suivi de Yaley.* Paris: Éditions Silex.

———. 1989. Interview with Bennetta Jules-Rosette, Paris, Sept. 15.

———. 1990. Interview with Bennetta Jules-Rosette, Paris, July 19.

———. 1997. "Essan, le savant du vingtième siècle." Unpublished play.

Towa, Marcien. 1971. *Léopold Sédar Senghor: Négritude ou servitude?* Yaoundé, Cameroon: Éditions Clé.

Towet, Taita. 1959. "Le Rôle d'un philosophe africain." *Présence Africaine,* 2d. ser., 27–28, special issue (Aug.–Nov.): 108–28.

Tribalat, Michèle. 1995. *Faire France: Une Enquête sur les immigrés et leurs enfants.* Paris: Éditions La Découverte.

Tyler, Stephen A. 1985. "Ethnography, Intertextuality and the End of Description." *American Journal of Semiotics* 3, no. 4:83–98.

Urbain, Amoa. 1992a. *Les Braises de la lagune.* Abidjan, Côte d'Ivoire: Éditions des Lagunes.

———. 1992b. Interview with Bennetta Jules-Rosette, Abidjan, Côte d'Ivoire, Aug. 7.

Vansina, Jan. 1985. *Oral Tradition as History.* Madison: University of Wisconsin Press.

Vieyra, Paulin Soumanou. 1959. "Responsabilités du cinéma dans la formation d'une conscience nationale africaine." *Présence Africaine,* 2d ser., 27–28, special issue (Aug.–Nov.): 303–13.

———. 1968. "Cinematic Art: In Search of Its African Expression. In *First World Festival of Negro Arts: Colloquium on Negro Culture,* ed. Société Africaine de Culture, pp. 539–58. Paris: Présence Africaine. First presented in French as a paper, "L'Art cinématographique à la recherche de son expression africaine," at the First World Festival of Negro Arts, Colloquium on Negro Art, Dakar, Senegal, 1966. File GN 460-A315-F41-M87, Musée de l'Homme, Paris.

———. 1975. *Le Cinéma africain des origines à 1973.* Vol. 1. Paris: Présence Africaine.

Vincileoni, Nicole. 1986. *L'Oeuvre de B. B. Dadié.* Issy les Moulineaux: Éditions Saint-Paul, 1986.

Vogel, Susan, ed. 1991. *Africa Explores: Twentieth-Century African Art.* New York: Center for African Art.

Volet, Jean-Marie. 1993. "Calixthe Beyala, or the Literary Success of a Cameroonian Woman Living in Paris." *World Literature Today* 67, no. 2:309–14.

Walker, Margaret. 1988. *Daemonic Genius.* New York: Warner Books.

Walmsley, Anne. 1992. *The Caribbean Artists Movement, 1966–1972.* London: New Beacon Press.

Waterman, Christopher Alan. 1990. *Jùjú: A Social History and Ethnography of an African Popular Music.* Chicago: University of Chicago Press.

Wright, Richard. 1956. "Tradition and Industrialization: The Plight of the Tragic Elite in Africa." *Présence Africaine,* 2d ser. 8–9–10, special issue (June–Nov.): 347–60.

Young, Robert J. C. 1995. *Colonial Desire: Hybridity in Theory, Culture and Race.* London: Routledge.

INDEX

BENNETTA JULES-ROSETTE is a professor of sociology at the University of California, San Diego, and was director of the University of California Study Centers, Bordeaux/Toulouse (1995–97). She is a specialist in the study of contemporary African cultures, literature, religion, and art. Jules-Rosette is the author of several books, including *Symbols of Change: Urban Transition in a Zambian Community* (1981), *The Messages of Tourist Art: An African Semiotic System in Comparative Perspective* (1984), and *Terminal Signs: Computers and Social Change in Africa* (1990). She also has served as a consulting editor for *African Arts* and for *Revue Noire,* France's leading contemporary African art magazine.